LOOK WHO'S TALKING

BUSINESS LEADERS

The San Francisco Giants provide another compelling example of Conscious Capitalism. Bruce Bochy's down-to-earth approach unequivocally demonstrates that leadership—conscious leadership and culture matter. Bochy Ball is a testament to those who believe that people give their best when you trust them, believe in them and give them ownership for the outcome you are trying to achieve.

John Mackey,
CEO, Whole Foods Market

A powerful invitation to play for something bigger than yourself, Bochy Ball is a manual on gutsy leadership with heart—a primer on how to build team chemistry and why it is essential to the performance of any enterprise. The Freibergs have captured the spirit and strategy of a remarkable organization.

Dawn Sweeney,
President and CEO,
National Restaurant Association

As a sports fan and someone who loves great leadership, I have always admired what Bruce has done with his teams. Bochy Ball is a blueprint for all organizations that understand team chemistry is essential to their success.

Rob Katz,
CEO, Vail Resorts, Inc.

If "exceptional success requires exceptional circumstances," Bochy Ball captures what it takes to create exceptional circumstances in baseball and in business. Read this relevant and entertaining book and you will capture it too!

Bill Whitacre,
President and CEO,
J.R. Simplot Company

The San Francisco Giants have built one of the most enduring brands in the world. The Freibergs put the emphasis right where it should be—on how they make "ONE FOR ALL, ALL FOR ONE" a driving force people are passionate about; not empty spin. This practical and entertaining book is not only for coaches, athletes and sports fanatics, but also for business leaders who aspire to bring a whole new level of positive energy to their organization and create deeper bonds within the team and within the community. Walk into the clubhouse and learn!

Kent Thiry,
Chairman and CEO,
DaVita Inc.

Levi Strauss & Co has much in common with the San Francisco Giants. We are both iconic brands built by a committed team of people who "bring it" every day. The values that have guided Bruce Bochy's three World Championship—courage, empathy, unwavering originality, integrity, and fearless exploration—are the very values that have guided Levis Strauss since day one. If you want to build a celebrated culture and a strong, enduring brand, read Bochy Ball.

Chip Bergh,
President and CEO,
Levi Strauss & Co.

Bochy Ball provides a lively and penetrating analysis of how great leaders think and what they do. A true "Giant" in the world of baseball, Bruce Bochy is one of the most successful managers in the history of the game. The Freibergs give you a behind the scenes look at how you, too, can be a "Giant" in your field.

Mike Murphy,
President and CEO,
Sharp HealthCare

A business book on a baseball franchise—an inspiring tale of the remarkable results possible when a team chooses service over self-interest and plays for something larger than themselves. If you're a CEO who believes that success is built on great leadership, dive into this entertaining and actionable case study. What the San Francisco Giants have accomplished, from the front office to the field, is truly extraordinary.

Lloyd Dean,
President and CEO,
Dignity Health

Every winning team needs a great "Manager!" This is true in Baseball, Business and the Military. A leader brings together the best skills of their team, prepares them for the competition and then is the Team Leader as the game is played. Everyone wants to be a part of a winning team! Bochy Ball will give you the formula for creating a winning team.

Cutler Dawson,
President and CEO,
Navy Federal Credit Union

Everyone can learn something from a world class coach at the top of his game. As soon as I started reading this book, I added some "to do's" to my daily list. Bruce Bochy gives practical and actionable advice for anyone leading a team or needing to get things done through people.

David Perkins,
Founder,
High West Distillery

THOUGHT LEADERS

Bruce Bochy's three World Series rings give him insight and credibility that few leaders possess. In Bochy Ball, you'll learn how to apply his wisdom – a maniacal drive to win coupled with a deep sense of humility and community – well beyond the baseball diamond. This book is so good that even a Los Angeles Dodgers fan will love it

Daniel H. Pink,
author, WHEN and To Sell is Human

I'm a raving fan of Bruce Bochy and the Giants organization is world-class. Since he took over in San Francisco, he's been able to show us the lessons about winning and losing in a way that is helpful to anyone, no matter what kind of enterprise you lead. If you believe that character counts, culture matters and team chemistry is one of the great differentiators, don't miss this book!

Ken Blanchard,
co-author, The New One Minute Manager
and co-editor, Servant Leadership in Action

This is an outstanding leadership book with valuable insights across any organization in any industry. Bochy Ball puts a personal face on leadership, detailing through examples what it takes to get the most from your team over the roller coaster of events and personalities that are largely out of your control. Baseball fans will go ga-ga over the insider view of the SF Giants' experience, but the book is a home run for those who want to know how they can construct and sustain a championship team within their own organizations. The Freiberg's don't dote on Bochy, in providing an astute 360-degree look at what a leader does to create a winning culture. Bochy Ball should be read by every would-be, emerging, and contemporary leader, and it would be a shame if it ends up only in the hands of sports enthusiasts.

Barry Posner,
author, The Leadership Challenge

This delightful and insightful book is proof that you can preserve your humanity and humility and win. And do it under the spotlight and pressure of an unforgiving, soul consuming entertainment business. Most of us have trouble maintaining our humanity and humility when nobody, including our boss, is really watching. The book is an endearing counter cultural surprise.

Peter Block,
author, Stewardship,
An Other Kingdom and
The Empowered Manager

Charmingly self-effacing and refreshingly vulnerable, Bruce Bochy wins at lifting others because he works at getting an accurate view of how he "lands" on his players. Then, he changes. This book is more than just a baseball book about a celebrity sports personality. It broadens the San Francisco Giants experience to a more fundamental issue—what great leadership looks like.

Marshall Goldsmith,
author, Triggers, MOJO
and Lifestorming

CELEBRITIES - COACHES - ATHLETES

Reading through the engrossing BOCHY BALL, I was struck at how similar Bruce Bochy's work managing the storied San Francisco Giants is to a film director. He operates in the foreground by staying in the background, he listens more than he talks, he never draws out a great performance but makes the conditions possible for one to emerge. He puts the necessary puzzle pieces together but the success belongs to the team alone.

Francis Ford Coppola

I love baseball. I love the San Francisco Giants. I love Bruce Bochy and I love this book!

Huey Lewis,
American singer/songwriter/actor

A priceless dialogue with arguably one of the most successful managers in the history of the game. Filled with exciting triumphs and gut-wrenching defeats that leave no doubt in the reader that team chemistry is a great differentiator. Thoroughly enjoyed this book, you will too!

Joe Montana

I covered the Padres for the San Diego Union-Tribune at the time when Bruce Bochy was hired to manage before the 1995 season, and while there was an expectation he would be a strong leader, no one could have foreseen what he's accomplished. For the way he works with players and navigated through challenges and for his World Series titles, he will be elected to the Hall of Fame in the years to come, as arguably the greatest manager of his era.

Buster Olney,
Sports columnist for ESPN: The Magazine,
and author, The Last Night of the Yankee Dynasty

There is only one Bruce Bochy! He just might be the most respected manager in the game—ever. Players come and go but they all love playing for him. And, if you talked to every other manager who knows him and has competed against him, they'd say the same thing, "He's smart. He's the guy." Three different teams, three World Championships. Bruce is the link and in this detailed account of great leadership, Kevin and Jackie Freiberg show you why.

Hall of Famer Bobby Cox,
former manager, World Champion Atlanta Braves

Bruce Bochy has proven that leadership does not always require the loudest voice in the room. Through the highs and lows—in baseball and in life—a trusted voice is more important. With unflappability and quiet confidence, Bruce created a culture in San Francisco that consistently allowed his teams to rise to the occasion when it counted most. Kevin and Jackie Freiberg give great insight into not only a classic baseball man whose approach has resonated with ballplayers for nearly a quarter-century, but also a special individual who sets a powerful example for all those who aspire to lead.

Hall of Famer Joe Torre,
Four-Time World Champion Manager of the New York Yankees
and Chief Baseball Officer of Major League Baseball

Long before Bruce managed three World Series Championships, his peers recognized that he belonged in the conversation with MLB's greatest managers ever! Those titles keep adding to his credentials. Bochy Ball provides all of us a championship learning experience that translates wherever competitive challenges exist!

Hall of Famer Tony La Russa,
Three-Time World Champion,
Chief Baseball Officer, Arizona Diamondbacks

A great listener. A brilliant strategist. Flawless in managing the bullpen. Bruce Bochy is a master at putting players in positions to be their best when their best is needed. This book offers a tremendous opportunity for you to do the same in your life and in your organization. The Freibergs give you an exclusive look inside the mind of a fearless competitor and one of the game's truly authentic leaders.

Rick Sutcliffe,
Cy Young Award and Roberto Clemente Award winner,
ESPN broadcaster

Bruce Bochy is a master at drawing the best out of others and leading them to heights they never thought imaginable. Many competitors have miscalculated his low-key, down-to-earth approach—at their own peril. If you want to go behind the scenes and see what a world-class manager does to connect with, inspire and challenge people to give it their all, this book is a gold mine of concrete examples and actionable suggestions. Thanks Skipper!

Trevor Hoffman,
Former Major League Baseball pitcher

Chemistry is one of the hardest things to get right, but the San Francisco Giants and Bruce Bochy obviously cracked the code. In a game that is increasingly driven by analytics, the Giants haven't forgotten that players are real people, not robots or statistics on a spreadsheet. Using Bochy's straightforward, no-BS approach, Kevin and Jackie Freiberg show you how to find your own "championship blood" and inspire it in others.

Hall of Famer Goose Gossage,
World Series Champion

A coach/manager is the glue, the visionary, the driver of a great team. My best coaches and I had an unbreakable communication between us. It brought confidence and focus to my mission--you need both to throw yourself down a mountain at 80 mph! Bochy exemplifies great leadership and brings the best out in his players. You can too through this book.

Steve Nyman,
U.S. Ski Team member,
Three-Time Olympian and
World Cup Champion

An enlightening, entertaining and engaging book. Bochy Ball describes what I've always felt, a deep connection to San Francisco and its people. This is the story of how a great manager thinks and what he does. It is also the story of how the Giants created one of the most successful sports franchises in the world. Don't miss this one.

Hall of Famer Willie McCovey,
Six-Time All-Star

We have the greatest fans in the greatest city because they are always there—whether the team is winning or losing. Bochy's guys appreciate this because he has challenged them to play for something bigger than just themselves.

Hall of Famer Willie Mays,
World Series Champion

BOCHY BALL!

THE CHEMISTRY OF WINNING AND LOSING IN BASEBALL, BUSINESS, AND LIFE

KEVIN AND JACKIE FREIBERG

EPIC WORK EPIC LIFE

San Diego   San Francisco   Chennai

Credits and permissions are listed on page 356, and are considered
a continuation of the copyright page.

Published in San Diego, California by Epic Work Epic Life, Inc.

Library of Congress Cataloging-in-Publication Data

Freiberg, Kevin, 1958—

BOCHY BALL! The Chemistry of Winning and Losing in
Baseball, Business, and Life /by Kevin and Jackie Freiberg

ISBN 978-0-9997001-0-5

I. Freiberg, Jackie, 1963-- II. Title

Library of Congress Control Number: 2017962726

Book website: www.bochyball.com
Publisher website: www.epicworkepiclife.com

Printed in the United States of America

Cover and Book Design by: Emma Strong

To Ken Blue

Personally, professionally and spiritually, our lives have
been enriched by your wise and candid counsel. You
are no shrinking violet, yet your warrior spirit is always
grounded in grace and unconditional love.

You have been a friend in the truest and deepest sense of
the word. Thanks for being our die-hard 10th player.

LINE UP

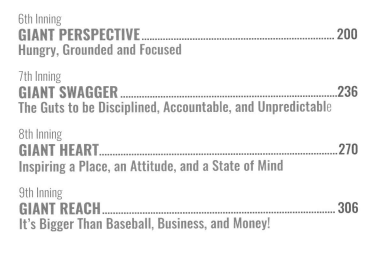

FOREWORD

1962. I was just seven years old. My dad, Jim Berman, had taken me to a couple of Yankees games . . . as we lived on the New York–Connecticut line. It was the first World Series I was aware of, and the Yankees were in it. I didn't care. I rooted for the San Francisco Giants. Dad had told me they had the best player and his name was Willie Mays. That was more than enough for me.

The next May, for my eighth birthday, Dad took me, my brother Andy, and a few friends to the Polo Grounds because the Giants were in town to play the Mets. I learned about Willie McCovey, Orlando Cepeda, and Juan Marichal, and Gaylord Perry. I was hooked. The Giants were my team…for life. At least for those of us in my generation, we've come to realize there are three things you cannot change in life: your date of birth, your Social Security number, and your childhood baseball team.

Polo Grounds, New York City c. 1905

You know what being a Giants fan was? It was cool. Especially 2,500 miles away when you often didn't get the Tuesday night scores until the Thursday morning paper. Back then they were always good. But they were always finishing second. The darn Dodgers and Cardinals were always in the way.

In 1971, the Giants broke through to win the NL West. Yes, I snuck a transistor radio into school so I could hear the Championship Series games against the Pirates. It was the last hurrah of Mays and the old guard. Then the doldrums . . . until 1987. I flew to St. Louis to watch games 1 and 2 of the NLCS, which were played in a 24-hour span. Like 16 years earlier, the Giants were valiant, but came up short.

Then 1989. The World Series. The Bay Area Series. The earthquake. I was covering it for ESPN, and the auxiliary press area was in the upper deck. Between those 20 seconds of the stadium shaking and our live 3-hour coverage immediately afterward, through the disaster, I saw something else. It wasn't just cool to be a Giants fan, it was honorable. The way the organization handled the unforeseen, from owner Bob Lurie through Stadium Operations Manager Jorge Costa, was a sight to behold. It was more impressive than the team getting to the World Series.

> **Between those 20 seconds of the stadium shaking and our live 3-hour coverage immediately afterward, through the disaster, I saw something else. It wasn't just cool to be a Giants fan, it was honorable.**

Soon it was 1992. The Giants might really be heading to St. Petersburg, Florida, at season's end. I flew out to go to a couple of games in perhaps the final home stand. Through the sadness, though, something happened. San Francisco class prevailed. Lurie took less money from a group of local investors so the Giants could stay where they belong. This new group—headed by Peter Magowan, full of energy and vision, and partners like Larry Baer—didn't just acquire the team. They gave us hope. And they gave us Barry Bonds in left field, Dusty Baker as manager, and a momentarily below-the-radar front office hiring in Brian Sabean.

At once, the Giants took, well, Giants steps. One hundred and three wins. Amazingly, one short of the amount needed to catch the Braves. It was hardly the goal, but history will show that those 1993 Giants are a huge reason why the next time baseball played a full season, it had a Wild Card team in the playoffs so that couldn't happen again.

Now it was like the '60s again. The Giants were seemingly always good. The long-awaited replacement to Candlestick Park was a marvel. Baseball's first privately financed stadium in 38 years opened in 2000. And what's now AT&T Park remains the absolute best of its kind. Division crowns came in 1997, 2000, and 2003, and, oh yes, a Wild Card berth in 2002. That resulted in an amazing five-game win over Atlanta, followed by a mauling of St. Louis, and now it was the World Series. No Giants fan needs to be reminded of the Fall Classic against the Angels. So close . . . yet so far. Game 6 in Anaheim, the disappearance of a 5-0 lead. And the next night's loss in Game 7. Maybe the San Francisco Giants were just one of those teams, destined to never win a World Series. The Chicago Cubs and Boston Red Sox miseries may have been more documented nationally, but the Giants sorrows were every bit as real.

The team soon became one of transition, and one quite a bit below .500. Before the 2007 season, GM Sabean hired Bruce Bochy, with a strong track record in the division in San Diego, as manager. While not apparent to the outside at first, what was being assembled on the field mimicked what had long been established upstairs. A team. A team with ability, accountability, camaraderie, and—most importantly—a team with loyalty. Everybody is in it to win. These Giants were in it to win the right way.

What follows in the pages here is an account of three successive even-numbered seasons that not only rewrote San Francisco Giants history but also rewrote baseball history. A 55-year drought that extended back to the old Polo Grounds and the New York Giants and a very young Willie Mays in 1954 was ended. Not only that. Misery became a dynasty: three World Championships in five years.

This account is far from a pitch-by-pitch recall of those glorious seasons. There is so much more to it behind the scenes than many folks would guess for a sport that has a winner and loser every day for seven months. Championships don't just happen. Surely not when you haven't experienced one in over half a century, and never in your longtime Bay Area home. These pages reveal that a special kind of leadership, deployed at all levels, made the difference.

If you think about it, most baseball teams who win three times in five years have a great deal of the same contributors on the field. But for the Giants of 2010, 2012, and 2014, that really wasn't the case. Of course, Buster Posey was behind the plate for all of them, catching stellar pitching that was the backbone of these crowns. Tim Lincecum got each round of the 2010 postseason started with a bang . . . as he won Game 1 against Atlanta, Philadelphia, and Texas. Matt Cain was right on his heels and will forever be remembered for finishing off the amazing comebacks in 2012 against Cincinnati and St. Louis. Down 0-2, the Giants beat the Reds in five, with Cain wining Game 5. Down 1-3, the Giants beat the Cards in seven, with Cain winning Game 7. By 2014, Lincecum was deep in the bullpen and Cain was sidelined with an injury. The lone constant in the starters category was Madison Bumgarner, culminating, of course, with his legendary 2014 World Series against the Royals. Bum had two dominating starts and a spectacular five-inning save in Game 7 in Kansas City.

Charging out of the bullpen to close things down in 2010 was Brian Wilson and his beard. In 2012, it was Sergio Romo and *his beard*. In 2014, it was Santiago Casilla. The effervescent Panda, Pablo Sandoval, was a constant at third base through these championships. He will forever be part of World Series lore for his three home runs in Game 1 of the 2012 World Series against Detroit, two off ace Justin Verlander. Don't forget two other members of the infield who were so important in those 2012 and 2014 titles: first baseman Brandon Belt, of 18th-inning home run fame against Washington in 2014 and the maestro at shortstop, Brandon Crawford—both of whom were in the minors in 2010. Also, hardnosed right fielder Hunter Pence, another pivotal cog in 2012 and 2014, was playing for the Houston Astros in 2010.

> **This account is far from a pitch-by-pitch recall of those glorious seasons. There is so much more to it behind the scenes.**

So what was the constant? An organization that first and foremost kept old-school values and blended them into 21st-century reality. An organization with smarts. An organization with class. An organization with continuity and alignment. There is a direct path from upstairs to the manager's office, just as there is a direct path from the field to the manager's office. That's why the eyes, ears, and mind of Bruce Bochy are a perfect conduit to tell the championship story of the San Francisco Giants.

Their win in 2010 was for fathers and mothers, grandfathers and grandmothers. Their win in 2012 was for us, the current fans of the team. Their win in 2014 was for all sports fans, even the casual ones, because everyone can identify excellence when they see it. I was thrilled to be a Giants fan as a boy of seven. I am honored and even more thrilled to be one now.

Enjoy Bochy Ball! Just as you, and I, have enjoyed these Giants.

Chris Berman
November 20, 2017

THE STORY BEHIND THE STORY
A 20 Year Relationship

We met Bruce Bochy—Boch, as his friends call him—in 1995 shortly after he had become the manager of the San Diego Padres. Having spent the prior five years managing in the minor leagues he knew that dealing with the media was going to be a big part of his job in San Diego. He also knew that he would periodically be asked to give presentations to various groups inside and outside of Major League Baseball (MLB). Boch doesn't like to do anything half-assed. So, with a desire to build mutual trust and respect with the media, improve his communication skills, and become a more well-rounded manager, he called our mutual friend Felix Oroz and asked for help.

Felix and Kevin attended the University of Wyoming together. Boch and Felix played together in the minor leagues. Felix connected us because he knew that we write, consult, and speak about leadership, change, and innovation. We have a business that has provided leadership and team development, executive coaching, and keynotes to more than 2,000 companies in 60 industries across the globe. So, Boch and Kevin met at a restaurant in San Diego.

Although we admired Boch for getting out of his comfort zone and wanting to improve, we were cautious, having coached executives who similarly spoke sincerely about facing their fears yet failing to follow through. Unwilling to dig in and carve out the time to do the hard work, they had conveniently let the demands of their jobs distract them. But this wasn't Bruce. Immediately, Kevin could see and hear just how serious he was about improving his communication skills.

> Kevin came back to the office and said, "Jackie, I think this guy is the real deal."

We began to work with Bruce in a variety of ways. Whether it is to help him with inspiring players, team building, finding ways out of a funk, or taking the high road when handling challenging questions from the media, Boch has used us as a sounding board to get a different perspective. We've been doing this together for better than 20 years.

Lessons for Business and Personal Success

During the last three decades, we have been chasing down stories about unconventional leaders in disruptive companies who are blowing the doors off business as usual. We go deep and get to know leaders who stand out. Our books profile gutsy, go-for-it leaders who are creating the future of business and brands that are tied to a noble and worthy cause. These are the kind of people who fill a room with energy, draw the best out of others, and do things others say cannot be done. As you could imagine, they are also extraordinary magnets for world-class talent. That's why competitors envy them and customers can't live without them. Bruce Bochy is one of these leaders.

After the San Francisco Giants won the 2012 World Series, Boch stood out. The baseball world came to grips with the fact of the Giants winning the championship in both 2010 and 2012 wasn't just a fluke. People from all walks of life—journalists, talk show hosts, bloggers, coaches, entrepreneurs, and business executives—started to ask questions like: "How do the Giants prevail when they are outmatched by their opponents? How did they overcome seemingly insurmountable odds? What special ingredients cause this team to gel? Why do they seem to perform better on the biggest stages in baseball where the pressure is so intense? And what role might the Giants culture play in all of this?"

We approached Boch with the idea of collaborating on a book that would speak to how they did it. The good news was that working together over a long time would give us a great vantage point for a project like this. The bad news was, we knew he wasn't excited about it.

In Boch's mind, winning in 2012 silenced the critics who said winning in 2010 was just luck. It also silenced the demons of doubt in his own mind that pestered him with the question, "Can we do it again?" But he still wasn't convinced the story was worthy of a book, so we dropped the subject completely. Meanwhile, as we continued to work on issues Boch wanted help with, we felt strongly that there were many business and life lessons to be learned from the Giants journey to success and from the way they handle the not-so-great years as well.

They've done a masterful job of organically developing talent inside the organization and then supplementing it from the outside to fill holes. Getting the right people in the right seats on the bus—to use Jim Collins's phraseology—is essential. As we will see, however, finding talent is not enough. Roster strength is essential, but getting that talent to come together as a unified front and function as one is the ultimate differentiator in baseball—as it is in business and everyday life. Riddled with injuries and setbacks in each of their World Series runs, the Giants adapted, changed, and built an organization that was capable of self-renewal on the fly.

In many respects, baseball, like business, is a game of chess. You do an in-depth study of the market, the shifting trends, and your competitors. Then you anticipate every move they can make and plan for it accordingly. It involves thinking two or three innings—or even games—ahead of where you are, rehearsing moves and counter moves in your head, always looking for that little something that will give you a competitive advantage. Survey the smartest people in MLB and they will tell you Boch does this as well as anyone. He is a brilliant strategist.

> **Roster strength is essential, but getting that talent to come together as a unified front and function as one is the ultimate differentiator in baseball.**

What makes the Giants such a compelling story from the game-of-life point of view are the glaring lessons about passion, perseverance, and the art of the comeback that pour out of this franchise. You see what happens when players unselfishly play for each other and find a cause worth fighting for. Then you can watch how this sense of purpose and destiny turns individual performance into a powerful movement that wins championships—and learns from the experience when the team doesn't. You can see what happens when people aren't hog-tied by bureaucracy and excessive rules. When a clubhouse is turned over to the players, they own it. The glue that makes this possible is trust. The result is a spirit of community that binds people together. These observations just scratch the surface of what's in the Giants DNA.

No Doesn't Necessarily Mean No

Not long after the Giants won the 2014 World Series, we got to talking with Boch about many of the principles and themes that have been consistent in the Giants way of playing—winning and losing—baseball. "Bruce, there's definitely a story to tell here," Kevin said, "and it should be told from an insider's perspective, from someone who can take readers behind the scenes." This time, he agreed. As we envisioned the project, it became clear to all of us that it should be a book that equips, enables, and enriches people's lives. So, we teamed up to write what you now have in your hands.

The book is not only the story of how the Giants won three World Championships in 5 years; it outlines a game plan for leaders anywhere to build great chemistry and achieve great things too. Periodically, you will get the other side of the story as well. Having just finished the worst year in franchise history (2017), the book also speaks to how Boch and the Giants slug through the really hard times and focus forward. They not only teach us how to win with humility, they also teach us how to lose with dignity.

You will find Boch's thinking throughout, in his own words, highlighted in the orange sections labeled Boch. Our complementary insights come from either 2 or 20 years of research, depending on how you choose to look at it. We have spent the last 2 years, almost weekly, talking with Bruce about the ingredients that make chemistry happen. But this is against the backdrop of a 20-year partnership.

In addition to our ongoing dialogue with Boch, we conducted interviews with the Giants front office executives, players, coaches, trainers, clubhouse staff, and other executives in MLB. We tapped more than 300 articles from Giants beat writers, reporters, and other journalists who basically live with the team during the season. We sifted

> We hope this book will inspire leaders to create their own best place, where the best people can do their best work to make the world better.

through the 100-plus videos of pre and postgame interviews, short features, and documentaries provided by MLB Productions and Giants Productions.

It is our hope that Bochy Ball! will inspire you to think big and to act boldly; to not back down from your dreams. If you run a business, we hope it helps you develop a critical mass of enlightened people who want to do whatever it takes to create a best place, where the best people can do their best work to make the world better. If you're a parent or coach, we hope this book helps you cultivate the mental, spiritual, and emotional makeup in your children and athletes that enables them to be world-class team members. If you are an athlete, we hope the stories and ideas here motivate you to play at full throttle and become a catalyst for drawing other players together to achieve more than you ever dreamed you could. But first, a caveat.

Guilty as Charged

When we wrote our first book, *NUTS! Southwest Airlines' Crazy Recipe for Business and Personal Success,* the reviews were mostly great. The ones that weren't said that it was too Pollyannaish. The critics said we wrote from a biased perspective, as though we had a love affair with the company and its founders. They were right; we did. Our passion is to find what's right and good in the world, what's worth emulating, then write about that. That's why we write positive stories about standout leaders and standout brands.

Let cynics and skeptics write the other stuff.

Make a list of your Top 100 all-time great leaders. Are they perfect? No. We are all flawed. From Herb Kelleher at Southwest Airlines to Boch and his colleagues in the Giants organization, there are no exceptions. If you dig deep enough, you can always find a way to demonize someone who has achieved great success—particularly if they live in a fishbowl. Frankly, we think people are tired of analysts who dig for the dirt and then play "gotcha." You know

the type. Instead of evaluating the overall trajectory of a leader's body of work, they "pole-vault over mouse turds" by dissecting that person's every imperfection.

Nevertheless, we suspect that this book, like all books, will draw some criticism. Why? We have become close friends with Boch over 20 years. We are biased. So, feel free to evaluate our part of what you read from that perspective. And, you should know, the person most uncomfortable with our holding Boch up as a great leader who understands chemistry is Boch himself. But we've also traveled the world and made careers out of identifying what makes great leaders tick. The companies we've worked with and written about are excellent reference points for comparing Bruce Bochy and his colleagues to other gutsy and benevolent leaders.

As you will see, Boch and the people who surround him stand with the best.

Kevin and Jackie Freiberg
San Diego, California

Warm Up

GIANT CHEMISTRY

Igniting a Legacy

1
THE PERFECT GAME
It Doesn't Happen Alone

On June 13, 2012, starter Matt Cain did what only 22 pitchers have done in the history of Major League Baseball (MLB)—and what no one had done in the 129-year history of the Giants franchise. He pitched a perfect game. To pitch a perfect game, no runner can reach base. This means you have to retire 27 hitters in a row. Not only that, Cain matched Dodgers' iconic ace, Sandy Koufax, with 14 strikeouts, the most ever in a perfect game[1]. Here are a few of the game's other highlights.

- Cain threw 125 pitches, the most thrown in an MLB perfect game.
- The Giants scored 10 runs, the most by any team in a perfect game.
- Cain scored a run in the fifth inning, the only pitcher ever to have scored a run in a perfect game.

Depending on which baseball aficionado is doing the math, the experts have calculated the odds of pitching a perfect game at 1 in 18,000 and 1 in 29,000. Either way, it's a very exclusive club.

The unflappable 27-year-old pitcher shut down the Houston Astros in a performance that was nothing short of brilliant. He would emerge the hero, deservedly so. But, he would be the first to admit that it was only possible because of a team effort. Think about the critical elements in the system that enabled Cain to do the nearly impossible.

The offense gave Cain huge run support with 10 runs. Catcher Buster Posey called a game that leveraged every one of Cain's pitches. No hesitation. No shake-offs. Cain went with whatever Posey called—any pitch, anytime. "I can't thank Buster enough. I didn't even question once what he was calling. I just let him go. Buster did an unbelievable job back there."

Every player on defense knew his role and played it passionately, not knowing what would be at stake until the middle of the game. In the sixth inning,

Matt Cain strikes out 14 in the first perfect game in San Francisco Giants history.

Melky Cabrera chased down Chris Snyder's one-out fly ball, scurrying back to make a leaping catch at the wall. Cain showed his enthusiasm by raising both arms and slapping his glove in gratification when Cabrera made the catch.

Then, in what might have been *the* defining play of the game—and one for the ages—right fielder Gregor Blanco ran deep into right center to make a spectacular, desperate diving catch on the warning track, which robbed Jordan Schafer of a base hit and secured the first out of the seventh inning. When Blanco came up with the ball and held it high over his head, the sellout crowd roared and gave him a prolonged standing ovation. "It's unbelievable," says Boch. "I still don't know how he made that catch." Cain hugged Blanco in the dugout after the inning and then again after the dog-pile celebration cleared at the end of the game.

Cain later said: "In the seventh inning, when Blanco makes that catch in center field, I literally felt everybody on the mound with me. I mean the whole stadium was electric right there." Speaking of Schafer's hit, first baseman Brandon Belt said: "I thought it was going to get down, but then I saw how good a jump he [Blanco] got on it, just like he's done all year; that's why you can't say enough

Gregor Blanco a major contributor to Matt Cain's perfect game.

about what he's done in the outfield. So, I saw that he had a good jump on it and thought maybe he's got a chance, and then he just made one of the most spectacular plays I think anybody's ever seen considering the circumstances. It's probably one of the best catches in baseball history."

Cain said of Cabrera and Blanco: "We can talk about the sixth inning and seventh inning and those two unbelievable catches. That right there, that changes the whole thing."

Boch also did everything he could to support Cain. In the later innings, he inserted strong infielders Brandon Crawford and Emmanuel Burris in the middle infield and replaced Pablo Sandoval at third base with the agile Joaquín Árias. In the eighth inning, with Cain's pitch count rising, Boch sent reliever Shane Loux *behind* the dugout to warm up secretly. It was simply a precautionary measure. Boch would've let Cain go at least 130 pitches, maybe more. Cain had incredible stuff and maintained, in fact increased, his pitch velocity through the last inning.

In the ninth inning, with two outs, Árias took a ground ball with a tough hop at third. With little time and no margin for error, Árias turned and fired a long rocket ball to Belt at first for the final out.

Game over!

Cain fist pumped. The Giants dugout emptied. Dog-pile on the mound. Fans who were strangers jumped up and started hugging each other in the stands because Matt Cain and his supporting cast had brought the city of San Francisco something historic. A perfect game!

Powerful Chemistry

While he never used the term, Cain clearly understood the power of what can happen when a team has chemistry. He summed up the game this way: "I can't explain what these two guys (Posey and Blanco) and the rest of the guys did to make this happen. It definitely was not just me. I mean, running down balls, hitting home runs, making plays; it was an all-out effort tonight. Everybody did a lot of work and it turned out perfect."

What if Cabrera's timing on Snyder's fly ball is a second too late and the ball bounces off the wall? What if Cabrera, Belt, and Blanco each *don't* hit two-run homers? What if bench coach Ron Wotus doesn't place Blanco to "shade Shafer toward center field?" Would he have caught the ball? What if Árias can't get the ball out of his glove at third base and the runner at first beats the throw by a split second? What if Posey gets away from Cain's strength and gives up a hit on his third or fourth best pitch?

A lot of space and time lies between the sixth and seventh innings and the final outcome of a baseball game. A catch made in the sixth inning is far removed from the final score, right? Cabrera and Blanco could not have known that each of their clutch plays would make a major contribution to the perfect game, but they played as if they did. That's how chemistry works. Playing at full throttle way over *here* in the sixth could have a cause-and-effect relationship with the final, game-winning pitch way over *there* in the ninth, officially making the game one for the record books.

And, don't doubt for a minute that the sold-out crowd wasn't a factor. Giants fans hung on every pitch. Comcast SportsNet Bay Area journalist Amy Gutierrez interviewed Cain in front of the packed house at AT&T Park. When she asked Cain if he could feel the pull of the fans, he was in awe. "Yes! I don't think there's an empty seat right now. That's unbelievable."

Posey said the game had a postseason feel to it and Cain agreed. "You know what? It felt like the World Series, but it almost felt a little bit louder, a little bit crazier than that. Every strike, they were going nuts for. It was truly amazing. I've never had that much excitement in every pitch, every strike, every swing."[2] Center fielder Ángel Pagán said: "I've never been in the World Series, but I'm pretty sure the World Series feels like that because it was pretty intense. It was awesome." Pagán's words were almost prophetic. In three months he would indeed get to feel the adrenaline rush of a World Series.

The point is, there are so many variables and so many moving parts over 125 pitches that must be in sync to pitch a perfect game—plays that have to go just right. The parts have to function as a whole. One lapse in concentration, one botched play, one missed signal, and the opportunity for a perfect game is gone.

Boch: It was a night we will all remember. After Blanco's catch we could sense something special was happening. So, every pitch, every play you're just living on the edge hoping he gets it done. The crowd was loud, like in a playoff game. They were so into it. The players said the same thing. You could viscerally feel the energy.

And our guys . . . I know they were feeling the pressure in the ninth inning. I told Árias at the time, "I wouldn't have wanted to be the one out there taking that grounder for the last out."

You can imagine the intensity. You come all this way in a game, you've shut down 26 batters, and then we don't make the last out. That's how much tension there was.

We were all pulling so hard for Matty. He got in a little bit of trouble, ran a couple of full counts, but he handled it with incredible composure. You know, this is not the first time he had knocked on the door of a perfect game. There were a couple of times during the season when I thought he had the opportunity to do it, but this time he got it done.

To watch a guy—a group of guys really—make history together and do something that's never been done in the Giants franchise, that's special. It's a lifelong dream for every pitcher. I don't know how to describe how hard it is to do what he did. It was my first one, and I was so happy for Matt. I was happy for Buster too. A catcher can go his whole career and not catch a no-no [no hitter] let alone a perfect game.

After Belt caught Árias's throw to end the game, he put the ball in his back pocket and rushed the mound to celebrate. Later he recalled giving it to Cain in the clubhouse: "Handing him the ball was one of the coolest things. You see stuff like that on TV and you wonder how you'd feel doing that for a teammate. Honestly, it was one of the best feelings I've ever had playing the game. I was just so happy for him. He deserves this so much. He goes out every game with good stuff, and you knew it was just a matter of time before something really special was going to happen. He's a bulldog. He fights every day."[3]

Chemistry in baseball—and in any other human endeavor for that matter—depends to a large degree on how team-oriented the individual players are. Blanco chose to play all out. His heroic catch was a turning point for the team. He got people thinking: "Hey, this might be possible. We could actually do this."

Javier López leads the charge as players take a victory lap around AT&T Park. Another sold-out crowd at AT&T Park.

The Championship Run

In 2014, the Giants won their third World Championship in five years. It was the Giants eighth World Series title in franchise history, and they became the first National League team to win eight since the 1940s Cardinals. More than 1 million fans showed up to honor the Giants in a victory parade that blanketed downtown San Francisco's Market Street in confetti—just as they had in 2010 and 2012. The boys were world champions again. And, again, they did it harmoniously, with humility and a collective sense of humor. They also did it with a deep sense of gratitude for the 10th player—the 40,000-plus fans who showed up at the park every day. Fanatical, loud, eccentric, and loyal, they never stop believing—they bleed orange.

The team's connection with its fans mirrors the chemistry within the club. Giant chemistry goes beyond teamwork: It is a bond unlike any other. It shows up in different people, runs in multiple directions, and can always be counted on. It's about the connection between the Giants front office and the team; among the players themselves; between the front office, team, and broadcasters; and between the entire organization and the fans. Even in the not-so-magical years, these people remain faithful to each other and to the shared vision that unites them. Everyone in San Francisco knows it and feels it. As Giants CEO Larry Baer said to the fans, "Our story is a collective one." Indeed, it is; they all do it together.

It all came together in 2010, again in 2012, and in 2014, the third time *was* a real charm. Three different Giants teams. Three different roads to the postseason. Three World Series trophies. But each followed a familiar story line: Everything is going well, then something goes terribly wrong; a thrilling battle must be fought—a battle that requires the players to muster everything they've got. In the last minute (almost always with the Giants it is the last minute), the heroes do something extraordinary to take the win. Over five notorious years, these crowd-pleasers took their fans on a thrilling roller-coaster ride and gave history a shove.

2010
Beat Atlanta, 3-1 in NLDS.
Beat Philadelphia, 4-2 in NLCS.
Beat Texas, 4-1 in World Series.

2012
Beat Cincinnati, 3-2 NLDS.
Beat St. Louis, 4-3 in NLCS.
Beat Detroit, 4-0 in World Series.

2014
Beat Pittsburgh, 1-0 in Wild Card.
Beat Washington, 3-1 in NLDS.
Beat St. Louis, 4-1 in NLCS.
Beat Kansas City, 4-3 in World Series.

One of the common factors in all three of the Giants championship runs is a guy who never took an at bat or threw a pitch or fielded a ball; a guy whom many nevertheless consider to be a lock on the Hall of Fame. Bruce Bochy is the 10th manager in baseball history with three World Series rings. The other nine are revered and celebrated in Cooperstown.

Bochy's rise to MLB fame was not meteoric; it was a slow and steady climb with a few twists and turns and lots of patience. He did it the old-fashioned way. He apprenticed and learned and then apprenticed some more. After 40 years in baseball, Bochy has developed an uncanny feel for the game, for his players, and for working with the Giants front office.

It is extremely difficult to win a World Championship in any sport, let alone the MLB World Series three times in five years. This book is the story of a manager, a team, a franchise, and a city—and the extraordinary kind of chemistry that contributed to their uncommon feat. For fans of the game, in the San Francisco Bay Area and around the globe, it's a chronicle of the Giants world-class achievement. It's also a playbook for leaders everywhere—whether in business or baseball, in professional or personal life—who want to borrow from what's special about the Giants.

2
DUGOUT LEADERSHIP
Lifting Others

When spring training camp started in 2010, affable Giants reliever Jeremy Affeldt was clowning around with the rookies and a few of the coaches. He was conducting an informal survey, game show style. "Of all the MLB players you admired when you were growing up, who was your favorite?" he asked. Now, you'd think there couldn't be a wrong answer to a question like this, but no one, not even Ron Wotus, San Francisco's tenured bench coach, got it right. Of course, Affeldt was the judge.

The correct answer, according to Affeldt? Bruce Bochy.

Besides being a stellar veteran reliever, Affeldt was just doing one of the things Affeldt does best—having fun and keeping it light. While his informal quiz was tongue-in-cheek, the inference behind the ribbing conveyed a larger message: Not only is Bruce Bochy the most decorated skipper in the game at this writing, he has also solidified his legacy as one of the greatest managers of all time.

Jeremy Affeldt, undoubtedly thinking up his next game show–like quiz to stump teammates.

Sheer Numbers

After 24 years of managing in professional baseball, 12 with the San Diego Padres and 12 with the San Francisco Giants, Boch is the only manager in history to win at least 900 games for two different teams. The winningest manager in both San Diego and San Francisco, Boch has led his teams to eight postseasons and three World Championships. He has been to the World Series four times—more than any active manager in the game. (He also went once as a player.) He is just the fifth manager in the history of the game to lead a team to three World Series titles in a five-year span.

During Boch's tenure, the Giants have won 11 postseason rounds, the longest streak ever by a manager—equaled only by Joe Torre with the New York Yankees between 1998 and 2001. Boch's .679 postseason winning percentage is currently 10th all time among managers with more than 10 career postseason games.

In the 40 seasons that have passed since the advent of free agency in 1975, only four managers (Tony La Russa, Bobby Cox, Joe Torre, and Bruce Bochy) have won as many as 1,600 games and four pennants. With 1,815 regular season victories (the most of any active manager), Boch ranks 15th on the all-time list. All 22 previous managers who have won four pennants have been elected to the Hall of Fame.

> Boch is the only manager to achieve 900-plus wins with two different clubs (San Diego and San Francisco). He has led his teams to eight postseasons and three World Championships. He has been to the World Series four times—more than any active manager in the game.

In 1996, the Baseball Writers' Association of America named Bruce Bochy National League Manager of the Year, and in both 1996 and 1998, Sporting News named him National League Manager of the Year. Between 1995 and 2015 he was voted into the top three candidates for this recognition six times. Keep in mind that the voting for this prestigious title doesn't include a manager's performance during the postseason.

With a third World Series ring, Bochy joined an exclusive club. Only Tony La Russa, Sparky Anderson, Miller Huggins, and John McGraw have also won three each. Only Joe Torre, Walter Alston, Connie Mack, Joe McCarthy, and Casey Stengel have won more.

If you look outside baseball, it would not be a stretch to put Boch in the same camp with Bill Belichick (New England Patriots), Phil Jackson (Chicago Bulls and Los Angeles Lakers), and Gregg Popovich (San Antonio Spurs). Each has built strong team chemistry and contributed to powerful standout franchise brands.

Respect from Peers

Baseball is loaded with talent—on and off the field. So, to be recognized by your peers as a force to be reckoned with is a big deal. "I've never been shy in saying he's a manager I have a lot of respect for," St. Louis manager Mike Matheny said of Bochy. "People who get to see him day in and day out . . . they see somebody that is a constant source of leadership on that club."[4] Dodgers manager Dave Roberts, who played for Bochy in San Diego and San Francisco, put it succinctly: "He's the best manager in the game."[5]

At MLB's general managers (GMs) meeting in November 2014, Arizona Diamondbacks GM Dave "Stew" Stewart talked about his opponents. "You know the challenge with beating the Giants?" Stewart said. "It's Bruce Bochy. He's the key to that team. We would need him to be kidnapped and taken away someplace for us to have an opportunity."[6] Boch is an imposing figure. Stew might need a U.S. Navy SEAL team to make that extraction. Certainly, no one would ever consider hog-tying the Giants skipper and hauling him away, but many agree that Boch is an essential ingredient in the Giants success.

Los Angeles Angels manager Mike Scioscia, the second-winningest active manager in the game, told the *LA Times*: "He's very quietly putting together a Hall of Fame career. When you talk about Joe Torre, about Tony La Russa, about Bobby Cox, about guys that have made it, Boch is going to be right there when it's all said and done. And it will be very deserving if he gets in."[7]

One of those Hall of Famers, Tony La Russa, identified Boch as a complete manager. "A manager needs three things: a brain that knows the percentages, a heart that has instincts based on what's happening in the game, and the guts to pull the trigger. He relates to the players, they play hard for him, they want to learn, they want to compete. He's got excellent judgment during the game. He's creative offensively, he's got a very special feel for handling pitching. He's one of the best."[8]

After losing to the Giants in the 2010 National League Division Series (NLDS), retiring Atlanta Braves manager Bobby Cox received a standing ovation from the crowd, including Giants players. After the game, Cox, another Hall of Famer, said: "That was a nice gesture by the Giants. I love Bochy. He's one of the best guys in baseball. If we couldn't win, I'm glad he did."[9]

Drawing Players Up

Bochy knows how to get the best out of his players and turn what many analysts have thought to be average teams into division and World Series champions. In his book, *Evaluating Baseball's Managers,* Chris Jaffe examines 89 managers between 1876 and 2008, most of whom managed 10 seasons or more. Using various metrics to establish a manager's patterns (Do they tend to value base hits or wait for the three-run homer?), along with key issues they faced during their tenure, he discusses their approaches and how effective they were.

Jaffe noted that Bochy's teams scored 270 more runs and won 26 more games than expected during his 12 years with the Padres. Moreover, Padres veterans such as Phil Nevin, Ryan Klesko, Mark Kotsay, Mark Loretta, Mike Cameron, and Wally Joyner all produced better-than-expected results in notoriously pitcher-friendly parks under Bochy's leadership. Even the freakishly good Tony Gwynn put up some of his best numbers in his 30s and finished his last season at 41 with a .324 average, his 19th consecutive season batting at least .300. Boch recorded 951 victories and four NL West titles in San Diego, more than any manager in Padres franchise history.

Now, the cynics will be quick to note that performance-enhancing drugs were at play with

Bobby Cox, former manager of the Atlanta Braves.

the hitting surges players experienced in the late 1990s and beyond. And, Gwynn being Gwynn, was just from another planet. But what happened when Bochy moved to San Francisco? Same thing.

It looked like it was over for the 32-year-old Aubrey Huff who hit .241 in 2009. Then he came to San Francisco in 2010, hit .290, his on-base percentage was .385, and his slugging percentage was .506. In 2010, he was also voted into the Top 10 for Most Valuable Player (MVP) of the year.

Pat Burrell was finished with Tampa Bay. His offense was so miserable that the budget-conscious Rays released him and ate the rest of his $16 million contract. The Giants signed him to a minor league deal for a song and then, seven games later, he was in the majors hitting .266/.364/.509—contributing to the Giants success. A relatively similar story could be told about Ángel Pagán and Marco Scutaro.

At some point, you have to look at the common denominator—a leader who inspires people to bring their best selves to work.

A lot of variables go into a player's performance. But is this coincidence? At some point, you have to look at the common denominator—a leader who inspires people to bring their best selves to work.

During Bochy's tenure as manager of the Padres (1994–2006), the club finished 24 games under .500. Jaffe concluded that Bruce Bochy was the 30th best manager of all time, given his ability to draw the best out of often talent-starved teams and exceed the pundits' expectations. It should be noted that Jaffe's book was published in 2009 and his data collection only goes through 2006, Bochy's final season with the Padres. In other words, what Boch has done with the Giants doesn't factor into Jaffe's research.

Chris Haft of MLB.com follows the Giants closely. He gives Boch a lot of credit for the way he handles his staff. Here's how he delineated Boch's strengths.

He rarely puts people in a position to fail. He puts people in a position to succeed. That sounds basic, but sometimes a manager will send a guy up to bunt who's got no business bunting. Bruce won't do that. He knows his players' limitations, and he never criticizes them in print. That's another thing that sounds like something that most normal people wouldn't do, but he just doesn't do it. He may rip guys off the record, but it stays off the record. I don't think it affects the way he uses them, either, [. . .] he may come back with them the next day.[10]

With the Giants, Boch might have the world record for the number of rosters he's managed. Given this volatility, he managed to keep egos in check and create a bond among players—even with season-ending injuries dealt to Buster Posey, Scutaro, Matt Cain, and Pagán; serious injuries to Brandon Belt,

A players' manager is a person that the players just ultimately respect. And the reason they respect Boch is because [he] is invested in making each one of them successful.

—Giants CEO Larry Baer

Michael Morse, and Hunter Pence, daring to try numerous options at second and third base before landing on Joe Panik and Matt Duffy and then Eduardo Núñez; and demoting Tim Lincecum, Sergio Romo, Santiago Casilla, and Ryan Vogelsong. The ability to do more with less throughout his career is signature Bochy.

Kevin Towers was the Padres GM when Boch managed in San Diego. They are longtime friends. "He's an incredible leader and he's able to take ballplayers and make them usually better than what they are," Towers said.

"Every year, Bochy gives a talk he prepares for all off-season. It's about 45 minutes to an hour, no notes. And I'll tell you what, when he's done with it, myself, the players, they're ready to run through a frickin' wall for the guy."[11]

A Players' Manager

Giants CEO Larry Baer is a hands-off executive who hires talented people and then turns them loose. Boch, of course, is one of those people. "A players' manager is a person that the players just ultimately respect," Baer said. "And the reason they respect Boch is because Boch is invested in making each one of them successful." The players agree.

> "Boch is the only manager I've ever played for. He's the leader of this team. It would be tough imagining someone having a better baseball mind and being a better leader for the team."
> —**Madison Bumgarner**

> "It's an honor to play for a manager like Boch. To have somebody at the helm like him is a big reason why we have won three titles in the last five years." —**Buster Posey**

> "To be a part of [Bochy's] program and his team is such an honor. That's why coming here was a big thing for me. Everybody comes here happy to be here, nobody ever has a bad attitude. Everybody has one goal, and that's to win together. To me, it's the perfect balance of having fun and having success." —**Michael Morse**

> "He's got a lot of poise. When your leader is a rock, it leaks into your team." —**Hunter Pence**

> "I'm glad I'm playing for a guy like him, for sure. He just seems to have the right intuition with every move he makes." —**Travis Ishikawa**

> "He speaks, people listen. He's a game changer."—**Jake Peavy** [who played for four other men][12]

Media-Friendly

To a large degree, the fans build a relationship with a club through the media, which can be a cynical outpost. But, even there, Boch gets high marks because he makes time for the media. He enjoys reporters, learns from them, and values their role in the game. "Many managers have set times when you can see them," said Bill Center, longtime sportswriter for the *San Diego Union-Tribune*. "Bruce always is approachable, and if he tells you something, it's pretty much gospel."[13]

The Giants skipper is personable and down-to-earth. He can tell a good baseball story, of course, yet he can also take you on a deep dive and give you tremendous insights. Frequently accused of deadpanning, he actually has a great sense of humor and is witty, which makes him more quotable than he gets credit for. But he is also not afraid to confront dicey issues. He can tell it like it is without throwing a player, or any other member of the club, under the bus—almost always because he assumes responsibility for things that go wrong. Brian "Sabes" Sabean, the Giants Executive Vice President, Baseball Operations and former GM,[14] told us this talk-straight approach is why the media trusts and appreciates him.

"People forget that these guys [managers] get their ass grilled twice a day. Good, bad, or ugly, you gotta meet with reporters every day. You have to keep your cool, protect your players, and not air your dirty laundry in public or make a misstep, and that wears on you. And, all this happens in a world where everyone is going to put their spin on it, no matter what you meant. That's why I marvel at how he handles it. He's got a great relationship with the media."

Best Overall

When ESPN released its 2015 results of a survey that polled 50 scouts, front-office executives, big league coaches, and media analysts, Bochy's rankings were nothing short of impressive. Here's how he ranked in each category.

First.   Best overall manager
First.   Best at handling pitching staff
Second. Best tactician
Third.   Best at relating to players
First.   Best at using entire 25-man roster
First.   Best leader

ESPN also asked 117 players, "If you could play for any manager (other than your current one), who would it be?" Boch ranked second behind Joe Maddon of the Chicago Cubs.

Brian "Sabes" Sabean, Giants EVP, Baseball Operations & Former GM.

In 2016, *Sporting News*[15] ranked Boch number one among all current managers, and Yardbarker[16] had him number three in 2017. There are other statistical surveys and pundit rankings, but they all put Boch in the top three among stellar managers.

Let Go and Move On

Baseball can be a fickle game. Superstition runs rampant in the culture. So, when a team goes into a downward spiral and the fans start barking, it's usually time for someone to go. Sometimes it's deserved and sometimes it isn't. In a business where you are only as good as your last season, Boch might be the only current manager to have never been fired.

With one year remaining on Bochy's contract in San Diego, Padres CEO Sandy Alderson indicated that the club wasn't ready to give him an extension "for now." From the outside looking in, the cost-conscious Padres were a club in search of themselves. Weighted down by the their lean years, Boch was ready to turn a corner. He was excited about finding a home that was a cultural fit and where he had the potential to establish some real chemistry with a front office that shared his passion for winning.

When the Giants asked for permission to talk with Bochy and it was granted, the rest was a whirlwind. Within a week Boch was in front of the media, beaming as he held up his new No. 15 San Francisco jersey.

That Bochy has never been fired speaks volumes about his well-rounded leadership. He understands and appreciates the role of the *entire* front office, not just the GM. He cares about their jobs and wants to know how he can help. He fully grasps that baseball is entertainment and that without the fans there is no club. Bochy participates in in community events and encourages his players to do the same.

Boch has a commanding presence and confidently skippers the ship, but he also shows great admiration and appreciation for the coaching and clubhouse staff who make the ship seaworthy. Down-to-earth, approachable, and curious, he has a natural ability to make people feel comfortable, appreciated, and valued.

Bigger Than One Player

How many teams get nominated for *Sports Illustrated*'s Sportsperson of the Year Award? That's what happened in 2010 after the Giants won the World Series. The editors make their selection from among the best athletes, male and female, in every sport based on their performance, sportsmanship, and contributions off the field.

The nomination was the sports world's way of recognizing that the Giants are bigger than one player. The way they came together with each other, with all levels of the franchise, and with the city of San Francisco represented sports at its inspirational best. Nelson Mandela said: "Sports has the power to change the world. It has the power to inspire, the power to unite people that little else has . . ." The Giants are a living example of the power to inspire, unify, and unite.

Scan the sold-out crowds at AT&T Park and chances are you'll see the fist-pumping, 91-year-old Rosalie Alioto, aka Dancing Granny, seated among Little Leaguers with big dreams, and everyone in between. In 2010, multiple generations, extended families, and an entire community were brought together around a World Series title long in the making. Orange fever swept the City by the Bay. The Giants did for San Francisco what the 1955 Dodgers did for Brooklyn, the 2004 Red Sox did for Boston and most recently, what the 2016 Cubs did for Chicago. As Sabes put it, San Francisco had finally become a "baseball town."

Sportsperson of the Year is one of the athletic community's highest honors. The Giants and other nominees were ultimately beat out by Drew Brees, quarterback for the New Orleans Saints. Nonetheless, to have been nominated as a team says something special both about *how* the Giants made it to the pinnacle of the game and about the person who led them there.

When it comes to passion for the Giants, young people have nothing on 91-year-old Rosalie Alioto.

It's all about chemistry. And, as with any organization that rises to greatness, the formula is complex. But, leadership is always an indispensable part of the mix.

He "Gets" Leadership

Somewhere in our first couple of years of working with Boch it dawned on us: "We've worked with many iconic leaders in our career. Herb Kelleher and Colleen Barrett at Southwest Airlines; Ratan Tata at India's esteemed Tata Group; Nandan Nilekani, cofounder of Infosys; Rob Katz at Vail Resorts; Graham Weston and Lanham Napier at Rackspace; and General Bill Cooney at USAA, just to name a few. Boch is as gifted as any CEO I've ever met. Intelligence, strategy, creativity, courage, heart, and leadership presence—he's got the whole package. This guy *gets* leadership."

In a game that has enough data, statistics, and sabermetrics to tax a supercomputer, you can't adequately measure these character strengths, and you would certainly be hard-pressed to put a price tag on them. Like all great leaders, Boch is a blend of many attributes and actions that are paradoxical. His success is anchored in how he manages these paradoxes. Here are a few examples to illustrate his finesse.

Be **for** *your players, but not one of them.* Boch easily puts himself in the shoes of his players and thinks like them because he was one of them. This empathy informs his decisions. Today, he is an integral member of the team, but he is not a player and doesn't try to be. Approachable and affable, he is relevant to his players, yet he respects their space. He is their greatest advocate and often their toughest critic. He is the general, the commander in chief, but he does not see himself as being above anyone. Players respect him and love playing for him because he strikes a balance. Too much separation and he would be out of touch. Too much of trying to be "one of the guys" and he would compromise his credibility.

Be tough, but not mean. You can't create a World Series—winning franchise without big expectations, tough discipline, and focused execution. Players will test boundaries. They will evaluate how strong a manager is before they wholeheartedly devote themselves to the vision he sets for the team. They want to know: "Does he have the courage to make tough decisions that are best for the team? Can he stand up to players who are not living the culture? Is he stalwart in looking out for the good of the group?" The problem arises when a leader confuses being tough with being mean. Boch is not domineering, controlling, or brash. He doesn't force himself on his coaches or his players. He doesn't lean on the power of title or pedigree; yet, he's very much in charge. He demands a lot from his players and coaches. He is tough, but never mean.

Be in control, but let go. In his first few years of managing, Boch tried to do everything. He quickly learned, however, that he could be in control without controlling everything. Delegating did several things. It gave him more freedom. It connected his coaching staff and made them feel more engaged, more a part of the team. And, it put people who were really good at those things in charge of those things. It *is* paradoxical; he has gained more control by relinquishing it.

Be constrained, but not limited. When you are part of a small-market club like the Padres, you learn to do more with less or you lose big time. We have never heard Boch complain about payroll constraints. It seems he always considered it a challenge to see what he could do with what he had. When competing against clubs with deep pockets, he seemed to quietly draw from the well of defiance and show the baseball world what his teams could do. Often, his players exceeded the experts' expectations. Whether it was playing through pain, pushing through self-imposed psychological constraints, or bouncing back when all the prognosticators said it was over, Boch saw constraints as an opportunity to be more creative and draw more from less.

Be a servant, but not a pushover. The only reason to be in leadership is because you have a desire to serve—to right a wrong, to enrich a condition, to draw the best out of others, to make the world better. Boch intuitively understands this. He would do anything for one of his players or coaches; he has their backs. When his teams play poorly, he doesn't shift blame; he assumes responsibility. When they play well, he doesn't absorb the accolades; he deflects them and gives his players the credit. Players see in Boch an other-centered person who is not weak; he is confident, yet humble. He's no pushover. He's direct and firm, yet compassionate when it comes to telling players the difficult truth. He doesn't shy away from the brutal facts of reality in the media, with his bosses, or with franchise owners either. Boch owns the losses, shares the wins, and handles the rest with dignity and honor.

Know that the more you learn, the less you know. Boch is a lifelong learner who doesn't believe he has arrived. He knows he can learn something from anyone. He also has enough confidence to own his shortcomings, to be vulnerable and grow. He is competitive. If Boch is going to do something, he's going to dig in and do it well. And, he's dedicated to baseball. From his first years as a manager it was clear that he wanted to be a great ambassador for the game. That meant being well-rounded and becoming proficient in those parts of the manager's role that were outside of coaching. In 20-plus years, he has created an impressive body of work and racked up a boatload of experience. But the game has changed dramatically and with those changes come more questions about managing effectively in this new era. The hunt for new and better ways of doing it is what keeps Bochy in the game.

> **Great leaders believe that they are there to serve the team—not the other way around.**

Speak without responding, act without reacting. When you manage 25 different, often eccentric personalities, there is plenty of room for drama. Yet, Boch has had very little of that in his clubhouses. One reason for this is the calming effect he has on his players. He doesn't overreact. If a player is "amped" about something, he doesn't mirror that behavior. Instead, he will just listen and let the fellow get it out, whatever "it" is. Boch intuitively knows that reacting to a situation could exacerbate it. The better part of prudence is often to do nothing and let time play a role.

We've watched him do this with players who said something derogatory or questionable in the media because they were upset about something that happened during a rough game. We knew Boch was ticked. We know how most people would have reacted. But he took a different tack. He took a step back, made sure he had all the facts, reflected on what the player might be thinking. He patiently gave it a day or two before reacting and then he rationally moved to resolve the conflict.

Boch is an action-oriented leader. He's not prone to denial or putting things off because of fear. There is wisdom in his restraint. Boch has often cut cycle time and accelerated conflict resolution by not forcing a situation prematurely.

Be proud, but not arrogant. Boch has always been extremely proud of his players and what he has accomplished as a manager, but he has never been cocky or arrogant. This remains true today, even after winning three World Series titles. He is pleased with what his teams have done for San Francisco; he is equally grateful for what the city, the fans, the front office, and his coaching staff have done for his players. With Boch, it's never been about Boch. Nothing happens in isolation. It's always a collaborative effort.

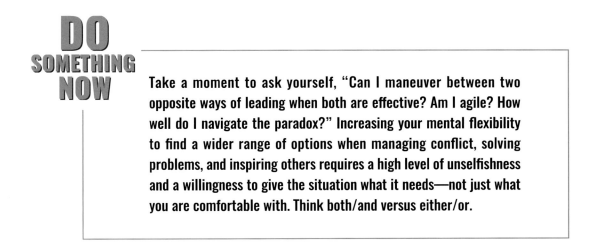

DO SOMETHING NOW

Take a moment to ask yourself, "Can I maneuver between two opposite ways of leading when both are effective? Am I agile? How well do I navigate the paradox?" Increasing your mental flexibility to find a wider range of options when managing conflict, solving problems, and inspiring others requires a high level of unselfishness and a willingness to give the situation what it needs—not just what you are comfortable with. Think both/and versus either/or.

The overwhelming majority of baseball experts agree that Bruce Bochy is a remarkable leader. He has demonstrated almost every attribute that you would look for in a Hall of Fame manager. He has won in multiple places under varied conditions. His success has been sustained over time. Most importantly, he holds an enviable postseason track record. He has won not one, not two, but three MLB World Series championships.

Are we talking about innate qualities that are gifted to only a cherished few? No! What we are talking about is a special set of leadership characteristics that all of us can learn from, leadership qualities that have inspired and enabled a team, a fan base, a community, and a franchise to gel. We're talking about a leader who is willing to work hard at blending divergent talents, personalities, and experiences to collectively accomplish incredible things. A leader who intentionally paves the way for creating a best place, where the best players can play their best game to make the experience for all stakeholders so much better.

And we believe Boch is this kind of leader!

3
CHEMISTRY
Art and Science?

What causes teammates to rise to the occasion? What's the difference between underdogs who emerge as champions against more talented teams that come up short? What causes a team to form such a bond that they can overcome insurmountable odds? What is the intangible but common element in each of these scenarios?

Chemistry

It's hard to describe, but you know it when you see it. Chemistry brings a team, an organization, a family, or a marriage together and makes it gel, makes it click. The signs are obvious: people who understand each other, respect each other, like each other, and are loyal to each other. People who support each other and lift each other up. Individuals who share a desire to achieve common aspirations collectively.

Chemistry springs forth when people value collaboration, cooperation, and connectivity over self-interest, individuality, and personal achievement. When there is chemistry, people take the initiative to build deep-seated, meaningful, and fulfilling relationships. Integrity, accountability, honesty, trust, respect, humility, compassion, and love are some of the elements that make chemistry happen. Chemistry is the prerequisite for profoundly rewarding achievements, the kind that blow our minds by demonstrating the extraordinary heights to which the human spirit can rise.

Chemistry is what people talk about after an athletic team wins a championship, a project team creates a game-changing innovation, a start-up beats the odds, or a sales team lands a huge piece of business. Chemistry is the pilot light that sparks talents, skills, and passions and sets them ablaze. Chemistry is what makes a team a formidable force.

Chemical Bonds | Chemistry Defined

A challenge in writing about chemistry is to not oversimplify it on the one hand and to not overthink it on the other. Can chemistry be reduced to a simple formula? We'd like to think so, but we know better.

Yet, as metrics for everything permeate the game of baseball, one of the next frontiers will be to figure out what chemistry is and how to measure it. The people who crack this code just may find the Holy Grail of baseball. We'd like to offer a *working* definition of chemistry as a starting point.

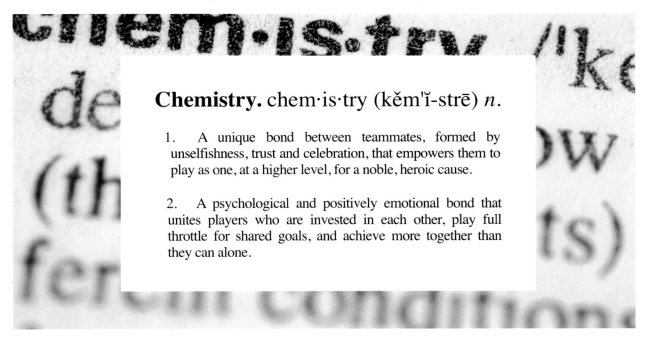

Chemistry. chem·is·try (kĕm'ĭ-strē) *n.*

1. A unique bond between teammates, formed by unselfishness, trust and celebration, that empowers them to play as one, at a higher level, for a noble, heroic cause.

2. A psychological and positively emotional bond that unites players who are invested in each other, play full throttle for shared goals, and achieve more together than they can alone.

Think of a time when you were a part of doing something significant that energized, fulfilled, and enriched your life. We're betting that it involved a special bond with others who shared a common goal and commitment to a cause worth fighting for. We're betting that you cared more about what you could achieve together than any glory you got on your own. We're also betting that you were undeterred by a lack of talent or insufficient resources, by odds that seemed insurmountable, and by critics that said you couldn't do it. That's what chemistry does. It's the X factor that makes the impossible possible and leaves people asking, "How did you do that?"

Chemistry is what brought the San Francisco Giants together—especially in the critical moments—to win three World Series playoffs over five seasons. The thing that set them apart in their three improbable runs to the top was that their belief in each other, and their unwavering ability to act on that belief, was dialed up higher than it was on most other teams they faced. And it's chemistry that holds the San Francisco Giants together during the slumps and funks of a long, slow not-so-winning season too. And, if used correctly, chemistry can be a powerful bond that continues to unite before, in between, and even after the championship years.

Chemistry doesn't guarantee success, of course, just as losing doesn't mean a team doesn't have it. But show us a clubhouse of guys who don't get along and we will show you a team that, even if it reaches the top, doesn't enjoy the ride or the victory nearly as much. And, isn't this why we play the game—any game? A trophy alone is empty; the journey to its achievement is what makes it fulfilling.

You can't legislate chemistry. You can't deploy it like a training program, but you can create an environment that is conducive to producing it. When it begins to take hold, it must be protected and promoted. When you see something that creates a bond between team members, you lean into it, reinforce it, repeat it, and make it work for what you are ultimately trying to accomplish.

To push the metaphor, when we talk about chemistry we are talking about the molecular makeup of a World Championship team and a world-class organization as seen from behind the scenes of the San Francisco Giants.

Boch's teams have always had chemistry. Each player believes the other guys have his back and will do whatever it takes to help the team. Their confidence in the team enables them to play as one and this, in turn, enhances their individual performance. When we asked him, "How do you achieve this elusive blend of extraordinary team bonding?" his response was classic dry-wit Boch.

Boch: I'd like to tell you it was charismatic leadership and superior coaching, but I suppose you want me to be honest, don't you?

DO SOMETHING NOW

Break down the definition of chemistry above and use it as criteria for unifying your team:

1. Do unselfishness, trust, and celebration characterize your players?

2. Do they play as one? For a larger cause?

3. Does a positive emotional bond unite them?

4. Do they play at full throttle for shared goals?

Chemistry Outplays Talent

Can a team loaded with superstar talent make chemistry irrelevant? Some people think so. History has shown that some teams with little or no chemistry have won. The 2000–2001 Lakers, the 2002 San Francisco Giants, and the 2009 Yankees come to mind—all made it to the championships despite awkward, less-than-friendly clubhouse dynamics. The Oakland A's won three consecutive World Series titles between 1972 and 1974. But they were better known for another kind of chemistry—the combustible kind. They had clubhouse brawls and self-inflicted black eyes to prove it. If you're cynical, there's plenty of such evidence to undermine the case for chemistry, and you'd have more than a few iconic baseball people on your side.

Jim Leyland, former manager of the Detroit Tigers and a World Series champion himself, apparently thinks chemistry is a bunch of BS. Clearly one of the standout characters of modern day baseball, Leyland opened up to a group of reporters about the Washington Nationals in 2010 and suggested that talent, not chemistry, wins games. Craig Calcaterra of NBC's blog HardballTalk quoted Leyland as saying: "Take all that clubhouse [bleep] and all that, throw it out the window. Every writer in the country has been writing about that [bleep] for years. Chemistry don't mean [bleep] . . . That don't mean [bleep]. They got good chemistry because their team is improved, they got a real good team, they got guys knocking in runs, they got a catcher hitting .336, they got a phenom pitcher they just brought up. That's why they're happy." Kansas City Royals manager Ned Yost echoes the same sentiment. "You're talking about talent. Without talent, it don't matter what kind of chemistry you got."[17]

Leyland and Yost have a point: talent counts. Without it, you don't win games. The Giants won each of their three World Series on the back of a dominant postseason ace, be it Tim Lincecum in 2010, Matt Cain in 2012, or Madison Bumgarner in 2014. But what happens when the talent isn't working up to their potential? What happens when key talent finds the most inopportune time to slump? Or, when a team crashes, like the Giants in 2017? What is it that puts talent back on track? And how do you account for a team that goes up against another team with arguably more talent yet pulls off a win?

> **Boch:** Do we make too much of culture and chemistry? I don't think so. It matters . . . a lot. We've had our backs against the wall so many times, and here's what I've observed. When it gets tough, when it looks like it's over, players who play for each other step up and do amazing things. Camaraderie causes people to dig deeper and reach higher because you care about the guys you play with and you don't want to be the one to let them down.
>
> There's another thing about chemistry. It sustains you in the off years. It gives you something to build on. We were down in 2011, 2013, and 2015. Right now [2017], we are having the worst season in Giants history. And believe me, it's painful. But I'll tell you something. I'm as proud of how our guys have hung together during these extremely difficult and trying times as I was in the good years. Now, does losing make you have to work harder at building chemistry? Yes. There's more stress when you are losing. Stress creates tension, and tension divides—if you let it. So, you can't let it. You have to focus on protecting unity that much more.

Sabes agrees with Boch. He believes that one of the reasons the Giants were able to win three championships in five years has to do with how they handled the off years. Here's how Sabes put it.

> During the regular season, we actually pitched better in 2011 than we did in 2010, but we couldn't score any runs. And the one big trade we made, Carlos Beltran, got injured when he came over to us. So, we ended up three games out of the Wild Card and didn't make the playoffs. The ability to weather that and not have everybody pointing fingers at each other is a

big differentiator. In many respects, the pressure of not going to the playoffs, of not repeating [winning a championship] is intense. But nobody cracked. There was no bullshit flying, no infighting. It actually drew the group closer together and galvanized our organization because we spent more time with the players, more time with each other, saying, "This will pass."

Let's be clear. We're not suggesting, even for a minute, that chemistry is the only thing that wins baseball games. Homegrown talent, acquired talent that fills gaps, veteran intelligence and experience, and even a little luck are ingredients that must be added to the ultimate formula for winning. But, when nine guys function really well together versus individually, the competitive advantage is powerful.

> **Boch:** We've had great talent, no doubt about it—marquee pitching, incredible athletes that take a lot of pride in their defense along with their offense, and guys who can get that clutch hit at the right time. But if you look at our history, it's the underdogs who have come up with some of our biggest plays that kept us in it when we should've been done. In terms of heart, they were second to none.
>
> Now, where does "heart" come from? It comes from an inner drive and a will to win to be sure, but more than that, the roots of a team with our kind of resolve are anchored in a special bond and a collective chemistry our players have. Chemistry is about believing in each other, and when people believe in you, I mean *really* believe in you, it makes you feel invincible.

In the postgame show after the Giants won Game 5 in the 2014 World Series, Al Leiter asked Hunter Pence how much he buys into the idea of team chemistry. "I think it's the strongest thing this team has."[18] To say that Madison Bumgarner's 2014 postseason performances were utterly dominant is an understatement. Words can hardly describe what he accomplished, although we try later in the book. In the same postgame commentary, MLB Network's Greg Amsinger asked a follow-up question: "What's more important—team chemistry or the best pitcher on the planet right now?" Pence piped in with more behind-the-scenes insight on Bumgarner and the team.

> You know what, he's [Bumgarner's] doing outstanding, but he is one of the most humble guys. He'll get out there and do anything for any one of us. That's the biggest thing. This guy, it's not, "Oh, me, me, me. This is my game." It's our game. If you talk to Bumgarner, you talk to Buster Posey, you know that they are always going to share credit with everyone else. [MadBum is] going to talk about his defense. You don't find that. You don't find people who are that good and that humble. He never makes himself bigger than what it is.[19]

Winning Catalyzes Chemistry

The skeptics will also tell you that *winning* is what creates chemistry. Of course, a winning club is a happy club. The more you win, the more it solidifies an expectation to win again. Winning sustains winning by igniting passion, growing confidence, strengthening resolve, and cultivating optimism. No argument there. But then we are back to asking, how do you account for less talented teams, that haven't won yet, and ones that topple teams that significantly outmatch them? Personal and relational bonds create team chemistry.

The Giants have gone from the best record in baseball to a free fall of epic proportions twice: once in 2014, and again in 2016. Both times they made it into the playoffs. Listen to how Sabes explained the 2016 experience.

> We came into the season high as a kite [best record in baseball] and then we fell flat on our face. If we didn't have chemistry, how in the hell could you handle blowing a division lead, becoming irrelevant in terms of winning the division, and then being reduced to worrying about whether you can even get into the playoffs from the Wild Card Game? It came down to the last ten

games of the season, and we were able to pull it off. We didn't get back to the World Series, but we came through what could've been an epic collapse and beat [Noah] Syndergaard, one of the best pitchers on the planet, on the road, in New York. Big friggin' deal! We kept our sanity. That doesn't happen without chemistry.

At some point during these painful slides, why didn't the Giants just check out and call it a season? Why didn't they wave the white flag? If winning alone creates chemistry, why didn't they disintegrate? They were losing, after all. Most of the players will tell you that they weren't giving up because they didn't want to let their teammates down. Did they get into the postseason, then, because of talent or chemistry? If you say "both," we wholeheartedly agree. We're just not willing to discount chemistry.

> **"The way a team plays as a whole determines its success. You may have the greatest bunch of individual stars in the world, but if they don't play together, the club won't be worth a dime."**
>
> **—Babe Ruth**

A More Meaningful Win

History shows that the route to the top varies, but chemistry is often the special something that gives top teams an edge. And perhaps more importantly, chemistry makes the victory more delicious. Winning is wonderful, but winning with people you like is so much more meaningful. It's clear that baseball is a bottom-line business, and winning puts fans in seats and makes players more marketable. Ask most players whether they'd rather win a championship or the league's MVP award, however, and most will choose a championship ring.

Ask the players and coaches who win with great chemistry, "What do you remember the most about winning? What do you cherish the most?" They will tell you it was the experience of seeing elated teammates accomplish something extraordinary; it was the exuberant feeling of doing it—together.

Is talent more important than chemistry when it comes to winning? Not necessarily. Is chemistry absolutely necessary to win? No. But if you do a statistical analysis of the great teams and powerful athletic dynasties throughout history, it's a good bet that the majority had great chemistry. And, if you study the lives of athletes who achieved truly meaningful careers, their meaning and significance came more from the chemistry they experienced than from their numbers. Extraordinary numbers put you in the Hall of Fame, but meaningful memories, created in the heat of battle with people you like, love, and respect, make the ride so much more worthwhile.

Baseball is a long season. Players spend more time with other players than they do with their families. If you don't enjoy coming to the park, if you don't have fun with teammates, the season can feel even longer and your chances of winning diminish. When there is animosity among the players, they turn on each other and things get toxic. If someone gets hurt or has a bad day, the motivation to pick each other up just isn't as strong.

In a club like the Giants, where the lineup is always being shuffled because of multiple platoons and injuries, and where roles frequently shift, chemistry can be a big differentiator. When things are constantly in flux, a gloomy clubhouse can make everyone more agitated and less flexible. Players question the manager's decisions; some are tempted to throw teammates under the bus; the clubhouse becomes divided; and the toxic mess spreads through the entire organization. By taking chemistry seriously and focusing on the attitude and spirit that players bring to the clubhouse, the Giants reap a huge return on their investment (ROI) in team bonding.

The ROI of Chemistry

Many years ago Boch introduced Kevin to country superstar Garth Brooks, the number-one-selling solo artist in U.S. history. When Kevin asked Garth how rigorous he is about who he brings into the band, the singer's response was unexpected, but it highlighted the power of chemistry.

> Well, that's a tough one because I'm not really all that selective. I trust God a lot that there's some reason why we're together—me and whoever I'm working with. Like with the band. I didn't care how good they played, I wanted to know what kind of people they were the other 22 hours I was with them in a day. Because that's what matters. Those 2 hours on stage—hell, if you can't play a guitar solo after 160 shows, you're in trouble. So really, playing wasn't the big [issue]. The more important[criterion] for me is: "How are they to live with on the bus?"
>
> You live in a little cramped area with twelve guys. One asshole in the bunch can make the tour seem like dog years. The question I always want an answer to is, "Is he or she a sweetheart of a person or not?"
>
> One of the last guys we hired was a musician's musician that everybody loved. He turned out to be one of the sweetest, most hardworking guys you'd ever meet. We were lucky to find the exception to the rule—a player's player who doesn't have to

Garth Brooks, the number-one-selling solo artist in U.S. history, performing live.

be some eclectic asshole that hides in a closet and is hard to get along with, yet when he plays everybody says, "OOH." Our guy, Jimmy Mattingly, is a great entertainer, but the other 22 hours of the day he was funnier than hell—and a sweetheart of a guy.

Garth Brooks is not only one of the world's most gifted entertainers (after a 14-year retirement, he was crowned Entertainer of the Year, again, at the 2016 and 2017 Country Music Association Awards), he is also a talented entrepreneur with tremendous business acumen. The total number of past and announced shows for his 2017 world tour has already broken the record for the most all-time concerts (220) in a tour.

How do you perform that many shows? How do you log that many miles with roadies and band members unless you have incredible chemistry? Of course, you can ask the same thing about baseball. Here are some of the reasons why chemistry can be such a game changer no matter where you find it.

Chemistry Is Hard to Emulate

Conditioning, individual skill development, reinforcing fundamentals, reading signs, studying your opponent's profile, pitching smart, and hitting with swagger are critical if you want to be competitive. But in a sense, every club brings these necessary ingredients to the game. And if they don't, they can get them.

Plenty of pitching and hitting gurus in baseball know how to develop talent and know how to the play the game—and play it really well. Many competent training staffs know what it takes to get a player in top physical condition or minimize the cycle time of rehab after a player has been injured. Plenty of smart quants can analyze a player from 21 different angles. You can buy great talent and support that talent with the best facilities and equipment in the world.

Most of these things are replicable, right? Right. If one team needs better conditioning, it can look to other teams that never seem to run out of gas in the dog days and then emulate what they do to keep their players in shape. One manager can study the way another strategically uses his players to ensure longevity. If you work hard enough to learn, you can reverse engineer most of these best practices to address what you realize you're lacking.

Chemistry isn't as easily replicable as the best practices mentioned above, however. It is something you have to work at every day. Theo Epstein, the former GM of the Boston Red Sox, helped create great chemistry for the Red Sox between 2003 and 2007. But in 2011, his final year with Boston, things fell apart. The point is you can never take the chemistry for granted. You can never take shortcuts or stop doing the things you are doing just because everything is going well. You have to be able to walk through a clubhouse and notice when things are right and when they're wrong. It's a constant effort. "If you want to win, you gotta sweat" has more than one meaning. Most organizations aren't willing to work that hard at creating and maintaining chemistry.

Chemistry Fosters Fierce Loyalty

When players come together to know and be known, to fight for something they all believe in, to give unselfishly and graciously receive, something is created together that is more than they are by themselves. Call it synergy, synchrony, harmony, seamlessness or oneness, getting talent to pull together, to be truly unified, can produce extraordinary results, but it's not easy. Egos, agendas, salary differentials, insecurities, factions, power struggles, extremely diverse personalities, and lack of a common vision and shared values all sabotage unity. They eat away at bonding and keep a team from performing at its highest level.

Chemistry is all about having mutual respect, valuing differences, and tolerating eccentricity. Chemistry is what happens when teammates genuinely care for each other, have a deep-seated trust in each other, and share a passion for accomplishing the same thing. It is hard to think of a better example of this type of cohesiveness than the U.S. Navy SEALs. Thrown into some of the most dangerous and extreme conditions, the SEALs succeed on an "I have your back" mentality. Marcus Luttrell, author of Lone Survivor, illustrated that mindset with a vignette from June 28, 2005, when he and SEAL Team 10 were on a mission to kill or capture a high-ranking Taliban leader in the mountains of Afghanistan.

Three goat herders stumbled upon the four SEALs, compromising their position. After an intense discussion about whether to execute the goat herders or let them go, the team released them. Within an hour, the SEALs were ambushed by a force of some 120–150 Taliban fighters. SEAL Team 10 went from being the hunters to being the hunted. Not only were they flanked by fighters on their left and right, the enemy had the high ground and therefore the major advantage. A brutal gunfight ensued as the Taliban fighters pushed the SEALs down a very steep mountainside, over cliffs.

With multiple fractures, shrapnel wounds, and a broken back, Luttrell managed to crawl and walk seven miles to evade his enemies. Pashtun villagers took him in and alerted U.S. forces of his presence. Six days after the horrific gun battle that killed his three teammates, Marcus Luttrell was rescued by another Special Operations team.

Keep in mind it was four SEALs against nearly 150 Taliban fighters. But, Luttrell said, "At no time during the gunfight did I or any of my teammates think we were going to lose." Against those odds, it's hard to imagine that kind of resolve. And yet, when you are fighting with guys you deeply care about, there is an unabashed refusal to give up. His teammates were his friends. He liked, loved, and respected them. No one died alone, Luttrell said. They died while he was trying to save them. Referring to the unbreakable bond these guys had with each other, he described what we've all come to know about the SEALs: "The only way you are going to break a Navy SEAL is to kill him."

The difference between giving up

RESOLVE

and getting up

Veteran reliever Javier López asked Boch if he could invite SEAL Team 6 into the clubhouse for a visit. Not only did Boch say yes; he wanted these soldiers who have been through extremely intensive physical and psychological training to talk with the players about chemistry, resolve, and resilience. Baseball can hardly be compared to combat, but Boch thought his guys could learn from the SEALs. He wanted to give his players a vivid example of how unity makes a team stronger and more resilient to negative forces. And, he wanted them to be inspired by how indefatigable the human spirit can be when put under tremendous pressure.

Boch: The thing that stands out for me about Marcus Luttrell as well as the members of SEAL Team 6 is that they are so maniacally focused and so mission driven that there is no ambiguity. No one stands around and argues about who is in charge or who's responsible for what. No one complains about the role they play. When lives are on the line and time is of the essence, you spring into action and move as one or someone dies. Sadly, in Luttrell's team, people died anyway. But the SEALs—really, all emergency response teams—are such a great example for our players about what it means to be fiercely loyal to each other.

Chemistry Emboldens Risk

Some people have suggested that baseball is an individual sport. What they seem to mean is that you are alone on the pitcher's mound. You are alone in the batter's box. You don't have to have a lot of chemistry to wave off another outfielder from a fly ball. Boch disagrees.

> **Boch:** It may not be the same dance that happens in basketball or football, where the choreography happens in real time, but there's a lot to chemistry in baseball. It's a catcher knowing his pitcher, reading the moment, and calling the right pitch. It's a shortstop anticipating where the ball is going by the swing of the bat. There's chemistry with two outfielders going after the same ball, and there's chemistry with a third base coach who is like an orchestra conductor giving signs to both the runners and the hitters. If there's chemistry on the field, guys play with a lot more freedom. They approach it more aggressively and take more risks.

Chemistry Releases Energy

There's energy in every organization and every relationship. Good energy and bad energy. If the clubhouse is cohesive, if people feel like family or a band of brothers, the outcome is collaboration, mutual support, trust, and levity. If people are having a good time, energy will be focused on what elevates the team and what needs to be done to realize the bigger vision.

If the clubhouse is a collection of self-centered or self-indulgent players, the outcome is conflict. There will always be some type of conflict because that's the nature of 25 different personalities working and traveling together for half the year. But, selfishness breeds a different kind of conflict. It becomes difficult and divergent versus collaborative and complimentary.

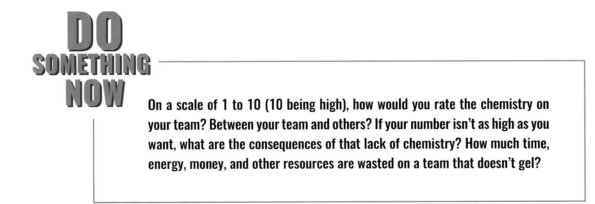

DO SOMETHING NOW On a scale of 1 to 10 (10 being high), how would you rate the chemistry on your team? Between your team and others? If your number isn't as high as you want, what are the consequences of that lack of chemistry? How much time, energy, money, and other resources are wasted on a team that doesn't gel?

Chemistry Is Magnetic

If a team has good chemistry, the intensity of competition draws people into relationships that have greater emotional depth. Think about it: when the stakes are high or the challenge is rigorous, like staying motivated and performing your best for 162 games a year, good chemistry causes people to want to bond versus divide. And, with each opponent the team faces, relationships grow stronger because an outside foe threatens to take away something valuable—the opportunity to stay together.

There's something about team chemistry that says something like this: "Break me off a piece of that; I want in! I want into the battle. I want into the camaraderie. I want to take a risk and stand on the edge with others who fought their way here and share the same aspirations." Watch any team's victory celebration. The release of emotion and energy is palpable. It's one thing to win, but knowing that you were a crucial part of an epic story, written with others, makes it so much sweeter.

Obviously, chemistry can't be legislated or willed into existence, but you can create the conditions in which it can mature and grow. To better understand how chemistry played out in the exhilarating and unforgettable moments that led to three World Series rings, as well as how it protected the team in the lulls and tensions of those not-so-memorable seasons, come behind the scenes of the San Francisco Giants organization. See where the grit, determination, and passion come from to create one of the truly great success stories in the history of MLB.

1st Inning

GIANT DNA

Creating a Championship Culture

4

THE GIANT WAY
The Foundation of a Championship Culture

When he came to the San Francisco Giants in 2007, Boch knew he was coming to a storied franchise and a unique culture.

"Storied" is a way to express the rich and colorful history of an enterprise. When the roots of a club go as far back as the Giants do, it elicits a sense of reverence and respect. Boch knew that the club originated in New York City in 1883 as the New York Gothams and had played on a field once used for polo matches. The Gothams became the Giants in 1885 when, legend has it, owner/manager Jim Mutrie called the players "his Giants" after they won a hard-fought victory against Philadelphia in extra innings. New time, new era, new team (no name change likely), Boch affectionately calls his players his "misfits."

"Storied" also comes from the stories and events that echo through the corridors of time to celebrate those magical moments you never forget—even if you weren't there.

> **Boch:** When I became the manager [in San Francisco], I read up on the club's history—some of the great managers and legendary players. I already knew a lot about the Giants, but out of my own interest and respect for the club, I wanted to absorb as much of that as possible. I read John McGraw's biography. He was the hard-nosed old-school manager who won 10 National League pennants, 2,500-plus games, and three World Series. Just an incredible run.

When New York Giants outfielder Bobby Thompson hammered a game-winning homer off Brooklyn Dodgers pitcher Ralph Branca to win the National League pennant in 1951, it was known as the "Shot Heard 'Round the World." Legendary Giants announcer Russ Hodges shouted, "The Giants win the pennant! The Giants win the pennant! The Giants win the pennant!" Boch understood the significance of this event as a cherished part of Giants lore. How could he predict that one day in the not-too-distant future legendary broadcasters Duane Kuiper and Mike Krukow would shout, "The Giants win the Series!"

The Giants won their first World Series title in 1905, and then again in 1921, 1922, 1933, 1937, and 1954. In Game 1 of the 1954 World Series against the Cleveland Indians, Willie Mays, in a dead sprint—his back to the infield—made a dramatic over-the-shoulder catch 450 feet from home plate in the deepest part of center field. It was off a fly ball by Vic Wertz. "The Catch" made history by keeping Cleveland from scoring and thus giving the Giants a 5-2 victory. The Giants ultimately swept the Indians in four straight games. The 1954 World Series win would be the Giants last playoffs appearance as New Yorkers. When Boch came to San Francisco, he was painfully aware that the fans had waited 53 years for another title. Boch was hungry and he knew they were too. He was determined to be part of rebuilding that winning tradition and contributing to a historic brand.

"Storied" is part of the narrative you use to describe epic battles, such as the 100-year-old rivalry between the Giants and the Los Angeles Dodgers. This fierce tug-of-war intensified when both teams moved to the West Coast in 1958. That year the Giants won the historic opener 8-0 in Seals Stadium. Of course, the heated competition between these two historic franchises continues to this day.

"Storied" is also the word you use when you come to a club that is home to some of the greatest names in baseball, including Hall of Famers Juan the "Dominican Dandy" Marichal, Willie the "Say Hey Kid" Mays, Orlando the "Baby Bull" Cepeda, Willie McCovey, and Gaylord Perry. Brian Sabean remembered former Giants President and General Managing Partner Bill Neukom saying, "We are standing on the shoulders of soldiers who have come before us." These icons represent a powerful sense of tradition.

> **Boch:** As a kid growing up in this sport, and then as a player and manager, I'm still amazed by the legends who have walked the halls of this club. When you think of Willie Mays, Willie McCovey, Gaylord Perry, and others, these are the guys on whose shoulders this club was built. These are the guys we idolized as kids. These are the guys who showed us how the game should be played. What they accomplished and what they've done for the game will forever be etched in all our hearts and minds.
>
> Many of them are still here. Sometimes I have to remind myself that the guy who just walked out of my office is the great Willie Mays. To have met him is an honor, but to have him here and work with him throughout the year and call him my friend—I don't have the words to describe how special that is.
>
> I'll never forget the first time I met Willie. He said, "You may need these." And he handed me a dozen signed balls. He wasn't being self-aggrandizing; he just knew how many requests I would be getting for them. He was just trying to take a weight off my shoulders.

Young players in the Giants minor league listen intently as they hear from the legendary Willie Mays.

Imagine walking into the Giants spring training clubhouse, looking over at a wise old sage holding court with a few players, and asking, "Is *that* who I think it is?" Yep. That's Willie Mays. Throughout spring training he hangs out at his own roundtable where players can sit down and talk or simply engage in a game of cards.

> **Boch:** I'm amazed by how much he cares and how much he knows about what's going on with our players, year after year. He follows us closely. He knows who's struggling, who's in the zone, and who might need a shot of humility.
>
> Just his presence in our clubhouse, along with Willie McCovey and others, sends a powerful message to our players. It says, "Don't let your ego get out of line and don't get too caught up with yourself because you are among the *Giants* of the game." When you are around guys like this, every day, you see the history of this organization in *them*.

"When our young players, and even the veterans who've been around for awhile, come in [to the clubhouse] and see these great names," Larry Baer told us, "something very powerful begins to happen. Our culture seeps into them. It's like they see a baton being passed down through history. And now it's being handed to them. You get a tremendous sense of pride in being part of that amazing history. You also realize that there is a tremendous responsibility." "Storied" is what you think about when you take the baton from managerial greats such as Hall of Famer John McGraw, Bill Terry, Mel Ott, and Leo Durocher. Honored to join an organization with so much history and so many legendary figures, Boch didn't step into it lightly. He came to San Francisco with the immense respect one should afford a 133-year-old franchise, a deep admiration for the legacy of the club, and a passion for helping to make it storied all over again.

"Storied" was also certainly a compelling reason for Boch to seriously consider a move from managing the Padres to the Giants, but who doesn't have some trepidation about going to a new job in a new place with new people? Who doesn't wonder: "Will this be a fit? Will I gel with this organization's way of doing things?"

Walk In, Fit In

What Boch sensed, but couldn't have fully known at the time, was how good a fit the Giants culture would be with his personality and demeanor, his values and his approach to the game. Some cultures are more conducive to leveraging a person's gifts and talents than are others. Some environments just seem to have a combination of things that accelerate high performance, while others lack the right stuff.

Every season baseball shows us clubs where the talent is strong and formidable but the team is not. Most everyone agrees that during the three twenty-first century World Series playoffs they participated in, the Giants, outmatched by their opponents, overachieved again and again. Through five years and three championships some of the Giants core players remained the same. But many changed. What didn't change—and hasn't to this day—is the club's focus on building a strong, purposeful culture throughout the entire franchise. Talent, statistics, unconventional wisdom—they all play a critical role in the club's success. But the one constant, the essential glue that brings all these things together, is its culture.

> **Culture isn't just one aspect of the game—it is the game.**
>
> **—Lou Gerstner, former chairman of IBM**

Culture is the force that determines "the way we do things around here," particularly when no one is looking. It says: *"This is what we believe. This is how we think about our business. This is how we feel about what we do and who we do it for. And, this is what those beliefs look like when they are lived out loud."*

Culture is a multidimensional blend of values, attitudes and beliefs, rites, rituals and rules, and heroes, heroines, and outlaws that, when combined, can create a world of pleasure or pain. A healthy culture creates passionate brand of ambassadors. A dysfunctional culture creates "dead people working." Culture can be the animating spirit that lifts people up or the dampening spirit that drags them down. Some cultures are toxic and undermine "team-ness." Others are powerfully positive and catapult a team to peak performance. Culture can accelerate the momentum and growth of a firm or grind it into status quo and mediocrity. It can make a brand iconic or obsolete.

The point is, culture counts.

Call it the organization's DNA, or character, or personality, culture is the X factor that separates one franchise from another. Every MLB franchise has a culture. Every company has a culture. Every family has a culture. Some are thoughtful, intentional, and nurtured on purpose and by design. Others are accidental, evolve haphazardly, and grow in a vacuum, by default.

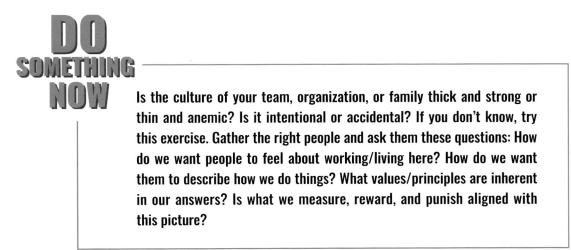

DO SOMETHING NOW

Is the culture of your team, organization, or family thick and strong or thin and anemic? Is it intentional or accidental? If you don't know, try this exercise. Gather the right people and ask them these questions: How do we want people to feel about working/living here? How do we want them to describe how we do things? What values/principles are inherent in our answers? Is what we measure, reward, and punish aligned with this picture?

It didn't take Boch long to figure out that the culture of the Giants organization would give him the freedom to do more, become more, and help others achieve more. There was a lot of chemistry: a "can-do, we believe in you" chemistry versus a "prove yourself, watch your back, be careful" kind of chemistry, and it played out in various ways.

> **Boch:** As I came up through the majors, I had never been with a storied franchise. Initially, I saw a significant part of the Giants culture from the other side of the field. The fans were dedicated, unified, and loud. Whenever we played San Francisco in their house—even in ours—you could just feel the energy from their fans. As an opposing manager, you're just thinking about how to help your guys deal with that intensity and find ways to counteract it; you're not necessarily thinking about what creates it.
>
> I got here, it was apparent that the Giants culture was bigger and stronger than I could've imagined. I was blown away by how the ownership group trusts and supports the front office; how frequently they communicate and how seamlessly they work together. Baseball is a big business and there's a lot of pressure to win, but I could tell that these guys genuinely liked being together. They were more like family. And rarely, if ever, have they refrained from giving us the resources we need to do our jobs.

You know, when there's trust and camaraderie at the top, it flows down into the organization. I was also impressed by how the front office supported, but didn't meddle in, the baseball side [of the business]. They're in it, they care, and they voice their opinions, but they let us do our jobs without a lot of interference or second-guessing. There is a powerful level of mutual respect on both sides of the organization.

When I came here Sabes and I didn't know each other all that well, but it didn't take me very long to see that he is incredibly good at what he does and he's a great collaborator. Even though my first couple of years here were not easy because the team didn't perform as well as we thought we would, the chemistry between Sabes and me developed very fast. I couldn't have known at the time, but believe me, I know now how fortunate I am to be teamed up with a guy like Brian.

By the time Boch had been hired, the Giants were in the throes of a turnaround. The front office was committed to rebuilding; their superstar, Barry Bonds, was transitioning out of the club; and the farm system was turning a corner with bright new prospects on the verge of breaking through to the majors. Sabes and his team were the architects; Boch was charged with making the turnaround work.

"If you reduce it to just Boch and me, which you can't, and to a space and time, and how we played off each other, we needed each other," Sabes told us. "When you look at how his teams competed with a lot less money, he came here and got swept up in it [the support we get from our owners, the front office, and the fans] much like I did when I came here. I put it that way because there is cultural fabric here that underpins everything we do."

Boch: The other thing that struck me about the culture of the Giants in my first year here is the number of fans that traveled with us and showed up at games on the road. It soon became obvious that the commitment and passion of our fan base isn't something that just happens; it's cultivated. It's something the front office works at very hard. And believe me, our players feed off that energy!

Sure, it helps when we win, but our fans are there in full force even when we are losing. You don't sell out as many games as we have unless there's a culture in place that makes fans feel like family—and they are. The kind of ballpark we have, the experience our fans have when they come here, the way we reach into the community—there's a Giant way of doing things that drives all of that.

"There's a Giant way of doing things." Boch's observation sums up in plain English what we mean by "culture." And where culture starts. And what needs to happen for it to develop and flourish. Culture is fueled and ignited by the what, the how, and the why. By passionately engaged leaders who genuinely care about not only *what* the

Boch was attracted to a strong culture that had been built and nurtured by design. That's what great cultures do; they summon people to come play a role in something big, important, and fun. Is your culture this magnetic?

organization achieves but also *how* it achieves it and the impact (the why) it has on people along the way. Strong cultures honor, respect, and empower people; celebrate their gifts and talents; and give them very clear roles and responsibilities. And then, they hold people accountable to improving or having a positive impact on their corner of the world.

How Leaders Shape Culture

An overwhelming majority of business leaders believe that culture is a source of competitive advantage and that an organization without a winning culture is destined for mediocrity. And while it's easy to agree that a winning culture is what separates the likes of Southwest Airlines, Wegmans, SAS, Patagonia, Virgin, and others from competitors in their respective fields, shaping a new culture is one of a leader's toughest challenges because the old culture is designed to protect itself.

When Boch joined the Giants in 2007, he came to an esteemed franchise with a lot of history and a rich legacy, but he also inherited a dysfunctional clubhouse culture. All cultures have a strong immune system. You can't change a culture using its own ways. You have to establish new values and new priorities, and you must do so with unwavering commitment and relentless resolve. When you challenge its tenets and values, the existing culture launches a strong counteroffensive. That's why shaping a new culture requires strong leadership and a clear sense of purpose—something Bruce Bochy and Brian Sabean have in common.

Sabes is a quiet, behind-the-scenes kind of guy. He also has one of the sharpest minds in baseball and an intuitive read on people. Even though superstar Bonds helped turn the Giants into a winning team and led them into the 2002 World Series as the best home run hitter of all time, Sabes knew the club needed to rebuild. Life after Bonds would have to be a more nontraditional, anti-star kind of system, one where everyone understands that everyone else is a critical link in the chain. Winning would have to be achieved by a little bit of everything instead of a lot of one thing.

As GM, Sabes changed the architecture of the club by building from within. He brought in more homegrown players who came up through the Giants system and knew the Giants way. He wasn't afraid to give young players such as Tim Lincecum, Pablo Sandoval, and Brandon Belt, who hadn't had a lot of time in the minor leagues, an opportunity to learn on the job.

> **Boch:** Brian knew we needed to get younger. He wasn't afraid to take the risk and bring young players up sooner than the norm. But it wasn't a quick-fix strategy. A lot of these guys went through growing pains together, on the job. They made mistakes, but it brought them together, made them stronger, and created the kind of chemistry we're talking about here. The fruits of that structural change started to show in 2010 and beyond. I'm convinced that so many of our guys have performed well in the heat of postseason battles because they've logged so many Major League miles at such a young age. Brian was the mastermind behind this and, obviously, his instincts and patience paid off.

Boch figured into Sabean's change in architecture as well. Sabes sensed that, by bringing in Boch, he would naturally change the clubhouse from a superstar culture to an "all for one and one for all" culture. But it wasn't easy, nor would it happen fast.

> **Boch:** I noticed right away that there were a few factions. It didn't appear to be a group of guys who were close-knit or who played for each other. We had a superstar, and I wanted to get him more involved because of the influence and impact he could make on the club.

The clubhouse itself was not physically conducive to spontaneous meetings, open communication, and great chemistry. Separated by posts and walls and other minor barriers, guys could walk into their locker on one end of the clubhouse without ever seeing a teammate at the other end. Instead of drawing people together it separated them.

Boch didn't mount a huge culture change or create a big brouhaha; he quickly, yet quietly moved to align the team and break down the physical and psychological barriers. Even though the GM had already eliminated the entourages accompanying some players, Boch started to make the clubhouse more of a sanctuary. He got rid of the elitist symbols communicating that there were "haves" and "have-nots" among team members. And, he used every opportunity he had in spring training speeches, clubhouse meetings, and one-on-ones with players to simply and strongly communicate a new set of values. Chief among them was choosing service over self-interest and adopting a team-first mentality.

He also enlisted veterans and the club's most famous player, Barry Bonds, to be key influencers in driving this change. He wanted them to have skin in the game.

Boch: I tried to make a case to Barry and some of the other guys that if we didn't shake it up and create more unity or become more team-oriented, we would never play to our full potential. I also knew that if our players didn't have some ownership in what we were trying to accomplish, our success would be limited.

So, I got some of our starting pitchers, role players, and veterans together to cast a vision of what they wanted to accomplish and how they wanted to rebuild the unity of the team. Culture is lots of little things, you know. So, they decided who got to come into the clubhouse and when; they decided our dress code on the plane; who

Barry Bonds unleashes another home run against the Los Angeles Dodgers.

would choose the music played in the clubhouse; and when the TVs would be shut off before a game. All of this was about giving them ownership. I said, "You decide and then you police it." And they did.

Peter Drucker is credited with coining the catchphrase "Culture will eat strategy for breakfast!" It was a concept that Boch intuitively grasped from his early days as a manager. In baseball you can have great talent (Bonds was arguably the best player in the game—maybe ever); you can know your opponents better than anyone else does; and you can have a well-honed strategy. But, if you don't have a culture that enables you to successfully deploy a winning strategy, the culture will overpower and eventually defeat it. A vibrant culture is the oil that makes the strategy engine—from sabermetrics and recruiting to filling out lineup cards and choosing relievers on the field—run smoothly.

Of course, all of this took time. Boch would say it was at least several years of constantly reinforcing the values of the clubhouse and the attitudes and behaviors that make those values tangible to this day. But he worked at it every day. He tried to be consistent with his message because the lightbulbs go on for different people at different times. Eventually, the message started to permeate the clubhouse and a "new way of being" took shape.

> **Boch:** Somewhere around 2009–2010 I could see that things were starting to change. Our guys were coming together more often and the factions were disappearing. We were moving from disharmony to more of a cohesive unit. Much of this happened because of our homegrown players, but Brian wasn't afraid to go outside [our minor leagues] either. He brought in Aaron Rowand, a center fielder and Golden Glove winner, without giving up any of our top young pitchers.
>
> I wanted our clubhouse to get back to a warrior mentality where everyone played the game hard for nine innings. Aaron was that kind of guy—a gritty, hard-nosed player who could help us put some swagger back in the clubhouse.

Rowand did two things that contributed to the Giants culture change: He played the game in a way that held other players accountable; and he had a knack for drawing guys together socially. In the clubhouse and on the road, Rowand provided key leadership to support the culture shift.

A change in architecture, younger players with a team-first mindset, a veteran outsider who exemplified the way the Giants thought the game should be played, and a manager and GM who understood the power of what can happen when they are intentional about shaping clubhouse culture—it all laid the foundation for the kind of chemistry that characterizes the storied franchise of the San Francisco Giants.

DO SOMETHING NOW

If you are leading a culture change, keep in mind that old ways die hard. The status quo is designed to protect itself. Be stalwart in your approach, involve "influential" others to be ambassadors for the change, and be prepared for the long haul. Change (and buy-in) takes time.

The point here is that the culture change happened because *changes were made first at the top*, and the new values and behaviors permeated the organization because leadership made them a strategic, forward-thinking priority. Even today, after three World Championships, Boch is still working at protecting and promoting the Giants culture because, left on its own, culture takes the path of least resistance and atrophies into something that is unintended. Consequently, his messages in the media, his spring training speeches, and his talks during the season continue to have consistent themes. Boch doesn't fall into the flavor of the month trap. He looks for new and creative ways to convey the core values and demonstrate the essential behaviors to grow a culture where his players gel with a team-first mindset on all dimensions.

DO SOMETHING NOW

Confronted with change, the lightbulbs go on for different people at different times. The most iconic leaders we know are willing to change strategy and tactics, but when it comes to the core values that drive culture, their message is consistent—even repetitive. This is one reason why such leaders breed "thick" cultures with a critical mass of turned-on, all-in followers.

The X Factor

You can look to a whole cadre of leaders who shape the Giants culture, but it certainly starts with Baer and ripples out into the organization. Baer is an energizer. Always on the go, he is the epitome of "full throttle." But he does it with a joyful spirit that seems effortless.

> **Boch:** I don't know anyone who has Larry's energy. He just goes and goes, but what amazes me is that he's so genuine about everything he is committed to. He cares about the club and the club's involvement in the community; he wants to make the Giants the best organization in the world; he wants our fans to experience something here [at AT&T Park] they can't get anywhere else; and he wants that for our players and coaching staff too. The tone he sets is one of the reasons players love being here.

Under Baer's leadership the Giants have won three World Series; built an award-winning, privately financed ballpark that has become a San Francisco destination of choice; established several successful Giants subsidiaries; and are currently developing Mission Rock, a 27-acre multiuse urban real estate project adjacent to AT&T Park.

Baer's Harvard Business School classmate and friend Beth Hardin observed: "Larry knows what brings him joy, and he actually chooses to spend his life doing that. Not only that, but he lives in the place he loves and devotes his time to places and people he loves. He lives a powerful life."

In a Huffington Post interview with *Finding the Right Work* author Leni Miller, Baer described what it feels like to be the Giants CEO.

First of all, I definitely think I am in [the] right line of work and you have probably hit on somebody who is maybe a poster child for the right line of work, because this is shared with a lot of people here. The Giants organization is more than work; it is viewed as a much larger part of life and existence and our being than the workplace. That is because there is so much emotion associated with the connection of going to a game or following a team, especially when it is your team, in my case as a fourth generation San Franciscan . . . there is a crusade element to this or passion element that goes well beyond work. It is messianic.[20]

Larry Lucchino, the president and CEO emeritus of the Red Sox, called Baer "one of baseball's most versatile and effective executives. He leads the league in energy, drive, smarts, and executive imagination, yet people still like him!" As Lucchino points out, there is nothing lukewarm about Baer's leadership. The Giants are a $2-billion enterprise that operates like a Silicon Valley start-up. And Baer is the torchbearer consumed with drawing as many talented people into the fire as he can.

CEO Larry Baer, holding the 2014 National League trophy.

Boch: Larry has been a Giants fan all of his life. To be the CEO of the Giants is a childhood dream come true, and it shows in everything he does. His enthusiasm is infectious. It just makes the rest of us want to go out and raise the bar. He's a risk taker, so you don't have any reticence about trying to be innovative and shaking it up on the field. His spirit of hospitality extends to our players and their families, so you can proudly recruit talent without hesitation. He's a competitor, so when we are fighting our way out of a hole, he's there in the trenches with us. Yet, he doesn't meddle; he gives us the freedom to do our jobs.

When we rub shoulders with people so dedicated to their work, so committed to creating an environment we can flourish in, and so energized by what they do, it rubs off on us. There is something so alive in them that it awakens something that needs to be alive in us. It intensifies our own commitment. Their faith, focus, and drive cranks up our own faith, focus, and drive and we, too, are called upon to make a dent, have a positive impact, and raise the bar.

5
NOT BY ACCIDENT
Lead with Heart and Head

The rebirth of the modern-day Giants is a story about saving baseball in San Francisco and enriching the community by giving people a world-class cultural experience on and off the field. It's also a story that highlights the hallmarks of the Giants formidable culture.

When the Giants moved to San Francisco in 1958 they first played at Seals Stadium until Candlestick Park was opened in 1961. Located on the bay's shore south of downtown San Francisco, Candlestick was a disaster from the very beginning. Access to it by public transportation was limited, it was inadequately maintained, and it did not have enough concession stands. Giants CEO Larry Baer described it as "a cold, windy, and miserable place to watch a ball game." Few players and fans would disagree.

After suffering through four failed elections to get a new ballpark built, Bob Lurie, the club's previous owner, accepted an offer in 1992 from a Tampa Bay investor group to buy the Giants for $115 million. The Bay Area was devastated by the prospect of losing the Giants. How could this be? How could the celebrated franchise that brought MLB Willie Mays, Willie McCovey, and Orlando Cepeda not make it in the City by the Bay?

> **Doing something big and risky requires thick skin and strong conviction.**

In a last-ditch effort to save the team, Baer reached out to Giants board member and former Safeway CEO Peter Magowan. Together with San Francisco's new mayor, Frank Jordan, they gathered a group of civic-minded investors—the who's who of the San Francisco business community—to purchase the Giants and keep them from leaving San Francisco.

It was a long shot.

Fortunately for San Francisco, the team couldn't be moved to Tampa without the approval of other owners in the league. In November 1992 the proposed agreement to sell the franchise to Tampa Bay was rejected, creating an open door for the investor group led by Magowan and Baer to buy the Giants. Still, it was a huge risk and Magowan wasn't convinced the whole thing could work.

But, Baer remembered: "[Magowan] had grown up in New York when the Giants moved from New York to San Francisco. He saw firsthand how that move devastated a community. He was determined not to let the same thing happen in San Francisco. I'm proud to say that ultimately our investors led with their hearts and not their heads. They decided that if the Giants left San Francisco it would be too much of a blow to the people of the Bay Area."

Professional sports franchises sometimes become a hobby that gives billionaires bragging rights. In this case, purchasing the Giants was more than a brag line or a business deal; it became the noble, heroic cause for which Larry Baer, Peter Magowan, and the investor group would fight.

The purchase was noble because it was about giving something back to the community, which, if lost, would create a significant cultural vacuum. When you pay $100 million for a franchise that is losing more than $10 million a year and that many believe has no future, the motive has to be something more than just profit.

The purchase was heroic because it was a mammoth undertaking and there were so many reasons why it wouldn't work. The Giants brand was pretty much shot. The community was tired of the uncertain future of the team. They were tired of asking whether the Giants would leave or stay. They were tired of the team losing. And, they were tired of wealthy owners asking for public money to build a new ballpark. But it had to work; this world-class city deserved a world-class team, and the city dwellers didn't want to lose baseball, one of their favorite pastimes.

Looking back, the cause that incited Baer and the Magowan-led investor group to buy the Giants in 1992 was instrumental in shaping the championship culture the Giants have today. To understand the chemistry of the team and the team's success, you have to know what's in the cultural DNA of the Giants organization.

Peter Magowan, one of the Giants principal owners.

Competitive Mindset

Baer and Magowan knew that just keeping the team from leaving San Francisco was not going to be enough. If they were going to be successful, they'd have to bring in top-level baseball talent—both managers and players. So, for starters, they persistently pursued Barry Bonds (even before they officially owned the club) and stepped way out on a limb by signing him to a six-year deal for $43 million. The duration of that deal outraged owners of other clubs, and the players union required that if the investor group *didn't* get ownership of the club they would have to make up the difference between the $43 million they offered Bonds and whatever offer Barry agreed to from another club.

The Giants also hired Bob Quinn as GM. In 1990, *Sporting News* had named Quinn Executive of the Year for turning around the Cincinnati Reds and leading them to a World Series title. The Giants also promoted Dusty Baker from hitting coach to manager.

Decisions like these set a precedent for the way the Giants do things. They are competitive. They have a burning desire to win so they aim high. This means that good enough never is. Talk to anyone in the front office and you will get the distinct impression that none of these people are satisfied with the status quo—even after attaining sellout crowds at the ballpark year after year. Whether it's expanding non-baseball revenue, developing Minor League Baseball (MiLB) players, or growing the Giants fan base, staff in the Giants organization are always pushing to go farther by getting smarter, better, and faster. They know that everyone and everything around them is constantly getting better. Rest on what you did yesterday and there may be no tomorrow.

> **Boch:** I remember one of my first meetings with Peter Magowan, Larry Baer, and Brian Sabean at Peter's house in Pacific Heights. Peter said that the owners were committed to take the Giants profit and reinvest it in the club. They were sincere about it. After Barry Bonds left, they went out and signed Barry Zito to a huge contract, hoping he would be the face of the franchise. Now, it's true that Zito struggled, but he was always the "character" guy we signed and, of course, helped us write history with a clutch win in Game 5 of the National League Championship Series [NLCS] and starting Game 1 of the World Series.
>
> My point is that our ownership group and our front office were committed to making this franchise an exciting ball club. They were willing to put the money they made into winning, not their own pockets. To me that said a lot about how competitive this organization is.

This drive to constantly compete and excel has energized the clubhouse as well. In fact, if you talk to Sabean long enough, you'll see that it's one of his major hot buttons.

> Competitiveness is a mindset. It starts with how our guys get ready for the season and how seriously they take their roles. It's about the effort they bring and how invested they are in every game. If you're not invested, if you don't have that competitive spirit, the rigors of a long season will crush you. Our guys can be down for the count in the middle of the season, but because they are so competitive they never let up; they push to the end. Everyone in this organization loves to win, but we hate to lose even more.
>
> And frankly, you can see the true character of a team when things aren't going well. In 2011, 2013, and 2015, our players carried themselves like champions. When they struggled they never gave in. What makes me most proud of our guys is that they demand more of themselves than we could ever demand of them. When they knew we were out of the postseason, they were still bringing it every day. That's what influences the personality of a club. That's what builds character and the survival instinct you draw on when you are in the postseason and have an opportunity to do something special.

Dare to Do

The new owners clearly understood that they needed a new ballpark to be competitive and that being competitive was essential to keeping the Giants in San Francisco. Yet, between 1987 and

> **If you can dream it, you can do it. —Walt Disney**

1992, San Francisco voters defeated four referendums seeking public funds to replace Candlestick Park. A majority of voters polled said they loved the idea of a new stadium, but not if it was going to be built on the backs of taxpayers.

At that point the ownership group decided to take a huge risk and fund the ballpark privately.

The risks and constraints that came with privately funding the ballpark forced the entire Giants community to dream big and dare to try. The franchise would have to approach potential corporate sponsors and season ticket holders in a way that provided the club with capital before it ever broke ground. It would also have to show bankers that it would have sustainable revenue over the long haul.

Multiyear sponsorship contracts were awarded to corporations for the first time and a "Winner's Circle" was created for sponsors who signed on for three years or more. These long-term sponsors paid 20 percent of their total investment an entire four years before the new park would open in 2000. The remainder of their total commitment would be paid over the period of their contract, starting when the new park opened.

Everyone assumed that the Giants would clutter the new park with sponsorship signs, but as Mario Alioto, Senior Vice President, Business Operations, pointed out, "We wanted to do something classy and tasteful with the advertising opportunities." Alioto and a team member spent an entire day ensconced in a hotel room reading architectural blueprints and looking into the proposed building site for the new park. Their goal? To answer the question, "What if we could give each of the Winner's Circle participants something unique as a part of their deal without overwhelming the park with signage?"

The answers they came up with are what make AT&T Park one of the most attractive, unique, and appealing baseball venues in the world. Chevron, one of the first big sponsors, had a car sign in which the headlights are illuminated during games. Dignity Health built a medical clinic on the port walk of the park. Old Navy acquired the signature space of the ballpark in right field and named it "Old Navy Splash Landing." Dozens of kayakers rally in Splash Landing for every game and scramble for the ball when a home run is hit out of the park. One of the most exceptional features of the ballpark, it adds color and texture to an already unique Giants baseball experience. The children's playground behind the left field bleachers features an 80-foot Coke bottle with a slide built by, of course, Coca-Cola. Many of these features contributed to why the Sports Business Journal named AT&T Park the 2008 Sports Facility of the Year and Sports Business Daily as part of the inaugural Sports Business Awards program.

The children's playground behind the left field bleachers features this 80-foot Coke bottle with a built-in slide.

Up-front revenue was generated with a unique approach to consumers as well. For the first time ever in baseball, the Giants identified a limited number of the best seats in the house and assigned each one a lifetime license fee. People who purchased a seat license had the right to buy a season ticket for that seat for a lifetime. Additionally, the Giants were the only team in baseball that sold only full- versus partial-season ticket plans. They encouraged potential buyers to develop partnerships and then created an online service where season ticket holders could resell their tickets on the club's website.

Instead of spending lots of money on elaborate advertising campaigns and celebrity endorsements, the Giants fueled a movement that created a grassroots approach to funding the project. As corporate sponsors and season ticket holders came on board, the club sent gifts, invited them to special events, and acknowledged them in public. It was the club's way of saying "thank you" for joining the cause, being a part of this movement, and helping us realize the dream. The Giants created a buzz by making the people of San Francisco feel part of the team that was building a dream. And as the ballpark went up, the buzz intensified.

Yet, in the midst of the creativity and growing momentum and buzz, the inevitable cynics and skeptics chimed in. "You'll never get it financed, and if you do, you'll never be able to generate enough revenue to pay down the debt. And if you do pay down the debt, you'll never have enough money to field a competitive team." It would have been easy to buy into their arguments. Think about it: the annual debt service on the $320-million park would be $20 million. That's approximately three times the average annual rent paid by a team playing in a publicly financed stadium.

But, only eight days after the election to approve zoning changes for the site, the club announced that Pacific Bell had acquired the naming rights to the park for $50 million. Two months after that, Chase Manhattan Bank agreed to finance the $170-million debt portion of the new park. The corporate and charter seat license programs raised $150 million ($75 million each) in advance payments, and the team generated another $10 million up front from a contract with the food and beverage concessionaire.

The rewards? When the new park opened in 2000, the Giants won their division with 97 games and generated a $6 million profit. In 2001, the team won 90 games and finished second in the division behind the Arizona Diamondbacks, who ultimately won the World Series. That was also the year Barry Bonds made history hitting 73 homers in the new park and breaking Hank Aaron's home run record. Then, in 2002, the Giants won 93 games and went to the World Series as a Wild Card team.

What did all of this mean? In their first three years, the Giants led the National League in attendance because Giants fans purchased 99 percent of all available seats. The club had the strongest base of corporate sponsorship and the largest fan base of season tickets (28,000) in baseball. In the long term, the club would have a stadium they own, free of debt, with a great degree of operational control.

Empathy and Conviction

The financing of the new ballpark contributed another strand to the cultural DNA of the club—the creativity to blow the doors off business as usual and the courage to "gut it out" when things got messy and difficult. It foreshadowed the Giants brand of baseball for which this franchise has become famous.

Doing the unconventional—going left on red, taking the road less traveled, and bushwhacking a new path— requires thick skin and tremendous resolve. When the cynics weigh in and the demons of doubt come calling, passion and conviction are what keep you in the game.

> **Boch:** When I got here [in 2007] I didn't know all the details and background that went into getting the new park built, but I knew enough to know that this was a club that was hungry, that wanted to win and was willing to do whatever it takes, ethically and legally, to build a competitive franchise. You sort of connect the dots, right? If the owners and front office of this organization were willing to take that kind of risk [to privately finance the park], wouldn't they bring the same creativity and entrepreneurial spirit to rebuilding the team?

The club's now-famous "Never Say Die" culture can be traced to a small band of renegades and risk takers who were committed to keeping America's favorite pastime in one of America's favorite cities.

These entrepreneurs were resolute and tenacious. They didn't give up easily, which was fortunate for Boch in his first two years with the franchise.

Boch: Brian and I knew that my first couple of years here would be rebuilding years, but to say that the team got off to a rough start is an understatement. In 2007, we won 71 games and finished fifth in the NL West, 19 games behind Arizona. It was horrible. And, pretty much the same the next year. In 2008, we won 72 games and finished fourth in the division, 12 games behind the Dodgers.

As you could imagine, the fans wanted my head. Who could blame them? But I never felt pressure from Sabes or from our owners. We were all frustrated, of course, but I never felt like my job was on the line, and I've been in this game long enough to know that it easily could've been. Instead, they gave me the freedom to take risks and the support to do what I thought was right.

I think some of that is because our owners had been through tough times in building the new park. They knew what it's like to struggle, to face the cynics. So they were very patient. Now, they may have been plotting my removal, but not once did they ever let on like that was the case.

Hospitality and Benevolence

Part of stabilizing the newly acquired franchise was changing the fans' experience. Because it would be a long time before the new ballpark would be finished, the Giants worked on rebuilding the club's brand. Baer wanted it to convey the customer friendliness of Nordstrom or Ritz Carlton, the reliability of FedEx, and the convenience and simplicity of Amazon.

Baer and company insisted on a friendly workforce and then invested countless hours in customer service training. They launched a major effort to reconnect the organization and its players to the fans. They brought in a new food and beverage concessionaire and completely changed the guests' eating and drinking experience. No detail was overlooked. The Giants even ensured that every hot dog wrapper that landed on the field was immediately picked up so the park didn't look messy.

Cocreating products and services with customers is a popular strategy among innovators. The Giants were into cocreation with the club's customers long before the term had ever been coined. When the *Sunday Examiner* called somewhat apologetically to inform the club it was going to do a story on improving the park entitled "Fix the Stick," the Giants embraced it immediately and offered to implement the best suggestions they received from readers each week. This loaded the pipeline with all kinds of new ideas, and winners were rewarded with front row seats at the games. For example, a foghorn was installed in center field that went off every time the Giants hit a home run, and every time they scored, a cable car bell behind home plate would ring. The Giants were the first MLB franchise to have a female announcer at the games. Every employee, from the ushers to the front office executives, wore a button that said, "We're listening."

If the Giants couldn't immediately build a new house, they focused on what they *could* control by making the existing house more of a home. Transforming the entire feel of the park, combined with a much-improved team, radically changed the game. The payoff was dramatic. In 1993: the Giants won 103 games, giving them the second-best record in baseball; Barry Bonds was named MVP; Dusty Baker received the *Sporting News* Manager of the Year Award; and attendance soared to 2.6 million from 1.5 million the previous year.

Even after the new park was built, Baer knew that people wouldn't flock to it year after year. At some point the novelty of the park would wear off. The fans had to have a compelling reason to come back again and again, and, beyond fielding a winning team, that meant creating an exceptional ballpark experience.

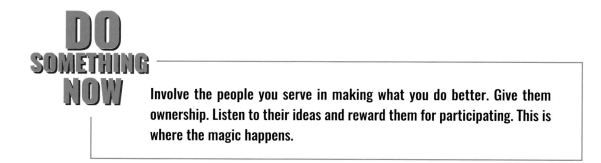

DO SOMETHING NOW

Involve the people you serve in making what you do better. Give them ownership. Listen to their ideas and reward them for participating. This is where the magic happens.

Today, AT&T Park is considered one of the game's crown jewels. Dubbed "baseball's perfect address" by the press, it has a vintage-inspired but ultramodern décor that communicates it's a place you want to be. Festive and fun, the park is a haven for foodies: it features hip bars that offer local brews, some of the best stadium food in America, and a wine bar that resembles a Napa tasting room. It's also the first baseball stadium in California where you can charge your electric vehicle. And don't forget the sustainable garden right behind center field. There you get a field-level view of the game in an urban farm setting replete with overflowing vegetable boxes, enchanting fire pits, and comfortable Adirondack chairs.

One of the hidden gems at AT&T is the Gotham Club, which is housed behind the team's right field scoreboard showing out-of-town game scores and takes its name from the Giants renowned history. (They were the New York Gothams before becoming the New York Giants remember.) Consider it a one-of-a-kind baseball country club for diehard Giants fans who are willing to pay a handsome fee for a members-only place to hang

Majestically located on San Francisco's waterfront, AT&T Park is a hub in the city.

out before and after games. Featuring baseball memorabilia, wood paneled lounges, a pool table, a bar, and a two-lane bowling alley, the Gotham Club has a speakeasy feel to it.

The alluring attractions inside AT&T Park undoubtedly seduce the senses and generate a great vibe. Where the Giants really excel, though, is in the often invisible, hard-to-define yet very tangible "something" that makes the organization so human—a spirit of hospitality. It's a state of mind, a way of being that shows up in the way Giants employees think about their guests and the greater community.

Bowling alley within the Gotham Club inside AT&T Park.

Alioto told us that the Giants are about more than just baseball; they're about enriching lives. "Everyone comes here for different reasons. You have fans who know every statistic; they have on every piece of Giants clothing you can imagine and; they're so emotional about the team. You have other fans who come here because it's the place to be, like being at a great restaurant everyone wants to be seen at. You have other fans who want to do things with their kids and they have lots of other choices. We want to give them a reason to come here; and, when they are here, it needs to be fun."

Take, for instance, Amanda Nichols, Premium Seating Coordinator, one of those individuals who live the Giants culture out loud. For example, a season ticket member had accepted an invitation to a field visit from Amanda as a small gesture of apology after his car had been broken into twice during the season. When they were planning the details, the ticket member indicated it might be a perfect time and place for him to propose to his girlfriend. Amanda was on it. When the day came, she had people on the field with cameras and phones ready.

> I escorted them out onto the field like it was just a field visit. As they got settled on the field, the girlfriend asked my client for the baseball she was hoping to get signed by a player or two. Instead, he handed her a ball with "Will You Marry Me?" written on it. He got down on one knee, all the staff came closer to snap pictures and video the moment, and she said, "Yes!" They were so cute. Once we finished the field visit, I surprised them with congratulatory glasses of champagne that I had prepared before the visit. When they got home, they had an email from me that included all the photos and videos that my colleagues had taken.

Hospitality is about how you make people feel. Whether it's handing a ticket to an usher at a turnstile, buying a beer at a concession stand, or getting a ball signed for a child, do you feel that the person on the other end of the touch point is warm, friendly, generous, and genuinely glad to be there? Do season ticket members really feel respected and appreciated for their loyalty? Jim Broedlow, a Vietnam veteran and longtime season ticket member, does. In 2013, Cindy Hernandez, part of the Giants Client Relations group, invited him to be one of the select few to carry the World Series banner into the park on Opening Day. Jim said it was one of the best days of his life. Stories like these pour out of the franchise's archives.

Hospitality also motivated Greg Marinec, Client Relations Account Manager, when he surprised a few long-standing season ticket members with an opportunity to walk in the 2014 World Series parade and experience a million cheering fans from the players' perspectives. It's the personal letters from Larry Baer or video recordings from Matt Cain and other players sent to fans who need to be cheered up because they are going through really hard times. And, it's Bob Tobeber, a lifelong Giants fan and cancer patient, who said he always felt better when he was watching a game in his box seat behind home plate. When Bob lost his final fight to cancer before the start of the 2014 season, everyone, including his pastor, family, and close friends, talked about how much the Giants meant to Bob.

You can't fake these kinds of relationships. They come from somewhere beyond good service; they come from a spirit of benevolence. Benevolence is an expression of care and kindness. It is doing the right thing, the kind thing, because you want to, not because you have to. Benevolence is altruistic. It is transformative, not transactional.

Hospitality is all about thoughtful foresight, preparation, and attention to detail that make you feel anticipated and appreciated—like you belong. To deliver this kind of hospitality the Giants have hired people who have a spirit of hospitality in their hearts. You can train servers to clear a table properly or be knowledgeable about the wine list, but you can't teach them to care about how their actions and attitudes affect others. You can train ushers to offer directions to a guest in the ballpark or guide them to their seats, but you can't train them to tell that special story, ask that inviting question, or notice when a season ticket member should be checked on because they have been absent from several games.

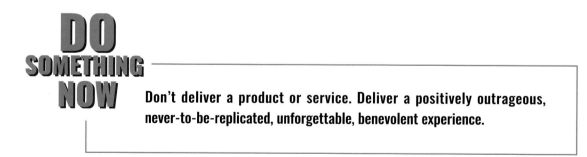

DO SOMETHING NOW Don't deliver a product or service. Deliver a positively outrageous, never-to-be-replicated, unforgettable, benevolent experience.

The Giants CEO and his team understand that it costs the club five times more to win a new season ticket holder than to keep an existing one. Making fans feel special gives them a compelling reason to come back to the park again and again. It's an essential part of the Giants culture because in a world that is conditioned to expect poor service, it's the most effective way to expand your fan base. Beyond the business reasons for nurturing a spirit of hospitality, that hospitality is simply a reflection of how the Giants feel about their fans— they are family.

Design and Disrupt

Baer says the Giants have this motto: "If it hasn't been done before, let's be the first to try it."

In the spirit of trying to give fans a ballpark experience that stays fresh and exciting, the Giants are constantly asking questions like these: "How do we make the experience better? How do we differentiate the business more? And, how do we grow the business faster?" When the Giants set out to do something they don't look at what everyone else doing. They know that if you are trying to replicate someone else's *best* practice the best you are ever going to be is a good number two.

As Alioto told us, finding a way to say "yes" fast is part of the Giants culture. For instance, when home run

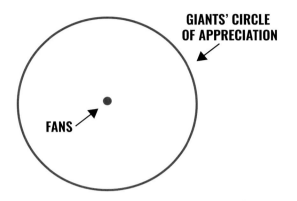

Adapted from the Carl Richards graphic titled "Circle of Gratitude."

hitter Barry Bonds played for the Giants, opposing pitchers often walked him. Someone thought it would be fun to put rubber chickens in fans' hands so they could wave them every time a pitcher walked Bonds. Within a couple of weeks, the club had sourced the chickens, put fans behind home plate where they could be seen waving them on television, and then sold them at the park. "It was a small thing," said Alioto. "It wasn't a moneymaker, but it was fun. It created buzz and excitement and elevated the fans' experience."

This involves innovation. And innovation is the result of a culture in which everyone is expected to flex their creative muscle, people aren't afraid to challenge established ways of doing things, and failure is not a dirty word. It also means that the design of anything you're building is driven by a deep-seated empathy for the people you serve—internally and externally. Here are a few examples.

The Giants were the first franchise to create a secondary market for season ticket holders to sell their unused tickets. Think about it. You're trying to figure out whether or not you are going to renew your season tickets because you don't know if you will attend enough games. Now the club makes it relatively painless to sell your unused seats.

Or, imagine going to a Giants game and being able to upgrade your seat. With a smart phone app you can check in automatically, find a better seat, and pay the difference. It's a win-win solution that puts another weld on the bar of customer loyalty.

The Giants were also the first team to come up with dynamically priced tickets, much the same way the airlines sync ticket prices with demand. A lot of variables affect demand for tickets. For example, a rock-star pitcher such as Tim Lincecum or Madison Bumgarner might create greater demand than a lesser-name starter. A Monday night game against the Rockies won't see the same demand for tickets as a Sunday afternoon game against the Dodgers. A game when there will be fireworks or a concert, or when a player has a chance to break a record, will draw more interest than a regular game.

When dynamic pricing was fully deployed in 2010, revenues increased by $7 million, while the face value of a ticket actually declined for 75 percent of the available seats. This new model enabled the Giants to drive revenue while maintaining modest price increases for the club's most valuable customers: season ticket holders.

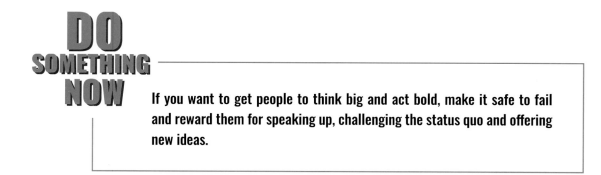

DO SOMETHING NOW

If you want to get people to think big and act bold, make it safe to fail and reward them for speaking up, challenging the status quo and offering new ideas.

The Giants see themselves not just as a sports team but also as a media and entertainment company. AT&T Park has more than 1,600 Wi-Fi access points to keep fans connected to whatever kinds of "second screen" experiences they want. A fan could be watching a couple of games on TV, getting statistical data from the club's website, and calling up replays while texting friends and tweeting. With an estimated 24 billion connected devices coming online by 2020, the franchise of the future—particularly in the Bay Area with its myriad tech-savvy fans—will engage fans through multiple channels.

To engage a new generation of fans eager to be part of this storied franchise, the club opened a social media café inside the ballpark in 2013. Now, fans can visualize what people—in the ballpark, in the city, and around both the Bay Area and literally the world—are saying about the team. Real-time visualizations from Twitter and Instagram posts from players, other fans, reporters, and pundits are displayed in the café. The dashboard tracks followers across various platforms and presents trending topics, comments, and fan photos, all of which is designed to give fans in a fresh new way to experience a ballgame.

As of this writing, the Giants have more than 3.1 million Facebook followers, 1.6 million Twitter followers, and 1 million Instagram followers. Additionally, the club uses every other social media outlet it can think of—Pinterest, Snapchat, LinkedIn, and more—to strengthen the bond between fans and the team. In 2012, the Giants had the same Klout score (which measures social media impact) as then-President Barack Obama did.

When the Giants built the new park, they envisioned a year-round gathering place for the whole community. "We saw the potential to create not just a special place to watch baseball but also a new San Francisco landmark and a premier entertainment venue," said CEO Baer. To that end, the franchise created one of the top hospitality, intimate and large-scale event, entertainment, and sports consultancies in the world: Giants Enterprises, a wholly owned subsidiary responsible for filling AT&T Park with non-baseball events such as corporate meetings and parties to full-scale concerts.

Fans can get real-time posts from players, reporters, and other fans at the Giants Social Media Café.

Today, almost every part of the park can be monetized. If you want to host a sit-down dinner in the Giants clubhouse or dugout you can. If you want to have a party in the Gotham Club, host a fantasy batting practice, or play a game on the field, you can do that too. If you want Willie Mays, Willie McCovey, or Orlando Cepeda to be part of a special event, Giants Enterprises will make it happen. These one-of-a-kind events provide new revenue streams by leveraging the use of the stadium beyond the club's 81 home games.

Giants Enterprises has also produced such events outside the park as the 34th America's Cup spectator experiences, AVP Beach Volleyball competitions, the City Hall Centennial, and the San Francisco Bowl. When the Giants are out of town, the firm hosts more than 150 non-baseball events each year.

Fireworks at an AC/DC concert at AT&T Park.

The Giants clubhouse doubles as special events dinning.

The Giants had and continue to have the audacity to dream and do big things. Innovation is a thick strand in the DNA of the club's culture. Located near Silicon Valley, the innovation capital of the world, the club has owners, season ticket holders, and fans who are building new technology, launching new business models, and disrupting not just the experience of baseball but also the business of baseball and the positive impact the game has.

The difficulty of winning a championship in baseball is unreal. This is true in any professional sport, really, and it's even harder when leaders aren't on the same page and the organization is off balance. Survey the NFL, the NBA, the NHL, and MLB. The teams that win consistently create, work, operate, and manage "as one."[21] Stakeholders from top to bottom see eye to eye about the organization's culture, strategy, team makeup, style of play, technology, and communication.

6
CONTINUITY AND ALIGNMENT
Thinking Different in the Same Direction

As *Sports Illustrated*'s Tom Verducci observed, "The bedrock of the San Francisco championships is a manager-front office relationship that's as stable as it is sublime."[22] The Giants culture is so thick, well-defined, and enduring because people come into the organization and stay. Leadership continuity reinforces the values driving the culture. Operationally, it makes the club seamless.

Add to this that people respect each other's expertise and truly enjoy working together. From the front office to baseball operations, no one is stuck in a Master of the Universe syndrome. The relationships are collegial and collaborative. Larry Baer has been a fan of Giants baseball since childhood. He obviously has a good grasp of the game, but he knows what he doesn't know and defers to Brian Sabean, Bobby Evans, and Bruce Bochy to manage baseball operations. These guys, in turn, appreciate the fact that Baer usually runs 90 mph, juggling multiple priorities and inspiring every person in the organization to bring their best selves to the club. It is a symbiotic relationship anchored in each leader's choice to serve. Sabean explained it like this.

Early on, our players—even in Bruce's first two years when it was pretty rough—saw that he was not only joined at the hip with them, but he was also joined at the hip with me, which made me a part of them and them a part of the front office and ownership. There was no escape valve where you could point the finger and blame "them" because we were all *"them."*

> **When vision becomes the boss and everyone is committed to this boss, turf battles, internal politics, pettiness, and power plays give way to synchronicity.**

Then, you add the fact that I had a great relationship with the ownership group. Thank goodness that Larry, Peter Magowan, Bill Neukom, and the entire group were so accommodating. They wanted to win, they didn't meddle in baseball operations; they believed in us, trusted what we were doing, and they cared. We were very lucky to create that atmosphere, to have that continuity all the way through the organization.

When vision becomes the boss and everyone is committed to *this* boss, turf battles, internal politics, pettiness, and power plays give way to the kind of synergy that ripples through the system. Doors open, people look for a way to support each other, to say "yes" quickly, and the organization shifts gears smoothly. Exciting things get done faster and more cost-effectively.

Arrive Together

Continuity doesn't come from thinking alike in a groupthink kind of way; it comes from thinking different in the same direction. It comes from trusting that your colleague, who sees things differently, is as committed to achieving the same goals and realizing the same vision as you are. Sometimes you take the scenic route to get there—navigating a lot of arguments, give-and-take discussions, and the kind of pushback where you agree to disagree—but you arrive together. Boch has confidence in the fact that, no matter what the approach, Sabean is constantly thinking about what he can do to improve the team.

The two men have a lot of respect for each other. If one has a hunch or an idea, the other takes it seriously. Here's a simple example that illustrates their mutual esteem.

One of the great things about managing an All-Star Game is that you get to see a lot of incredible talent under one roof at one time. When Boch was managing the 2011 All-Star Game he picked up on Houston Astros outfielder Hunter Pence's leadership and affability.

Boch and Sabes outside the White House after the team met with President Obama.

Boch: Managing the All-Star Game is such an honor and one of the benefits is that it allows you to meet players and learn more about them. I told Brian that Pence had a lot of energy and that I thought he would be a great clubhouse guy at some point. I could see the way other players responded to him. He just had a presence that made him stand out as someone we could use. The thing I appreciate about Brian and Bobby is that those observations are valued. They will follow up and investigate. If someone in our organization has an idea, it doesn't fall into a black hole somewhere. Fortunately, that one [signing Pence] worked out pretty well.

Scouting Pence shows how collaboration works inside the Giants organization. Boch's radar was on and his antenna was up. He noticed something extraordinary and then communicated it. Instead of blowing it off, Sabes and his team logged it into the "follow-up" file and then pursued it. Pence became a force for the Giants—on and off the field—yet he would be the first to tell you that he was just one among many moving parts that contributed to the Giants 2012 and 2014 World Series wins. That said, it's hard to imagine the Giants without the presence of the scrappy right fielder.

Got Your Back

By 2007, the Barry Bonds era was coming to an end and the club was rebuilding. Still, the franchise lost 91 and 90 games in Boch's first two seasons. Impatient fans labeled him "Botchy" and called for his ouster. But in those dark days Sabes didn't flinch. "You don't have the bloodletting here that you do in most franchises or the corporate world," he told us. "Larry Baer and Peter Magowan put their thumbprint on the organization from the very beginning. They are fiercely loyal and have very little turnover." Clearly, those qualities roll down through the whole Giants organization. "A lot of organizations wouldn't have allowed us to soldier on and have some continuity," Sabean continued. "They allowed us to soldier on, and they were proven right."[23]

> **Boch:** Those first two years weren't pretty. We were tested. We knew we were in rebuilding mode, but still, to suffer through two years of under .500 ball was so disappointing. It would've been easy for the organization to make a change [in the manager]. No one would have blamed them. But I've gotta give Sabes a lot of credit. This is where character gets revealed. He stuck by me—he carried me.

During the time Boch has been in San Francisco, he and Sabes have established an uncommonly tight friendship. They socialize often and their wives are close friends. It helps that the two have offices next to each other and they live in condos in the same building across the street from AT&T Park. The good news is that they have the luxury of walking home together. The bad news is that they have the luxury of walking home together, which often means they're "holding court" into the wee hours.

> **Boch:** We talk baseball a lot. We ask each other's opinion. I don't tell Sabes what he *wants* to hear, I tell him what I think he *needs* to hear. And he does the same with me. I'm happy we have that kind of freedom. I feel respected because I have a voice with Sabes. Believe me, I know how fortunate I am.

Close friends, Amanda Sabean and Kim Bochy clicked immediately.

> The other thing is, if we are going to release a player or call a player up from the minors, there are no surprises. Whether the decision is Larry's, Brian's, Bobby's, or mine, it's always talked about. And that conveys respect. We would never make a decision without discussing it with those who are affected by it.

> It reminds me of what Bill Parcells [former head coach of the New York Giants and other NFL teams] said. "If they want me to cook the dinner, at least they ought to let me shop for some of the groceries."

Sabean said he also appreciates the luxury of being able to decompress after games.

> The time we spend together and the relationship we have allows us to have the kind of conversations where you can come back to work with a clear mind the next day, or if things are really hitting the fan, you could stay there all night, exorcise the demons, and then come back the next day making sure you have a plan going forward.

> When Boch first came here, we developed the ability to talk freely without being judged or worrying about where the conversation is going. Fierce loyalty goes along with that.

Both Boch and Sabes are completely immersed in the game, but when they finish with the pre- and postgame debriefs, the conversations usually spill over into any number of non-baseball topics. Sabean is a versatile and entertaining storyteller who loves to talk about his old days with George Steinbrenner's Yankees.

> **Boch:** More than a few times, Brian, Lee Elder [senior scouting advisor and close friend of Sabean's], and I sit around talking baseball and then the Steinbrenner stories start to come out. Before you know it, time gets away from us and it's 1:30 or 2:00 o'clock in the morning.

Giants CEO Baer puts it this way. "Nothing is more important in sports than the relationship between the GM and the manager or coach. It works here because they respect each other. Boch can have a say in acquisitions and Sabes can have a say in lineups. They know the other one has the final decision, but they know their opinion is respected."[24]

We all have egos, and there is a time and a place where, if you are the boss, you have to play that role. But "being the boss" just doesn't seem to be all that important to these guys. Here's what Sabean told us.

> I've always looked at the manager as "talent," just like the players. I've never had to be the smartest voice in the room or the loudest voice in the room or the first and foremost opinion. Boch is the same way. If you were to sit us both down and talk about our backgrounds, both of us came from very humble beginnings, and both of us worked our way up in the game, which doesn't happen as much today. So, there's a lot of respect, but not the need for attention. In many respects, you don't even want to attract the attention.

When you look at the Giants success it's hard to talk about either Boch or Sabes without talking about the other. Both guys have obviously bought into the idea that finding the right solutions to make the Giants better is a collaborative endeavor.

> **Boch:** I don't know if I have the words to adequately describe how I feel about Sabes. Had Brian and his team not gone out and got the talent, we wouldn't have won three World Championships. I'm grateful to work with a guy like Sabes. He's a genius at finding resources. He's passionate about the game. He's emotional. He cares deeply about the players, the fans, and about winning.
>
> But, Brian is more than just a boss. He's a world-class strategist who rarely tires of talking baseball. He's a courageous buffer when I need one and a hotheaded critic when I need one of those too. Most of all, he's a friend. And that makes managing so much easier.
>
> Don't get me wrong; we don't agree on everything. We have our moments where we'll have it out. But that's the beauty of our relationship. No punches pulled. Nothing gets unsaid. Everything's on the table. When you have the freedom to say what you want and still have that respect [for each other] so much more gets accomplished.

Sabes believes that the relationship he and Boch have is tighter than most GMs and coaches or managers have. Spending time together, enjoying each other's company, sends a message to the rest of the organization. "[I]t rubs off into the clubhouse," Sabean said. "In a lot of places you can develop an us-vs-them mentality. We don't have that here because I'm so visible. I have a little office, removed from the clubhouse, but on the same level. [Players and coaches] see us interact a lot before games. They know we're in it together."[25]

Of course, Sabes and Boch have dramatically different personalities, but they complement and strengthen one another. Sabes is emotional and fiery. Tightly wound. Boch is more laid-back and calm. Both are demanding and fiercely loyal. And both share a passion with Baer for challenging the status quo and finding the next new thing.

They keep their offices open to each other, which creates a "boundaryless" environment where communication easily flows back and forth. It's the same with Evans now that he has moved into the role of GM. Unlike some clubs where the GM dictates lineups and choreographs the way players are used, the relationship between Bochy, Sabean, and now Evans is collaborative. They know each other well enough to cross boundaries yet respect one another's space.

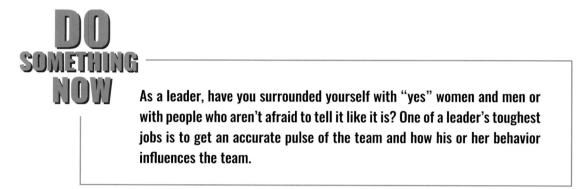

As a leader, have you surrounded yourself with "yes" women and men or with people who aren't afraid to tell it like it is? One of a leader's toughest jobs is to get an accurate pulse of the team and how his or her behavior influences the team.

In the off-season, they remain in constant contact about potential signings and trades and how they are going to modify the roster. It all comes down to radical collaboration. This is the basis for what sportswriter Tom Verducci labeled "the winning team within the winning team."

Giant Among Giants

Friendship aside, is it any wonder that Boch has so much trust in Brian Sabean? After all, he's the architect of the rosters that Boch and his coaches parlayed into three World Series trophies in five years. Unparalleled among active GMs, Sabean's résumé reads like the vita of a Hall of Fame inductee:

- Three World Series Championships (2010, 2012, 2014)
- Four National League pennants (2002, 2010, 2012, 2014)
- Five National League Division titles (1997, 2000, 2002, 2010, 2012)
- Three National League Wild Cards (2002, 2014, 2016)
- Sporting News Executive of the Year (2003)

As for the senior executive of any large enterprise, being the GM of a baseball club is a balancing act. You juggle baseball economics, ownership and fan expectations, and media pressure alongside being able to make the right deals at the right time. When there is a need to massage your roster, you must be willing to act. You also must know when to be patient and hold off. In a role that requires a quick grasp of big data, knowledge of the game, the ability to spot a bargain, tremendous negotiating skills, and a knack for handling unprecedented scrutiny from increased media attention, Sabean is exceptional. Consider just this handful of examples.

In 2006, Sabean and his scouting staff saw something in a skinny little pitcher from the University of Washington that other teams didn't. A freakishly funky delivery, combined with his small frame, didn't scare Sabes. That kid turned out to be Tim Lincecum, who has two Cy Young awards, two no-hitters, and three World Series rings to his credit.

In 2007, under Sabean's watch, the Giants signed Madison Bumgarner, and in 2008, Buster Posey. If you are not a Giants fan and don't know their stories, stay tuned. Calling these guys "world-class" is an understatement. In 2015, the Giants entire infield was homegrown. It included first baseman Brandon Belt, second baseman Joe Panik, shortstop Brandon Crawford, and third baseman Matt Duffy—plus catcher Buster Posey. Together, the killer foursome made up one of the best infields in baseball. Bumgarner, nicknamed MadBum and sometimes just Bum, is yet another huge success story. Stay tuned for that one too.

In the trade market, Sabean has not been shy about taking risks. He acquired reliever Javier López from the Pirates, right fielder Hunter Pence from the Phillies, left fielder Ángel Pagán from the Mets, and Cy Young winner Jake Peavy from the Red Sox.

Even with a robust farm system and solid trades, no roster is without some holes. So, Sabean made several free agent deals—ace reliever Jeremy Affeldt, slugger Michael Morse, and veteran starter Tim Hudson—that worked out nicely for the Giants.

Call Sabean's approach whatever you like—astute, judicious, discerning—it combines with his unconventional deep-seated belief in his manager to draw the best out of anyone and makes him as good as they come. He knows what it takes to find guys who can add value from unlikely places. The scrap heap in baseball refers to ancillary players who have run out of opportunities elsewhere, which means a franchise can pick them up for a bargain. This is where left fielder Travis Ishikawa, starter Ryan Vogelsong, closer Santiago Casilla, long reliever Yusmeiro Petit, and middle reliever Jean Machi all came from.

Homegrown draft picks. Trades. Free agents. The scrap heap. Putting quality players on the roster isn't just luck. It's the result of experience plus spirited give-and-take discussions with a highly competent and shrewd baseball operations team that Sabean trusts. Together, they have a proven eye for finding high-impact, cost-effective players to build out Bochy's toolbox. Boch in turn has drawn something special out of each of these guys and melded them into teams that exceeded everyone's expectations.

Many speculate that Boch is a shoo-in for the Hall of Fame. The question is, will Sabes join him? Most people don't think of Cooperstown in terms of GMs; they don't go there to see bronze plaques of guys wearing ties. (Sabean rarely wears one.) The Hall of Fame currently includes only five GMs: Branch Rickey, Larry MacPhail, Ed Barrow, George Weiss, and Pat Gillick. MacPhail was the last inductee, in 1978. This decades-long hiatus means that very few GMs have been successful for more than a few years. And, the higher you go in a baseball franchise, the more variables play into your success—payroll, player availability, managerial acumen, ballpark layout, and fan enthusiasm.

Yet Sabean has the entire package—versatility, restless curiosity, a desire to constantly improve, and a die-hard, all in, team-first work ethic.

> **Boch:** Sabes has built a tight-knit group of unsung heroes around him. You want to talk about continuity; we have a lot of it in that group. Bobby Evans has been with Brian from the beginning—24-plus years. Dick Tidrow. Felipe Alou. Joe Lefebvre. Paul Turco. Lee Elder. Matt Nerland. Tony Siegle. And the guys who have passed—Pat Dobson, Ted Uhlaender, and Joe DiCarlo. Just to name a few.
>
> These are all seasoned guys who know Giants baseball. Any one of them would take a bullet for Sabes, and I know he'd do the same for them. These are the guys in the background that you never hear about, and yet they are so consequential to our success.

These are the guys that shake the bushes and find your Pat Burrells, Mark DeRosas, Travis Ishikawas, Marco Scutaros, and Michael Morses. Their scouting reports ring true because they know that Sabes values substance over hype. This kind of tenure among staff puts everyone on the same page in terms of what we are trying to accomplish.

Even though you rarely hear about them, these unsung heroes—scouts, player development officials, and on-field personnel—have been with the Giants most of their careers. "Those guys are worth their weight in gold," Sabean has said. "The good thing is that we have a lot of long-term employees, a lot of smart people. We have a lot of collective collaboration that has helped sort a lot of things out."[26]

Many of the front office executives who were instrumental in getting the new ballpark built and key in launching the Giants transformation two decades ago are still with the club too. Since 1992, the Giants have had only three field managers, two GMs, two CFOs, three CEOs, and one lawyer. In a world where GM job security has dropped precipitously, Brian Sabean was the longest-tenured GM in MLB until he handed the reins to assistant GM Bobby Evans in 2015. In terms of continuity, few people were more prepared for the demands of the GM role than Evans was.

Boch, now the winningest active manager in the game, is in his twelfth year with the club. With a couple of exceptions, his coaching staff has remained intact for the last six years, and the same is true for the Giants scouting network. The same scouts who identified Pat Burrell, Cody Ross, Buster Posey, Brandon Crawford, and Madison Bumgarner in 2009 and 2010 are the same guys who had Hunter Pence and Marco Scutaro on their radar in 2012 and Joe Panik, Matt Duffy, and Jake Peavy in 2014. They understand that the Giants are looking not only for extraordinary talent based on analytics but also for people of character who will fit into the culture. They don't have to look up the character strengths the Giants want in a player; they've been in the culture long enough to know what it means to live them.

General Manager, Bobby Evans.

All this continuity breeds cultural consistency. From Larry Baer and the front office to baseball operations, from Brain Sabean and Bobby Evans to Bruce Bochy and his coaching staff, the Giants have created a culture where one message can have many messengers but still sound unified. "We've got a great culture here," Sabean has said. "We love and appreciate everyone's loyalty and commitment, their work ethic. We feed off each other, and we have a hell of a time together. We're fully invested."[27]

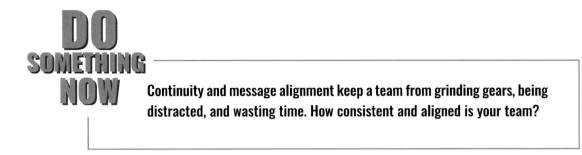

DO SOMETHING NOW

Continuity and message alignment keep a team from grinding gears, being distracted, and wasting time. How consistent and aligned is your team?

Surrounded by Competence

Great leaders admit that others see things they cannot see and do things they cannot do on their own. Boch is surrounded by a cadre of world-class coaches who shore up the entire operation.

> **Boch**: I have such a great coaching staff. I trust them. I lean on them. And they support me. Even among coaches it's always a team effort—they don't get the accolades they should.

For example, pitching coach Dave "Rags" Righetti's fingerprints are all over the Giants success. Rags has a great eye for spotting weaknesses in hitters and for motivating pitchers. He works seamlessly with Bullpen Coach Mark "Gardy" Gardner who is a master at fine-tuning pitching mechanics. If you look back at all the strategic pitching decisions that have earned Boch a reputation for being one of the best bullpen managers in the business, few have been made without collaborating with Rags and Gardy.

Even Bench Coach Ron Wotus's influence is pervasive in what the Giants have achieved. Responsible for many details, Wotus is the guy who painstakingly positions infielders. And, on that rare occasion when Boch gets ejected from a game, Wotus has Bochy's complete trust and free rein to manage the club. He is like a COO who gives Boch the freedom to think strategically. Then there is Hitting Coach Hensley "Bam-Bam" Meulens who can "talk baseball" in five languages—literally. Yet he has an impressive knack for keeping it simple for hitters; many say he has a calming effect on them. Collectively, these coaches are Boch's go-to guys.

> **Boch**: In my early days as a manager I was much more hands-on. Inexperience tricks you into believing that you need to control everything. But there's an arrogance in that because you can't know it all, do it all, and be it all, particularly when you are surrounded by talented coaches like I have. I delegate a lot more now. I still maintain final authority over how we do things, but when you've got guys like I do, it's almost criminal not to be tapping their expertise. I'm still a work in progress, but I'd like to think it's much more collaborative now.

And Boch's former charismatic Third Base Coach Tim Flannery (Flann, as he is known to his friends and colleagues) was just one of the guys who fostered harmony on the team. Flann gave his heart and soul to the players, and his read on their psychological and emotional well-being was invaluable to Boch. Not to mention that he brought fiery passion and inexhaustible energy to the club. When waving in a runner from third base, Flann was nothing short of entertaining.

With the talent and experience these coaches bring to the game Boch has no problem saying, "I don't know, what do you think?" He knows he doesn't have all the answers. He knows that creativity feeds on multiple points of view. This collaborative spirit fosters a sense of interdependence and creates space for his staff to step forward with their ideas and become more engaged. It gives people an opportunity to express their gifts and talents, and it sets a tone of inclusiveness. That energizes people.

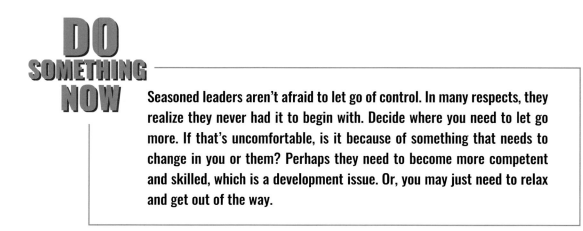

Seasoned leaders aren't afraid to let go of control. In many respects, they realize they never had it to begin with. Decide where you need to let go more. If that's uncomfortable, is it because of something that needs to change in you or them? Perhaps they need to become more competent and skilled, which is a development issue. Or, you may just need to relax and get out of the way.

The Power of Continuity and Alignment

"There's a special kind of continuity here," pitcher Javier López told us. "We know how each other thinks; we know when were in the zone and when we're struggling; we know our strengths and weaknesses and idiosyncrasies. We know what to expect from each other and how to support one another. Add to this the fact that Boch and the coaching staff are really good about keeping us informed. There's a level of comfort in this that creates a special kind of chemistry."

It's not just continuity and alignment among the players. There's a unique brand of alignment in the Giants organization too. Alignment is more than a lack of disagreement. Just because there's minimal conflict in an enterprise doesn't mean people are all on the same page. But in the Giants organization, people are. For example, in many clubs there is a great divide between the statisticians and the old-school guys. For the Giants, Sabean, Evans, Bochy, the sabermetrics gurus, and the scouting organization achieve extraordinary results—together. The scouting organization doesn't feel threatened by the analytics team, and the analytics team members aren't bashful about putting the data in front of Boch. In this franchise, alignment is all about everyone actively owning the club's vision, strategy, and top priorities; all about arriving together from different directions.

Giants Equipment Manager Mike Murphy started with the club in 1958.

Walk the hallways of the Giants front office and talk to the people there about what they do and you can see and feel the results of the club's continuity and alignment. Mutual understanding, mutual self-giving and support, mutual celebration of each other's accomplishments, and mutual pride in the Giants is what you will see. The sense of unity and togetherness is strong and deep. You get the same thing on the baseball operations side. Sabean, Evans, Bochy, and the coaches and unsung heroes who support them say their victories are much sweeter because it's a collective effort.

It's the same story when you listen to Giants broadcasters Duane Kuiper and Mike Krukow, Jon Miller and Dave Flemming, or Erwin Higueros and Tito Fuentes. Even though they tell it like it is, you can just feel how in tune they are with the team, the fans, and the community.

One of those unsung heroes is a Giants legend in his own right. He has ordered bats for Barry Bonds, rubbed baseballs for Juan Marichal, and polished spikes for Willie Mays. Around 11:30 p.m., after games, you'll most likely see him—stogie in his mouth—listening to Frank Sinatra while he's vacuuming the clubhouse. Mike Murphy, affectionately known as "Murph," has worked in the clubhouse and managed baseball equipment for the Giants since the team moved west in 1958. Murph might be the longest-tenured employee in any MLB franchise. He is the guy who makes sure everyone has the gear they need. Tremendously popular among past and current coaches and players, Murph is a best friend to everyone. He is part of what makes this storied franchise "storied."

> **Boch:** I've known Murph since I was called up to the major leagues in 1978. Murph really has created such a family atmosphere in the clubhouse. He's got that everybody's-favorite-uncle charm. Murph is one of the guys who keep me sane around here. When things are going rough, I'll ask, "Hey Murph, it didn't go to well last night; you want to write out the lineup card today?"

After the Giants won the World Series in 2010, Brian Sabean had this to say about Mike Murphy. "When I saw him on the field afterward, I got teary-eyed. Murph is as important to this organization as anyone. He makes all the players feel so comfortable in a family way, and that should not be overlooked."[28] In recognition of his contribution, the Giants named the clubhouse at AT&T Park the Mike Murphy Clubhouse.

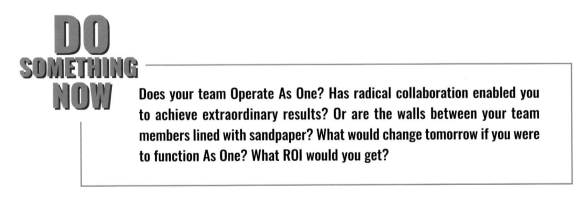

DO SOMETHING NOW Does your team Operate As One? Has radical collaboration enabled you to achieve extraordinary results? Or are the walls between your team members lined with sandpaper? What would change tomorrow if you were to function As One? What ROI would you get?

Continuity and alignment are part of the foundation and framework that make chemistry possible. They are also something that makes the Giants culture unique. Mehrdad Baghai and James Quigley make an observation in their book, *As One: Individual Action, Collective Power*, that essentially describes the Giants way of being: "Adding the phrase 'as one' to another word changes its entire meaning. Working *versus* Working As One. Winning *versus* Winning As One. Stronger *versus* Stronger As One . . . Believing As One. Succeeding As One."[29] The possibilities are endless, but those words describe how continuity and alignment can strengthen a culture.

What works inside the Giants organization is that people who have different personalities, are from different departments, and have different perspectives demonstrate a powerful ability to think and act "as one."

2nd Inning

GIANT FIT

Targeting the Right Stuff

7

BEYOND TALENT
See the Whole Person

In March 2013 the Giants signed catcher Buster Posey to a landmark nine-year, $167-million contract. It was the largest contract in Giants history and the longest MLB deal ever given to a catcher.

It was a huge risk for the Giants. Posey plays one of baseball's most grueling and demanding positions. Plus, it's one of the most dangerous. Giants CEO Larry Baer said that Posey's contract was the "largest and boldest" commitment the Giants had ever made to a player. In explaining why the Giants did it, Baer said that the club looked beyond the player to the person and spoke to Posey's "professionalism, work ethic, maturity, and the way he plays the game with humility. The biggest consideration for us when you get into a commitment like this is: *Who* is the person you're committing to? And that became a very easy call on our part when we thought about Buster—what he'll mean to the Giants going forward and what he'll mean to this community of Giants fans."

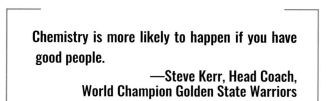

Chemistry is more likely to happen if you have good people.

—Steve Kerr, Head Coach,
World Champion Golden State Warriors

To be sure, Posey is a superstar. Before completing three full years after signing with the Giants in 2009, he earned a Rookie of the Year award, a batting title, an MVP trophy, and two World Series rings. But Boch will tell you, Buster isn't about flash; he's all business—the business of baseball that is. After the 2010 World Series victory, Boch told the catcher, "This is your team now, Buster." It was a rite of passage. It's the type of affirmation you get when another sees that you have the character as well as the talent that makes for good chemistry.

A Branded Mindset

The Giants have built a world-renowned brand because the players and people they bring into the organization don't just support the brand; they *are* the brand. That's why Larry Baer, Brian Sabean, Bobby Evans, and Bruce Bochy aren't just hiring people to win ball games; they are hiring people to position the Giants as a world-class organization— people who will live the brand out loud and protect its legacy.

Buster Posey, talent and character earned him a long-term contract.

Boch: Leaders have to live, eat, and breathe talent. It's something that's in the back of your mind 24 hours a day, seven days a week, year after year. In our business, it's always a war for talent. We compete for it every day. And every year we live and die by our ability to recognize it when we see it. With the kind of investment our owners make [in players] and what's at stake, we have to be very discriminating about who will be a fit for our culture and who won't.

It starts with our scouts. They are the backbone of the organization. If they're not full-blown, full-throttle obsessed with talent, we'll never have chemistry.

In our game that might not seem like rocket science, but I'm talking about the kind of passion that wakes you up in the middle of the night thinking about the talent you have and the talent you want. I'm talking about always being tuned in so that you are constantly learning about the pool of talent that's out there. This is why we lean on our scouting organization so heavily.

If it's a new player, our scouts want to know who they played for, who they played with, what motivates them, what kind of circumstances caused them to excel, and what held them back. Same thing with existing players. We don't assume we've got a player wired just because they've been in the game for awhile. The landscape is constantly changing, so you never stop reading, watching video, getting the scouts' perspective, talking with other players, and studying other clubs to stay in the know.

Boch is acknowledging that the Giants manifest a superior talent mindset. Think Hollywood or Broadway casting. Think presidential cabinet. Think the team you would assemble for a dangerous mission to Mars. Having that outlook is *that* critical. And, he's talking about building a body of knowledge about people in the game that enables the Giants to continue the legacy of a storied franchise.

Data and Instinct

Sabean and Bochy both understand that chemistry makes talent dance. Essentially, they look for both, but if you've got the talent and aren't a fit with the Giants way of doing things, they'll take a pass.

Boch: It's so easy to focus on what you know, right? You look at the field or at your bench and determine where the holes are. Then, our scouting organization goes to work. We have scouts all over. We look everywhere—in foreign markets like Venezuela, Korea, Taiwan, Mexico, Panama, and Japan, and into the draft for the skills we need. It's like putting a puzzle together. What pieces are we missing and who has the right stuff to fill those holes? It's easy to fall into the trap of focusing 90 percent of your attention on a player's athleticism; never mind what they're like in the clubhouse. Never mind how they treat other players or interact with the fans.

You can't win ball games without all the necessary puzzle pieces, but if I've learned anything in my career, it's that the attitude and mentality of a player is every bit as important as their raw baseball skills. Sabes and I have always been on the same page, making character a priority. And, fortunately, the "Propeller Heads" who crunch all the numbers are on board with this philosophy too. I get all the data I need from them—very helpful data—but I've never felt pressured to dismiss the importance of character.

Both Sabean and Bochy have been branded as eyes-over-numbers guys who approach the game in a traditional way. But those public personas aren't entirely accurate. Both are learners who are constantly trying to get better at their craft. Both will try anything to get a competitive edge. And, both believe in the importance of analytics.

They are not anti-sabermetric and never have been. The Giants have been using statistical modeling for 20 years. They are quite sophisticated at leveraging the data. They just don't make a big deal of it in public. In fact, Boch has been recognized for generally making moves that are consistent with the preferences of the sabermetrics gurus.

What Sabean and Bochy reject is managing solely by the numbers. With millions of dollars invested in every franchise, baseball is a business, and business runs on certainty and predictable outcomes. The predominant way front offices have tried to reduce uncertainty is to put their faith in the numbers. Measure and analyze everything. Then, consistently manage what you measure. It makes sense, right? If 1+1 always equals two and 4+4 always makes eight, it limits the uncertainty of managing. Except that it doesn't.

What happens when 1+1 equals two, but two is not a real number—two is altered by a player's impact, positively or negatively, on an entire clubhouse? What if two is really eight or minus two because a manager's intuitive sense of where a player is psychologically and emotionally suggests he should be played or pulled from a game?

The key idea here is balance. The Giants have replaced the tyranny of the "or" with the genius of the "and" by blending sophisticated analytics with a player's makeup and character. They're not in one camp *or* the other; they're in both camps. Every team in the majors has access to the same sabermetrics. One could argue that the advantage it gives one team over another is getting marginalized. In a sense, if the metrics are being commoditized, what is the great differentiator? One of the keys to the Giants success just may be that Sabean, Evans, and Bochy do that "blending" as well as anyone.

> **Not everything that can be counted counts. Not everything that counts can be counted.**
> **—Albert Einstein**

The point is in a game where the volume of statistics available is staggering, there is more to evaluating a player than sheer numbers. For example, how do you measure the worth of Barry Zito's perseverance and work ethic during the years he struggled? How do you account for the tremendous example he set to younger players? How do measure the passion, energy, and enthusiasm Hunter Pence brings to the clubhouse every day? And, how do measure the negative impact of marquee players whose superstar power and disruptive presence suck the life out of the clubhouse?

So often, teams go after a player because he is super-talented, without considering if he's also a cultural fit. How do you generate good chemistry, however, when a superstar who's making millions comes into the clubhouse like a prima donna? He might be ultra-talented, but if he is ultra–high maintenance, the impact on chemistry is draining. The Giants are more interested in creating a *team* of rock stars who deeply care about each other and care about the larger organization as well as the community.

Hiring Formula

The Giants have a formula for attracting the kind of players who will protect and promote the club's chemistry and special culture. It has been a key ingredient behind each of their three World Championship rings. It's a novel and relatively sophisticated idea:

We can build a much stronger franchise if we simply . . . **hire people who don't suck.**

In every organization there are two types of people: those who add and multiply—people who add something to what the other players offer and multiply the flexibility of the team, giving it more options and elevating its power to perform; and those who subtract and divide—people who take something away from other players and have a divisive effect on the team, limiting its ability to perform to its potential. The adders and multipliers are a fountain; the subtractors and dividers are a drain.

There are people who can find opportunity in adversity. Good-humored and optimistic, they play the game to win versus playing it not to lose. They exude enthusiasm and inspire others to dig deep when it seems like all is lost. They unify people and help others believe in themselves, making the team stronger. We're all better for having them around.

> **In every organization there are two types of people: those who add and multiply, and those who subtract and divide.**

Then there are people who can find the difficulty in every opportunity. They are cynical, sarcastic, and pessimistic. They take themselves way too seriously and create drama that doesn't need to exist. Unless we have extraordinary resolve, if we rub shoulders with these people long enough, we get sucked into their shit storm and jaded by their worldview.

Bad attitudes suck.

They quite literally suck the passion, energy, teamwork, unity, and life right out of an organization. People with bad attitudes and a flawed character drag other people down versus lifting them up. They make excuses instead of making things happen. Their unchecked egos won't let them revel in the success of others so their energy is spent drawing attention to themselves. And, ultimately, they suck chemistry out of the team as well.

The solution seems so obvious. Except it's not.

Why do so many teams, and businesses for that matter, end up with toxic people who screw up what would otherwise be great chemistry? Well, someone looks at a guy on paper and says, "We have a deep hole to fill and this guy has the stuff to fill it, even though 'fit' might be a little questionable." Or a player points out another player's negative impact on the clubhouse, yet the manager says, "I know, but he's one of our most productive guys; we need him."

Bit by bit, player by player, management builds a dysfunctional team under the assumption that raw talent trumps culture. Until it doesn't. What to do about underperforming players who negatively disrupt a clubhouse is a no-brainer. It's the toxic guys who excel on the field that tempt us into denial. Initially, we fail to realize that our compromise corrupts chemistry. And then, when the infection eventually shows up on the field, we wake up to realize we have compromised fit, conceded character, and corrupted our formula—all at the expense of culture.

> **Boch:** You can't be held hostage by great talent. There's no question about it, we want players who can perform under pressure, just when you need them the most. We want guys with some swagger. But I've seen managers—I've done it myself—who put up with a player who is toxic in the clubhouse because they have tremendous skill. Just when you've had enough of their attitude they come up with a burst of brilliance in a game, so you let it ride. It never works out because what you don't realize when you capitulate like that is the drip, drip, drip negative effect on other players. Then you wake up one day and say: "How did we get this way? Why are we so disjointed?"

Here's the question: Do you go after the best talent, with stellar numbers, who will obviously fill a gap, and hope they will be a cultural fit? Or do you hold out for talent that has the statistical pedigree *and* the right character, which usually isn't easy, fast, or convenient?

When the *Wall Street Journal* asked CEO Larry Baer to prioritize character versus talent in hiring an employee—whether a director of ticket sales or a shortstop—his response was unequivocal: "When we sign a player, we make repeated calls to people who know him and know about his character. Same thing when we hire someone in the front office. We really do a deep dive into the character and values to see if the values are a match. If the values are a match, that's probably the most important thing. And I'll tell you a good way to do it: About 70 percent of our new hires have come through our internship program."[30]

Baer said that he was influenced by a top venture capitalist who told him that he would rather invest in a person with strong values and "B" talent than the other way around.

You can't legislate or fake chemistry, but you can create the conditions to make it flourish. You can bring people into the club who are naturally predisposed to contributing to chemistry and making it a priority. That starts with the GM and the front office. "We want well-rounded people who fit with the culture here," Sabean said. "Even the most talented athletes can screw up good chemistry if they aren't aligned with our values." The club's results are a testament to his unabashed fanaticism for finding players who can flourish in the Giants culture and perpetuate its chemistry.

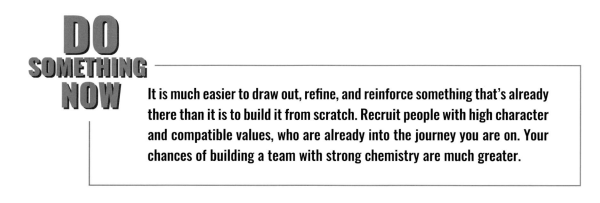

DO SOMETHING NOW

It is much easier to draw out, refine, and reinforce something that's already there than it is to build it from scratch. Recruit people with high character and compatible values, who are already into the journey you are on. Your chances of building a team with strong chemistry are much greater.

Know the Target

A franchise is who it employs. The people you hire today will establish the culture you enjoy—or endure—tomorrow. This means you have to know what you're looking for. Consider the following dialogue:

Let's get pizza for dinner.

What kind do you want?

A good hot pizza.

Thanks, now I understand.

If you don't know precisely what you're looking for, how will you ever find it? If the target is vague or undefined, you severely limit your chances of success. Every club wants "good hot" players, but what does that really mean? The sabermetrics guys can tell you exactly what that means in terms of a player's technical skills. And they can certainly help you look at it from hundreds of different angles.

Take position players, for example. Do they have power and speed? Can they hit, run, and throw? Or take pitchers. Do they have great stuff? Can they move the ball? Do they have good velocity coupled with good control? These are the essentials, the price of entry. But what the sabermetrics gurus can't define—not yet anyway—are the intangible qualities of a player that factor into chemistry. Look at the following list of situations that reveal those qualities, for example:

- How does a player handle victory or a devastating loss?
- Have they been through adversity?
- How did they deal with it?
- When they are in clutch situations, do they rise to the occasion or cave in?
- Are they coachable?
- Are they willing to share their experience and insights with other players?
- What are they like with the fans?
- Do they have a genuine love for the game or want to be a star?
- Are they high energy or low energy?
- What are they like on the bus, on the plane, or in the restaurant after the game?

Choosing players is both an art and a science. The key is the right baseball talent packaged *with* character that protects and promotes the desired chemistry of the clubhouse.

Fit, Not Flash

If the Giants have taught us anything since winning the 2010 World Series, it's this: unbelievable things can happen when a group of people with strong character come together to pursue something big. Making character a strategic priority in the signing and drafting of players pays. Sabean, Evans, and Bochy are veterans. They've been in the game long enough to see how hard it is to build chemistry when there is a vacuum in character.

> **Boch:** You wouldn't think it should be this way, but over the years, character has become more of a priority for me. I think Sabes would agree. It's always been important, but the more miles you log and experiences you have, the more you realize what a big role it plays in the makeup of a team. So, you work harder at evaluating it.
>
> I was incredibly fortunate to work with one of the best GMs in the game. He's a visionary and a fellow connoisseur who never tires of looking for the next great player. Brian has the unique ability to look beyond a player's numbers, beyond their age and history, and see something that others don't see. I've watched him respond to the media for years now. Almost always, he starts into questions about a player by talking about their character.

As a former scout for the New York Yankees, Sabean honed his ability to identify those special intangibles that cause even the most talented players, with their extraordinary physical tools, to stand out. Think Derek Jeter, Andy Pettitte, and Mariano Rivera. Sabean's recruiting philosophy can be summed up in his motto: "If the man is equal to his ability, we have a hell of a baseball player." For the architect of three World Championship teams it's more than a throwaway line; it informs who gets in and who doesn't. Chemistry seems to be ever present in the back of his mind. "We do as much work, if not more, on guys' background and how they fit into the clubhouse than all of the other analysis. We think it's very important from a professional standpoint, a coaching standpoint, and a team standpoint. We don't have a star system here. Everybody has got to be a link in the chain, and they have to accept that responsibility and pull that weight every day."[31]

GM Evans echoes Sabean's philosophy.

> We're looking for a well-rounded person, so we evaluate the whole player, on and off the field. On the field, do they listen? Are they coachable? Do they love the game? Off the field, what are they like to be around? Do they have composure? Do they handle themselves professionally? Can they keep their emotions in check?

> This game is hard. It will relentlessly test you mentally and physically every day, for six or seven straight months. You fail way more than you succeed, so nothing comes easy. Some personalities and temperaments are more suited to that than others.[32]

Before signing a new player, the Giants put a full-blown investigation in motion. It starts with the scouting organization. They tap into a network that gets very small very fast. Someone has either played with the prospect, coached him, or represented him. If Boch doesn't know anything about a player, he or one of his coaches is most likely only two or three degrees of separation from someone who does.

College coaches. Trainers. Equipment managers. You name it. The Giants will talk to anyone who can shed light on the character of a prospective team member. The more data the better.

> **Boch:** Sabes has spent a lot of time thinking about what it means to be a Giant. He has such a great ability to assimilate all of this data—the qualitative data we get in interviews combined with a player's performance metrics—and then make a decision. We look for a special type of person, even if it means bypassing someone with great numbers.

The Giants had been watching and learning about Hunter Pence for two years prior to acquiring him in 2012. Through their reconnaissance they learned what Boch suspected when he met Pence at the 2011 All-Star Game. Pence comes to play every day, and every day he leaves it all on the field. As everyone who follows the Giants knows, Pence has been as instrumental to the club's success off the field as he has been on the field.

> **Boch:** We recently went through the same process with starters Jeff Samardzija and Johnny Cueto. Across the board—and we talked to a lot of people—we got glowing reports on both of these guys. People talked about Cueto's work ethic, what a tough competitor he is, and how devoted he is to his craft. Same with Samardzija. They talked about the energy he brings to the clubhouse, how he genuinely cares for his teammates, and how he never gives up. And he's consistent. He's the same when he is struggling as when he's crushing it.

Contrast this with a reliever we were looking at a while back. His numbers were outstanding. He would've filled a gap in our bullpen nicely. But more than one person told us he would be a cancer in the clubhouse. So, we took a hard pass. Sure enough, what we learned came to fruition in a rather significant incident in another club.

Taking a pass on a super-talented player is how important character and culture are to the Giants. They learned that you have to be very clear about what you stand for, about the values driving your business, and how you want to realize your vision. And, you can't be afraid to pass on or dismiss players (even if you have to eat salary) who aren't in it for the right reasons, who can't passionately opt in to your cause.

All of this means you have to investigate, dig deep, and be creative. This could mean Googling a player's comments over their career to see how he responds to defeat, what he says about teammates, how he handles injuries, how he adjusts to change, how he deals with pressure, and what kind of work ethic he has. What have other players said about the kind of clubhouse guy he is? It could mean talking to previous coaches, dissecting what fans have to say about him on social media, and reviewing the comments he makes there as well. The world is more transparent than ever; the information is there. The Giants care about culture, character, chemistry, and talent; they have the motivation to go get that relevant information and the fortitude to use it.

The Giants have won three World Series Championships, but not on talent alone. They've won by being fanatical about building a team of people whose talents and characters gel in extraordinary ways in wins and losses. Chemistry is so important to the Giants that this "cultural fit" has become a nonnegotiable.

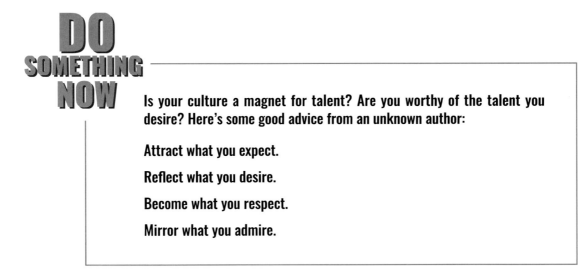

DO SOMETHING NOW

Is your culture a magnet for talent? Are you worthy of the talent you desire? Here's some good advice from an unknown author:

Attract what you expect.

Reflect what you desire.

Become what you respect.

Mirror what you admire.

8
STRENGTHS OF A GIANT
Character is Core

Imagine making 80-plus trips a year with your coworkers—after spending six weeks with them at a camp. Tough assignment. It's risky. And, it's fraught with danger, because if it doesn't work out, it could be a really long and miserable journey. And, if you don't accomplish the mission that brought you together, it could be even longer and more miserable.

Now, consider that this trip includes 25 guys from different countries who think, act, speak, and feel differently. While we're at it, let's throw in the fragile and sometimes flawed humanity of these individuals that creates multiple opportunities for conflict and discord. You're not only asking them to get along; you're asking them to coalesce in such a way that they can accomplish something truly extraordinary. Wouldn't you agree that the makeup of these characters is pretty damn important?

It's no secret that people become more energized and impassioned when they look forward to coming to work and look forward to being with teammates they like and respect. As discussed in the previous chapter, the *who*—as in who you will team up with—is crucial.

> **Life is short. Work somewhere awesome.**
>
> **—Tierney Brothers**

To be this selective about who you bring into the fold is extremely difficult. In his well-researched book, *The Psychology of Baseball,* psychologist Mike Stadler suggests that, "You have to be one in two million to have the total package of physical and psychological abilities required to succeed in baseball at its highest levels of competition." Add the character component to the selection process and it gets even more difficult.

So, what do the Giants look for when they go after a player? What are the virtues or character strengths of a San Francisco Giant? The profile looks something like this.

Championship Blood

Professional baseball players all share colossal physical talent, but what separates the standouts among the pros is something Boch calls "Championship Blood." Running through their veins and sweating through their pores is an iron will to compete. They love the heat of battle. They also love to win and hate to lose. Think Michael Jordan with a stomach virus before Game 5 of the 1997 NBA Finals against the Utah Jazz. Dehydrated and visibly weak, Jordan was told by the Chicago Bulls trainers he was too sick to play. Then he went out and scored 38 points, giving the Bulls a 90-88 victory that took the series back to Chicago where the Bulls clinched the title.

Players with Championship Blood are scrappy. When they face defeat, they never stop trying. When they are exhausted, they don't quit on each other. When they are in a funk, they push through it until they find their stride again. When they say, "I've got your back," they mean it.

If you want a symbol of Championship Blood, go no further than former starting pitcher Jake Peavy. A polite southern boy in person, Peavy turns into something else on the mound. He is an intense, fiery, ultracompetitive presence who attacks the game and barks out loud—mostly to himself. A Cy Young Award winner, one of 38 players with a Pitching Triple Crown (leading the leagues in wins, strikeouts, and earned run average), and with two World Series titles to his name, Peavy is a fierce competitor.

Peavy's famous barking is how he pumps himself up. It's what he does to elevate his game. His emotional outbursts are both startling and endearing. You can see he loves the challenge. It's as though every game he gets to pitch in is special—an opportunity to be perfect. And even though that's unrealistic, he doesn't back down from the goal.

Jake Peavy, Mr. Intensity, and a Cy Young winner, has the warrior spirit.

Boch: Jake *is* a good example of what we're talking about here. He's as tough a player as there is; he goes all out, full bore all the time. He just wears how much he loves to compete right there on his sleeve. It's raw and transparent, but it's authentic too.

If you're a hitter, he wants to get you out more than you want to get a hit off him. And that's what you want in a player.

His presence in the clubhouse and on the bench has been invaluable. He's helped a lot of our guys turn up their intensity and elevate their games. Jake is contagious. His passion infects everyone in a positive way.

Guys like Peavy—and there have been many of them in the Giants clubhouse—set the tempo and tone for the club. And that tone and that competitive drive have brought this team back over and over again when everyone else counted them out.

Team First

It might seem like a no-brainer, but in a game where performance is everything and everything is measured, guys get pretty focused on their own performance. Even more so when they are up for contract renewal and there is a lot at stake—pride, prestige, and money. Then, the "me versus we" debate in a player's head isn't so easily resolved. Brian Sabean and company are looking for guys who are clear about their priorities, guys who are willing to sacrifice for the greater good of the team.

So, the questions become: How do players see themselves in the world? Are they the center of the universe or are they part of something bigger? Do their egos need feeding or do they naturally convey a graciousness toward others who have helped them succeed? Does their language reflect someone who primarily defines himself as an individual contributor or one who is interdependent on a larger group? Are they all about their own numbers or concerned about what's going on with the rest of the team? Do they focus their energy on their rights or their responsibilities? The answers to these questions are very telling.

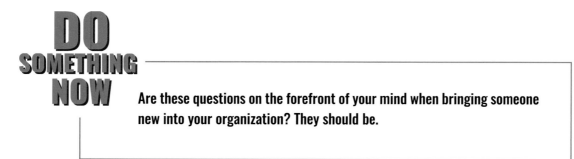

Are these questions on the forefront of your mind when bringing someone new into your organization? They should be.

Boch: Me-first will corrode a team's unity, and when unity goes, a collective self-confidence goes with it. Certainly, with the players, but also within the larger Giants organization, we are a family bound together by a common sense of purpose and shared fate. And really, "family" is how we see it. Larry [Baer] lives it in the front office; Brian, Bobby, and I reinforce it on the baseball side.

I know that word [family] can sound insincere and overused. But, that's why we look for guys who relish the idea of training for battle—together; deploying a game plan—together; coping with losses and celebrating victories—together. When you go after guys who take pride in watching each other's back, you're already a long way toward building the kind of chemistry we want here.

Love to Get Better

The Giants are looking for players who are obsessive about honing their craft: the ones who are in a constant state of improvement. They look for the consummate pros who understand that, every day, what they do affects others. Teammates depend on them to get smarter, better, and faster. These are the players who assume responsibility for being crystal clear about what's expected of them. They are fanatics about covering their assignments. Then they move with a sense of urgency to make the play, in the right sequence and at the right time. They know more about their opponents than their opponents know about themselves. These guys are watching video of an opposing hitter "one more last time" or digging at 2:00 a.m. for that last little detail that just might be what gives them an edge.

Boch: We look for the guys who are so passionate about the game that they love to get better. The opportunity to drill, to run through plays again and again puts them in a category of their own. Even in practice their concentration level is remarkable. When they are there, they are *there*. It's why they are so confident when they face tough challenges or nonroutine plays.

I've told our players, "If you're not prepared, it's not pressure you feel, it's fear, because you are competing against guys who are constantly getting better."

Malcolm Gladwell talks about 10,000 hours in his book *Outliers*. Name your field, the elite put in 10,000 hours or more of practice to become the best at what they do.

Working to get better, striving, looking for the next skill, the next bit of knowledge, the next adventure or breakthrough is a way of thinking and being. When a group of people who really believe there are no upper limits come together, the results can often defy the impossible. Mastery is about loving to get better. It's the pursuit of the ongoing "almost." You almost get there, but "there" keeps moving outward and upward.

Grit and Resolve

When you're in a slump, when the dog days of summer are wearing you out, or when the pressure of the postseason closes in on you, it's almost impossible to access talent without mental toughness.

> **Boch:** In our game, talent alone is never enough because it's a game of adversity. It's long. You get hot and then you struggle. Players get injured and those injuries can have a domino effect on other players. If one of our guys in the bullpen goes out with an injury, we will inevitably put more pressure on other guys to fill that void. To shake off the bad days and stay focused, to maintain the necessary level of intensity, day in and day out, you've got to be mentally and emotionally tough.
>
> It's a funny thing. Every time you face adversity and come through it, you expect to come through it again. And the more times you come through it, the stronger that expectation becomes. Believe me, I don't take it for granted, but our guys have faced so much adversity over the last five or six years that there is an unspoken belief in the clubhouse that says we thrive under pressure. I think that when new players come to our organization they know this because they've either heard about it or witnessed it from the other side of the field. So, when they come here they immediately pick up on it.

When you're around a group of guys who display emotional control and a steely-eyed resolve, it's kind of like osmosis; it permeates the clubhouse and makes everyone tougher. The guts and grittiness Boch is talking about doesn't just happen. It's the result of Sabean seeing something in guys who have gone through the brutal grind of just getting to "the Show."

For example, reliever Yusmeiro Petit, known for pounding out extra innings, kept his hopes alive for playing in the majors by playing in Mexico. Starter Ryan Vogelsong had to play in Japan, was let go from Triple-A, and then played winter ball in Venezuela to prove that he could still pitch at 33. Travis Ishikawa, first baseman turned outfielder, gutted it out in the minor leagues for a long time before earning a chance to bring the gauntlet down on the St. Louis Cardinals, taking the Giants to the 2014 World Series.

> **Mastery is a journey. It's not about perfection in the end. It's about being 2 or 3 or 5 percent better today than you were yesterday.**

Many others just like these guys could be mentioned here, but the point is, when it doesn't come easy, you appreciate it more and you fight to protect it more. Going through trying periods built character and gave these players grit.

Thrive on Uncertainty

Baseball is a cat and mouse game of strategy. Near captures. Repeated escapes. And the constant pursuit of victory while one team tries to outsmart, outmaneuver, and outplay the other. In the span of an evening or a season, the game changes constantly. Sometimes you anticipate these changes and sometimes you don't see them coming. But they are almost always accompanied by uncertainty.

Uncertainty can cause us to hunker down and play not to lose or it can open us up to new opportunities. Sometimes the opportunities demand bold action and big leaps of faith. Sure, the sabermetrics data can mitigate that risk, but when you are forced to make decisions in real time, your players have to do more than just *deal with* unsettling and unforeseen circumstances; they must be able to thrive on them.

Over the course of three World Series Championships, the Giants have had to adapt to player injuries and inconsistent performances. For example, during the regular season in 2014, the Giants lost Matt Cain, Ángel

FAITH moves mountains. DOUBT creates them.

Pagán, Marco Scutaro, and periodically Michael Morse and Brandon Belt to injuries. This meant asking other players to step out of their comfort zones into roles that were unfamiliar to them. In many organizations, fear, insecurity, and egos would get in the way of these changes. Players would gripe to their agents and their agents would complain to the club's management. Not so with the Giants. Boch's players never made excuses and never caved in. That's because Sabean and Evans attract the kind of players who think team first and focus on contributing.

When Boch does something unconventional, rather than moving into self-protection mode and withholding a part of themselves, his players lean into the ambiguity. In the spring of 2011, after winning the World Series, Boch imparted some harsh news to his veterans. He told first baseman Aubrey Huff that he might be moved to left field. Left fielder Pat Burrell, who was instrumental in the Giants 2010 playoff run, was informed that his playing time would be limited. The deck was being shuffled to make room for a rookie first baseman, Brandon Belt, who had played only one season in the minor leagues. How'd it go?

> **Boch:** It couldn't have gone better. These guys are consummate professionals who want to do what's best for the club. Huff not only went out and played left field [in spring training] for the first time without complaining, he got behind Belt. When a rookie is displacing you and you tell him that you are confident he can do the job, that's a strong vote of confidence in what we are trying to accomplish.

In the spring of 2016, the Giants signed speedy center fielder Denard Span to a three-year, $31-million deal. Span would hit leadoff. This meant that Ángel Pagán, *another* speedy center fielder who hit leadoff, would move to left field. What did he have to say about that? "Well, I'll be honest—really honest. First of all, I was surprised by the move. Like anybody, when that's your position and you're asked to play a different position, I was surprised. But at the same time, Span is a great center fielder, a great player. Every player has pride, and you have to sit down and understand that at some point, you have to make a move . . . I'm on board 100 percent. I'm here to do whatever the team needs me to do".

And when Pagán was asked about moving from leadoff hitter to a spot lower in the batting order, possibly even the ninth spot, behind starting pitcher Madison Bumgarner, he said:

> I'm in. I'm in. Because I think when you have two leadoff hitters rolling, and Bumgarner who can hit the ball a long way, he's a great hitter too, that makes the lineup even more dangerous.

I can get on base, put pressure on the bases, and Denard can get a hit-and-run going; we get first and third, nobody out, we've got a great chance to score and that might be the difference in the game. So I like it. We just have to wait and see how the lineup is going to play out, but I'm ready for anything.

Boch: When you have a team that's flexible and willing to adapt, it gives you so many more options to be creative and use your imagination, to experiment and maybe do something unpredictable. When you bring in guys who are willing to do whatever it takes, even if it takes them out of their comfort zones, it gives you the capacity to change before the need for change even becomes obvious. If you have a Swiss Army knife versus a single-blade knife in your tool kit, it changes your whole mindset about what you think is possible.

If culture and chemistry are important; if you are part of a family you cherish; if you are trying to protect a storied legacy; and if you are passionate about accomplishing something extraordinary in the future . . . *precise, painstaking, scrupulous*, and *demanding* ought to be the words used to describe your vetting process.

Boch: We try to be as rigorous about evaluating a player's character and attitude as we are about their numbers, such as batting average, on base percentage, earned run average, runs batted in, and all the other things we keep track of. It's just that important.

I think Larry Baer would tell you the same thing. We're in the entertainment business and the cast determines the quality of the show. Our guys in the front office try to be as disciplined about who gets into the front office as they are about measuring the number of seats sold, season ticket memberships, and sponsorship revenues.

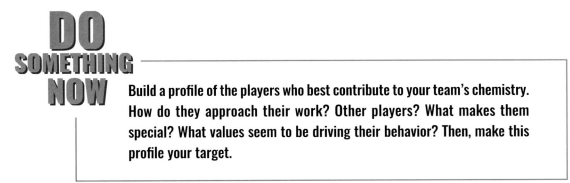

DO SOMETHING NOW Build a profile of the players who best contribute to your team's chemistry. How do they approach their work? Other players? What makes them special? What values seem to be driving their behavior? Then, make this profile your target.

Chemistry doesn't just happen. You come at it from hundreds of different angles and work at it. The prerequisite is starting with people who crush it in terms of already possessing the values driving your culture.

Here's how the Giants look at it. They cherish the club's relationship with the Bay Area community. Players are part of that community. The Giants have a world-class brand. A brand is a promise of the experience you will have when you come to the park, watch a game on TV, or interact with a player. Players are ambassadors of this brand. The Giants are a family. Family members rely on each other to step in, be there, and do whatever it takes. Players are members of this family.

Community member. Brand ambassador. Family member. *Who* these players are affects, positively or negatively, the chemistry of the club and the brand of the franchise.

9
MI CASA ES TU CASA
Hospitality is Pervasive

Most players come into a new clubhouse for the first time feeling alone and isolated. But, if it's a clubhouse like the Giants have at AT&T Park, a player will quickly feel known, wanted, and welcomed. Someone, many "someones," will have anticipated his arrival.

Call it human decency or just good manners, but whatever you call it, the Giants clubhouse exudes hospitality. *Philoxenia*, the Greek word for "hospitality," means "friendliness and love shown toward strangers." That means graciously receiving outsiders, putting them at ease, and making them feel at home when they arrive.

That's what hospitality does. It notices and then anticipates. It says to a newcomer: "We were excited when we heard you signed. Everyone was pumped when you got called up. You're in the right place." It's obvious that the team talked about and planned for his arrival.

> **Boch:** One of our biggest assets—and, I'm convinced, one that carried us to three World Series—is the way our more tenured guys accept and adopt new players. It has created a clubhouse atmosphere where every guy on the team believes that the guy next to him has his back and will do anything to make him better and make the team better. When they believe in the team as a whole, and they know that the team believes in them, it creates a special kind of chemistry that expands their ability to make individual contributions.

Hospitality quickly breaks down barriers and takes relationships to a new level. When people extend hospitality to you, it means you matter to them. It creates a space at the table, a place for a new player to settle in. It says: "We need you. You are essential to what we're trying to accomplish. You are one of us now. Be yourself and let 'er rip." You can imagine what this does to a player's confidence.

> Hospitality creates a space at the table. It says, "You're in the right place. We're glad you're here. We need you."

Pitching Coach Dave Righetti believes that a lot of young guys coming up through the farm system have what it takes to pitch in the major leagues. Creating the right environment is essential to drawing out this talent. "You keep them fired up and make them feel at home. My job is, the minute [they] come in here, to make them feel comfortable and give them a chance."[33]

Hospitality creates a picture of who a new player is, how he fits in, and what his role will be in making things happen. Hospitality is also about who the veterans are and how they make people feel. It's players being personable, warm toward one another, and generous with their time. It's about engaging new guys by asking questions and giving them your full, undivided attention. Being neighborly is about helping them make friends with the other guys and drawing them into the kinship already established in the clubhouse.

Make It Safe

When people know your name and embrace you enthusiastically, your defenses start to melt. You feel included. You can relax. As kids, ballplayers dreamed of individual greatness. But as adults, they also see themselves locking arms with others, playing an important role in an epic story. It is the longed-for camaraderie of doing what you love to do with a group of guys who accept you and value your contribution.

Boch considers Giants former Pitching Coach Dave Righetti the best in the game.

Beyond the dream of making it into a big league clubhouse, who doesn't want to be known and accepted? Who doesn't want to be a real ingredient in realizing the team's shared vision? To be part of its quest for greatness? Who doesn't want to be "one of the guys" and enjoy real conversation and fellowship? Who doesn't want to be on the "inside," sitting next to a more experienced player, listening intently to their insights about the game? And, if your clubhouse includes the likes of Willie Mays and Willie McCovey, who doesn't want *that?*

Home, if it is truly a home, is a safe place that makes connection easy. As a newbie, you can be *in* the life of the clubhouse or you can be on the outside looking in, wishing you had an invitation. Imagine going into a new group of guys who already know each other and you don't know anyone. It can get insecure and lonely real fast as you start asking yourself whether you have what it takes. Hospitality disarms all notions of someone being an outsider, being cut off from the fraternity.

Spread the Love

One of the greatest needs of human existence is the need to be loved and accepted. No matter how mature or successful you are, no matter what kind of front you project or how strong you are emotionally and psychologically, this need of acceptance cuts across culture, gender, and age. And, it doesn't go away when you walk through the doors of the clubhouse. Hospitality is one of many ways love is expressed.

Peace, joy, contentment, and happiness flow out of love. Fear produces anxiety, shame, guilt, and disharmony. You cannot feel these opposite emotions at the same time. Love and fear cannot coexist. People who are loved act differently from those who are not. When we feel loved our hearts are aroused, we're more fully alive and we bring more of ourselves to work. Love dissolves fear and creates a sense of security in people that gives them the courage to risk more, engage more and be more human. Eliminate fear and you make room for passion.

When starter Tim Hudson came to the Giants, he and Madison "MadBum" Bumgarner quickly struck up a friendship. They are country boys who have a lot in common. At the same time the Giants made it into the 2014 postseason, Madison and Ali Bumgarner's lease ran out. They needed a place to live. Tim and Kim Hudson did what friends do. They graciously opened their doors, and the two couples became even closer. "You know, he's been amazing. We've got a special friendship over this year. I feel like he's my little brother. I love him to death," Huddy said.[34]

Most guys are not quick to open up about feelings. More often than not, they express their love for each other through harmless harassment and by giving each other shit. Getting below the surface to find out what makes them tick can be like going on an archeological dig. But Huddy's relationship with MadBum is characteristic of a group of guys who live in a home, make it safe, and spread the love.

Hudson had waited 16 years in his career for this moment. "These guys are like my brothers," he told the media. "I love 'em to death. I can't express how happy I am and how thankful I am to be able to experience this."

Tim Hudson, holding the 2014 World Series trophy, Kansas City.

After winning another do-or-die Wild Card Game in 2016, Bumgarner was asked how he has been so successful in these nail-biting postseason scenarios. The press got an all-too-familiar answer. "It gets said a lot, but our team and all our guys, we love each other," MadBum said. "We love coming to work every day and going to battle for each other. We just really enjoy and have fun coming in and competing."

Bond and Belong

If you think about it, our greatest joys and deepest wounds have to do with relationships. Human beings are *relational* to the core. Any way

Twitter
@kimberlybhudson

LOVE that the Bumgarners stayed with us this postseason.
This just happened:
Tim: Goodnight, man, I love you.

Madison: Love you too, man

you look at it, our need to feel closely connected and bonded to others carries tremendous emotional weight. This is particularly true in baseball, a game where players spend so much time together, much of it on the road away from family and friends. If the relationships are healthy, the house becomes a home; commitment runs deep. If not, separation, isolation, and loneliness can make time with the team—on the plane, on the bus, or in the clubhouse—feel like a prison.

Exclusion cuts off chemistry and causes pain. If you walk into a clubhouse that isn't welcoming, it's much easier to become insecure—and insecurity creates self-centeredness. Players become preoccupied with being okay, with their own sense of well-being and place. If you are not assured that you belong, you will try almost anything to fit in because the emptiness drains your spirit. This is when guys start getting greedy about playing time and grow even more insecure when they don't get it.

When you are trying to fit in, the temptation is either to be overly hard on yourself for making mistakes or to be cocky and cavalier about it. Other symptoms include pressing too hard at the plate or being too aggressive on the mound and playing tight. Whatever it is, if you feel insecure, you can't be yourself and you can't play with the kind of freedom that brings your athletic best to the game.

People who feel left out and live on the fringes often find each other. This is how cliques and factions are born. But if a caste system develops in the clubhouse, it will create a "dis-ease." It infects the ties that bind and breaks down "at-homeness." Eventually, there will be a breakdown in performance. Even when the team wins, disharmony will dampen the experience. Harmony, union, and togetherness make the victories sweet. The game is more enjoyable when you are playing it with friends.

Such bonding isn't easy, though; it's hard.

If you think this all sounds too soft—and that soft is weak—think again. It takes more guts to be vulnerable with people than it does to be distant. It takes guts to lead with love and trust versus authority and fear. Revealing

> **Leadership would be a lot easier if people weren't involved.**

the caring, inquiring, intuitive, and spiritual aspects of ourselves takes guts because it feels unsafe. That's why so many people don't do it. It takes more guts to come down from the ivory tower and talk to people in a human voice that's intimate, inviting, and authentic than it does to dictate and control. When an organization feels lifeless, perhaps the reason is that we bring so little life to work.

Soft is not weak; soft is hard.

Leadership would be easy if it weren't for the people. Relationships can be messy, they take time, and they are complicated and unpredictable. The so-called hard stuff is more quantifiable and easier to measure. It isn't moody. It doesn't argue with you. It doesn't pout. And, it makes for a good hiding place; you can bury yourself in the numbers. But, messy as it is, human interaction is what breeds the loyalty, trust, and love that spark chemistry.

Soft is hard.

Come to the Center

Legendary basketball coach Phil Jackson famously recognized the importance of relationships by using a "bull's-eye" test with his players to determine who felt like they were really connected to their teammates and who didn't. Jackson gave each player a drawing of a three-ring target. Explaining that the bull's-eye was the epicenter of the team and the outer rings represented more and more of the fringe, he asked them to place themselves somewhere on the diagram. Those who felt extremely connected, often the everyday players, put their names in the very center. Those who had a weak sense of belonging put their names on the outermost ring. And then there were players who felt somewhat connected who were on the middle ring. You get the idea.

A master tactician, Jackson's forte was getting his teams to move together in a "spirited way." He used the results of the bull's-eye exercise to have individual discussions with his players, focusing on questions to determine why they felt the way they did and how the team could pull them into the center.

Jackson gets it. To be met with excitement and know that you belong, that your presence adds something, fulfills a deep-seated longing in his players. What player doesn't want to know that he is a source of connection and completion to the rest of the team? What family member doesn't want to be a significant factor in the family's completeness?

This is what makes hospitality so powerful. We are wired for union, not separation. Hospitality is a sign of solidarity. When you truly feel part of the family, playing *for* your teammates isn't a punitive, prove-yourself kind of thing; it's an all-in, collaborative, want-to-support-them kind of thing. As we've defined it here, hospitality creates assurance, and assurance is the lubricant that makes chemistry work.

> **What family member doesn't want to be a significant factor in the family's completeness?**

Michael Morse, who played a crucial role in the 2014 World Series, described how the off-field hospitality fosters on-field unity. "Usually, position players kind of stick together. When I'm in the dugout, I'm talking to the starting pitchers—I'm talking to Tim Hudson, [Madison] Bumgarner, Matt Cain. It's so great. It's such a family. Everybody's done so much in their career and no one acts or thinks that he's better than the other guys. Everybody comes here happy to be here; nobody ever has a bad attitude. Everybody has one goal, and that's to win together. To me, it's the perfect balance of having fun and having success."[35]

Baseball is a game of risk. You fail more often than you succeed. When players truly believe they belong, they aren't paralyzed by a need for perfection. They have the freedom to be imperfect, which increases the chances that they actually will be perfect—or closer to it.

> **Boch:** If you are new to the organization, particularly if you are a young player, you are still feeling your way around. What are the rules and the *unwritten* rules? If you make a mistake on the field, how will the other guys respond? There is a lot of uncertainty. If you're nervous, walking on eggshells, worrying about screwing up in front of your teammates, you're not focused on making plays or getting hits. You are playing not to lose. That chews up a lot of mental and physical energy. You're just asking to make a mistake.
>
> Building rapport cuts the cycle time down by making our new players feel included and keeping them loose. The more you know people, at least our kind of players, the more you can relax because you're accepted. Essentially, we are saying: "You're here because we believe in you. We know you are going to make mistakes. It's not the end of the world. Learn from it and move on. We want you to play your heart out—don't hold back, give it all you got."

Rookies Are Family

How did Buster Posey come up into the majors in 2010 and play with maturity beyond his years? How did a young rookie like Joe Panik have the kind of composure that enabled him to make a game-changing play in the World Series? How did Matt Duffy make an impressive jump from Double-A to join the Giants for a postseason run in August?

Each of these guys told us how comfortable he feels in a clubhouse shaped by team-oriented veterans.

> **Boch:** Our veterans just have a way about them. You can see it in the way they welcome our young guys when they come up. It makes it easier for the rookies to make that transition and do well.
>
> This sense of belonging starts in spring training. We bring the minor leaguers over, even when they're not in big league camp, to hang out and talk with the coaches and veterans who are here. It goes on every year. It gives our minor leaguers a higher comfort level when they *do* come up because they've already been around the veterans. Our minor league guys aren't afraid to talk to them. They're not afraid to make mistakes around them.

I can take you back to when Posey, Bumgarner, Crawford, and Belt came up, and more recently Panik and Duffy. It's pretty special to see how these guys welcome the younger players and help them feel comfortable.

When Duffy first came up from the minors, Tim Lincecum immediately sat down with him and started a conversation that made Duffy feel welcomed. Lincecum wasn't glad-handing either. A day later he continued the conversation by picking up right where the two players left off.

Duffy was impressed by Lincecum's sincere interest in getting to know him. Perhaps there are players with Lincecum's credentials who wouldn't give a rookie the time of day. But then, that's not the Giants way.

The clubhouse rubs off on these guys, and they pick up on the vibes of other players—even players who are long gone but have left a mark on the culture. The new guys breathe in the culture and start to take on the characteristics of these more tenured players. In a piece he wrote for the *Players' Tribune*, Matt Duffy talked about hospitality as a key factor in the success of the Giants young players. "I was 23 and just up from Double-A (in 2014). Nobody had ever heard of me. But Hunter [Pence] didn't treat me like an outsider who was just passing through, filling a roster spot. He made me feel as if I was exactly what the team needed. Thus began a succession of welcoming handshakes and confidence-boosters from Buster and Brandon Crawford and everyone else. 'Play big,' they told me. 'Let's win some games,' they told me."[36]

> **We've just got a bunch of guys who come together. There's something magic that happens in this clubhouse.**
>
> **—Tim Flannery,
> Giants former Third Base Coach**

When the Giants needed a relief arm in 2012, they called right-hander George Kontos from Triple-A. The first weekend after he arrived, a group of players, including Bumgarner and Posey, invited him to dinner. No big deal. Right? Except that it is.

A band of brothers celebrates after the 2012 World Series victory parade.

The simple act of sharing a meal is a classic form of hospitality. Food and drink bring people together. Inviting a new player out for a meal or a beer taps into one of the most ancient forms of building authentic community. When you invite someone to dinner, they start to move from being a colleague to becoming a friend. Something we so often take for granted can have a profound effect on the relationship. It means you are relaxed enough to let down your guard, put away self-defense mechanisms, truly enjoy each other, and start to build trust.

Breaking bread together facilitates communion and camaraderie. When you have a meal with others, you learn about them. They become more human. It's not as easy to make unwarranted assumptions about or judge them.

When veterans like Lincecum, Pence, Posey, Bumgarner, and others set this kind of tone, it reinforces chemistry. Hospitality doesn't just happen. It takes hundreds, maybe even thousands, of little gestures. A sincere welcome reaches out and figuratively pulls a player into Phil Jackson's bull's-eye, making them feel like they made a great choice.

And, at some point, Duffy will have an opportunity to do for a rookie what Lincecum did for him, and he will rise to the occasion. So will Panik, Kontos, and a host of other rookies who have appreciated how they were enculturated into the Giants organization.

Here's the thing. The more accepted and comfortable you feel in a new environment, the less distracted you are about trying to fit in—you feel like you already fit in. It's liberating. It enables you to concentrate on making a contribution. When you take that freedom onto the field, good things often happen. When people honor you with their respect, the reciprocal effect is to be worthy of that respect.

> **Boch:** Believe me, players talk. Even across franchise boundaries, players talk among themselves. "What's *your* clubhouse like? What's it like to play with this guy or that manager?" They compare their experiences. So, it can be a small world fast. You've either created a place that players are curious about and attracted to or one that they try to avoid.

The familiar adage rings true here: *The way you treat your people is the way they will treat your customers.* Except in this case, the way you treat your players not only influences the way they play the game; it also influences your club's brand among other players and your ability, for example, to sign a free agent or get a player to waive a no-trade clause. These aren't necessarily the reasons behind the Giants brand of hospitality; they are the positive by-products of it.

Players don't belong because the terms of their contracts say they do. They belong because a spirit of hospitality shows them they are wanted and welcomed. Beyond merely having legal standing, they have been included—adopted, to be more accurate—into the inner circle of the Giants family. When a place has been made for you at the table, you are drawn into the center, invited to engage, connect, and bond. The Giants know soft is hard so they are relentless about spreading the love and making it safe for new players to relax, play big, win games, and add to the franchise.

You can't legislate hospitality and friendships, but you can put newbies in a position to spend time with more tenured folks. You can teach your people about the importance of making others feel comfortable by reaching out and extending a welcoming hand.

GIANT EXPECTATIONS

Leading, Coaching, and Connecting

10
PLAYERS ARE PEOPLE FIRST
Valuing Humanity in the Business of Baseball

What separates the truly great clubs from those who perform at a level of mediocrity? As we've noted, an obvious answer is talent. There's just no substitute for it. But extraordinary talent never reaches its full potential without good chemistry, and good chemistry improves with great leadership. The manager's ability to fully engage that talent—every single person, every single game, all season long—makes chemistry work. For many clubs, this requires a fundamental shift in how management sees players.

With the advent of television coverage, professional and college sports became big business. Of course, to get the best contract you have to have the best ratings, and winning attracts viewers. Baseball is no exception to this phenomenon.

Athletes who put themselves on the bidding block for millions of dollars become the unofficial "property" of clubs who will program and hone them into winning revenue machines. Players become "our most important assets." They are "our payroll," our "acquisition costs," and "commodities" traded in the open market. As America's favorite pastime, baseball offers an escape into the world of high-stakes drama, adventure, and heroics. It's called putting the best "product" on the field because the fans are buying entertainment. Property. Products. Assets. Commodities. Players are objects. Interchangeable parts. Teams buy, sell, trade, and own them.

> **What if our organizations were as human as the human beings in them?**

GMs and managers will often say they don't want to get too close to their players, anticipating that a player will eventually be traded. And when he stops performing or grows too old, he will be discarded, although it's called "designated for assignment" or being "released."

In a world where you have a job today and could lose it tomorrow, players even objectify themselves. Witness the use and abuse of performance-enhancing drugs. When your performance is your worth, you do whatever you can to get an edge and improve it—even if it means doing long-term harm to yourself.

Professional broadcasters, beat writers, and fans on social media analyze the skills of players and the strategies of managers, often with a sense of detachment that leaves little regard for diplomacy. One day you're a hero, the next day you're vilified. It doesn't matter that you're talking about a real person, with a real family, who has real feelings; it just goes with the territory. If you don't like it, put your big kid pants on and toughen up.

What if our organizations were as human as the human beings in them? Randomly ask 10 people walking down the street what they think and you'll discover that many of the places they work are not very human. Who or what is to blame? One of the many things that make the Giants organization unique is that it hasn't lost its sense of humanness. The owners, CEO Larry Baer, and the entire organization have created a $2-billion enterprise. It's not without checks and balances, but it's still human. Even though Brian Sabean, Bobby Evans, and Bruce Bochy have grown up in this game—and occasionally use the dehumanizing language of business when talking about the team—they see players as more than tradable commodities; they are people first.

Chemistry fails or flourishes based on how we see people and treat them. How a manager sees his players in a clubhouse, for example, will spill over into how they see themselves and, ultimately, how they treat each other. It starts with the tone set by the leader.

> **Boch:** For me it's about what or who you see first. Do you see a player or a person? An opportunity or a person? A statistical profile or a person? A person or someone who can be leveraged in a trade?
>
> I've been on the other side of this with hard, old-school managers. I know how our players feel. I know how dehumanizing it can be. So I try to remind myself that these guys are people first. Do I always get it right? Not even close.

Bottom line: You have more influence and more impact on players when you treat them like human beings, not property.

Moneyball Doesn't Tell the Whole Story

In the search for more objective knowledge about the game and the performance of individual players, sabermetrics is defining the future of baseball. Anything that can be measured will be measured. So, besides referring to players as property, management talks about players as numbers that show up on spreadsheets and proprietary databases. Analytics equip us to go granular, and granular determines a player's worth.

Think about it: How many GMs have you heard say: "My spouse is my most important asset. I went back and looked at her numbers. I think her market value has gone up. Might be time for a trade"? Or, "Our expenses are too high; we have to designate a few of the kids for assignment"? Don't answer these questions. You get the point. We never talk about our families in those objectified, dehumanizing terms.

Admit it or not, when you talk about players primarily in numbers it reduces them to faceless facts and creates a culture that is soulless. This is especially true for the "Propeller Heads," as Boch likes to call them: that is, the folks who can give you all the statistical ins and outs about a player they've never met.

> **Boch:** Believe me, I look at the numbers. The metrics are incredibly valuable. And in our club, we have some of the best analytical people in the business. When the spray charts are showing a definite tendency about where hitters are hitting, it helps [bench coach Ron] Wotus position our defense. I want that data.

But sometimes it [analytics] can go too far. I rarely, if ever, feel the pressure from our guys, but I know other managers who hear, "You have to play this guy or that guy today because that's what the numbers show." That doesn't happen here. For example, with pitchers such as Bum [Madison Bumgarner] or [Johnny] Cueto we may not shift our defense as much. That's because we have confidence in their stuff and their ability to get the ball where they want it. We even let them override what the analytics suggest we should do.

Numbers don't tell the whole story. They don't tell you what kind of impact Hunter Pence or Pablo Sandoval is going to have on the psychology of the team. They don't tell you about Gregor Blanco's passionate and enthusiastic support for his teammates in the dugout, even though he isn't an everyday player. They don't tell you that there's something in a player who hasn't played for two months and is aching to make a contribution.

It's easy to manage solely by the numbers because they don't feel anything, they don't talk back to you, and they don't show their disappointment or passion—they just are. I don't have that luxury in the clubhouse or in the dugout. Reading and managing people is the most important and the most difficult part of the game.

So far, sabermetrics can isolate the elements that define a player's individual performance and tell us everything we want to know about that player compared to other players. What it *can't* do, yet, is tell us how a plethora of other variables—leadership, culture, chemistry, environment, fan participation—impact a player's performance.

In a 2014 article entitled "Moneyball 2.0: The New, Team-Oriented Study of Baseball," Hayden Higgins wrote: "If the first wave of sabermetrics was largely about finding a holistic metric for comparing players, the next wave might be about figuring out how best to fit those players together as a response to a given situation. The key question from Moneyball 1.0 was: Who is the *better* player? The key questions from Moneyball 2.0 are: Who is the *right* player? And what is the best way to deploy him?"[37]

As analytics departments grow, we will most likely answer Higgins's questions, but the point still remains, when players feel like they are numbers only and that their fate is in the hands of the statisticians, they grow fatalistic, leaving a crack in the door for learned helplessness—a passive attitude in which players believe they have no control over what's happening to them. With that, morale goes out the door. Larry Baer said as much.

> We've invested a lot in technology and generating data, but we've also made a conscious decision to be low-key about it. We don't want our players to feel like their fate is already established by the statisticians. And if you look at the way Brian approaches it and the way Boch manages his guys, it isn't [preordained]. They use the analytics, but there is no preestablished template [based on data] that we are trying to force them into.

> And I think it's the right approach because Brian's big on accountability. You know: be clear about your role and what's expected of you [as a player] and then commit to being one of the strongest links in the chain. Our brand of baseball is creative. In all three World Series, our victories didn't come from an analytical template. They often came from less familiar faces stepping up at different times, in unexpected ways, to execute because they believed their future was in their hands.

Giants GM Evans said the same thing applies to coaches.

> Every club has access to the same data. But data is data. It's how you digest it, assimilate it, and leverage it that makes the difference. That's the human factor. There are many variables that data doesn't account for, variables that only Boch may know about at any given moment.

> Boch has such an intuitive feel for his players and that intuition has served us well. Boch likes to say that our players 'aren't robots.' Well, our coaches aren't robots either. We're not a club that says, 'Here are the analytics so here's how we want you to manage.' We don't get so enamored with data that there is no room for Boch and his staff to apply their experience, intuition, and the insights they get from having a relationship with the players.

If you are sabermetrically inclined, you might be feeling a little pinched right now, but don't write us off just yet. Our intent is not to level a scathing criticism on the statistical part of the game. We are not suggesting that big data isn't important. "DataBall" has made the game better. It can make players better too. Players who perform better are happier and contribute more to team chemistry. We get it.

But data alone will tempt you to dehumanize people without even knowing it or meaning to. If you want chemistry, expand your data points. Get to know your team at a deeper level. Combine the quantitative with the qualitative.

Tell Them Who They Are

With Jake Peavy on the mound, the Giants got blown out in a 0-10 loss to the Kansas City Royals in Game 6 of the 2014 World Series, tying the Series at three games each. Since 1980, 22 of the 26 teams that forced a Game 6 at home went on to win the World Series. The last 7 teams to force Game 7 by winning Game 6 at home ended up winning the Series. Home field. Home crowd. Home rules. In the most pressure-packed game of the season, beating a pennant-winning team with these three variables in its favor is scary difficult.

You go into a game like this with the best information analytics can provide. You also go in with a deep understanding of what will build confidence in your guys given their psychological and emotional makeup.

On the evening of Game 7, Boch gathered his boys together to put some perspective on what they were about to go do. "I think I need to remind them of who they are," he had said to Kevin earlier that day. That's what great leaders do. They tell us who we are. They remind us of what's in us that is creative, courageous, and noble. And they do it when we need to hear it the most, because when we get blown out, when we face seemingly insurmountable challenges, we forget. We often lose confidence, focus, and that true sense of ourselves.

Behind closed doors, with only players and coaching staff present, Boch did what every great coach does before a monumental game; he set the stage.

> **Boch:** Okay, so the pundits will be saying: the momentum has shifted, we're in *their* house, the odds are with Kansas City. Even the best of us are tempted to believe that. You start to entertain thoughts: *Are we really that gutsy? That resilient? Do we really have what it takes?* I want to remind you of who you are.
>
> *You* are the club who silenced the crowd in Pittsburgh in *their* house.
>
> *You* are the club that beat Washington, twice, in *their* house.
>
> *You* are the club that beat St. Louis in *their* house.
>
> *You* are the best postseason club in the recent history of the game!
>
> Remember who you are. You have defied the odds again and again.
>
> I want you to listen to me very carefully right now. No one, nobody, believes in you guys more than me and this coaching staff. You know why? Because we've seen what you are capable of— we *know* what you can do.

Boch talked to the players individually, reminding each and every one of them that their individual contributions were the basis for believing that they could beat the odds. He wanted each player to know how much he mattered.

> To Hunter: You've shown us what it means to leave it all on the field.
>
> To Pablo: I've watched you rise to the occasion in the postseason so many times.
>
> To Buster: You carried us in the second half; we're not here without you.
>
> To Bum: A complete game shutout in Pittsburgh; without you we're done.
>
> To Huddy: You've brought so much character, depth, experience to this staff.
>
> To Ishi: Your historic hit put us here.

To Petit: You've been the unsung hero in this run.

Tonight, we have an opportunity to make history. We have an opportunity to do what's never been done before in this franchise and what only a few have done in the history of the game. And, we have an opportunity to do this for the guys who haven't been here before: Huddy, Morse, and Panik.

I want you to envision flying home with a trophy and watching a million San Francisco fans pouring into the streets of our city because *you* gave them something special. I want you to think about the stories you're going to tell.

Some of us may never be here again. We may never play together again. This is our moment!

What do you want the world's last impression of the 2014 San Francisco Giants to be?

Guys, what we do tonight will echo throughout history.

I can't tell you what an honor and what a privilege it's been to manage such an incredible team of warriors. Let's get this done!

The speech moved everyone and united them. Win or lose, it reinforced the idea that a special kind of chemistry had brought them to this place. Peavy remembered Boch's message that evening as "historic." He said it touched him at a deeply, a gut level.

When Boch called us together in the clubhouse, we were in a tight, close circle. He connected with almost every player. [Peavy still got emotional talking about it.] When your manager, who has done this already, talks about how damn bad he wants to win tonight, it does something to you. When he asks you to look in the eyes of the guys standing next to you and play for them, it gets real—real fast. He just knew what we needed, when we needed it.

I promise you, we didn't go out and give that effort without his genuine call to arms. It was *that* special. I'm telling you, he didn't throw any pitches and he didn't get any hits, but it [winning the Series] doesn't happen without him. People can't understand who Bruce Bochy is as a leader unless they understand who he is in the biggest of moments.

In speaking to the team that night, Boch was real. No fluff and no rah-rah BS. He spoke to their past achievements. He gave them something tangible they could reflect upon and draw from; he reminded them of who they are; and he tapped into their strengths and highlighted what they could control.

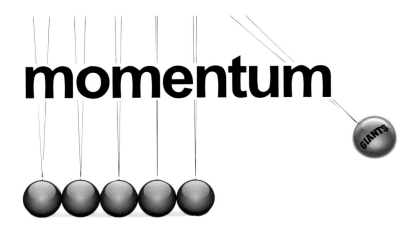

He made it all personal. He had watched these guys all season. He knew them well. He looked each one of them in the eye, calling out their individual contributions as if to inventory all the goodness that brought them to this moment in time. He helped them remember how they personally pushed this team forward. In doing so, he shifted the momentum psychologically.

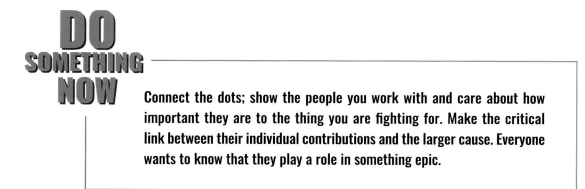

DO SOMETHING NOW

Connect the dots; show the people you work with and care about how important they are to the thing you are fighting for. Make the critical link between their individual contributions and the larger cause. Everyone wants to know that they play a role in something epic.

They're Not Robots or Toys

In February 2015, Boch had just finished working out on the elliptical machine in the training room at the Giants spring training facility in Scottsdale, Arizona. He walked up a flight of stairs and felt "that pain." The one where you can't breathe and your chest is closing in on you. Fortunately, the training staff rushed him across the street, literally, and within 45 minutes, physicians had inserted two stents into his arteries. It was one of those wake-up calls that make a guy think about life.

The further down the road you go age-wise, the more you start thinking about legacy. Boch has talked about what he's learned from the game over the years and the mark he would like to leave. Mind you, he doesn't see himself as a big man having a big impact on the game. It's just not the way he thinks. But when he is pushed on these kinds of philosophical questions, he's very thoughtful about it. There is a theme he always comes back to. He articulates it this way.

> **Boch:** I want our players to know that through all the frustrations, disappointments, victories, and celebrations I care about them—I care about them as people. They aren't toys we can pull out of the box and play with anytime we want. They aren't robots who perform exactly the way we think they should just because we punch in a code based on some statistic. And, they aren't pawns in a game.
>
> They are real people, with real lives, who have real feelings.
>
> We are here to do a job and win ball games for sure. But if we ever lose the spirit of baseball— the people, the relationships, and the camaraderie—to the business of baseball, we will have missed the real reason for being here. And, I believe, missed the essence of what it takes to create great chemistry.
>
> We're not just building ballplayers; we're building character. If I can look back and say that I helped our guys mature as human beings while we won some ball games, I'd be good. I'm pretty sure you can't take the rings with you when you check out [pass on], so what are you left with? It's the relationships that matter. It's the impact you have on people's lives.

Boch has lived this philosophy out loud. Perhaps most vividly in the epic battle with the Royals in the 2014 World Series. A lot of people—pundits and fans alike—hoped that Boch would start Madison "MadBum" Bumgarner in the clinching Game 7 of the Series. Three days earlier MadBum had thrown a 117-pitch, complete game shutout against the Royals.

> **Boch:** We had ridden Bum pretty hard in the postseason and I was concerned about his workload. I didn't want to overwork him and have him get hurt. Hey, I'm competitive. I told the press that I wanted to win another championship as much as anyone. But Bum's not a toy; he's a human being. So, I didn't start him, but I knew I had him available to be a bridge to [Sergio] Romo and [Santiago] Casilla. But I didn't expect him to be a bridge and the closer too.

You can say "people come first," but with the world watching, the pressure of millions of hopeful fans on your back, and a World Championship on the line, you are looking for any way to win. That's when character reveals itself and your words mean something—or not. Boch put Bum's health first.

Bumgarner eventually *did* come into Game 7 as a reliever and pitched five shutout innings. It was one of the most impressive performances in the history of baseball. But it happened only after Bum—who is big and durable and has a pitching motion less prone to injury—convinced Boch that he was good to go.

Most of us would agree that people are to be loved and things are to be used. Yet, if we are honest about it, too many organizations get it backward. They *use* people and *love* things. And then, they spend boatloads of money on engagement studies and consultants trying to understand why the place is so lifeless and uninteresting.

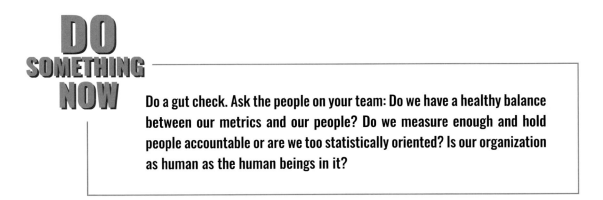

DO SOMETHING NOW

Do a gut check. Ask the people on your team: Do we have a healthy balance between our metrics and our people? Do we measure enough and hold people accountable or are we too statistically oriented? Is our organization as human as the human beings in it?

The Giants are certainly not perfect; they aren't immune to the things-matter-more-than-people thinking so common in our society. But there is a culture in this organization that gets the equation right more often than not. For the most part, they are not tethered by the boredom, cynicism, and selfishness that characterize so many organizations today. This is because the Giants don't see people as a commodity to be managed to grow revenue; they see revenue as a commodity to be managed to grow people and grow the community. And, they have figured out that chemistry is born from treating individuals as human beings, not units of production.

Boch is right: If we lose the heart of baseball to the business of baseball, we lose something timeless and sacred.

11
CONNECT! CONNECT! CONNECT!
The Art of Making Players Feel Special

Boch is a big, intimidating guy. When he talks, he growls. He's often a man of few words. You would be tempted to think that his personality and approach are not conducive to mining the depths of relationships. And because strong relationships are essential to chemistry, it might seem odd that his teams have created so much of it. But then again, if he expects it among players—and you know he does—it's fitting that he'd model it as their leader and coach. And he does!

Interesting and Interested

Boch has two qualities common to all great leaders: He is both *interesting* and *interested*. Baseball has enabled him to meet a lot of people inside and outside the game that have filled his life with color and texture. Sit down over a glass or two of bourbon and the stories start to roll.

You might hear about how the late country music legend Waylon Jennings used to call Boch before every Opening Day and advise, "Do it your way." He might tell you about the incredibly brave soldiers he's met at Walter Reed Army Hospital or the one-on-one meeting he had with President Obama before Obama addressed the team at the White House. The president asked him if they could trade places—he'd fill out the lineup cards and Boch could take care of world affairs. Boch passed.

You might learn about the time he crashed a motorcycle in order to avoid hitting Ryan Klesko (his Padres first basemen at the time) who was stalled in the middle of the road on a blind corner. That gnarly injury (his foot was completely turned backward) compelled his wife, Kim, to exclaim ixnay to storing the motorcycle at home. The Indian bike resided in his clubhouse office for the better part of a year.

He'd probably tell you about stalking a 2,000-pound bull on an open prairie while buffalo hunting with a bow on the Durham Ranch in Wyoming. Or the time he stood 20 feet away from a stampede of wild buffalo on the Rick Paul Ranch in Oregon.

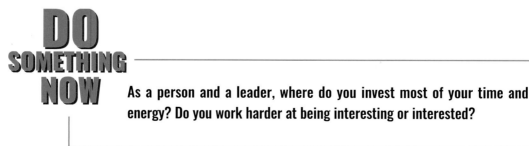

DO SOMETHING NOW

As a person and a leader, where do you invest most of your time and energy? Do you work harder at being interesting or interested?

Boch could describe how life flashed before his and Tony Gwynn's eyes when wind shear caught former Padres owner John Moore's jet and a near-fatal landing had to be aborted. Woven through all these stories you would hear about his two sons, Greg and Brett, his new daughter (in-law) Kelsey, and Kim, whom he loves to affectionately tease.

The best leaders grab our attention and pique our interest. Their stories captivate, fascinate, and inspire us. We seek out people who are interesting, right? There is something about their lives that stimulates our imagination and calls us to be different or to reach higher. In their presence we feel our best selves expand.

We rarely have chemistry with someone we *don't* find interesting.

One of the many reasons players love playing for Boch is that he frequently shakes it up in the clubhouse. He has inserted TV and movie clips and songs into his pregame speeches countless times, but he's always up for trying something new to keep it fresh. He's invited Mohammed Ali, Joe Montana, members of the Navy SEALs, and professional magician Michael Finney into the clubhouse to make things interesting.

While most people see Boch's straight-faced demeanor during press interviews, Pitching Coach Dave Righetti said he can do the "Knute Rockne thing" too. That is, he gives great inspirational speeches. Closer Trevor Hoffman, who spent a lot of time with him when Boch managed the Padres, has said: "People who hear Boch on TV may not think of him as verbal, but his communication skills with players are through the roof. He's also grown as an X and O guy and in knowing how to delegate to his staff. I'm a great admirer."[38]

Boch, Bum, and Bert Bradley, Minor League Pitching Coordinator.

Boch is interesting, but he works a lot harder at being *interested*.

Everybody Wants to Be Known

Giants broadcaster Duane Kuiper told us: "If you asked Boch to give a brief synopsis on everybody in our travel party—and that's about 65 people, and not the same 65 people all the time—he'd give you a pretty good 'scouting report' on each person's job, their personality, and who they are. He's just very unique in that respect."

Great leaders make people feel significant simply by *being interested* in their lives. When something momentous happens in a player's life—getting married, having a baby, a child going through something traumatic, the loss of a parent, or some personal accomplishment outside of baseball, just to name a few—it's common sense to think that they would want the most important people at work to know about it. If a manager doesn't care enough to ask, it sends a very bad message: "We really are not interested in you outside of baseball, beyond what you can do for the team. Check your personal life at the door."

When someone ignores what's important to you, it hurts. It's dehumanizing. Nobody wants to be anonymous. No one wants to be a cog in a wheel or a pawn in a chess game. We were made to know and be known. When people are interested in us it says: "We value you because you are valuable. You matter." It makes you feel like a human being rather than an insignificant weed waiting to be pulled for a better crop.

Indifference. Anonymity. Neglect. Lack of interest. If the volume is turned up on any one of these for very long, it crushes the spirit and poisons the culture of an organization.

Perhaps this happens in a lot of clubs, but the power of what's going on in the Giants organization is that people are treated like family—because they are. How can the most important things in these players' lives not be important to Boch, Brian Sabean, Larry Baer, and the rest of the organization? How can a player feel a part of something bigger if management and coaches aren't interested in him as a person? Where does commitment, loyalty, and dedication originate? It starts with leaders who are interested.

In the world of baseball, there are challenges with getting close to a player because he might only be with you for a year or two. On the other hand, when you travel together for half the year and spend an inordinate amount of time together, there are ample opportunities to get to know people faster. All the same, it's fairly simple: You can't know your team and address their needs if you don't hear what those needs are. That means you have to take time to stop and ask, then listen and learn. And when you listen, you have to *be there*, not somewhere else.

Most people don't listen with the intent to understand; they listen with the intent to reply. They ask, you respond, and then it's as if what you say falls into a black hole while they jump into their "me-too" story. Boch isn't like that. When he talks to his players, they will tell you that he's fully present. When he listens, he does more than just stop talking. They seem to know that he has shut down the internal chatter and turned off the mental noise to genuinely and nonjudgmentally tune in.

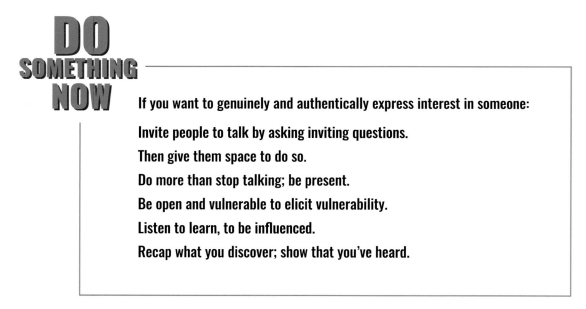

DO SOMETHING NOW

If you want to genuinely and authentically express interest in someone:

Invite people to talk by asking inviting questions.

Then give them space to do so.

Do more than stop talking; be present.

Be open and vulnerable to elicit vulnerability.

Listen to learn, to be influenced.

Recap what you discover; show that you've heard.

Ballplayers may be guarded, but they are not undiscovered mysteries. Like most of us, they constantly send signals that reveal who they are below the surface. Giants shortstop Brandon Crawford captured the power of Boch's attentiveness when he told us: "It's hard to explain, but I feel like he really knows me. Not just how I play, but who I am. I know that sounds quasi-mystical, but that's how I feel sometimes, like he knows me better than I know myself."

Find the Story Behind the Story

Each of us has a story that makes us who we are; the story that influences our behavior and affects our emotions; the story that drives us to excel or holds us back; and the story that provides a clue to our hidden or underlying interests. Great leaders are interested in mining this story behind the story.

> **Boch:** If you can figure that [the story behind the story] out, you can figure *them* out. Granted, you never figure anyone out completely. You know, after 39 years of marriage, Kim is still a mystery to me [grinning]. But if you can unpack some of the story and really get to know your players and coaches, you're in a much better position to show them how important they are to you.
>
> Our pitching coach, Dave ["Rags"] Righetti, does this so well. I'd put Rags up against any pitching coach in the game. He's just that good. Rags has the whole package: He's not only a master of [pitching] mechanics, he can get in our guys' heads and talk to them individually because he knows them so well. He's *interested*. I think if you talked to our catchers and pitchers, they'd tell you he's more than a coach, he's a friend.

When you spend years managing really young guys whose professional lives are under the microscope and who feel a lot of pressure, you get ample opportunities to deal with emotional highs and lows. Simply dealing with the first story you hear often yields a superficial result. But paying attention to the story behind the story can help you discover things about a person that teaches you how to get their attention, earn their respect, and tailor your approach to coaching them. This is why Boch tries to get below the surface and understand his players at a deeper level.

> **Boch:** It's only natural to see the actions of others solely through the lens of how their attitudes and behaviors impact us, especially if it's negative. It's also selfish, because it's all about me and how I'm affected.
>
> Nobody in our club wakes up in the morning and says, "How can I screw it up for the other guys today?" But if a player does something to negatively affect me or another player or the team, it's easy to demonize them without ever asking: "What's driving this? What's behind the behavior?" If we don't get to what's going on underneath it, we might miss an opportunity to make a bad situation better.
>
> Sometimes you've got to get yourself out of the way to get to the root of an issue, and that's hard because you have to swallow your ego. You have to let go of your automatic [defensive] reaction. But in a business where your team's performance is always out there, front and center, for the world to see, you have to ask yourself, "Do I want to protect my ego or to solve a problem so we can win ball games?"

When it comes to drawing people out and getting the best from a player, getting to the story behind the story is paramount. How many times have you watched someone miss an opportunity to lead or screw up an opportunity to instill confidence in another because they couldn't get past the veneer? They didn't care enough or perhaps know enough to dig deeper. How many times have you written someone off because of a stereotype or outward appearance, only to eventually find out that they were *more* than you thought they were? You got hung up on the first story.

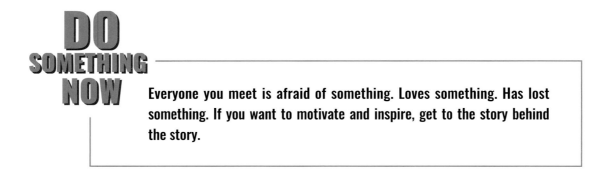

DO SOMETHING NOW

Everyone you meet is afraid of something. Loves something. Has lost something. If you want to motivate and inspire, get to the story behind the story.

The people you lead right now want to know: Do you hear me? Do you understand me? Do you care about me? Do I mean anything to you? The story behind the story isn't going to present itself on the spreadsheets and printouts prepared by the statisticians. To lead effectively you have to *be there* when the story is being told.

Be There—Go to the Conversation

Every leader has blind spots. In baseball, blind spots can be the difference between what the players and coaches need and what the manager thinks they need. Blind spots can be the difference between what the investors, media, or fans want and what the manager thinks they want. How do you keep your finger on the pulse of your coaches and players? Of your front office folks? Your fans? You don't do it sitting in the manager's office or the dugout day in and day out. You go to where the people are.

Anyone who has children knows that kids will talk when *they* want to talk—on *their* time, not yours. If you're driving carpool or shuttling them to a dance recital and they are in a chatty mood, you learn. If you're not there when they are ready to talk, you missed it. Leadership functions the same way. The only way to get your finger on the pulse of your people, the only way to truly understand your organization's culture, temperature, and tone is to be where your colleagues are when they are talking.

Boch has an open-door policy. He spends a little time in the clubhouse, but for the most part, he wants it to be *their* clubhouse. He walks a fine line here because that's the players' inner sanctum and he doesn't want them to feel pestered. He's present and available, but he doesn't hover.

Tune-in to the Spoken and Unspoken

After a career of catching, he has knees that are shot, a cranky left hip, numerous surgeries, and the ailments that come with age. Boch is a walking patchwork. Or, as *Giants* magazine writer Joan Ryan put it so perfectly, "He moves as if his body has been issued to him just this morning and he's still figuring out how to work the thing." If you've ever watched Boch walk out to the mound, you know exactly what she's talking about.

That's the bad news. The silver lining is that he has plenty of reasons to spend time with his trainers and physicians in the Giants training facility.

> **Boch:** Even in a clubhouse it's easy to get sequestered in your office. I enjoy being with Dave Groeschner and our training staff before a game. It's always entertaining listening to the guys ribbing and badgering each other.

Getting out of his office and into the trenches with his players and staff enables Boch to get a feel for the tenor and mood of the club. He tries to do this with the front office as well. To Larry Baer's credit, the Giants have regular meetings with the 35 owners of the team where they get to hear from Brian Sabean, Bobby Evans, and Boch about the club. This is another way Boch stays in tune firsthand with what's going on in the bigger picture.

> **Boch:** Those meetings are invaluable. I get to hear their concerns and get a feel for how they interpret what we are doing on the baseball side of the organization. And, they're interested in our needs and what we're trying to accomplish as well. It's unbelievable how supportive our ownership is. They listen intently to where we think we have gaps in the roster and then lean into problem solving that. In the 2016 off-season when we were replacing some of our marquee players, our owners didn't hesitate to step up and invest in what we thought we needed. I'm convinced that's because of the relationship we have. You can't have that kind of relationship if both sides aren't available.

It's difficult to get the pulse of the organization from text and emails while locked away in your office. If you really want to find out what's going on and what's needed, you have to be in the trenches. Best-selling business management author Tom Peters called it "managing by wandering around" and he was right. You have to be in the conversation when it is happening.

Boch makes it a habit to hang out after a game or occasionally go to the back of the plane where the players sit on road trips to have a beer or join a card game. His way of hanging out could be sharing a meal with a player in the clubhouse kitchen or simply chatting it up with a coach or player behind the batting cage when players are taking batting practice (BP). It might mean walking the outfield when players are taking Fungo balls (ground balls from a Fungo bat) or shagging balls during BP. Tim Flannery said Boch does his best work in the back of the team's plane: "He'll go get himself in a card game with three or four guys. They get to see he's a guy you can trust, that you can talk to, and who understands what it's like to be a player. Then he'll take $600, $700 of their money."[39]

Tuning into your team is about being *out* where the conversations are taking place; it's catching people when they are relaxed and raw, listening, with your radar on and your antenna up, to what's being said and what's *not* being said. It's picking up on a player's tone of voice and reading his body language to get a sense of his mood. It's why Starbucks's founder Howard Schultz visits a minimum of 20 stores every week. It's the reason Southwest Airlines founder and chairman emeritus Herb Kelleher used to go out to work side by side with the baggage handlers on the Wednesday before Thanksgiving, the industry's busiest day of the year.

DO SOMETHING NOW

So, you've decided to "be there" and connect with your team. Now what? Be relaxed and self-effacing when you have an opportunity. It can open others up. Find out what's going on with your players off the field. Ask for ideas and recognize contributions. Be the bearer of good news. Share what's working and why you are optimistic about the future. Ask about hobbies, interests, and passions outside of work.

Connection is the way you get below the surface and get a gut feel for what's really going on in the head and heart of your organization. This is how you pick up on the psyche of the club. You gain a nugget of insight here or a moment of discernment there. It's how you build a culture where people feel comfortable voicing their concerns. It's the way you make players feel special.

Chemistry is built on connection.

12
EXPECT THE BEST
Believe in Your Players

Every team wants to be in the playoffs. Every team wants to make a run at the World Series. Many teams have the raw talent to do it, but only two teams get there each season. The challenge comes when what a team wants is not what it expects. If there is a disconnect between the two, the team is far more likely to get what it expects than what it wants.

To a large degree, how far a club goes in baseball depends on the weightiness and magnitude of its dreams, the height of its expectations. No team can rise higher than its aspirations. Boch is keenly aware of this. He's walked in the shoes of his players. He's been there. He knows that a manager plays a powerful role in setting the tone of the clubhouse. He knows that what he believes about *them* makes a huge difference. And, what they believe about him—his competitiveness and passion for winning—makes a difference as well. Players take their cue from him. They watch his mannerisms, they listen to what he says, and they pick up on his expectations. In a very significant way Boch influences what players believe about themselves.

> Regardless of the pressure they're under, when players look into the eyes of a coach, what they should see is somebody who believes in them.

How Expectations Fuel Outcomes

Expectations create the context in which a team plays out its season. A manager who expects a lot from individual team members creates an atmosphere where team members expect a lot from themselves. Players who expect a lot from themselves also expect a lot from other players. This cycle elevates the entire team. Here's why.

Expectations affirm. The questions that haunt all of us at some point in our lives are these: Do I have what it takes? Can I support the people I love? Do I have the guts to fight for the things I believe in? Can I make a mark in the world?

Professional athletes are no exception. In fact, the high-stakes drama and pressure-filled world of the pro only exacerbate the doubts, adding more weight and salience to a leader's influence.

Cy Young winner Jake Peavy started his major league pitching career with Boch and the Padres. Peavy is thrilled to have joined the Giants and come full circle in his career with Boch. "When I look back, the things he has said to me molded me and gave me a chance to be who I am. I really think he had a huge role in helping me become a man as well as a player."

The day Peavy made his MLB debut with the Padres against the Yankees, Boch called him into his office. "I'm a kid who's never been above Double-A and now I'm about to start against the Yankees in front of 50,000 people at Qualcomm Stadium [in San Diego] on a Saturday," Peavy told us. What Boch said was: "You've got nothing to lose, so let it hang out there. We've got your back." Then he said something Peavy will never forget: "Take it all in, man. I want you to step off that mound and take it all in. This is the big leagues and you deserve this moment." What Peavy heard was, essentially, "We believe in you. Don't let the expectations of the moment get in the way of this. It only happens once, so savor it."

"That gave me such a freedom to go out and pitch my game," Peavy continued. "I'm a kid who's never thrown a pitch in the big leagues and I'm scared to death. I don't know anyone who doesn't have some fear—particularly against the Yankees, who have so many recognizable names and superstars. I don't know what anybody else could've said to me on that day, in that moment, that would've given me a bigger shot of courage."

> The glory of friendship is not in the outstretched hand, nor the kindly smile, nor the joy of companionship, it is the spiritual inspiration that comes to one when he discovers that someone else believes in him and is willing to trust him.
>
> — Waldo Emerson

Roll the tape forward. Sabean picked up Peavy from Boston on July 14, 2014. To say that Peavy was struggling with the Red Sox is an understatement. He was 1-9, with a 4.72 ERA. By September, Peavy was 6-1 with the Giants, with a 1.35 ERA. As *Boston Globe* sportswriter Nick Cafardo put it, "The difference in Jake Peavy's performance from Boston to San Francisco is as great as the 3,000-mile distance between the cities."[40]

What changed? According to Peavy, he got back "with people . . . who believe in me in a special way. [Boch] believes in me like my high school coach believed in me . . . When you are shown that faith in you, you want to exhaust every option. So that really can fuel a fire."[41]

Peavy also credited Righetti's eagle eye for making some slight adjustments that made a huge difference in his delivery. Plus, he said, the chemistry he has with Buster Posey took his game to another level.

When someone of influence expects the best of you and invests in you, it inspires you to work harder. It gives you a spirit of liberty to draw upon your best self. It also has the possibility to close the gap between your performance and your potential—and perhaps even to expand your potential.

Expectations elevate. Leaders elevate us with their expectations. They push us to see beyond what we see. Their expectations whisper: "I see something in you that you don't yet see in yourself. But trust me, I wouldn't put you in this position or ask this of you if I didn't think you could do it." These expectations broaden our expectations of ourselves.

Reflecting on the 2012 run-up to the World Series Sergio Romo had this to say: "A lot of our leadership came from our manager, Bruce Bochy. He always knew what he had in us. He always put us in positions where we could shine. Bochy wasn't afraid to give us an opportunity to push ourselves . . . I can just hear his voice: 'I'm not gonna lie to you . . . I think you guys are better than this . . . I believe in you guys.'"[42]

Words and expectations are powerful. They can influence outcomes and achievements. If someone you deem credible tells you that you have Championship Blood, you start to believe it. If the coaches all around you call you the best late-inning, comeback team in the game, you start to believe it. If the people all around you build a narrative about how calm you are under pressure, guess what? You see yourself and your teammates as calm under pressure.

DO SOMETHING NOW

If you are a parent, what do your expectations communicate to your children? Are you intentional? As a child, what did your parents' expectations say to you? How has that shaped who you are?

Take it from Tim Lincecum. "I remember in my first no-hitter in San Diego . . . coming down into the tunnel and he [Bochy] said, 'You're the best I got, you gotta keep this going,' to encourage me and keep me going."[43] Tim and his teammates know there are no heights to which the human spirit cannot rise when someone believes in you. It makes you stronger. It lifts you up. Tim Hudson told ESPN's Steve Wulf that Boch and the iconic manager of the Atlanta Braves, Bobby Cox, have a lot in common. Boch has always held Cox up as one of his mentors in the game. Hudson, who has played for both managers, said: "They're players' managers, but more than that, they'll fight for you. Their goal is your goal; their passion is your passion."

Boch's belief in his players allows them to relax and stay focused on what's possible, making the possible more probable. If they are down by several runs in a game or several games in a series, his belief in them eliminates doubt and reduces the frustration that causes a player to press too hard. When you relax you become more patient, you slow things down, and you think more clearly. When you expect to ultimately prevail, perseverance intensifies. Instead of giving in, you double down.

Expectations strengthen resolve. Over the years, the Giants have beaten teams far more talented than they are—many times. Why?

Because there is a difference between what we *can* do and what we *will* do. The talent of a team determines what it *can* do. Expectations determine what it *will* do. When we talk about what a team can do, we are talking about its potential. "We can" is a positive statement, but in terms of drive and determination, "We will" has the firepower because it assumes the potential *and* expresses the conviction.

Over the course of three World Championships, people have said things like "The Giants pulled it out in the end by a sheer force of will." "On this day, they wanted it more." And "They willed it to happen." All these statements point to the raw determination and incredible resolve witnessed in all three of the Giants runs to the World Series.

> "We can" is a positive statement, but "We will" has the firepower because it assumes the potential and expresses the conviction.

Expectations guarantee nothing, but they do inspire the passion and perseverance to gut it out when the going gets tough. It's clear that Boch's expectations of his players have strengthened the collective will of the Giants, expanding their capacity to access the full weight of their collective talent.

Expectations overwhelm doubt. Players rarely bring their best selves to the game when they are faced with doubt. Who does? Doubt undermines confidence. It takes you down a dark road. Boch is a realist, but he has an extraordinary ability to give people the "benefit of belief." It's about seeing the potential in players, who they can be, and then communicating with no BS that you have confidence in them.

On June 9, 2015, a 27-year-old veteran named Chris Heston came out of nowhere to pitch what shortstop Brandon "Craw" Crawford called a "nasty" game for the Giants against the New York Mets. Crawford said that when Heston is "on" he's one of the best pitchers he's ever played behind.

Heston came into the starting rotation to fill in for a disabled Matt Cain. Getting to this game had not been without its struggles. A few weeks earlier, Boch had talked to the young pitcher.

> **Boch:** He was a really nice surprise, but once in a while his confidence would wane after a tough game. When things would go awry he'd have a tough time getting back on track. We just encouraged him to go back and think about what got him here—the fire in the belly—and pitch from *that* place. Essentially, I wanted him to feel like he should be here.

Crawford's word choice, "nasty," was a good description of the game. At the end of nine, Heston became the first Giants rookie to throw a no-hitter since 1912. It put the Giants in rarified air once again, making them the first team to throw a no-hitter in four straight seasons (Cain 2012, Lincecum 2013 and 2014, Heston 2015) since the 1962–1965 Dodgers.

> **Boch:** To pitch a no-hitter is unbelievably hard. And then, to do it in your first full year [in the majors], that's special. It commands respect. You've got a lot of pitchers out there with great stuff who have been in the game a long time but weren't fortunate enough to pitch a no-hitter. I'm sure they'd say the same thing—unbelievable! It really was a special night for Heston, especially with his family and coach at the game.

Crawford is another player who rose to excellence because Boch's faith in him never wavered. When Crawford became the Giants starting shortstop in 2012, he had a very rocky first couple of months. In the opening series of the season, against the Arizona Diamondbacks, Crawford made 3 errors, and the Diamondbacks swept the Giants. It got worse. Crawford's batting average fell to .219, and he made 12 errors in the next 60 games. This is a scenario ready-made for a club to trade the player for a more seasoned, veteran shortstop.

> **Boch:** Craw had one of those series against Arizona that I'm sure he'd like to forget. It was the kind of series that could cause a young player to lose confidence, and you don't want that. He handled it very well, but I still felt like I had to pull him aside and say, "Hey, you're it, man. Put your big boy pants on because you're not going anywhere."

Boch and Sabes stood by Crawford and his defense blossomed. In the next 102 games, Crawford would make only six errors. He got better at the plate as well. In the final two months of the season, he hit .288 and .281, respectively.

In 2012, Crawford ranked third among National League shortstops in defensive runs saved and was named the Wilson Defensive Player of the Year. He made huge contributions in the Giants sweep of the Tigers in the 2014 World Series. And in 2015, Crawford won his first Rawlings Gold Glove Award and Silver Slugger Award, the first Giant since Barry Bonds to win both awards in the same year.

Brandon Crawford's acrobatics as shortstop make him a favorite of the Giants fans.

Boch: You know, Willie Mays was spectacular in the minors, but when he made his debut in the majors, he went 0 for 12. Then he crushed one, and his rise from there was meteoric. Sabes's decision to bring Crawford up was prophetic. His growth on both sides of the plate has been phenomenal. And I think both players and fans agree he is fun to watch.

One of the Giants biggest assets is that they just don't doubt each other. Each player truly believes that the next guy has his back and will do everything he can to make the *team* stronger. Does this mean that everyone executes perfectly all the time? Of course not. But because of *what they believe* about each other, they will come through more often. Like every head coach, Boch has his moments when his frustration comes out, but he clearly believes in his players. Likewise, the confidence a player has in Boch, and in the team as a whole, strengthens that player's individual performance, amplifying his ability to contribute to the team.

"Boch sets the tone," Peavy said. "It's hard to describe, but he believes in all of his players, and not just in a general kind of way; he really conveys that he is behind us. And his decisions back that up. That confidence spills into the clubhouse from one player to another. When you're in a game battling it out with a hitter, to know there's a dugout full of guys who believe in you and support you, man, I can't tell you what that does for a pitcher."

Expectations are infectious. The belief Boch has in his players percolates through the entire organization. For example, Joe Panik, who was called up in 2014, has talked about the effect of the Giants expecting the best of rookies. "Once you get here, from the top down, the front office, Boch, they have faith in you. You can sense that. You are not just a young guy; you are not just a rookie. Last year, it was basically, 'Congratulations.' As a ballplayer, it makes you feel good, and it kind of gives you confidence."[44] And it shows up in the way players relate to one another.

When you are around teammates who expect a lot of themselves, it's infectious. Think of the many conversations that take place in the clubhouse, in the dugout, and on the plane. By their very example, players who reach high coax their teammates to reach higher. When they expect to win, it stirs something in others that raises their expectation to win. When your teammates refuse to give in or let down, it strengthens your resolve. When you watch the way a Buster Posey, Hunter Pence, or Madison Bumgarner goes about his business, you see how accountable each one of them is for the success of the team. It strengthens your sense of ownership.

In the end, an ethic emerges: The team knows that someone is going to come through in the clutch. It could be a different guy or two every day, but someone is going to fulfill this expectation. The mirror one teammate holds up to another is one of the most powerful images that player will ever see. For the Giants, these images aren't Pollyanna, pie-in-the-sky wishes; they are grounded in a history of seeing players dig deep in a club where the expectations are always high.

Even the fans create expectations. Notorious for pulling it out and winning in late-inning games, the Giants play a brand of baseball known as "torture," a term coined by Giants broadcaster Duane Kuiper for being the kind of entertainment you get when you go to a thriller movie. Fans pour into AT&T Park with the expectation "it ain't over 'til it's over." Too many times to ignore, they've seen the Giants do something spectacular when their backs are against the wall in the 9th or 10th inning. Being on a team whose fans are so fanatical and so supportive, who never stop believing, creates a complementary expectation among the players: "If they believe we can do it, if they refuse to go home when we are down by five runs, we are going to prove them right." And the Giants often do.

Expectations clarify. One of the greatest barriers to chemistry—and therefore team performance—is for players not to be clear about goals and roles. Great players want to know where a manager is going, how he plans to get there, and how they fit into the equation. They want precise answers to such questions as "What are the standards? What does commitment look like in *this* organization? Where does my role end and another player's role begin? What do you expect of *me*?" A leader who is laser clear about these things builds trust and instills confidence in a club.

> **Boch:** My goal is to leave no room for misunderstanding about where a player stands, where I am on an issue, or what I expect from our guys. Now, do I always succeed? No. There are times when roles are more difficult to define. For example, when you go to "bullpen by committee" [when a club does not assign relief pitchers to specific roles] as we did at times in 2012 and 2016.

That's when you need an unselfish group to buy into what you are doing. But as a player, that's [clear expectations] what I wanted. Sometimes I didn't like what I heard, but I knew where I stood and I could deal with that. Chemistry is stunted when players are left in the dark, forced to guess what the manager's expectations are.

Boch is known as one of the best bullpen managers in the game, and if you're talking about the postseason, he might be the best. It's a game of strategy where you don't want your pitchers—or anyone else for that matter—to run out of gas prematurely. The moves Boch makes today might be determined by what he is thinking about for two or three games from today. If his guys don't have the big picture and don't understand the goal, it compromises the objective.

"Bochy is a great communicator," Javier López told us. "He's always thinking out in front of everyone else, but he doesn't just assume that we know what he's thinking. He cares enough to give us a heads-up; he takes the time to make sure everyone is on the same page and they're good with it. That's one of the reasons we have so much confidence in him."

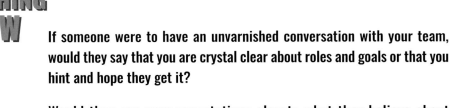

If someone were to have an unvarnished conversation with your team, would they say that you are crystal clear about roles and goals or that you hint and hope they get it?

Would they say your expectations elevate what they believe about themselves? Strengthen their resolve and determination? Make the team stronger and more cohesive?

What Goes Around Comes Around

Boch's players show up playing full throttle because *they* believe they count—their effort matters. And why wouldn't they? When your manager places tough, high expectations on you, you take it seriously and you begin to act in a manner that is worthy of those expectations.

In turn, Boch's faith in his players engenders their faith in him. They've watched him believe in guys that others couldn't get behind and then watched those players soar. They've seen him make unconventional moves that work. And, they've seen World Series expectations turn into three championship titles.

In an interview with Jake Peavy during the 2014 NLCS, the pitcher summed up how the players feel about Boch.

> Skipper gets the guys to be in the moment, to realize what's at stake. And the guys in that room know that this man has their back and is in it with them. He's in it with them.

> He's going to live and die and take a loss as hard as we take it. When you know that, the guys want to die for the guy they're playing for. When you can get that out of your guys, you're doin' something, especially when you talk about grown men.[45]

When Expectations Run Dry

The majority of this book focuses on the club's remarkable five-year run through three World Championships. But as we neared the end of this writing, the Giants were struggling through a season that can only be described as an epic breakdown. But think about it like this: If Apple were to tank over the next two or three years, it would in no way invalidate the principles behind the incredible success the company has had in the phenomenal years. We feel the same way about the Giants. And in many respects, chemistry is as much about losing gracefully and courageously as it is about winning humbly. Of course, if you are a Giants fan, the 2017 season was painful. The challenge for Boch then was to establish a different set of expectations in the clubhouse and keep those expectations high.

Boch: The truth is, we've had to grind pretty hard through our successful years and it may have taken a toll on some. Our core guys have given so much over the years, but it's a harsh reality in our game, players do wear down. As this happens, the smart ones adjust: they might adjust the pitches they throw, the nature of their workouts or nutrition, their approach to hitting, and many other things. But they adjust. Sometimes it works and sometimes time just takes its toll. Our job is to help them make these adjustments. The hard part is to stay up [inspired and motivated] when things go from bad to worse. Because when you are down [deflated] your confidence wanes, your creativity goes out the door, and you start to back off. That just exacerbates the damage.

> To throw in the towel now puts a chink in our armor for next year, because every time you compromise unnecessarily it weakens your resolve and the warrior spirit of the club.

When you are 35 games back in early August, it's statistically impossible to come back. But that doesn't mean you can't find the resolve to finish strong, to demonstrate the character to fight to the very end. Some guys would simply write off this season and ride it out, hoping for better next year. That's not where my head is, and it's certainly not where I want our players to be.

> I've told our guys to stay focused, to stay in it or have the balls to walk into my of my office and tell me they've quit.

To throw in the towel now puts a chink in our armor for next year, because every time you compromise unnecessarily it weakens your resolve and the warrior spirit of the club.

I've told our guys to stay focused, to stay in it or have the balls to walk into my office and tell me they've quit. I don't want them to start spring training next year looking back at a cowardly finish to this year. Because at some point you have to look in the mirror and admit, "We could have finished with more grit and more character than we did." There's no dignity in that.

This isn't about getting back into it [the season]. This is about the character and chemistry of the club. It's about who we are as individuals and as a team. What worked in 2012 and 2014 is that in 2011 and 2013 we didn't give in, we finished like warriors, and we lived to fight another day, with the confidence of *knowing* that we never checked out. We finished strong.

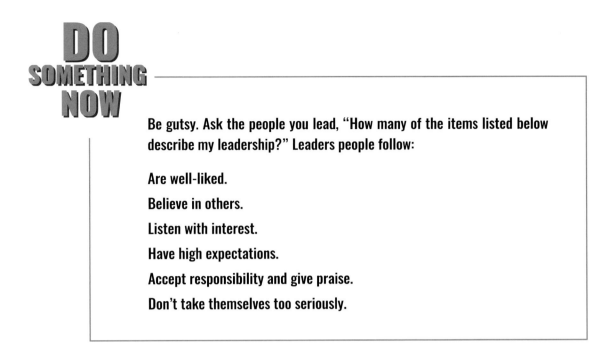

DO SOMETHING NOW

Be gutsy. Ask the people you lead, "How many of the items listed below describe my leadership?" Leaders people follow:

Are well-liked.

Believe in others.

Listen with interest.

Have high expectations.

Accept responsibility and give praise.

Don't take themselves too seriously.

There is no denial in Boch's words. But even in the midst of a losing season there is an expectation that essentially says: "Let's not be losers. Let's hold our heads up and show ourselves and our fans that there is an inner strength to this club. At some point in the future, when the stakes are high, we will look back upon this time and draw from the intestinal fortitude we demonstrated here." Of course, that assumes you've created something to draw from.

There is one last thing to be said about the good times, about a culture where people believe in each other and win: it's magnetic. A winning legacy, if it's protected, promoted, and perpetuated, is attractive. You come to the Giants expecting to win—because they have. You come expecting to overcome a deficit in late inning games because they do. You come expecting to demonstrate unflappable calmness in the postseason because that's what you see in the guy next to you. You come expecting to make a big contribution when the team needs it because, well, that's what your teammates expect of you. And, you come ready to change and adapt because you have a leader you trust.

4th Inning

GIANT SPIRIT

Service over Self-Interest

13

THE ULTIMATE CHAMPION
A Team-First Mentality

If we are honest with ourselves, we are all narcissistic and self-centered to some degree. Reading this may not be comfortable for you, but it's true. If you doubt this, just think children. They came into the world as little narcissists. Between them, Boch and Kim and Kevin and Jackie have five kids. No one remembers these little people coming home from the hospital, learning to talk, and asking, "Mom, anything I can do for you around here? Hey, Dad, need some money?" It never happens. It's all about *them.* So, we're born with a selfish "it's all about me" nature and we work the rest of our lives to transcend it or grow out of it.

If you're still not convinced, just ask yourself, "How much of what I read in the press or hear people talking about in society is focused on rights versus responsibilities?" Whether it's demanding political fairness and equality, safe work environments, justice in our communities, or compensation that reflects our value, we're quite good at standing up for our rights. We're less comfortable talking about our indebtedness, our ownership in and responsibility to our country, our organizations, and our colleagues.

In a baseball club the tension is about player's contracts versus management's need to get the most out of payroll. It's about individual playing time and a player's individual numbers versus making personal sacrifices that can help the team win. It's about the media's need for accessibility versus the players' need to get away and focus. Everyone has a right to something.

Getting Me Out of the Way

Added to this, a common problem in professional sports is that great athletes have been pandered to for a good part of their lives. The bigger the star, the more they've been coddled. And the more they've been coddled, the more tempting it is to become self-indulgent. Why wouldn't they be? Many of the key influencers in these players' lives *do* indulge their selfishness. The term "franchise player" means what? We will build a team around one or two marquee players instead of building it around a set of principles that inspire individuals to play best *together*. Giants starting pitcher and Cy Young winner Jake Peavy explained the mentality this way: "Guys come in and they are worried about their [pitching] mechanics or what they are doing in the [batter's] box. Then you get caught up in yourself. This game can do that to you. You can turn into, without even knowing it, a selfish player."[46]

It doesn't matter if we are leaders or players, at some point we need to wake up and candidly ask ourselves, "So, how's this me-first attitude working so far?" and then decide to get ourselves out of the way. Whether we know it or not, people around us know our motives. They quickly pick up on me-first. But this isn't where the power and influence in leadership lies. Influence expands when I believe that you understand me, care about me, grow my capabilities, and are genuinely interested in helping me reach potential I didn't even know I had.

This doesn't require a title or position of power; you don't have to be a veteran or a marquee ballplayer. You just have to have a desire to invest in others, get behind them, and help them prosper.

Boch deeply believes that one of the greatest obstacles he faces isn't always the talent in the opposing dugout, the constant scrutiny from a ratings-conscious media, or the inflated expectations of fans. It's the enemy within the team: selfishness. Like a cancer, selfishness has a way of destroying everything in its path, including chemistry.

> **Boch:** In our game, just like in business and in life, there is almost always a point or place in the game when you need a player to sacrifice himself for the team. It could be a sacrifice bunt or a suicide squeeze. It could be a hit and run or giving yourself up by advancing a runner from second to third base. It could be asking one of the guys to pitch during a time of fatigue or a catcher to play when he is beat up and really needs a day off. But you do it because that's what's best for the team.
>
> If a player is reluctant to make the sacrifice because he has a selfish agenda, it limits our options and it creates bad blood because you're doing whatever it takes to win a game. If the guys aren't pulling together you can sense it immediately in the dugout. On the other hand, it's amazing what we can do when our players willingly make sacrifices and play as a team.

Boch spends a lot of time taking the temperature of "the boys" and thinking about how they are doing mentally, physically, spiritually, and emotionally. He looks for teachable moments—everyday opportunities, big and small, to remind players that it's *Team Us,* not you. Once you become a Giant there is no I, me, or my; your language has to be we, us, and together. This was reinforced for Boch when he joined us for an accelerated public speaking course we did for the U.S. Marine Corps, a band of brothers and sisters who learn from day one at boot camp that to serve the Corps and the country they first have to serve each other.

Boch reinforces this idea by recognizing players' unselfishness in clubhouse meetings, in media interviews, and especially in one-on-one conversations with them. He truly is in awe of the unselfish way his guys play the game, and that just naturally spills out of him when people bump into him.

> **Boch:** I've said this in any number of interviews but it bears repeating because it is so uncommon in professional athletics. There is a critical characteristic that brought our club together in all three World Series wins—and that is the unselfish way our players played the game.
>
> They were willing to do whatever it takes for the good of the team. In 2010, the Dirty Dozen didn't care about having it *their way*; they simply wanted to find *a way* to get it done. No role was too small for our guys in 2012; it was all about accomplishing the mission, regardless of where I put them. Again, in 2014, they didn't care how we got there; they cared about doing what no one thought we could do [win a third World Series in five years]. They wanted to be part of something bigger and *that* was more important than their individual numbers.
>
> Their desire to make a contribution—no matter how many things we changed—was bigger than their insecurities and discomfort.

Step Out of the Comfort Zone

One of the preeminent examples of what Boch is talking about is Tim Lincecum. Dubbed "The Freak" for his contortionist pitching motion and the unbelievable leverage he generates with his mere 5-foot 11-inch, 170-pound frame, Lincecum has been one of the most feared starters in the game. He has multiple no-hitters thrown, multiple Cy Young Awards, multiple World Series championship titles, and multiple All Star selections to his credit. The only other player in the history of baseball to have done the same is the great Sandy Koufax.

Credited with creating one of the purest merit-based cultures in the major leagues, Boch finds a way to navigate around egos, star power, agents, and long-term contracts to put the players on the field who give the team the best chance of winning each game. In 2012, Lincecum tanked (10-15) during the regular season. How do you tell a two-time Cy Young Award winner that you are taking him out of the starting rotation and you'd like him to assume a role in the bullpen during the playoffs? That's what Boch did. Did Lincecum lash out at Boch in public? Pout? Throw a tantrum? Not even close. Instead of looking at it as a demotion, Timmy looked at it as another role where he could make a different kind of contribution. Righetti said Lincecum took it as a challenge—an opportunity to prove to himself and his team that he could do something he hadn't done before.

Lincecum flourished. Over five postseason relief appearances and 13 innings he struck out 17 and allowed only three hits and one earned run. He turned out to be a special weapon in Game 3 of the 2012 World Series where he struck out three over 2.1 hitless innings. Boch put the magnitude of this transition in perspective.

Boch: Do you know what can happen to a starting pitcher, with a Cy Young résumé, when you put him in the bullpen? It's a whole different mentality, a different way of getting psychologically prepared to pitch. It requires a different temperament.

Set aside the potential blow to the ego for a moment and just think about how this could rock his world. But it didn't. I said, "Timmy, we're going to put you in the pen." He didn't balk. He didn't waiver on it. He didn't complain. He just said, "Sure, whatever I can do to help the team win."

In all my years of managing, that conversation in our weight room will be one of my most memorable because, for me, it defined the meaning of "teammate." Little did I know then that it would set a precedent for Jake Peavy, another Cy Young winner with two World Series rings, in 2016. Timmy showed me that the ripple effect of unselfishness is long and deep.

Walk Tall in the Dark

Clearly, unselfishness is contagious. Lincecum drew inspiration from another superstar and Cy Young winner, Barry Zito. After a terrible regular season in 2010, Zito was left off the postseason roster altogether. After Boch informed him of the decision, Zito told reporters: "My heart and soul is in this clubhouse. I have no other options in myself than to pull for every one of these guys." A consummate professional, Zito continued to work out during 2011. He pitched to the bullpen and the taxi squad (substitute players who shuttle between the Giants major league team and its Triple-A affiliate when someone on the regular roster gets injured) just to keep himself game-ready.

Players and coaches alike were impressed with how Zito walked tall and stayed "up" through it all. Boch said Zito is a real class act.

Barry Zito and Tim Lincecum both exhibit unselfishness in difficult times.

Boch: "ZI" took a lot of flak in the press for not performing up to his contract [$126 million over seven years]. He must have been feeling it psychologically and emotionally, but you would never know. He never showed it. He was a real stand-up guy. He made himself available to other players. He made himself available to the media and always manned up to the scrutiny. Not once did I ever see him dodge the questions. He's just a competitor and a very unselfish player.

Then, in 2012, Zito came back to pitch 7.2 shutout innings in a clutch Game 5 of the NLCS against St. Louis. In front of 47,000 semi-stunned Cardinal fans, the Giants won with a final score of 5-0. Down three games to one in the National League series, it was a masterpiece performance that breathed life into the Giants postseason. Zito's confidence rubbed off on everyone on the team. Boch considered it the biggest game of the playoffs. "The momentum had switched," Hunter Pence said. "The Cardinals were rolling, the fans—you could feel it. There was a lot of confidence that we were up against and Zito silenced it all. It gives me chills just thinking about it."

Game 5 was only the start of Zito's redemption. He got the nod to start in Game 1 of the World Series against the Tigers. He called the opportunity "magical." Zito outdueled Justin Verlander, the 2011 American League Cy Young winner and one of the best starters in the game. He allowed only one run over 5.6 innings and even hit an RBI single off Verlander's 97-mph fastball. His outing started the momentum that would ultimately sweep the Tigers 4-0.

Zito left the sixth inning to a raucous standing ovation and tipped his hat to euphoric fans while Boch handed the ball to none other than "reliever" Tim Lincecum. For Boch, for both pitchers and their teammates, and certainly for those who love orange and black, it was one of the top feel-good stories of the season.

When the Giants were the World Champions for the second time, the players started chanting Barry! Barry! Barry! amid the champagne spray during the clubhouse celebration. Asked how he felt, Zito said, "To have the support of major league players, World Series Champion-caliber players, that meant so much to me."

The way Zito carried himself through his extremely difficult times spoke to Lincecum. In going in to the bullpen, Timmy wasn't thinking about his ego, and he wasn't thinking about whether or not he would have a starting role in 2013; he just wanted to contribute and help his team win another World Series. Of Zito, Lincecum said, "The way he handled it resonated for me."

Zito had his own thoughts about Lincecum. "Timmy and I have always been close, ever since

Barry Zito gets a standing ovation, Game 1 against Detroit Tigers, 2012 World Series.

the day he came up. But I think we got a little closer this year [2012] because I just tried to be there for him and help him out if he needed it this year."[47]

Contribute from Anywhere

Unselfishness coupled with accountability can be a killer combination. Who doesn't want another chance to make a contribution—particularly when you feel that you've let your teammates down during the regular season? Lincecum didn't care if it was one, two, or four innings; his goal was to do something for the team.

For the team and for Lincecum fans, it was downright strange to see Timmy in the bullpen. But in the fourth inning of the NLDS elimination Game 4, Lincecum threw 4 ⅓ innings of one-hit, one-run ball. Not only was it inspiring; not only did the 8-3 win over the Reds force a decisive Game 5; Lincecum got the win as well and the Giants got some swagger.

Boch sang his praises, saying that Lincecum was wholeheartedly all in. Starter Ryan Vogelsong agreed. "Timmy showed everybody what he's truly about. He could've been upset, could've protested to his agent, but he didn't. Not one time did you ever see him complain, even under the lights of the biggest stage."

"To have him in the bullpen, it's just ridiculous," Zito said. "It's such a tool in our pocket that we can bust out at any time, a guy that has made history with his two Cy Youngs. It was just really special personally, to watch Timmy carve them and just do what he does."[48]

How do you put a price tag on *that*? How do measure the value of *that*? Choosing service over self-interest is in the Giants cultural DNA. It's frequently talked about. It's celebrated often. And, it works. Besides Lincecum and Zito, there are countless other examples.

Unselfishness Makes You Agile

In 2012, when Marco Scutaro showed up at the trade deadline with his unstoppable bat, the Giants second baseman, Ryan Theriot, was relegated to the bench.

> **Boch:** I never underestimate how hard it is for a player to take a backseat like that—especially when they are used to being a starter. When you love to play baseball, you want to be in the game, not on the bench. Taking a backseat can be frustrating, I know [referring to his own playing time as a backup catcher for the Padres]. Especially when you've played on the biggest stage in the game. Ryan played for the Cardinals when they clinched the World Series the year before.
>
> But he never showed any resentment. He kept his head up and kept himself ready. He was a positive force in the dugout. He made the guys laugh, kept them loose, and never stopped cheering for his teammates. Every game he was "in it." I have a lot of respect for that.

In Game 4 of the 2012 World Series, Boch named Theriot the designated hitter. In the top of the 10th inning, Theriot led off for the Giants with a single to center field off Phil Coke, who had been virtually unhittable the whole season. Theriot moved to second on a sacrifice bunt by shortstop Crawford. Ironically, it was Marco Scutaro, the man who replaced Theriot, who made the two-out clutch hit enabling Theriot to score the decisive run. The Giants came from behind to win the game 4-3 and complete their sweep of the Tigers.

Boch: That's us. That's just the way we do things. You never know where the next contribution is going to come from. I couldn't have been happier for Theriot and for Scutaro. It was the perfect exclamation point on the end of the Series.

It's amazing what a group of guys who play like a team can accomplish. We've shaken up the roster a lot. We've had to. People typically resist change. But not once did anyone complain. Not once did a player walk into my office and bend my ear. Not once did anyone question what we were doing.

Our guys were willing to hang their egos outside the door—for the love of each other and for the game. Do you know what kind of flexibility that gives us as a coaching staff? Do you know what kind of versatility that offers us? On top of that, we waste no time on drama, distractions, and second-guessing. We can focus on getting the job done.

When you ask players to choose service over self-interest you also have to be ready to manage the creative tension that comes with this approach. On one hand, you look for players who are team-oriented. On the other hand, you want players with a warrior spirit and competitive drive—players who want in. Striking a balance between unselfishness and competitiveness requires some finesse.

Boch: If I go out and pull a Jake Peavy or a Madison Bumgarner off the mound, that's not easy for them. I know they get upset. They are warriors. They're competitive. And I want them to be. That's why they've had such great careers. I don't want them singing "Zip-a-Dee-Doo-Dah" when I take them out of a game. But even though they're ticked off, they also know that we are trying to do what gives us the best chance to win, and I think they trust that, in the moment, we [coaches] might have a more objective perspective.

DO SOMETHING NOW

If you want to engender a team-first mentality in your players, call it out and recognize it when you see it. People quickly pick up on what a leader rewards and punishes.

When players choose service over self-interest, three things happen. First, not only are the needs of other players and the team addressed, not only does it create more flexibility, but something very powerful also happens to those who give. Their lives are changed as well. The thrill that comes from advancing the larger cause creates a desire to give even more.

Second, serving others has a very natural side effect. When people feel served, something compels them to reciprocate and a spirit of service floods through the organization. Mutual giving elevates camaraderie and unity.

Third, the Giants have shown that when players figure out how to give more than they take, the team plays better over the long haul. And guess what? Every member of the team comes out ahead.

Make Other Players Better

Chemistry grows when players appreciate the specific contributions other players make. That appreciation is not just being happy for your teammates when they do well; it's about the effect that comes from making other players better. It releases pride and emotional energy and has you saying to yourself and your teammates, "I get to play with that guy and that gets me juiced!"

> **Boch:** Sometime deep into the 2014 playoffs I reminded our guys: "It's been teamwork that got us to this point and it's going to be teamwork that takes us through the playoffs on top. Your support of one another, your ability to forgive mistakes—in yourself and in others—and move on, your mutual respect, and your camaraderie have created a spirit of unity and a force to be reckoned with. And I'll tell you what, the team that becomes most unified is the one that's going to win the Series. It takes remarkable courage to ask the question, "Can I choose to make my happiness come from the success of others?" If you can answer with a confident yes, the payoff will be worth it.

In the Giants clubhouse there are many examples of players making each other better. For example, second baseman Joe Panik credits shortstop Brandon Crawford with helping him settle into the big leagues. Most rookies share a common experience. There is the excitement of being called up, emotions running wild, and questions about "how we do things around here" and "will I fit in." Panik says Crawford's calming effect on him made his job easier. There's plenty of evidence to show for it. Panik's composure and athleticism were highlighted in Game 7 when he made one of the most memorable plays of the entire 2014 World Series.

Joe Panik and Brandon Crawford have established a great friendship and one of the best double play combos in the game.

In the Royals house, in the third inning of a 2-2 ball game with no outs and everything on the line, the Royals speedy center fielder Lorenzo Cain was on first. Kauffman Stadium was loud and ready for a big hit. Panik made a diving catch and flip-of-the-glove throw to Crawford for a double play that prevented Eric Hosmer's 106-mph rocket from going into center field. Buster Posey called the play a "game changer" because it derailed a potential Royals rally. After Madison Bumgarner pitched five innings of history-making magic, the Giants pulled off one of the greatest clutch performances ever seen in the game and beat the Royals 3-2.

> **Boch:** It *was* a game-changing play. I don't know what happens in Game 7 if Panik doesn't make that play. It would have put us in an extremely tough position. [Jeremy] Affeldt is probably facing one more hitter and then we would've brought Timmy [Lincecum] into the game. But you go from getting two outs to having runners on first and third with nobody out. The difference is huge—particularly when you're looking at the depth of the Royals bullpen. I can't say enough about Joe's composure. You *can* win games on defense, and that play certainly won the game for us.

Panik's World Series performance was no one-act play either. In 73 regular season games in 2014, he played with the kind of poise rarely seen in a rookie, making clutch plays, starting rallies, driving in runs, and flourishing as a No. 2 hitter.

Panik and Crawford built a great relationship and a special bond in the heart of the infield. Together, they established themselves as one of the best double play combos in the game. Giving Panik one of the greatest endorsements a rookie can receive, Crawford said Panik's mental approach to the game and how he goes about his job is reminiscent of Posey's when he came into the majors.

In one of two games the Giants lost in the 2014 postseason—a 4-1 defeat to the Nationals in the NLDS—starting pitcher Madison Bumgarner made one off-target throwing error. Instead of throwing to first base for the easy out after fielding a sacrifice bunt, Bum fired to third, wide of Pablo Sandoval's outstretched glove, and two runs scored. The Nationals staved off elimination preventing a three-game sweep by the Giants.

In the postgame Q&A with the media, catcher Buster Posey stepped forward to take the heat and shield his pitcher. "We probably should have taken the out at first. I made a mistake telling him to throw to third. It happens."

Posey's choice to step in front of the bus for his teammate represents a culture of togetherness and, as Larry Baer pointed out, a bond that genuinely means something to these players. Lived out inside the clubhouse, on the field, and in the media, the courage to stand up for one another is a powerful catalyst for chemistry.

14
BETTER TOGETHER
Talent Wins Games—Teamwork Wins Championships

After a 9-0 blowout by the Reds in Game 2 of the 2012 NLDS, the Giants were one loss away from going home. One might even say they were in dire straits. Starting the very next night, in fact, the next three games would be do-or-die. History would say that no team had ever won three straight elimination games on the road in a best-of-five series. The Reds now had control. If the Giants wanted to keep their season alive, they would have to do something extraordinary.

> It takes remarkable courage to ask the question "Can I choose to make my happiness come from the success of others?"

Marco Scutaro and Javier López were having a conversation in the clubhouse kitchen that Hunter Pence overheard. Scutaro and Lopez had observed a defeatist attitude starting to take hold in the clubhouse and knew something had to change or the Giants season would be over. Lopez also knew that if someone was going to address the club, the rallying cry would get a much better reception coming from a player who was out there every day, not from the pitching staff.

Even though Pence had joined the Giants just nine weeks earlier, he said he'd do it. He was the perfect player to step up. He's an optimist philosopher at heart. He reads and reflects. And, he plays with passion.

Before Game 3, Boch spoke to the team in a closed-door meeting. He knew that a typical "you can do it" speech wasn't going to be enough. He had to make them believe by showing them how, by telling them of other teams who had bounced back under similar circumstances. He reminded them that his own San Diego Padres reached the 1984 World Series only *after* winning three straight games against the Chicago Cubs and that the Boston Red Sox beat the New York Yankees in four straight ALCS games to play in the 2004 World Series. Then he went back to ancient history.

Boch: I told them the Old Testament story of Gideon, a farmer chosen by God to lead the Israelites against the mighty Midianites. The Midianite army was massive—100,000 strong. Gideon assembled an army of 32,000, hardly enough to confront his enemy. But God said there were too many, knowing that, with so many soldiers, the Israelites would claim victory instead of acknowledging that God had saved them. So, Gideon goes to the men who were most afraid and gives them permission to go home. And just like that, his army is down to 10,000. You'd think that would make the point. Still, there were too many men. So, at God's request, Gideon reduces his army to 300 and defeats the Midianites.

I thought this story would put an exclamation mark on the meeting. Little did I know, I was just the warm-up act.

When Boch was finished, Pence asked to speak and gave what is now the most publicized speech in the club's history. He was loud and spoke with the kind of conviction you can't fake or manufacture. Scutaro and Lopez nodded their heads in support. Some of the guys were just mesmerized by Pence's passion. Others shouted in agreement. It was a speech charged with a fire and authenticity that left his teammates ready to leap tall buildings.

Flannery posted a summary of Pence's speech on his band's Facebook page that night. The post received 3,448 "Likes" from Giants fans.

> The Reverend Hunter Pence said, "Get in here, everyone get in here. Look into each other's eyes. Now! Look into each other's eyes! I want one more day with you. It's the most fun, the best team I have ever been on, and no matter what happens we must not give in. We owe it to each other. Play for each other. I need one more day with you guys. I need to see what Ryan Theriot will wear tomorrow. I want to play defense behind Ryan Vogelsong because he's never been to the playoffs. Play for each other, not yourself. Win each moment. Win each inning. It's all we have left."

Vogelsong later remembered, "It wasn't so much what he said as the emotion with which he said it. It was believable. It came from the heart."

Indeed, Vogelsong went out and held his own against Homer Bailey, who was making a bid for his second no-hitter in three starts. And in the second inning, Pence embodied his own words by throwing himself at a fly ball deep into right field. Nicknamed "Full Throttle" because that's the only way he knows how to play, Pence never slowed down. Maniacally focused on the ball, he made a sliding catch in foul territory while crashing into the wall. It was one of those collisions that make you wonder, "Is he going to get up?"

Here's another example of the only way Hunter Pence knows how to play—full throttle.

When they met in the dugout, Vogelsong told Pence, "You don't know how much that play did for me."

With a tie ballgame in the 10th inning, Pence rose to the occasion again by teaming up with Buster Posey to produce the two hits that ignited the winning rally. Third baseman Joaquín Árias hit a fastball to third, put his head down, and beat the throw to first base. The Giants won 2-1 and bought themselves a ticket to play another day.

> I was proud to be together as a team . . . brothers that play for the name on the front, not the name on the back.

Flannery put Pence's speech and winning Game 3 into his own words. "For me, an old coach, it moved me like I have never been moved before . . . purity, real, passion, soul. The last of the holdouts, this Pence . . . no arrows being shot, no hey look at me, no spotlight on me, no dance but 'play for each other,' honor the game and the game honors you . . . Don't know where and when it ends, but tonight I was proud to be together as a team, in a hostile environment, with just us . . . brothers that play for the name on the front, not the name on the back."

With his provocative speech, Pence became the de facto spiritual leader of the team. His heartfelt plea readied his teammates to throw down the gauntlet and find the kind of resilience that would carry the Giants through six elimination games.

Closer Sergio Romo said: "I can honestly say that I love that guy more than I love myself for what he helped us accomplish. Pence went to each of my teammates, and reminded us how important it was to have fun, to be kids, to play a game we truly cared about . . . He woke us up."[49]

Give People a Voice

Pence's performance shows what's possible when people are free to be themselves at work. Clearly, Boch has created a clubhouse culture that made Pence feel safe enough to step up and speak up.

The Giants went on to achieve 11 victories in the next 14 games, including a 4-game sweep against Detroit in the World Series. Most people have agreed that Pence's impassioned exhortations were a tipping point in the Giants postseason run.

Passion, confidence, vulnerability, determination, conviction, and unselfishness. These character strengths are contagious. They open the door to our better selves. They cause momentum to shift. But they must be unleashed. They must be given the freedom to run. This usually starts with a manager who isn't a control freak and a player who is brave enough to step in and speak up.

Hunter Pence did more than just speak up; he appealed to some of our deepest human needs, calling up meaning and significance and the things that *really* motivate us. He didn't want the season to end because he didn't want to let go of the special bond this band of brothers had created. He was vulnerable enough to express his love and respect and feelings for his teammates. His sense of conviction was bigger than whatever fears he had about looking foolish.

Pence talked about fighting for a compelling cause and the bigger YES. His ultimate WHY was bigger than just winning; it was about extending this incredible experience and being with guys he cared about—for another day. It was about belonging to something bigger than himself and bigger than anyone in the room. Then he asked his teammates to opt in and they responded.

They chose to play for each other and the fans. They took their eyes off putting up individual numbers and played to *not* let down their teammates, to play again. When it was touch and go for awhile, they didn't consider what they had to lose; they focused on what they had to gain. Pence appealed to something deeper than just winning. This was about the sheer joy of playing together one more time. He hit a nerve that perhaps awakened his teammates to their own deeper desires and the chemistry t it's touch and go for awhile hat holds a team together through 162 regular season games. Whatever you call it, winning was the by-product of this shared purpose.

Again, how do you put a price tag on *that?* If you're a coach, how do you manufacture *that?* One can only speculate what would have happened to the Giants postseason if Boch hadn't given his players the freedom to be themselves. Buster Posey knew. "Without his [Pence's] want and willpower, I'm not sure we would have done this."[50]

DO SOMETHING NOW

Leadership is not a position or a title; it's a choice. Hunter Pence made that choice and did something in a way and at a time that Boch couldn't. Make leadership a distributed virtue in your organization by expecting people to "step up" with their unique gifts and perspectives and then giving them the freedom to do so.

One of the things you have to admire about Hunter Pence is his raw, unvarnished vulnerability. He isn't afraid to show his emotions, and his teammates appreciate that. In 2013, Pence won the Willie Mac Award, named after Giants legend Willie McCovey and given annually to the club's most inspirational player. Here's what he said to a sold-out crowd at AT&T Park after receiving it. "It's tough to really quantify how much this means to me in my heart . . . My heart has never felt better than when my teammates put me up here in front of you today. I take every single game with everything I've got. I love every minute of playing with you guys. I tell you that every day, and Buster [looking at Posey], I know you don't like it when I say, 'I love you,' you think it's soft, but I actually think it's the strongest thing we've got."

Considered "one of the scariest hitters of his ERA," Giants Hall of Famer Willie McCovey.

Pence then excused himself for a sidebar chat with God. The player described as having an awkward practice swing, exhibiting an off-balance batting stance, and playing the outfield with the "grace of a dump truck" prayed in front of the entire crowd: "God, you didn't bless me with grace. You didn't bless me with very much style. But thank you for giving me heart and a chance."

His teammates might've joined in by praying, "God, thank you for giving us Hunter Pence." During 15 games in the 2014 postseason, Pence had six extra-base hits, eight RBIs, eight walks, and 11 runs, with an OPS (sum of a player's on-base percentage and slugging average) of .875.

Pence has clearly established himself as a "glue guy," a go-to leader who brings a daily dose of energy to his teammates and brings this team together. Giants broadcaster Duane Kuiper said of him, "Even when Hunter asks one of the broadcasters, 'How are things going?' if your answer isn't to his liking, you're going to get a pep talk."

> **Boch:** As a manager, you hope your words mean something to the guys. You hope you're getting through to them. But sometimes they need to hear from each other. Meetings can be overdone. I've been with clubs where the players are thinking, "Oh no, here comes another meeting." Besides, I'm just not that smart in terms of always having something valuable to say—especially with the culture of our club. So, I like to use players to get the mood and tempo of the team. I love players who own it, who are willing to step into the breach and rally the guys, or call them out or whatever is needed.
>
> Hunter's that guy. He dares to be a little different. But that's what makes him special. He stands out. The players listen to him because they are like brothers to him. And, he has credibility because he speaks like he plays—all out.

Play for Each Other

Boch doesn't call a lot of team meetings. He has such a respect for his players' time, their ability to think for themselves, and their passion for the game that he doesn't need to. For example, after a losing road trip or, worse, a losing home stand, he often feels that there is nothing he can say that will make his players grasp the severity of the situation more than they already do. So, he is cautious about overdoing it. But when he sees things the players aren't seeing themselves, he will speak to them.

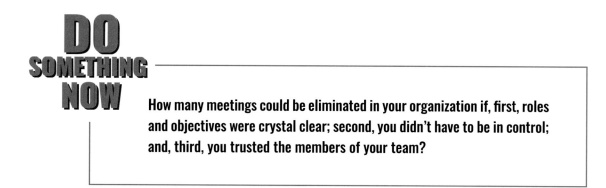

DO SOMETHING NOW

How many meetings could be eliminated in your organization if, first, roles and objectives were crystal clear; second, you didn't have to be in control; and, third, you trusted the members of your team?

Boch: In the middle of our horrific 2017 season, several staff and a couple of players observed that our clubhouse had gotten quiet. They noticed that players were in their own little worlds. Then, one day I'm walking through the clubhouse and I saw the same thing. Three guys, with lockers right next to each other, had their heads down, buried in their phones.

It might seem minor, especially in today's culture, but the scene was part of a bigger problem. I just felt the chemistry in the clubhouse—camaraderie, friends joking and ribbing each other, guys talking baseball, coaching each other, strategizing—was slipping a bit. We were missing the buzz we had before. So, I told them they were boring, that they needed to spend more time with each other, and then took the phones away an hour before each game.

I'm not a rules guy. I hate to be punitive, but sometimes you have to manage the exception and remove the things that get in the way of what you're trying to achieve.

Sometimes the heightened significance and consequences of the situation call for a rallying cry, like right before you play on the biggest stage in the world. Before Game 1 of the 2014 World Series against the Royals, Boch asked the guys who had won in 2010 and 2012 to play for the guys who didn't have a ring yet. He asked them to think about what that would mean, to know that they helped a teammate achieve something baseball players only dream about.

To emphasize *playing for each other*, he used a clip from *Longmire,* a contemporary crime drama set in Wyoming. In a gripping scene about loyalty and devotion, a tribal elder consoles Henry Standing Bear (played by Lou Diamond Phillips) for being a devoted friend in a difficult situation. Here's how Boch used this clip.

Boch: As many of you know, in the tribal community, elders speak words of truth and wisdom that reinforce the ways of the tribe. That's why their stories and words have been passed from chief to chief and warrior to warrior down through the ages. I picked up on this in the television series called Longmire when an elder of the tribe encouraged a warrior who doubted his own actions.

The team then watched the *Longmire* scene in which the tribal elder asks Henry Standing Bear what the young warrior said to the Great Spirit. He answered that the youth pledged to fight and win many battles for the Great Spirit in gratitude for all he had received. But the Great Spirit vehemently protested, urging him instead to fight for his tribe—his family, his fellow warriors, and his elders. "*They* are your home," he insisted. "Fight for *them.*"

Boch: Look around . . . *these* are your brothers and *this* is your home because *home* is where your brothers are.

- The reason we're here is because you guys have fought like warriors.
- The reason we're here is because you refused to back down.
- The reason we're here is because you guys have heart.

Look around . . . fight for *them!*

We have defeated our enemies and the victories were sweet . . . but that was yesterday. Today, we have come here to take on a new enemy and defeat the Royals on their own ground.

We came here to take on the guys in that opposing dugout; they're warriors too. But no team has the DNA you guys have, the DNA of a club that has defied the odds over and over again.

No one has demonstrated the passion to fight, the will to survive, and the determination to win like you guys have in the last three weeks.

But here . . . it's going to take all of that . . . and more!

Tonight we put on the armor, rededicate our commitment to each other, and show the world our warrior spirit once again.

So look around one last time: take a look at Huddy [Tim Hudson] and Hunter [Strickland], at Ishi [Travis Ishikawa] and [Michael] Morse, take a look at [Joe] Panik . . .

Let's fight for them!

The *Longmire* clip was a new way to reinforce an old theme—a theme that has been part of the Giants chemistry since the day Boch arrived: *play for each other.* It's commonplace for teams to give lip service to clichés like this, but for the Giants it's a visceral, long-standing, deeply rooted theme. After the Giants sweep of the Tigers in Game 4 of the 2012 World Series, Hunter Pence had this to say.

We bought into something you don't see happen very often; we bought into playing for each other. We bought into loving playing for each other. It's very unique because I've never really been a part of any other group that would buy in as much as we did. That everyone was pulling [in] the same direction. Everyone, it didn't matter if you had differences anywhere else, in the clubhouse we played, we loved every moment of it. It just speaks to the character of the guys, it speaks to the character of the people that put us together and their intelligence.[51]

Sergio Romo's elation at the win, like everyone else's, was overwhelming, but in the midst of the 2012 Series-clinching hoopla it was if he wanted every member of the squad to know how much they meant to him. He got face-to-face with as many of his teammates as he could. He told Marco Scutaro he had "big [*F-ing] Scutaros!" He grabbed Hunter Pence and said, "The rest of your life, you are a world champion. Eternity, baby!" And he described his deep sense of appreciation for his brothers. "The smile on my face does not mean as much to me as the smile on my teammates' faces. It makes it more special when you are not playing for yourself."[52]

If you look at the pictures in the coffee-table books from all three World Championship seasons, you can see it on the players' faces—this is a group of guys who love each other and play for each other.[53]

After the final out of the 2014 World Series, Buster Posey threw off his helmet, raced to the mound, and lifted 235-pound Madison Bumgarner off the ground in celebration. Bumgarner, who had just completed perhaps the most epic pitching performance in World Series history, hugged Posey and said, "I love you, man." They had played together since they were in the minor leagues. Both were key players in the Giants winning three World Series titles.

Yes, they were celebrating another epic win, but the moment revealed more than that. It was indicative of their bond, their connection to each other, the fraternity they have with their teammates, the trust and respect they have in their manager, and the kindred relationship they have with the entire Giant fan base.

Buster and Madbum were saying, in essence, "Together we're Giant."

15
PLAY FOR A CAUSE
Find the Why Beyond the Win

Larry Baer, who just might be the club's greatest ambassador, loves to mingle with the crowd at games. From the early days of rescuing the club and keeping it in San Francisco to spending every day thinking about how to enhance the fans' entertainment experience, Baer understands that the San Francisco Giants are not just a club; they are a cause. "I love the business I'm in," he insists. "On a good day, we bring fans joy, and even on a losing day, we provide an experience that helps them escape from their cares. Who else is lucky enough to have a job where they can do that?"[54] Larry makes a good point. Baseball (and sports generally, to a larger degree) has the power to captivate, to enable people to forget their worries, sorrows, and disappointments, and to celebrate—if only for a few hours—coming together around a shared passion, a pastime, an escape.

Baseball is a game of tradition—and routine. Most clubs are generally doing today what they did 5 or 10 years ago. Yes, sabermetrics has changed the game. Yes, strength and conditioning methods have changed. We've learned so much more about nutrition and hydration and recovery and stamina. And yes, the *business* of baseball has changed quite a bit. Yet, if you look at the way a club runs spring training today versus the way it did 5 years ago, for example, not much has changed, really. If you look at the pregame procedures of most clubs today, they're the same as they were 5 or 10 years ago. There is a pattern and rhythm to doing it the way it has always been done.

It's familiar. It's habitual. It's routine.

One of the greatest dangers ballplayers face (and this can be said for the rest of us too) is perfecting the *how* and forgetting the *why*. Boch is a big fundamentals guy. Perfecting the *how* is terribly important to him because in the heat of battle you have little time to think. Instead, you react, and those reactions must be ingrained in you. They must come naturally. But Boch, like CEO Baer, is also a big *why* guy. He wants his players to be deeply in tune with the bedrock that supports how they play the game.

When players forget the *why,* or never get in touch with it to begin with, they can lose the sense of adventure inherent in the game. Structure and routine keep things organized, predictable, and certain. But that habitual course of action can also dull the senses and numb the mind. When players become too familiar with the process, the process becomes *mindless*—the *last* thing Boch wants them to be. He wants *mindful* players on the field every day.

Understanding *why* you play the game is every bit as important as learning *how* to play the game. *Why* drives *how.* When you have a compelling *why,* you become more dedicated to the journey. Believe it or not, there are some extremely talented players whose hearts are far from the game. Maybe it's because the game comes to them so naturally. Maybe it's because they've been in the game so long that they've lost the awe they had when they first came into the majors. Or perhaps it's because with so many games in a season, it all becomes dull ritual. This is one of the reasons why Boch values having players such as Pablo Sandoval, Ryan Theriot, Gregor Blanco, Hunter Pence, and Sergio Romo in the clubhouse. These guys haven't lost their sense of wonder for the game.

The magnetic pull of *why* keeps the routine from becoming monotonous. It keeps a player's heart in the game. It lifts them out of mindlessly going through the motions and reminds them that there is something bigger to play for. *Why* draws you out of self-pity when a funk sets in and doubt wants to take over.

We live in a noisy, cynical world that is becoming more and more uncivil. Baseball offers a brief respite from all the craziness. It brings people together to share an experience, to celebrate the thrill of victory, and to comfort each other in the agony of defeat. Perhaps this sounds too ideal? Too romantic? Fine. Show us something better that works for you. The point is, playing inspiring baseball starts with something more enduring than winning. It starts with a compelling *why*; winning is merely a by-product of that noble, heroic cause.

Play for Something Beyond You

In every team there is something waiting to be awakened—*wanting* to be awakened. Great leaders reach below the surface and provide that wake-up call. One of the ways to get players to think about themselves less and about the team more is to help them think about playing for a cause or a crusade. It's about helping them see that their individual success is inextricably linked to something bigger.

Nicknamed the "Say Hey Kid," Willie Mays.

Boch: I want our guys to feel that what they do out there on the field and in the clubhouse, and what they bring to the game, contributes to something greater than themselves. They are building the brand of the San Francisco Giants, cementing our special relationship with the fans and the community, and ultimately contributing to the ongoing legacy of a storied franchise. This is why having legends like Mays and McCovey in our clubhouse is such a gift. They remind us that we are part of a greater legacy.

I want the players to see that they aren't just playing for themselves; they are playing for everyone in their lives who made some kind of sacrifice or some kind of investment that enabled them to be here.

Buster Posey gets it. During San Francisco's 2012 parade in celebration of the Giants second World Series victory, he talked about playing for something bigger. "I think for me, looking around and seeing all the excitement and happiness on everybody's face, you realize that an accomplishment like this means more than just winning a game. This is about making memories with your friends and family that will last a lifetime."[55] Winning is exciting, but there is something irresistible about the gratification and thrill of doing it together.

Boch: How can you not be happy making money playing the game you love? I don't just want them to be happy; I want them to find meaning in what they do. Happiness ebbs and flows, but meaning is deeper. Meaning reminds you about why you play the game. And incidentally, when you find the *why* you can overcome a lot of obstacles and generate a lot of staying power. Meaning keeps you humble when you are winning and keeps you going when you are losing.

The search for meaning and the desire to live a life that matters are powerful motivators. We are most alive when we have a sense of destiny, when we feel called to something greater than ourselves. And when we give ourselves to that calling, it draws out of us a drive to excel, a disregard for the impossible, and a willingness to win that is quite extraordinary.

Now for the Boys of Summer, you would immediately think that winning a World Series is the ultimate cause, right? But realistically, how often can that happen? There are very few dynasties in professional sports. So, if it's unrealistic to think you're going to win the ultimate prize year after year, what's the ultimate motivation?

Even though winning a World Series has lasting significance, and it is something you will cherish for the rest of your life, it also has a diminishing return. Every year you start over and every year there is (usually) a new winner. If the only reason why you play is to win, if that's your main source of significance, what happens when you lose?

Everyone wants to win the World Series, but what if there is something even bigger to play for? What if playing for it creates the exceptional chemistry that makes winning possible? What if winning is simply a by-product of the meaning, significance, joy, and aliveness that comes from *that?*

You might also be thinking: "Wait a minute, these guys are baseball players. They're playing a game they love for millions of dollars. Why do they need to be motivated?" And you'd be right. Their passion does pay—very handsomely. But even at that, how do you get "up" for 162 regular season games a year *after* spring training and do it year after year? How do you motivate different people, with different personalities and different interests, who come from different countries and speak different languages, to seamlessly work together—every day?

> **Make your players feel part of a team that's fighting for a noble, heroic cause.**

Boch's answer is to make his players feel part of a team that's fighting for a noble, heroic cause. Maybe it's about uplifting a man sitting in his wheelchair at home who looks forward to watching the Giants on television. Maybe it's an executive in a hotel room who just wants to chill from the day's business meetings and get his or her mind on something else. Maybe it's the kid who is coming to his or her first major league game. Maybe it's the family who couldn't afford a vacation but saved enough to come to the ballpark. Maybe it's the military soldiers who come to a game once a year to get away from the stress of serving their country. Maybe it's the father with a terminal illness who wants to do something enjoyable with his wife or children or friends before his time is up. Or maybe it's the season ticket holders who are there, like family, day after day cheering for and believing in their team.

Boch: Let's not forget that we're in the business of entertainment. No fans, no game. If our fans don't have a great experience and they don't feel a part of what we are doing, we don't get to play the game we love. So I tell our guys, "When a child asks for an autograph or the front office wants to introduce you to a season ticket holder, be gracious, be enthusiastic, lean into it, not because you *have* to but because you *want* to. *They* are the reason we're here. You have an opportunity to make their day." I want them to have a sense that we are playing for something bigger because we are.

What about the global impact of baseball? What happens when players from Cuba, the Dominican Republic, Venezuela, Japan, and other parts of the world share a season or a career with their American counterparts? It might not be the ultimate solution to the things that divide countries, but it has the potential to open doors and strengthen the ties that bind. Isn't this what the Goodwill Games were all about? When players from different countries converge, travel and work together, boundaries break down. It's no longer *us* and *them*. Cultural plurality is celebrated. More than just trophies won and records broken, baseball plays a role in strengthening the relationships between nations.

The larger cause can be defined in many ways, but no matter what it is, it is always bigger than just 25 guys trying to win ball games. There is always something beyond you and your team to play for.

Boch has been on both sides of the game—winning and losing. Like most of us, he's seen athletes become heroes only to be forgotten and replaced by new heroes. As a result, he not only thinks that "playing for something beyond you" has a positive impact on chemistry and winning, he also knows that it taps into an emotional and spiritual vacuum that leaves many players asking: "It this it? Is this all there is?" How many retired athletes do you know who are living in the past because they don't have a cause to fight for, because they can't see beyond themselves?

There are two striking aspects to what Boch is doing here.

First, it's believable. Players can be cynical and they are not easily impressed by fiery speeches and platitudes. They quickly see through the BS. But in San Francisco, the players have a direct line of sight between what they do every day and the larger cause. How does this happen? Through the chemistry cultivated between the front office of the Giants organization and baseball operations. Director of Client Retention & Services Joe Totah and his team make sure that Boch and his players are fed stories that expose them to the impact they have on the fans and the community.

For example, a season ticket member hosted a father and son for a Sunday afternoon game. The little boy had cancer and wasn't doing well so this was an especially poignant outing. Amanda Nichols, Account Manager in the Client Retention & Services department, put together a bag of items, including a baseball signed by Tim Lincecum, and brought it to them in their seats in between innings. The minute Amanda introduced herself and handed the bag to the little boy, the father started crying and thanked her over and over again for making the

Signing balls adds to player and fan chemistry.

day so special. Not only were the boy and his father touched by this gesture, the season ticket member called to say how impressed he was by what they did.

Stories like this, and they are many, give Lincecum and his teammates a sense that there is more to this game than fastballs and strikeouts. They are part of something bigger. And, when Boch reminds them of this, they know he's not just inflating them with empty idealism; he's very seriously asking them to connect the dots and see the influence they have on people's lives.

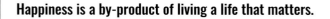

Happiness is a by-product of living a life that matters.

Second, the larger cause is transcendent. It's about honoring people, elevating spirits, enriching the human condition, and doing something to better society. When pitching superstar Lincecum takes a few minutes to sign some baseballs, maybe he sees the eternal significance in what he's doing and maybe he doesn't. But when the manager says, "Play for something beyond you," and then someone tells Tim about a memory he helped create for a family that might not have much time together, it becomes very real very fast.

If all of this seems a little too soft or sentimental, a little too far-fetched for you, ask yourself, "What would happen to the spirit of our nation if entertainment—baseball in particular—disappeared forever?" If we beamed America's favorite pastime off the face of the Earth, would it be missed? And if so, why?

In the end, Boch is reminding his players about the dignity and sacredness of the people they play for. They are not just fans occupying seats, pleading for balls and autographs; they're not just statistics on a spreadsheet or the numbers of a sellout crowd; they're not just consumers with a market value or an acquisition and retention cost. They are real people with real dreams and desires, and his players have an opportunity to use the game and use their platform to have a positive effect on each one of them.

Lots of us think happiness is the ultimate pursuit in life. We think happiness is a by-product of living a life that matters—a life that is useful, that stands for something, that enriches people's lives, and makes the world better. When ballplayers truly believe that the game they're committed to can do this, the game means something more, and the side effect is that win or lose, they enjoy it more.

Rally Them Around an Idea

In September 2010, the Padres collapsed, giving the Giants an opportunity to surge in their quest for the NL West title. Boch sensed the window of opportunity and laid down a call to arms. He held a pregame meeting with the team before BP at Dodger Stadium.

Boch told his guys and the media that this was a Players Association meeting, which meant that all members of the media were excluded from LA's small, outdated visitors' clubhouse. Then, after talking to his players about the history of Scotland and an iconic hero named William Wallace, Boch wheeled in a television monitor and played a scene from the Academy Award–winning film *Braveheart*.

Wallace struggles in the film to help the Scottish people stand against the formidable powers of their English oppressors. In this particular scene, moments before the Battle of Sterling, the Scottish nobles gather and prepare to negotiate a compromise, knowing that if they take their army and go home, they will each receive an estate and a hereditary title. Then Wallace rides in with his band of renegades and stirs the men to fight, ending with the immortal line, "They may take our lives, but they'll never take our freedom!"

After watching Wallace tell the Scottish troops, "This is your time," Boch told his players that the Padres, the team ahead of them, had faltered. "This is now *your* time," he said. This was their time to do something special for each other, for their families, for the franchise, and for thousands of Giants fans around the world.

Flannery remembered Boch's inspired meeting well. "It was a captivating moment. He got the guys so fired up that they took the field yelling, 'This is our time!' When something good happened, they yelled, 'FREEDOM!' When someone needed a lift, 'FREEDOM!' With each game we won going forward, 'FREEDOM!' It created a sense of urgency and a sense of resolve for all of us."

Conviction Is Contagious

The road into the 2010 postseason would be hard-fought. In bringing the clip from *Braveheart* into the clubhouse, Boch was looking for a way to rouse the warrior spirit in his guys, take them to a higher place, and prepare them for the intense battle that lay ahead. After the game, one of the San Diego sportswriters called it a "cheesy ploy," one typical of coaches who "trade in peak emotion." He either didn't understand or didn't care about why we are so drawn to movies like this. They speak to something we are wired for—an epic adventure, a larger calling, and an opportunity to do something heroic. Some ballplayers wait their whole lives for a moment in time to show their families and friends and fans how much they are appreciated. This is why Boch doesn't let journalists run his clubhouse.

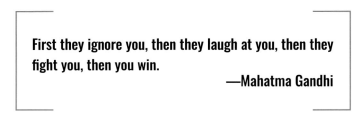

First they ignore you, then they laugh at you, then they fight you, then you win.

—Mahatma Gandhi

The players had a different perspective from the journalists. Sergio Romo's takeaway was that while the guys enjoyed Boch's way of delivering the message, they all understood its serious intent. There was a cause worth fighting for and the *Braveheart* clip reinforced an every-game-counts mentality. "I was like, 'What is this?'" former Giants right fielder Cody Ross remembered. "Next thing you know we're watching it and he talks afterwards, and we went on a run after that. It was one of the most awesome meetings that I've ever been a part of."[56]

Buster Posey had yet another kind of response to the meeting. "For me personally, it wasn't necessarily (about) the video. It was our manager putting himself out on a limb a little bit. For me, it showed this guy wants it. It was just reinforcing everything we wanted to do as a team."[57]

> **Boch:** You have to get in; you have to make it into the postseason to have a run at getting to the World Series. I was trying to get us refocused and give us the shot of adrenaline we needed. Playing for a larger cause cranks up the "want to" factor, but it also takes the guys' minds off pressing too hard. What our guys did in the next couple of weeks made me realize that this team was special.

For the next 12 anxiety-ridden days, the Giants and Padres traded the top spot in the NL West. With three games up on the Padres and three games left to play in the season, the Giants brought the fans one more round of torment, dropping the first game in the series to San Diego. You can only imagine the tension when the Padres won again the next day, 4-2. Here's what they were facing: The last game was critical. The questions loomed. Would the Giants have to play a tiebreaker in San Diego if they got swept by the Padres? If they lose the NL West, can they beat Atlanta for the Wild Card—in *their* house? What if this was hope disappointed and the season was over tomorrow?

Then Boch did something bold and audacious.

> **Boch:** I remember walking into our clubhouse. Michael King, our traveling secretary, was passing out the itinerary to the players, showing them the travel plans in case we lost. My first thought was, "What the hell! We're preparing these guys to lose?" I didn't want one negative thought in their heads.
>
> I felt that we needed to do something dramatic, to burn the bridges so to speak, so I talked it over with Brian [Sabean]. We told the players to leave their suitcases at home—literally not to pack their bags. I didn't want them bringing anything to the park before that last game except for the raw determination to finish the regular season at home. There was going to be no turning back. I wanted them to know we *were* going to end this thing—tomorrow.

The next day, October 3, the Giants threw down the gauntlet in a 3-0 victory over the Padres and clinched the division. Relief and anticipation filled the air. Before uncorking the champagne, Boch encouraged the players to take a celebratory lap inside the park to connect with fans who had faithfully endured the torture.

During the month of September, the Giants pitching staff was historic. They posted a record 18 consecutive games giving up three runs or less. The last team to do this was the Chicago White Sox in 1917. And the Giants jaw-dropping team ERA (1.78) was the lowest in a month since 1969, when divisional play started.

There is no question that superior pitching was a key to the Giants 2010 winning season. But where do the determination and the perseverance that empowered the Giants to emerge victorious after such a roller-coaster ride come from? They come from an opportunity to do something heroic, to play for a larger cause.

Matt Cain, and his teammates show their appreciation for the fans after winning the 2010 NL West Division Series.

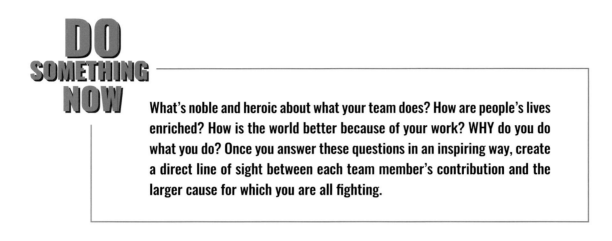

DO SOMETHING NOW

What's noble and heroic about what your team does? How are people's lives enriched? How is the world better because of your work? WHY do you do what you do? Once you answer these questions in an inspiring way, create a direct line of sight between each team member's contribution and the larger cause for which you are all fighting.

People follow passion. We are drawn to leaders who are good at communicating what they stand for—leaders who can inspire us to enrich others and make something better because of what we do. Leaders who have the guts to show "cheesy" video clips. Leaders who bear hug, listen, and love freely. They draw us up by showing us our place in something bigger. And, as we move toward that cause, we build a bond, a sense of belonging with others who are drawn there too.

That connection, that chemistry, has the power to transform good talent into World Champions.

These enthusiastic fans represent the larger cause that the Giants play for.

5th Inning

GIANT RESILIENCE

Never Say Die!

16
FEARLESS TOGETHER
Chemistry Forged by Crisis

Why do some professional franchises thrive under adversity while others crumble? Why do some MLB teams stand up to seemingly insurmountable odds while others give in to the pressure? When a team is in a funk, why do some players have an indefatigable hope that things will work out while others fall into despair?

Why does one innovator throw in the towel while another pushes past the first, easiest, most obvious solution to one that is elegant, fresh, and exciting? What causes one entrepreneur to stand up to the critics and naysayers and beat insurmountable odds when another gives up and quits?

To a large degree, the answer comes down to how these players handle adversity. Those who succeed find a way to keep going, keep trying, and keep exploring new ways to make something good happen. They find a way to play one more day when, by all measures, success appears to be impossible. Do these teams and players get discouraged? Sure they do; they're human. But they don't get discouraged easily, and when they do get "down," it doesn't last long. Despite being disrupted and derailed by one obstacle after another, they find the willpower to bounce back. And each time they do, resilience grows.

> **Boch:** To excel in this game, you have to be able to handle failure and disappointment. The game is loaded with missed signals, bad calls, strikeouts, errors, hostile crowds trying to get in your head, and physical setbacks. If you can't let go of failure, if you can't block out all the distractions—especially the voices floating around in your head—the pressure will get to you. It's almost impossible to relax. And if you can't relax, you can't access the full weight of your talent, you can't play to the upper range of your potential.
>
> It's been an amazing thing to watch. There is an uncanny level of calm in our clubhouse before crucial games—including the playoffs and World Series. I don't know if it's because we've played so many tight games, but our guys have learned to control their emotions. When things aren't going well, they have a lot of composure, and I'm convinced that that is why we have prevailed in so many heated battles.

Comeback Kids of the Century

The Giants have developed a powerful comeback narrative—one they developed in 2010 and relived in each subsequent run to the World Series. It's a narrative that includes the glory of "adversity ends in triumph" and the glory of heroes who were unwilling to let their collective dreams, and those of their fans, die. It's a tale of guys who have tremendous faith in each other, who stand on the side of hope, and who choose to see hardship as a challenge or a contest designed to test their limits.

This comeback narrative is also the story of a manager who breeds optimism in his club. Whether the adversity shows up as an injury, a defeat, the contempt of a loud and boisterous crowd, or an opponent's expanding lead, Boch explains these events in a nonnegative way that contributes to the resilience of his players. Taking a cue from their leader, players have a gut-level belief that misfortune can be overcome, failure can turn to success, and they *will* beat the odds.

Does it always work out this way? No. But it happens so often that this expectation is woven into the organization. The come-from-behind victory is now a part of the Giants brand of baseball. It's a reputation that has a psychological effect on other teams. It doesn't matter how talented they are or how big their lead is; opponents know they are never safe when playing the Giants. Opposing teams have seen this indomitable spirit too many times not to respect it. They know the Giants will be in it until the very last out. This is why the Giants hold the record for the most consecutive playoff wins and why Boch is considered one of the best postseason managers in the game.

> **When you stand on the side of hope and choose to see hardship as a challenge or a contest designed to test limits, resilience grows.**

In 2010, the Giants were 6½ games back in the NL West in August. In 2012, they were neck and neck with the Dodgers at mid-season. Then, the Dodgers made multiple blockbuster trades while the Giants best player got suspended for the remainder of the season. In 2014, after playing a Wild Card Game, the Giants lost Game 6 of the World Series 10-0, forcing the Series into a final Game 7. Somehow, some way, three seasons ended in champagne celebrations and ticker tape parades. How were the Giants able to overcome such adversity and stay united?

Playing not two or three but *six* elimination games in 2012, knowing that each one comes with the threat of going home for the season, tests the mettle of a team and reveals its character. Each affords an opportunity for a different player to make something good happen.

> **Boch:** Adversity can be a gift. Would we have written the script for less torture? Sure. But going through the fire together strengthened our resolve, unified our guys, and made us more resilient. It was like each battle tested our character as a club and showed us who we were. These words might make for nice sound bites, but every time we made it through another trial, our guys looked in the mirror and saw warriors.
>
> They saw that they could be flexible when we asked them to step into unfamiliar territory. They found out how quickly they could bounce back from dire circumstances. They maintained their warrior spirit no matter what they faced.

Adversity. It's a part of life and certainly inherent in the game of baseball. Even more so in the postseason. The clubs that recognize adversity as an inevitable part of the game embrace it and leverage it; they develop resilience because of it. Those that don't are often eaten alive. To say that the Giants love adversity would be just plain wrong, but they do seem to play at a higher level when the chips are down. When they hit a rough patch, it's as if a switch has been flipped that turns up the focus, crowds out the noise, dials down the anxiety, and brings on a sense of calm in the eye of the storm.

When their opponents have their foot on the Giants throats and the pundits start making overtures that losing is a foregone conclusion, the coaches and players draw deep from the wells of defiant determination and stubborn resolve. More often than not, they prove the critics wrong.

Fighting the Battle Together

Yes, the Giants had great pitching in 2010, but none of the baseball pundits would give you any reason to think they were the best team in baseball, or even close to it. And for the regular season that might've been true: the media predicted the Yankees and the Phillies would be playing in the World Series. But in the postseason it was a different story. San Francisco's Giants were the comeback kids. One minute the club was on the brink of disaster; the next minute someone makes a clutch contribution and everyone is riding high again.

Giants broadcaster Duane Kuiper observed that the late inning comebacks had a special effect on the club's chemistry. "It gave a lot of us a lot of gray hairs. But it did something else. We-ness comes from having fought the battle together, from a common struggle. The more intense the struggle is, the tighter the bond. This is true of the fans as well. There's a collective spirit in San Francisco that seems to say: 'We—we the fans and the team—went through this together. And because of this, there is a bond between us.'"

Kuiper's right. The more you have to fight and struggle for something, the more precious it becomes. The more battles you fight together, the more you learn about your teammates and the more there is to respect. The struggle unites all of those who live to tell about it. "We-ness" chemistry is the result of fighting the battle—together.

Initially, the Giants organization might not have been too keen on the word "torture" given all its implications in a world that's become increasingly more dangerous. But Kuiper gave the organization and the community a gift. He put a label on the ethos of the Giants and *branded* the characteristic spirit of the way this club wins.

Duane Kuiper Emmy award–winning broadcaster coined the term "torture" and it stuck.

Torture is a brand that glorifies struggles-turned-successes and gutsy, heartfelt contributions from likely and unlikely heroes who prove that the impossible isn't. Torture celebrates everything that demonstrates how the Giants prevail. It's become an integral part of the club's folklore and comeback narrative. And it establishes a code and raises the bar for the entire organization. As Kuiper so insightfully noted, torture is a catalyst for chemistry.

Would the Giants and their fans have liked less to agonize over on the way to three World Series titles? You bet. Who doesn't have an aversion to what's hard in life? But who among Giants fans doesn't like to recount those special moments when their hearts were on the line, about to be broken, and then, exuberance! Who doesn't enjoy reveling in having overcome impossible odds? It makes the story better, more dramatic. The more the story comes alive, the more fun it is to tell. That's why the come-from-behind type of win is weightier and more momentous than the sweep is.

Boch: Look, we'll take them [wins] any way they come. And a sweep in no way lessens the fearsomeness of the other team. But when you come from behind and do what no one thinks you can do, no doubt the guys prove something to themselves. I think the victory has more meaning for both our players and the fans. It really does bring them together like a band of brothers.

If you look at how the culture of this club evolved over the course of three World Series Championships in five years, there's another thing worth noting. It relates to that term Boch is so fond of: "Championship Blood." It can mean many things, but predominantly it is an expectation. Honed during those three major championships, each with many trials and obstacles that had to be overcome to achieve the end goal, an expectation to remain calm and not panic emerged. When the darkness threatened to envelope them, the players developed an expectation that went like this: "We *will* find a way out of this, we *will* come back; this is not over." They expected to go all out until the last out was recorded because you never know what can happen. And, as the Giants added to the number of torturous victories they put on the board, the stronger this expectation became.

Think about what this does to players coming up from the minor leagues or how it shapes the expectations of a veteran acquired from another major league team. Without it ever being articulated, it says: "You're joining something special, something exclusive, and something that's hard to come by. When you come here, expect to win. And when we're down by two runs in the ninth inning and it's the last out, with a 2-2 count, Never Say Die!"

Commitment right up to the end and membership are a big deal. Being accepted into a team with Championship Blood builds a stake in the club and feeds a personal commitment to reinforcing this Never Say Die culture. Chemistry is both the extraordinary magnet that draws players into this type of culture and the result of their steely-eyed resolve to protect it.

Making no apologies for squeezing into the 2014 playoffs as a Wild Card, Giants CEO Larry Baer echoed this resilient optimism in an interview with *USA Today*. "The mentality here was get in. Get in the tournament. Anything can happen once you get in. If you win the World Series, nobody says, 'Oh, but they were the Wild Card.' It's the same."[58]

You can't legislate a Never Say Die culture, but you can pay attention to the signs that it is emerging organically. Call it what it is and then proactively help it along. Eventually, something takes root, something sticks that defines the persona of a team and becomes its rallying cry. If you listen to the words and phrases Sabes and Boch use with each other, in media interviews, and when addressing the players, you can see how they reinforce a culture of resilience.

You Just Can't Kill Cockroaches

Cockroaches.

That's what Boch calls his players. Bench Coach Ron Wotus has adopted the same theme. The term originated when GM Brian Sabean told his team, "I can put you in a microwave oven, crank it up, and most of you will walk out."

It's an apt label for a team that refuses to let up, back down, or give in. Cockroaches have been around for millions of years—because they adapt. Through endless injuries, player suspensions, and erratic performances, the Giants, too, have adapted.

Every year that they won a championship the Giants faced adversity. Boch has drafted more different lineup cards than he can count. They simply choose to step through the fear of uncertainty and refuse to let circumstances dictate their emotions. Instead, they call on that irrepressible attitude, their uncanny knack for critical contributions at key moments and confidence under pressure—all honed in the experience of bouncing back over and over again.

On the road to World Series crowns in 2010, 2012, and 2014, the Giants dispatched 10 consecutive postseason foes. In 2010, they came back again and again to defeat the Atlanta Braves, Philadelphia Phillies, and Texas Rangers. In 2012, they got the best of the Cincinnati Reds, St. Louis Cardinals, and Detroit Tigers. In 2014, they took care of the Pittsburgh Pirates in the Wild Card Game, then toppled the Washington Nationals and St. Louis again before taking it down to Game 7 in the World Series and beating the Kansas City Royals.

Cockroaches. Looking in from the outside the term might be seen as an insult. But hearing it on the inside the Giants wear it as a badge of honor and a term of endearment. Players accept it because they can see the pride in their managers' faces when they use it.

> **Boch:** Brian's used the term, I've used it, and now others have picked up on it. When you look at how many times we've come back from being down and out, from having our backs against the wall, and you see the contributions we get from one guy tonight and a different guy tomorrow, they are like cockroaches. You can't kill 'em; they just keep coming back. And that's what makes our guys special.

On October 29, 2014, the Giants were knocking on the door of their third World Championship in five seasons. The night before, in Game 6, the Royals hammered San Francisco in a 10-0 victory. With momentum on their side, playing in their house, the Royals had the advantage going into the deciding Game 7. The Giants didn't see it that way. With just two days' rest, starter Madison Bumgarner came into the fifth inning *in relief* and was magnificent—virtually unhittable. More on his history-making performance later, but in the ninth inning things got tense.

With two outs, the Giants were clinging to a one-run lead, needing one more out to win it all. Royals left fielder Alex Gordon flared a ball into left field that dropped in front of outfielders Gregor Blanco and Juan Perez. Perez thought, "Blanco's got this" and started for the dugout. But he didn't get it. Perez then turned and scrambled for the ball, tried to barehand it, and kicked it instead, giving Gordon the go-ahead from second to third base.

Every third base coach in the National League knew the strength and accuracy of shortstop Brandon Crawford's throwing arm. Still, if the relay wasn't perfect, the Royals could send Gordon home and there would be a bang-bang play at home plate. Perez fired to Crawford, and Mike Jirschele, the Royals third base coach, held Gordon at third as the Kauffman Stadium crowd erupted.

It was a frantic nail-bitter that could have changed the outcome of the Series. It might've been one of the longest 12-second plays in World Series history. Most everyone agrees that Jirschele made a great call under tremendous pressure. But with Gordon on third and one of the Royals best hitters, catcher Salvador Pérez, at

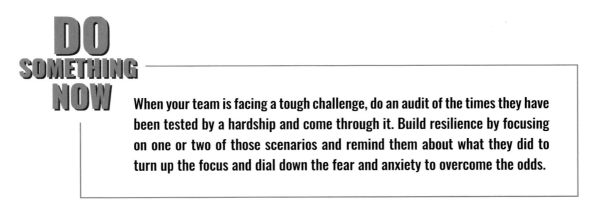

DO SOMETHING NOW When your team is facing a tough challenge, do an audit of the times they have been tested by a hardship and come through it. Build resilience by focusing on one or two of those scenarios and remind them about what they did to turn up the focus and dial down the fear and anxiety to overcome the odds.

the plate, the tension continued. One wild pitch, one hit, and the Royals tie the game—in their house. But MadBum was about to give history a shove. He entirely outmatched Perez, who hit a foul pop-up to Pablo Sandoval, and it was over—the Giants had won their third World Championship.

Adversity tests our mettle and challenges our beliefs. If we respond well, it reveals our inner strength. In the case of the Giants, quitting just isn't in their DNA, but adapting is. Each time they triumph over adversity the roots of their conviction about who they are and about what's possible run deeper. Each time adversity gets the best of them—as it did in the 2013 regular season—their determination to conquer grows—as it did in 2014. Either way, the Giants bandwidth for dealing with adversity expands.

What makes the Giants as tough and annoying as cockroaches? What puts teeth into the battle cry Never Say Die? There's more to it than just being fearless in the face of adversity. You also must have composure, resolve, and hope.

17
COMPOSURE, RESOLVE, HOPE
Building Invincible Players

Imagine trying to build chemistry without composure, resolve, and hope? Panic and stress multiply; grit weakens and people give up; and there is no expectation that tomorrow will be better. "We can do this!" gives way to "What's the use?" Things get dark and bleak. This is fertile ground for egos to get hurt, impatience to run wild, and tempers to flare. It has the potential to be contentious and divisive.

But when firing on all cylinders, these three components of hardiness and resilience—composure, resolve, and hope—can produce a completely different outcome. They can contribute to an optimistic way of explaining events that makes a brighter future reasonable, realistic, and therefore believable. They are an essential element in the Giants Never Say Die! mindset and a unifying force that makes chemistry possible.

Composure—Don't Panic

If you were looking for a character to cast in a movie on charismatic leadership, Boch most likely would not top your list. He's not flashy; he's stoic. He's not volatile; he's even-keeled. He's not a man of many words, he gravels and growls, all the while masking his quick-witted sense of humor. All of which just proves that charisma is an added advantage of great leadership but not a necessity.

The mental wheels are turning and the emotions ping-pong up and down, but you'd never know from watching Boch in the dugout.

Great leaders model what is acceptable behavior, and Boch is an expert at controlling his emotions. With the Giants, composure starts at the top. Boch models calm, steady, and strong. He does it in the dugout and MOST times he does it in the clubhouse. Why? Because Boch doesn't like to draw attention to himself. He doesn't have the kind of personality that makes for good print or television. He's a journalist's worst nightmare because he will make you dig for something juicy to print. You are not going to get a lot of colorful dugout reactions from Boch either. Dan Brown of the *Mercury News* dubbed him "Captain Calm." Boch has mastered the art of the poker face. He knows how to stay composed and keep everyone guessing.

Watching the Giants produces excessive mood swings and a lot of animation directed at the TV: "Really!? Yes! Aww, come on! Are you kidding me? Ahhh, nuts! Nice!" But when the cameras pan to Boch you don't know whether he's happy, ticked off, or deep in thought. If they took the score off the screen and you had to guess whether the Giants were winning or losing based on Boch's expressions—good luck! You've got a 50/50 chance.

Bottom line: That's just the way he wants it.

> **Boch:** Believe me, I'm emotional. There's a lot going on inside [me] during a game. I just think it's important to be consistent. Players take their cues from the manager. If they see me panic, they panic. If they see that I'm upset, they think I've lost confidence in them. Then, they lose confidence in themselves. Players have enough variables to contend with during a game. Guessing which manager is in the dugout—the one who's frustrated or the one who's optimistic and has your back—creates one more element of distraction they don't need. It causes them to lose focus.
>
> Our players know how passionate I am, but being erratic sets the wrong tone. When your mood is unpredictable it creates uncertainty and breeds fear. They don't need that.
>
> Mind you, this is how I try to be; it's not always the way I am. I do get frustrated and sometimes I wear it outside [myself]. I'm human just like everybody else. I "lose it" periodically. But when I throw my cap or yell, it just raises the anxiety in the dugout. Some players aren't affected by it, but others tighten up.

Where does Boch find ways to relieve the stress? In the Giants postseason bid for the 2010 World Series, he felt the pressure like never before. During the late nights and early mornings when his mind just wouldn't shut down, he watched the Military Channel. It helped in a couple of ways. First, there is something to be learned about strategy from the great military commanders of World Wars I and II. And second, it calibrated his perspective. The pressure of baseball hardly compares to the life-and-death scenarios a soldier faces, but those programs gave his ever-churning mind a break from the game and a more balanced perspective on life.

Giants broadcaster Mike Krukow sees a unique side of Boch from the booth. Krukow observed that Captain Calm is anything but cuddly with umpires. "He's got an open dialogue going, pitch by pitch, on the umpires. I mean, he's relentless on those guys. He does not let up. So, there is a side to him you

Mike Krukow, Emmy award–winning commentator loved by Giants fans.

don't often see. You see that big old St. Bernard in the dugout, and he looks pretty placid, but he lets his feelings be known as to what's going on."[59]

> **Boch:** Kruk's right. There are a lot of times I will bark at the umpires. It's part of the game. I try to take that away from the players because I don't want them arguing with the umpires and getting thrown out. I want our guys to know I'm fighting for them. I want 'em to know that I've got their back. That's what a manager should do.

Giants CEO Larry Baer said, "Boch is one of the steadiest managers I've ever seen." When you play 162 games with a wide variety of personalities (some players are high-strung and high-maintenance, some are all business, and some are quiet and reclusive), there are a lot of ups and downs. The potential for drama is high. What players need is an anchor point or a compass with true north. Hunter Pence says that compass is Boch. "It actually starts at the top. There's a unique, relaxed and encouraging feeling that starts with Bochy. He's always calm, and that keeps us calm."[60] Brandon Crawford agreed. "He doesn't get all mad or frustrated or worked up very often, which is nice. For the most part, he's pretty calm. If he *does* get worked up, it's something big."[61]

During 20 years of coaching and managing, when one of his teams was in the tank, Boch would say to Kevin, "I need to get us out of this funk; here's what I'm thinking about." They've had many conversations about getting unstuck, but countless times Bruce has said, "We're not panicking here." As we've noted earlier, he has an uncanny ability to sense when a meeting with his players is warranted and when to let it ride.

In 2014, the Giants came out of the chute hard and fast. In the first third of the season they had the best record in baseball. Then, over the next third, they massively imploded. This is the kind of scenario where fans start talking trash, owners get antsy, and GMs start calling for someone's head. But this isn't just any ball club; this is the Giants.

They don't panic.

Larry Baer, Brian Sabean, and Bobby Evans have learned to trust Boch's calm disposition. So have the players. When the tension mounts, Boch finds a way to lower the temperature. He's the "calm" in the eye of the storm and his players have grown to depend on this. Often, without a spoken word, he seems to convey a solid belief in what his guys are capable of doing, even in late innings when they've run out of road. In all three of the Giants championship runs, opponents caved in under the pressure while Boch's boys rose to a whole new level of performance.

> **Anyone can give up, that's easy. To hold it together and soldier on when no one would blame you for falling apart, that's resilience.**

In September 2012, the Giants had endured season-ending injuries to Brian Wilson and Freddy Sánchez, Melky Cabrera's suspension, and a string of blockbuster deals that threatened to put the Dodgers on top of the NL West. Instead, the Dodgers crumbled and the Giants cinched the division with 10 games to spare.

Former Dodgers manager Don Mattingly commented on the Giants resilience. "I don't think I ever expected them to stop performing the way they are because I've known Bruce Bochy for a long time. I know that the Giants are basically just going to keep coming at you. That's just typical Bruce Bochy. His teams are resilient. They never quit."[62]

Mattingly described what we've all observed. The Giants are not intimidated by the big stage, they're not tight under pressure, and they certainly don't blink when backed into a corner. And by the way, it's not just the veterans who display this poise; the young homegrown players have demonstrated a remarkable level of composure as well.

Righetti explained that rookies such as second baseman Joe Panik and reliever Hunter Strickland made significant contributions in the heat of the 2014 pennant race because they were relaxed. "We don't have a huge major-league type veteran bench. He's [Boch] got young kids. But they seem to be playing like they're not tight, right? It's got to be him. It's the atmosphere he creates."[63]

Composure Is Contagious

After Madison Bumgarner's historic relief outing in the 2014 World Series, Buster Posey said, "I'm still amazed at how he [MadBum] just sits on the bench and just seems so calm." Hunter Pence agreed. "He is so calm that it leaks into you, so confident that it leaks into us."[64]

Clearly, calm is contagious. Like Boch, the Giants hitting coach, Hensley Muelens—otherwise known as Bam-Bam—brings a reassuring calm to the clubhouse. According to Crawford: "Bam-Bam is probably the most easy-going and calm of all our coaches, which I think is huge for us. In past years, when we haven't hit well and everybody was getting stressed, he was the same calm guy. That's nice to get from a hitting coach when you're struggling and trying to find something. I think that's why we don't panic as hitters."[65]

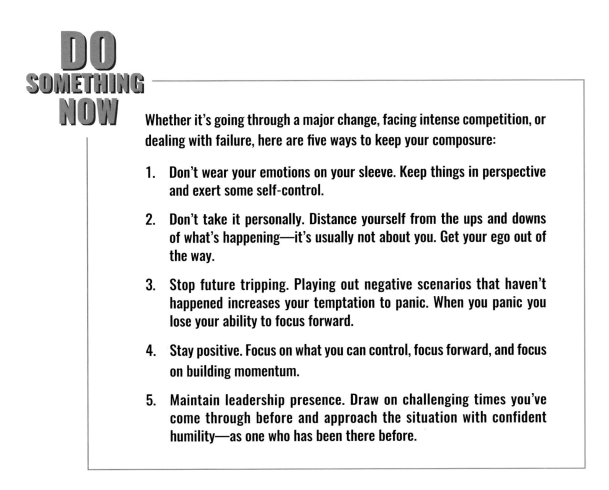

DO SOMETHING NOW

Whether it's going through a major change, facing intense competition, or dealing with failure, here are five ways to keep your composure:

1. **Don't wear your emotions on your sleeve.** Keep things in perspective and exert some self-control.

2. **Don't take it personally.** Distance yourself from the ups and downs of what's happening—it's usually not about you. Get your ego out of the way.

3. **Stop future tripping.** Playing out negative scenarios that haven't happened increases your temptation to panic. When you panic you lose your ability to focus forward.

4. **Stay positive.** Focus on what you can control, focus forward, and focus on building momentum.

5. **Maintain leadership presence.** Draw on challenging times you've come through before and approach the situation with confident humility—as one who has been there before.

Composure and champagne pair well. During Boch's tenure the Giants had never lost a postseason series until playing the Cubs in the 2016 NLDS. His levelheaded demeanor does several things for his players: It frees them to think clearly and avoid feeling trapped or out of control when things aren't going well. His players aren't ruled by the emotional highs and lows of adversity. They have choices. They decide how they will react and this creates options. Power over their emotions gives them more power over the situation—a huge advantage when playing against more formidable competitors.

Boch's composure also eliminates unnecessary distractions and allows his players to stay focused, to be in the moment. Losing composure can take you off your game plan, and once you lose that, you become reactive, powerless, and distressed—hardly the conditions under which an athlete performs successfully.

> **When players decide how they will react it creates options.**

Perhaps most importantly, composure also gives Boch's players the freedom to fully access their physical skills and leverage their talents when they are needed most. They don't dwell on errors. They don't get bogged down in perfectionism. They learn, let go, and move on. They stay in the right frame of mind to step up their game when the pressure is on.

In the 2014 World Series, after the Royals trounced the Giants 10-0 in Game 6 and the series was tied at three games each, someone posted on Pinterest a poster with a serious-looking Boch that said, "Everybody just chill. I F*&#in got this." It was funny because of the irony—Boch would never be that cocky. It was also funny because it lampooned his calm demeanor.

Resolve—Press On

"Resolve" is the undeniable power of a mind made up. It means to be committed to a course of action. It's a deep sense of determination to not give in under intense pressure. When you take a hit and all seems impossible, resolve challenges you to ignore the odds and keep going. Resolve is an unwavering, inflexible, and inexhaustible will to win. You're up against a force to be reckoned with when you face an opponent with considerable resolve.

In 2010, Boch's boys played more games (115) decided by three or fewer runs than any other club in MLB. They learned that by jettisoning the self-shaming and self-defeating narrative of failure they could relax and get down to doing their best work. The intensity of those closely fought battles prepared them for all they stood to gain or lose in the postseason. Game 3 of the 2010 NLDS is a great example of the Giants resolve.

Going into that game, the Giants and the Braves were tied at a game each. The Giants had blown an opportunity to carry momentum into Atlanta's Turner Field and would now have to win at least one game to stay alive in the best-of-five series. Starter Jonathan Sánchez no-hit Atlanta through 5 ⅓ innings, and the Giants held a 1-0 lead going into the eighth.

With third baseman and right-handed hitter Troy Glaus in the on-deck circle, Boch went to Sergio Romo for a "righty" against "righty" matchup. Atlanta's manager, Bobby Cox, countered by bringing left-handed hitter Eric Hinske to hit for Glaus. Romo throws a 2-2 hanging slider and coughs up a Hinske right-field home run. And just like that, the Giants were behind 2-1 going into the top of the ninth. Braves fans were electrified.

As he sat in the dugout, teary-eyed with a towel draped over his head, Romo's disappointment was obvious. His teammates tried to pick him up by reminding him the game wasn't over yet. Even though they were about to face Craig Kimbrel, a 22-year-old rookie with unbelievable numbers, there was no sense of hopelessness and no panic—just a stubborn and relentless resolve to turn it around.

Kimbrel came into the game with 21 previous appearances and one earned run in 20 ⅔ innings while striking out 40. A phenomenal 0.44 ERA! Three outs away from digging a hole in Atlanta's house, Cody Ross popped out in the first at bat. Pinch-hitting for Romo, Travis Ishikawa hung tough and battled to draw a walk on a 3-2 pitch. With Kimbrel still dealing ferociously, center fielder Andrés Torres was called out on strikes. Two down.

Second baseman Freddy Sánchez, up next, watched as Ishikawa worked the count and told himself that *his* wasn't going to be the last out. Even so, Kimbrel pitched ahead in the count 0-2. One strike and it would be over. The Giants would have to win two games in a row—the first at Turner Field—to advance. A daunting task in the shorter NLDS.

Sánchez hit a single up the middle. With runners on first and second base, Kimbrel was replaced. Another rookie, lefty Michael Dunn, faced left-handed hitter Aubrey Huff, who hit a game-tying single to right field, scoring Ishikawa. The once jubilant crowd was silenced.

The stage was set for Buster Posey to face right-hander Peter Moylan. Posey hit a gettable grounder directly to Atlanta's second baseman Brooks Conrad, who had already made two errors in the game. The ball bounced through Conrad's legs and Sánchez scored from second base. The Giants led 3-2.

In the bottom of the ninth, Giants closer Brian Wilson gave up a two-out single and then retired Atlanta, giving the Giants a one-game lead in the Series.

> **Boch:** That one game told me so much about our guys. It showed me how far they were willing to go and how determined they were not to give in. Talk about believing in what you can do! These guys "believed!" I'm looking at what just happened, the passion and commitment they brought to this Series, and I'm thinking, "With this kind of gutsy resolve they could go all the way."
>
> We're backed into a corner, one out away from having to dig out of a two-game deficit—in *their* park. That's why I called them the "Dirty Dozen"; they were not going to be denied.
>
> And really, even though we had played a lot of nail-biters during the regular season, it's so many games like this during the postseason that have reinforced the perseverance of this club. Even with players who weren't here in 2010, I think they know the history, they've heard the stories, they know the lore, and it says, "This is who we are."

Resolve is like a muscle. When taxed and then given a chance to recover, it grows stronger. If you watched the Giants between 2010 and 2016, you know that the opportunities to grow this formidable force through one late inning victory after another have been ample. And here's what happens.

> **Resolve is the undeniable power of a mind made up.**

The more resolve you have, the more you come back in late innings. The more you come back, the more you see yourself as resilient and unyielding. The more resilient and unyielding you become, the more you come back. It's seems like circular logic, but it's also a powerful self-fulfilling prophecy that establishes a precedent. String enough precedents together and the expectation to bounce back is secured in everyone's psyche.

Even though the Giants won three World Series with mostly different rosters, several things were constant. A purposeful, identifiable culture of resilience with a Never Say Die mantra; a mental pattern of positive expectations versus doubt; and a CEO, GM, and manager who all believed in the value of promulgating that culture.

"Torture" has a silver lining and its name is resolve.

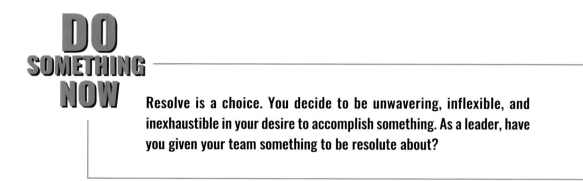

Resolve is a choice. You decide to be unwavering, inflexible, and inexhaustible in your desire to accomplish something. As a leader, have you given your team something to be resolute about?

Leaders Dispense Hope

When things go south in the course of a season, it's easy to get taken out by cynicism and skepticism. Yet these are the enemies of hope because they incite fear, and fear creates panic. As Boch points out, you can never play your best ball if you can't relax, and you can't relax if you live in fear.

Think about how Winston Churchill rallied a nation during World War II. Had he not been able to see beyond the dark clouds of war, had he not demonstrated the courage to inspire a nation, to stand firm in the midst of uncertainty and adversity, and had Hitler won the war, the world in which we now live might be a very different place.

Great leaders dispense hope. They make us realize how good we are. Their faith in us, in what we are capable of achieving, shapes and conditions the entire relationship. It is the electrical current that lights up a team and gives it life. Our faith is often a reflex response to their faith in us. Our composure under pressure reflects their calm. Our courage is their courage. We follow them into uncharted territory because their gut instincts have proven worthy of our trust. We rise to higher levels because their expectations of us say we can.

Hope is more powerful than any antidepressant on the market. It unleashes the will to fight and survive.

Hope is more powerful than any antidepressant on the market. It unleashes the will to fight and survive. In hope we find the courage to think big, act bold, speak firmly, and dare greatly. Hope stabilizes our runaway emotions and paves the way for a sense of calm. Hope cuts through discouragement and reaches for answers when solutions seem illusive. Hope opens us to possibility and inspires us to accept risk. Hope energizes and mobilizes us. And in doing all these things, hope stimulates resilience.

Leaders like Boch convincingly communicate a vision of a brighter future even when the immediate circumstances appear to be hopeless.

> **Boch:** Hope is not a strategy, but it *is* a powerful emotional asset that, when summoned, has pulled us out of some pretty dire situations. How do you hold on and overcome in so many come-from-behind scenarios without it?
>
> Without hope you lower your sights and stop reaching. Without hope you lose your will to engage and your motivation to make a contribution. Without hope you lose your ability to focus forward. You stop believing that your dream is still alive. Just because you can't measure it doesn't mean that it isn't pretty damn important.

Historically, when the World Series is tied and you lose Game 6, as the Giants did in 2014, you also lose Game 7. Boch knew this statistic well and even if he didn't, he certainly had plenty of media to remind him. But he never lost hope. He focused on the fact that there was one more game, stating that the best thing about Game 6 is that "we get to wash it off." Then he reminded his players about their past comebacks.

Without even knowing it, Boch was borrowing a problem-solving approach from the field of Appreciative Inquiry—the idea that you can solve problems by looking at similar problems or challenges you've solved in the past, not by identifying the root cause of a problem and then figuring out who's to blame. The latter is more of a traditional approach. Appreciative Inquiry challenges you to solve problems by asking questions such as: What elements were in play when we beat the odds then? What were we thinking? What brought us together? What worked? How did we confront the moment?

Questions like these inspire players to *remember themselves at their best* and then build on what they've *already* done that works. No pie-in-the-sky platitudes. The focus is on real strengths that have achieved *real* results. The focus is you, in a similar situation, performing well under pressure. When you are stuck, it's a hopeful and an energizing way to face a challenge. It has the potential to lift a team when it's down.

It is an understatement to say that during their participation in three World Series Championships in five years the Giants had a lot of practice navigating high-pressure situations. Each time they came back to win a crucial series it helped them get comfortable with being uncomfortable. It reinforced a collective consciousness that thinks, "We did it before; we can do it again."

Boch knew that since 1982, nine consecutive road teams had been beaten in Game 7 of the World Series. He knew that the Pittsburgh Pirates were the last road team to win Game 7 all the way back in 1979. He also knew that his club had the DNA to disrupt the odds. Wotus talked about Boch's speech before Game 7: "I've never seen a team love meetings, love inspiring each other, more. They're all good, but I think this was one of his best. I do."[66]

> **Boch:** I asked them to look back at 2012. A lot of people didn't think we had it in us to go deep [into the playoffs] then. But we did, and we did because this club knows how to let go and put things behind them. So, I wanted them to refresh their memories. We had come back against incredible odds before. I knew, and I wanted them to know that we could do it again.

This is what great leaders do. They rally people by disarming fear with the belief that things *will* get better. Leadership is about teaching people how to aspire and frequently reinforcing them for doing so. In the world of baseball, it's challenging players to push back against the prognosticators, soothsayers, cynics, and even their own demons of doubt to pursue their dreams. Hope helps our chances of success.

- Hope mobilizes. It moves us in the direction of our dreams.
- Hope challenges. It compels us to reach higher and bring more.
- Hope energizes. It inspires us to think in terms of possibilities, not limitations.
- Hope sustains. It summons us to get back up after taking a hit.
- Hope galvanizes. It draws people together.

Hope might not be a strategy, but it plays a critical role in growing resilience. Boch makes a good point. Perhaps we underestimate its power and take it for granted because we can't measure it. Or, maybe we think hope just happens. It's either there or it's not. In our collective opinion, hope is a choice—and a powerful one at that.

Boch shares something in common with all great leaders: he leaves nothing to chance. If he thinks something will help propel his club forward and he can influence the players, he will. As a dispenser of hope he has helped transform a clubhouse mindset from sacrifice and hopelessness to warrior-like survival and hope in some of the game's most difficult situations.

Composure. Resolve. Hope. In the Giants run up to three World Championships, the challenges they faced, no matter how daunting, rarely transcended the power of these three virtues. If we could peer inside the collective spirit of this club when things aren't going well, there, just below the surface of all that concentration we see on television, are players who don't panic, who can take a hit and recover, and who have the courage to dig deep and press on when all seems lost.

These are three more reasons why the Giants win under great pressure and after a loss remain calm, die-hard believers.

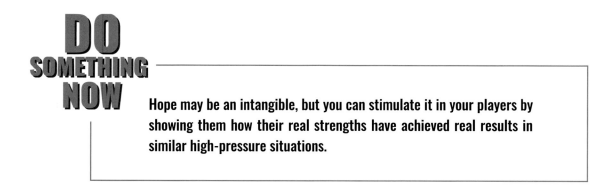

DO SOMETHING NOW

Hope may be an intangible, but you can stimulate it in your players by showing them how their real strengths have achieved real results in similar high-pressure situations.

18
EXPECT TO WIN
Refuse to Play Small

In November 2011, Brian Sabean traded the talented but erratic starter Jonathan Sánchez and the minor league pitcher Ryan Verdugo to the Royals for the switch-hitting left fielder Melky Cabrera.

Cabrera wasted no time validating Sabean's decision with a legendary start: On May 30, 2012, he tied Randy Winn's San Francisco record for the most hits (51) in any month; he earned a starting role in the 2012 All-Star Game; and he hit out of this world for most of the summer. Melky was an offensive rock star. He instantly became a fan favorite, inspiring the creation of the "Melk Men," a group of guys dressed in white pants, pressed white shirts, white caps, and orange bowties who were a throwback to the *real* early-twentieth-century milkmen. These fans garnered the attention of a packed house during games and were even periodically seen with "Melk Maids." When San Francisco fans become fond of a player, he becomes family.

The Melk Men became a crowd favorite during Melky Cabrera's time with the Giants.

In the months prior to mid-August 2012, due to injuries and slumps, Boch had reconfigured his lineup on an almost daily basis. While the constant juggling act is what Boch does best, he was thrilled to get back to normal, if there is such a thing in baseball.

Boch: Finally, on August 14, with Pablo [Sandoval] back [from a hamstring injury], the lineup included every regular starter for the first time. It was a thing of beauty. It had everything: power, speed, great defense. [Mario] Scutaro was hitting out of his mind. Buster Posey, after missing almost all of 2011 with a devastating injury, was having an MVP year. Melky Cabrera had been the MVP of the All-Star Game and was leading the league in hitting. Our young guys, Brandon Crawford and Brandon Belt, had matured into true major league starters. Ángel Pagán had become the leadoff hitter we needed. Now we had all of them on the field at the same time.

I loved writing that lineup. I thought, "OK, we're going to win this thing [NL West.]"[67]

The very next day—August 15—Melky Cabrera was suspended for 50 games for using performance-enhancing drugs. What? Are you kidding? The Giants were in a heated battle with the Dodgers for the NL West. Cabrera was hitting .346 and now this?

Boch found out about the suspension after filling out his lineup card, which included Cabrera, a few hours before San Francisco's series finale against the Nationals.

> **Boch:** Just like that, our best hitter was gone for the season—a particularly devastating loss in light of the Dodgers acquiring slugger Hanley Ramírez two weeks earlier.[68]

So much for the club's "Melk Men" T-shirt giveaway planned for September, and in the view of many, so much for the Giants hopes of getting into the postseason. That night the Giants lost to the Nationals and dropped a game to the Dodgers in the NL West. The entire incident felt like contending for the checkered flag at the Daytona 500 and then blowing a tire with just two laps to go.

Over all the years we've known Boch, he has never entered a season where he didn't expect to win—no matter what hand he was dealt. He's never had a game where his boys got smoked and not said, "Tomorrow's a new day; learn from this and shake it off."

Prevailing in adversity is a choice. Where you aim your energy and direct your attention moves you either toward what you want or away from it. You can choose to relive past injustices, nurse old wounds, and ruminate on the problem. You can play the worst-case scenario over and over again in your head, calculate the odds, and prepare for your imminent destruction.

That's one approach.

Or, you can choose to spend more time thinking about solutions and making your problems more manageable. You can look for the good in others and appreciate them more. You can imagine the possibilities of a positive future, elevating hope and feeding resilience.

Your future isn't in the rearview mirror. Don't give yesterday the power to define tomorrow.

That's a different approach. That's the approach Melky's teammates took after his suspension. They chose to prevail.

The Melk's All Gone

When Melky was suspended, the mood inside the clubhouse was one of shock and disappointment. It was almost surreal, as in, "This didn't really just happen, did it?" When Cabrera left his locker and equipment in place and just disappeared without saying a word to his teammates, their disappointment deepened. Sabean called it a gut punch, but then he added, "We've got a survival instinct . . . and [guys] who don't lack for character."

Sabes was right. The players chose to focus forward. Instead of asking, "Why is this happening to us?" or condemning Cabrera for his action, his teammates took a different tack and asked, "What do we want the outcome of this scenario to look like, and what can we, each one of us, do to move the team toward that picture now?"

As Sergio Romo recalled, "Buster was one of the voices in the clubhouse who helped us move on from Melky Cabrera's suspension."

You look at what Melky meant to the team. We were in playoff contention with him leading us—and then he's gone, just like that. It definitely hurt.

We understood Melky's absence had an effect on the team, but there's a reason we call it a "team." It's not built around one guy. Losing Melky wasn't the end of us. It was right around then when we'd gotten [Hunter] Pence, and he wanted to do so much for the team. You looked at the guys trying to fill Melky's gap, and you realized we had enough. You realized we'd be OK, because we never quit.[69]

"We are a team," Sandoval said. "We're going to fight." Pence, who had been with the team for only two weeks, was resolute. "It happened, and now we move on." Pagán, one of Cabrera's closest friends on the team, said, "We believe in what we have here."

Instead of ruminating on the problem, they reminded each other that there was something still worth fighting for. Instead of making Cabrera the scapegoat for a season lost, each player looked in the mirror and said, "We have it within ourselves to do this."

Instead of focusing on their weakness and bemoaning, "It can't be done without our best hitter," they chose to say, "We all have to hit better." They made every pitch count. Hitters were more patient, working the count to get on base. They got gritty, tightened the defense, and truly came together.

Think about it. You've been through the dog days of the season. Your guys are physically tired yet emotionally jacked up because they are in contention. Then, BAM! A devastating blow. At this point, your team has only a certain amount of energy, time, and talent to use each day. If you focus on what went wrong, what isn't working and what could've happened but didn't, you grow negative, cynical, and helpless. Can you hear that huge sucking sound? That's the energy and enthusiasm being drained out of a team that thinks like this.

> Instead of asking, "Why is this happening to us?" the players asked a different question: "What do we want the outcome of this scenario to look like, and what can we do to move the team toward that picture now?"

If you focus on what's right, what is working and how it *can* happen—even though a piece of the dream has been shattered—you build momentum and create opportunity because you become more hopeful, positive, and self-reliant.

The Giants were *victims* of what Posey called "a bad decision." Cabrera's choice affected the entire organization. But the players refused to be *victimized*, and each time they chose not to be victimized they boosted their resilience and catalyzed the chemistry of a winning team.

Boch: This is where Sabes and his entire team get all the credit in the world. If they don't hire men of character, as well as great ballplayers, we're screwed in a situation like this. It can unravel very quickly. You've got to have guys who are bigger than the situation, who can rise above it, pull together, and prevail.

Sabes has such an instinctive feel for finding these types of players. When I'm trying to do damage control, particularly in the throes of a heated battle for the playoffs, I can't tell you how much I appreciate that this is one of his priorities.

A lot has been said about Brian's architecture, about bringing in the right guy at the right time, and that's true. But the quality and the character of the guys he brings into this club has been a critical factor in our success.

The Giants could have let this scenario spawn the kind of defensiveness that drives a wedge between players. They didn't. Instead, they became more accountable to each other and engaged in the kind of collaboration that made them a force to be reckoned with.

The Giants played their best ball of the season after Cabrera's suspension. They took five of six games against the Padres and the Dodgers, including a sweep of Los Angeles in their house that put them back in first place. They split a four-game series with Atlanta and then swept Houston. In September, after winning six games in a row, including a sweep of Colorado, the Giants clinched the NL West on September 22 with 10 games left in the season. A dazzling finish under any circumstances.

> **Sometimes, due to circumstances outside your control, you are a victim. But you always have a choice about whether or not you will be victimized.**

Sabean puts it this way: "A wise baseball man a long time ago said you don't pick your time; the time picks you. Then it's a matter of how opportunistic you are to take advantage of it. Behind the ingenuity and leadership of Bruce Bochy, this team turned all the adversities into opportunities. Each time they were slapped in the face, they decided they were going to overcome it."[70]

Buster's Devastating Blow

Early in the 2011 season, the Giants had been dealt another such crushing blow in the last game of a series against the Florida Marlins. A horrible home plate collision with Scott Cousins sent catcher Buster Posey out of the game. At the time, no one knew for sure how bad Posey's injury was, but ballplayers are smart, and the longer you've been around, the more you know. This was serious.

This was the Buster Posey who came into the majors with a leadership presence that was years ahead of his résumé. In Game 4 of the 2010 World Series against the Rangers, Posey and Madison Bumgarner were the first rookie battery since 1947 to start a World Series game. MadBum pitched eight shutout innings and Posey hit his first World Series home run, putting the Giants up 3-1 in the Series. Posey caught every inning of the 2010 playoffs and was the first rookie catcher to win a World Series in more than 40 years. He was also named National League Rookie of the Year. Composure, poise, attack, and smarts behind the plate, Posey was the whole package.

The Giants flew to Milwaukee after being swept by the Marlins at AT&T Park. The next day the hangover in the clubhouse was palpable. With a fractured fibula and all three ligaments in his ankle torn completely through, Posey was out for the season. His 2012 season would be uncertain as well. Hushed tones, shared sobriety, and dejection filled the air. Losing a star player was bad enough, but everyone was concerned about Buster's well-being. When you've just lost a player everyone loves, and you can't control the future, you feel helpless. And yet, the season goes on, and there was a lot of baseball left to play.

Boch knew he needed to say something to acknowledge what everyone was feeling and help his guys rise above this calamity. Here is the gist of what he said in the clubhouse before the Giants first game against the Brewers.

Boch: Well, it's no news to anyone in this room that we limped out of San Francisco. And, there isn't anyone in this room who doesn't feel the loss of Buster. I'm angry. I'm sad. I'm frustrated. I'm shocked! What happened to him is unbelievably tragic.

But if you know Buster, you know this isn't final. He will bounce back from this. He will go into rehab with a vengeance. He will bring the same fire in the belly and determination to getting back behind the plate as he has to helping this club win a World Championship.

He WILL bounce back from this!

(Boch knew Posey's character well and believed deeply in the star catcher's resilience, but he had no way of knowing how prophetic those words would be. Posey *did* come back, with a vengeance.)

And he's going to expect us to bounce back from it as well. In fact, knowing him, he's going to expect us to widen the gap and get into the postseason so that he has a shot at joining us before it's all over.

The bad news is, our offense has been anemic and we've lost a key member of the "Dirty Dozen." The good news is, in spite of it all, we are still leading the division. Imagine what can happen when we start clicking. Imagine what can happen when we get back to the swagger that earned us a world title.

Guys, it's in us, but it's got to come out of us.

Look, we're in a game where you can't control everything that happens out there. But how we respond to what happens out there, how we approach what happens out there is our choice.

Right now, our mettle is being tested. So, we get to choose how we are going respond. We can find the "Dirty Dozen" again. We can disrupt the critics' expectations and we can give our teammate Buster a shot at coming back.

Or, we can tuck and run and let this accident deaden the fight in us. But let's be clear here. This team has never shown a propensity to tuck and run—backing down and giving in is not who we are. Let me tell you who we are:

- *We don't waste time ruminating.* What's happened has happened. Don't dwell on it. I need you to focus forward—on the next play, the next at bat, the next inning. I need your head in the here and now. Let's focus forward on what we set out to achieve this year.

- *We see limitations as opportunities.* Limitations don't have to be limiting—they can be a springboard to a more creative approach. In our case it's going to give some players an opportunity to play new positions—but that isn't foreign to us.

- *We understand the power of chemistry.* As we shake things up and move people around, I need you to go back to the unorthodox moves we made last year. We asked people to play different roles at different times. And each time, you guys stepped into the breach and got it done. Not once did I have a player crawl into a hole and quit because we moved him around.

Let's go back and draw from that well. Let's come together and focus on what we *can* control, on what we want to see happen.

Every baseball season, just like every season in life, is filled with moments of adversity where a team can focus forward and assume ownership for the outcome it desires or it can get stuck in the jaws of disappointment. But here's the thing: Players get to choose.

Choosing to meet adversity head-on isn't easy. Betrayal, as in the case of Melky Cabrera—intended or not—hurts. Losing a prominent and beloved player like Posey hurts. Choosing to get gritty and bounce back doesn't gloss over the pain—it's not about denial. Cabrera's suspension sucked. Posey's injury was devastating. Choosing to follow the team's Never Say Die motto means facing the brutal facts of reality and then deciding how you're going to handle it.

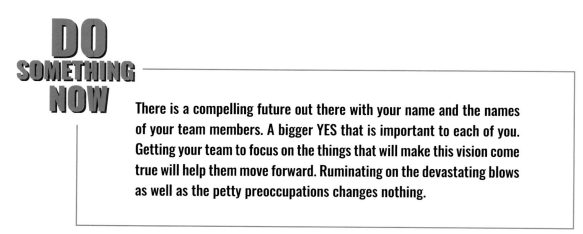

There is a compelling future out there with your name and the names of your team members. A bigger YES that is important to each of you. Getting your team to focus on the things that will make this vision come true will help them move forward. Ruminating on the devastating blows as well as the petty preoccupations changes nothing.

Sure, misery loves company, but there is no chemistry in complaining about things you can't control. Wallowing in your weakness doesn't build momentum. There is no ROI in self-pity. And, casting blame—whether at Melky Cabrera or Scott Cousins —changes nothing.

Change Your Thinking, Change Your Performance

Yogi Berra famously said, "Baseball is 90 percent mental; the other half is physical." Boch has always felt that one of his major challenges is to get better and better at managing that 90 percent. How a team thinks, what its players say to themselves, and how those players feel will have a dramatic effect on that team's day-to-day performance. And since the baseball season is so long, players have a lot of time to think.

Like every sport and every business, the world of baseball is filled with setbacks and failures, breakthroughs and triumphs. The tide can turn and the momentum can shift numerous times in a game, let alone a season. In this topsy-turvy world, nothing so impacts a club's ability to weather the emotional and psychological roller-coaster ride as the way players collectively choose to explain and interpret events that make up the game.

Choosing how you "frame" the situation is a skill that can be learned. In baseball, you can't script the unexpected turning points in a game, but you can choose how you explain them—to yourself and others. For example, some players let bad events contaminate everything they do. A bad game might affect their marriage, relationships with other players, eating or spending habits, and level of community engagement. Other players compartmentalize their problems neatly into a box so that they won't affect every other part of their lives.

Boch: With such a long season there are plenty of opportunities for things to go wrong. But you have to keep the bad events in perspective. A bad series is simply a bad series, not the end of the season; a tough meeting with a coach is a tough meeting, not a career-limiting event; a conflict with a teammate is a misunderstanding, not a collapse of chemistry in the clubhouse.

Future Hall of Fame closer Trevor Hoffman played for Boch with the Padres for 15 years. Hoffy was the first player to reach the 600-saves milestone and he ranks second (601 saves) behind Mariano Rivera in all-time saves (652).

Boch: Hoffy had a ritual after every game he pitched in. He'd take 5-10 minutes in the dugout after it was cleared to reflect on his performance. Was his strategy sound? Did he have the right read on the hitter? When he failed to execute, why? When he located the ball perfectly, what made it work? By going over it mentally, he had a focus both for what he would reinforce and what he would do differently in the next game.

Then, particularly with a bad outing or blown save (there weren't many), he let it go. He just had a remarkable ability to compartmentalize it. I'm not saying it was easy for him. He worked at it. He practiced learning from it and then putting it away. It was like he flipped a mental switch. That discipline is why he became one of the greatest closers in the game.

Hoffy had something in common with my good friend [Hall of Famer] Goose Gossage, who really was part of pioneering the role of the closer; they both have short memories.

Work on What You Can Control

America's favorite pastime is full of bad hops. You never know when a player is going to go down due to an injury. You think a key player's rehab is going to be three weeks; instead it takes six. You thought you were going to acquire a world-class pitcher; now you will have to face him. For the third time, the team plane sits on the tarmac for an hour and a half waiting for the club's equipment to be loaded; the players are irritated. The umpire's strike zone is so inconsistent that both pitchers have trouble executing their game plans. A 10-game losing streak causes the entire team to question whether or not the skid is unbreakable.

When adversity strikes, how much control does a player or a team perceive it has over the cause of it? Working on what you can control is an *inside-out* approach. Inside-out means that you choose to be the cause, not the effect. You "own" the things you can change. To be the *cause* of something is to "put it out there," to put a stake in the ground and be a positive influence. You may not control when or how adversity comes to you, but you *can* control how you react to it. To be the *effect* is to be reactive, to passively live with adversity—accept it as it is.

Coaches and players alike can encourage each other to focus on what they can control with statements like these:

- **"I'm not going to change the dimensions of a hitter's ballpark, so I'm going to change my strategy."**
- **"I can't change the fact that we just lost seven games in a row, but I can talk to the guys about eliminating the negative self-talk in the clubhouse."**
- **"I can't change the fact that the World Series comes down to a final Game 7 in *their* house. What has happened has happened—it's history. But I can do everything I can to sincerely and authentically remind them that they have Championship Blood."**

Inside-out suggests that if you want to engender a warrior spirit in your team, they need to see it in you first. It's a Hunter Pence stepping up when the Giants are seemingly down for the count and generating positive energy by asking for "one more day." If you want them to maintain their composure in the most intense of battles, they can't see you panic.

To work on what you can control is to get in the game, to be fully engaged, and, when shit hits the fan, to ask, "What can I do right here, right now to raise hope, strengthen resolve, and build our resilience?" This requires a different point of view, a sense of conviction that you have something valuable to offer, and the guts to try—even when you *feel* the same discouragement and despair as others do. If you think about how intimidating a pitcher is or how many times you've been thrown out when stealing second base, you're focused on something you can't control. This intensifies the pressure, unleashes your anxiety, and short-circuits you physically and psychologically.

During clutch moments in crucial games, the Giants have succeeded by drawing contributions from a wide array of players—often from players you would least expect. Why is that? It's because the players, coaches, and trainers believe that in times of adversity it does no good to complain about conditions and circumstances they can't control. If the game is going to change, that change starts with taking ownership. Their thinking goes like this: "I'm going to focus my attention and direct my energy on assuming responsibility for propelling the team forward. So, how can I become more resourceful, creative, collaborative, or proactive in making something good happen?"

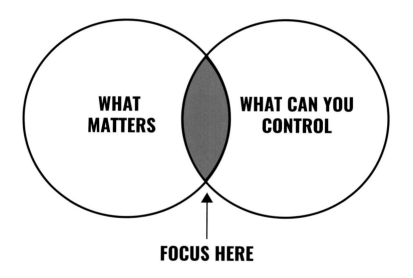

Adapted from a graphic by Carl Richards. If making complex financial concepts simple is one definition of elegance, Carl might be the most elegant guy we know.

Wallowing in worry, focusing on the things you're concerned about but have no control over is an *outside-in* approach. It essentially means that things outside of your control must change before your situation changes. Being convinced that the cause of adversity is *out there*—in another player, a coach or an umpire, an agent or a sponsor—disempowers a player from changing the game. If enough players choose this mindset, it depletes resilience in the entire team.

> **Boch:** We are known for shaking things up quite a bit. With the number of injuries we've had over the years we've had to be creative. Sometimes that means asking a player to step into a role that might be uncomfortable. The players who make these transitions most effectively are the ones who say, "It might not be where I am most comfortable, but I'm going to do everything in my power to learn what I can and master this position." They take control, which translates into playing aggressively versus tentatively, and usually end up exceeding their expectations.

When things go bad, it's not that the players pretend they aren't frustrated, angry, or disappointed, it's that they have subordinated these feelings to a sense of responsibility. Blaming the umpire, the ballpark, another player, or a coach shifts the responsibility to something or someone they can't control. It changes nothing.

Boch tries to help his players develop the discipline to take one of two approaches. Either they ignore the things they cannot do anything about—that is, simply don't let things outside their control take up too much mental space. Or they concentrate on bringing things outside their control into their control. It starts with asking, "Right now, at this moment, given this situation, am I focused on something I can control or obsessing over something I can't control?"

> **Boch:** We all do it [focus on things you can't control], but it's counterproductive. I've told our guys: "If you focus on how good a pitcher is or how many times you've been hit by an opposing hitter, you're focused on something you can't control. If you're focused on things you can't change, you empower those things to control you. Do you really want an umpire in charge of your performance? Are you really going to let another player determine your attitude? That's giving up a lot of control unnecessarily. Now you're mentally putting the outcome of the game in the hands of someone else."

> If we're focused on how difficult it is to pitch in Denver because the ball carries so well at altitude, it's wasted energy. We're not going to change that. Do we account for that in our strategy? Sure. But if that's a pitcher's focus, he's just disempowered himself because he's shifted the responsibility to the environment instead of focusing on his own responsibilities.

Working on what you can control energizes you to become more resourceful and action-oriented. This creates options, options create freedom, and freedom has a way of amplifying strengths and enlarging talents. When you perceive you have some control over unwelcomed events, you take more initiative. Instead of psychologically checking out and quitting, you act.

> **Boch:** I think we've come out of so many nasty situations because our players have a gritty resolve. They just believe that there is always something that can be done to change the momentum of a game or a series. They've proved it too many times.

> We've talked about this during crucial games. When you go into the other team's house in a playoff series, especially in places like Pittsburgh or Philly, you're in a hostile environment. You're not going to control the crowd. But we can get so locked and loaded on each pitch, each at bat, that the crowd fades into the distance.

> Our guys are either focused on the outcome—winning or losing—or on each and every play that puts you in the win column. Winning takes care of itself if you focus on competing.

> I've told our guys: "Focusing on the things you can control keeps you from getting desperate or hitting the panic button. It gives you the ability to relax and keeps you from pressing too much."

> Our players have demonstrated tremendous composure in tough games primarily because they are so focused on what they must be doing in any given moment. That leaves them little space for thinking about the things they can't control. Part of the Never Say Die motto is the belief that there is always a way to get back in a game.

Here's what's ironic. The more action you take, the more empowered you become and the more control you have. By working on the things you can control—namely, your attitude, mindset, energy, and effort—you begin to have an impact on the conditions, circumstances, and people you can't control. As you bring more of these things under your control, it raises your confidence, expands your influence, and gives you the determination to persist when adversity comes calling.

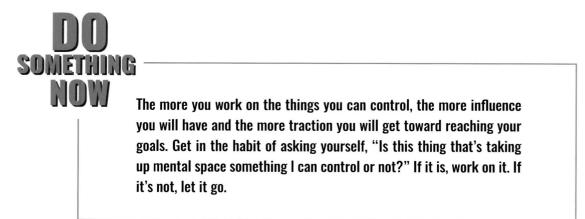

DO SOMETHING NOW

The more you work on the things you can control, the more influence you will have and the more traction you will get toward reaching your goals. Get in the habit of asking yourself, "Is this thing that's taking up mental space something I can control or not?" If it is, work on it. If it's not, let it go.

Working on what you can control means that you have to look past obvious limitations and constraints to see possibilities and alternatives. It's not easy. Like any skill, it takes practice. As with resilience, it is a muscle: the more you use it, the stronger it becomes. Make working on what you can control a priority and eventually it becomes a habit that can inoculate a player and immunize a team from hopelessness and helplessness.

In the 2010 NLCS against Philadelphia, outfielder Cody Ross hit .350. That means that 65 percent of his at bats failed. Yet, he eventually was named the MVP of the series.

Acquired from the Marlins on a waiver claim, Ross went from sitting atop baseball's scrap heap to becoming a major reason why the Giants made it to the World Series. That same year the Giants lost 70 regular season games and then came back to win it all. This just doesn't happen without the mental toughness to step out of your emotions, apply reason, and challenge your assumptions about what is not possible.

> **Boch:** The thing I want our players to understand is that they always have a choice about how and where they are going to focus. Good times, bad times, they get to decide how they are going to process what happens in a game or a series. Dwelling on the things that upset you, but you cannot control, only puts you further out of control. It only makes you more helpless and that creates a hopeless scenario.

Perceived control builds resilience. Players who work on what they can control—who choose to prevail—approach the game in terms of how they can proactively handle the flow of events. They are more likely to take action to improve bad situations rather than worry about them. They are also more immune to depression and better able to bounce back from adversity.

All of this not only gives a team a mental edge, it also builds chemistry because these very same principles, when applied to interpersonal relationships among teammates, help players manage and move through conflict more productively. A team that breeds candor and authenticity, yet constructively manages tension in the clubhouse, becomes more unified.

19
WARRIOR SPIRIT
Fierceness, Swagger, and Will

A warrior on the battlefield has a heightened sense of finality because the inevitability of death is always lurking over the horizon. Every day you step into combat you know it could be your last, so you make every minute, every day, and every decision count. With death in the vicinity, you have an acute level of awareness—clarity of mind, if you will—that summons you to seize the moment. Every training exercise matters. The skills you acquire are crucial. Your integrity can't be questioned. You must be accountable. And the quality of communication between you and your comrades must be frequent and flawless.

Although what unfolds on a baseball field can't be compared to the threats and sacrifices made on a battlefield, a similar spirit does prove invaluable on both. The metaphor of a warrior vividly communicates what Boch is trying to instill in his players. A warrior spirit is a mindset, a way of approaching your work.

> **Boch:** Every player who makes it to this level is competitive, but one thing that separates players at this level is fierceness. You can see it in the way they prepare physically and mentally, the focus they have, the calm before the storm, and the aggressiveness they bring to the game. It's an offensive attack that's always bringing it to the other team instead of reacting when they bring it to you.
>
> If we can awaken that ferociousness in our guys and connect it to playing for a larger cause, a very special thing happens. A warrior spirit starts to permeate the clubhouse. Sometimes I call it swagger. You read about warriors of old before going into battle. It's not a cocky or macho thing; it's almost a stoic, steely-eyed resolve that says: "We're going to do whatever it takes to get this done. Anything less, is unacceptable. Never say die!"
>
> I don't know how else to describe it. Every time we've come through, when we should've been down and out, I could see the warrior spirit in our guys.

Warriors Dare Greatly

Warriors relish a tough situation. They lean into doing the hard thing. Human and flawed, warriors don't wait to be "perfect and bulletproof" before entering the arena. When others back down, warriors have both the vulnerability and the courage to say: *I want in! Give me the ball. Let's go!* Think Madison Bumgarner. Considered the best postseason pitcher in the game right now—and maybe ever—he owns October baseball.

Chicago Cubs manager Joe Maddon recognized that in Bumgarner there's something more than his pitches. He unabashedly compared Bum to the likes of the greatest pitchers in the game. "It's not just purely his stuff. It's his competitive nature. I think that's what gets lost in this a lot, with what we do. Everybody's always analyzing numbers and pitches and how he does this and spin rotation and whatever. This guy competes. That's what sets him apart. It's not that his stuff is that special. It's really good. But how he competes is what sets him apart."[71]

When way behind in a game, down in a series, or facing elimination, the Giants have developed a warrior-like way of interpreting the overwhelming circumstances. They feed on the challenge, not the threat. Being down and then overcoming insurmountable odds is a rush; and neuroscientists confirm that it's a dopamine rush. When you achieve something big, when the success is significant, your brain releases chemical rewards— "good drugs"—into your body. One of these is the neurotransmitter dopamine.

When you take the first sip of your favorite coffee in the morning or the first bite of chocolate with a great glass of red wine, or when you do what no one thinks you can do in a late inning ball game, dopamine is responsible for the pleasurable sensation. The more pleasurable the sensation, the more we want to repeat the behaviors that created it. This is why dopamine is well-known for the role it plays in addiction. But it can also play a role in resilience.

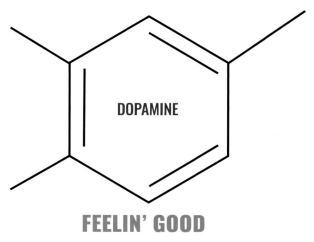

DOPAMINE

FEELIN' GOOD

Here's the thing about the dopamine response: it's not short-lived! The brain remembers it and anticipates it. Time after torturous time, when the Giants come from behind to win, something is going on inside the brains of the players and the fans. It's the thrill of being in a tight situation you've been in many times before and anticipating the dopamine buzz you will have if you succeed again.

Giants broadcaster Duane Kuiper made this observation when "torture" baseball ended with the Giants winning the World Series in 2010. "But it's funny how all the people were saying, 'This is killing me! This is too much!' Now those same people come up to me and say, 'We miss it! Life is boring! I need some more torture!'"[72] For fans, baseball is an experience, a pastime. When the ride is flat and unexciting, it's not memorable, and it sure isn't entertainment. When the ride is wild, it enriches us, invigorates us, and it unites us.

The dopamine buzz intensifies a player's resolve and the fans' hope. It entices both to keep battling, to be resilient. This might explain why the Giants often thrive in tight situations. The biochemical high that comes either from watching your teammates do something spectacular to change the momentum of a game or from making the extraordinary play that contributes to your teammates' joy when a game turns around is a good kind of addiction.

> **Boch:** Would we prefer to go into the second half of a game with a comfortable lead? Of course. I've got enough gray hairs. But if that doesn't happen, our guys don't dread the moment; they embrace it. By embracing the pressure, they make it fun. And by making it fun, they become more energized, think more clearly, and act with greater confidence.

When Boch's players see a deficit as a challenge, not a defeat, it changes the collective attitude of the team. Rather than being embarrassed or dejected by the hole they've dug, it becomes a defiant quest to beat the odds, prove the soothsayers wrong, and make the heroic comeback. They don't lose hope; they stay motivated. They don't succumb to helplessness; they dig deep and expect to find the meaningful contribution. They don't check out or back down; they step up and "dare greatly."

It's easy to be an armchair coach, a sideline critic. But critics don't create. They don't face hitters and pitchers; they don't chase down balls and score RBIs. They aren't on the field making the split-second decisions that win and lose ball games.

Critics have the luxury of hindsight when they analyze, deconstruct, and expose the flaws of those who stumble. But to a warrior, critics are of little consequence. They don't determine the strength of a warrior's

Rowdy, loud, and passionately engaged, Giants fans also bring a warrior spirit to the park.

resolve or the heroic nature of the cause for which he or she fights. Had the Giants paid attention to the critics each time they were considered down and out or in a funk, there would not be three World Series trophies proudly displayed at AT&T Park.

Warriors aren't bystanders. They're in the game, fully engaged, courageously stepping into uncertainty, knowing that they are exposing themselves physically and emotionally. Think Jake Peavy stretched out, throwing himself headfirst into first base to tag out a runner.

Warriors have a sense of conviction and confidence that they have something valuable to offer the team. If they see an opportunity to make the team better or they are outraged by the broken status quo, they speak up. They stand for something. They have a point of view about how to rally the team and make it better. Think Hunter Pence giving an epic speech after only being with his teammates for two months.

If you're playing with all your energy and effort in a game where you fail more than you succeed, you will stumble. For example, if you swing with swagger and conviction at the plate, you will miss the ball. If you take a risk and speak up in the clubhouse, your message might not resonate with everyone. If you are getting out of the comfort zone, reaching beyond what you think you can grasp, you will make mistakes. Warriors "bring it" anyway.

It's easy to be strong when you flourish; the real test is in being strong when the chips are down. Somewhere in the 2010 run-up to the World Series, the Giants dug deep and learned how to be strong when winning was elusive. They recognized it, defined it as a tremendous asset, and owned it. From that point on, an ethic of resilience started to take shape. With each successive trial the club has endured, and this temperament has been strengthened and fortified.

Faces sweaty, hands dirty, bodies bloody and bruised, warriors are more afraid of regret than they are of failure. They find a way to pick themselves up and keep going because what they fight for is so compelling. And each time they do, they expand their capacity to be braver more often. This is the story of the 2010, 2012, and 2014 Giants. They played for something beyond themselves. They played for each other. Each time they got knocked down they got up because the warrior playing next to them depended on them. Each time they rose they walked taller, became bigger, and exuded more confidence in each other.

Warriors don't play it safe. They refuse to play "small" because cautious, metered, and reluctant doesn't win battles. Warriors live dangerously because they don't want to live in the lukewarm water of neither enjoying nor suffering much. And even if they lose, they do so with dignity, knowing they've left everything on the field.

Warriors Are Determined

Common to every successful entrepreneur, a powerful movement, or a healthy, long-term marriage is a warrior spirit—people who refused to give up. They were determined to make it work. When faced with limitations, unexpected setbacks, fierce opposition, or disappointment, warriors step on the gas and become even more determined to achieve what they envision.

A warrior's determination often shows up as ambition. Ambition ignites the internal fire to go into battle. Ambition drives a warrior to train because he or she knows that confidence—and ultimately survival—comes from competence. If you want to stay alive on the battlefield or the playing field, you get better. One person's ambition challenges others to reach higher, raising the tide for the entire team. NBA great and former U.S. Senator Bill Bradley put it this way: "Ambition is the path to success. Persistence is the vehicle you arrive in." Ambition is what gets you out of bed in the morning.

> **Boch:** I think ambition has gotten a bum rap. I'm unapologetic about looking for ambition in our players. Not selfish ambition, but the kind of ambition that won't take "no" for an answer. When you're ambitious you work harder and hustle more because you want it more than the other team does. You endure more hardships. And, you bounce back faster because that ambition is driving you to get up and go again.

Ambition is often thought of as a negative word, but look at some of our most iconic world leaders. Winston Churchill's ambition and defiance saved England from Hitler's invasion. Mother Teresa was an ambitious warrior for the poor. If she hadn't been, how could she have created a movement that changed the world? Nelson Mandela and Desmond Tutu brought murderers and victims together for the cause of reconciliation. That's pretty ambitious. And in San Francisco, if it hadn't been for Larry Baer's ambition, the Giants would likely be playing in Tampa, under another name.

Warriors think "win" and, accordingly, act aggressively. Being a warrior is about being so committed to the cause you're fighting for, and being so prepared to face the challenge, that you have the confidence to meet your opponent on any level. When your life and the lives of others are on the line, your training is never complete: you are constantly pushing boundaries so that your skills become second nature, and you can never know enough about your enemy's strategy and tactics. In other words, you can never get comfortable. Warriors train harder than they expect to perform. Ironically, this kind of discipline enables a warrior to relax, think clearly, and move with speed and accuracy.

Boch is fond of saying "We never do anything easy" when referring to the many come-from-behind victories the Giants have had over the years. But those hard-fought battles have established a type of boot camp or proving ground that has given the Giants an opportunity to integrate their psychological and physical skills in a real-life setting—to actively train the warrior mindset Boch talks about so passionately.

Closer Brian Wilson's warrior spirit inspired the phrase "Fear the Beard."

> **Boch:** When I think about the players I've coached that have a warrior spirit, they all have one thing in common. They're never satisfied making it to the big leagues. They're not comfortable being a starter on a major league club; they want to be the best in the game. They aim extremely high and keep looking past the next milestone, yet they keep it real. There's no shame in not accomplishing 100 percent of your goal if you are reaching for it all.
>
> But because of this mindset they relish the battle. They want in because the battle is where you hone your skills; the battle is where you train yourself to handle the pressure, and the better you handle it the further you go. When our opponents attack, our guys don't lie down; they attack the attack. The battle is where you find out how much of a warrior you really are.

Most every ballplayer comes to the majors with talent and a sophisticated knowledge of the game. But, as Boch explained, not everyone has the determination to push through the physical, mental, emotional, and spiritual challenges of a long season. Not everyone has what it takes to throw down the gauntlet in the dog days of summer when all their faculties are being taxed. But this is what warriors do; this is what makes a true warrior extraordinary. The warrior says, "I will put myself on the line for you and for the cause we share." Warriors draw on every fume in the gas tank to focus their concentration, carry their weight, and be accountable to their teammates. They embody the Spartan philosophy of "bring back your shield or be carried back on it."

Warriors Are Decisive

Warriors act. Warriors intervene. Warriors are decisive. If the need or problem is worth fighting for, if the opportunity is big enough, they don't hesitate to rise to the occasion and take action. In the absence of clear direction or in the midst of uncertainty, warriors take charge.

Indecisiveness, hesitation, and timidity get people killed on a battlefield. On a baseball field it's not so dramatic, but you *do* lose. Decisiveness isn't random. It comes from being prepared, mapping out scenarios, studying video, and knowing the strengths and weaknesses of your opponent. In the heat of battle, warriors can't afford the luxury of overthinking it, of wondering what to do. They can't let the fear of making the wrong decision paralyze them. And they certainly can't wait for certainty to reveal itself before they decide because it never will.

> **Boch:** I've got to think, "One moment's loss of concentration in combat could mean your life." Obviously, the stakes are different in baseball, but to me, players with a warrior spirit are intensely engaged in every moment of the game. They've thought through every move they will make if the ball comes to them. So, when the time comes, the reaction is instinctive and proactive. They're decisive because if they hesitate they are going to get beat.

The same holds true for the interplay between a catcher and a pitcher. A catcher has to bear down on a hitter with a game plan that efficiently exposes his weaknesses. Once the catcher makes a decision, a pitcher has to unhesitatingly execute on that plan. If there is a collective level of decisiveness between them, a couple of things can happen. Opponents will sense the warrior spirit of two players who are in sync. It could put hitters on their heels and force them to play defensively. And, since decisiveness communicates confidence and chemistry, this dynamic has the potential to elevate everyone's game.

> **Boch:** I try to hold myself accountable to the same standard I ask of my players. Managers who are indecisive do not inspire confidence in their players or coaching staff. If your players lose faith, if they start questioning your decisions, that's the beginning of the end. It's not a dictatorial thing, though. I want our guys involved in as much of our decision-making process as possible. I want 'em to have ownership.

Decisiveness is self-reinforcing. Every time a ballplayer makes a hard decision, the warrior in him grows stronger. Every new decision gives him the courage to be even more decisive. Over time, "decisive" becomes his default setting. This doesn't mean that he doesn't hesitate or that every decision will be the right one. Warriors have no time for wallowing in a bad decision; they simply make a new decision and then move on with speed and determination.

DO SOMETHING NOW

Does your team approach the game with the mindset of a warrior? Talk to them about it. Mutually decide what it would take to create an environment where they dare greatly, play with fiery ambition, and are not afraid to make decisions.

There's a reason the warrior spirit has worked so well for Boch and his teams. He intuitively understands that there is a warrior's heart in every human being just waiting to be awakened. After our parents, the people best positioned and most capable of bringing it out in us are our coaches. By making this a priority in the kind of players he looks for, Boch is drawing on something that is already in them—something so natural that it longs to be summoned and expressed in full force.

The heart of a warrior gives the Giants their ability to keep their heads when opponents are losing theirs. A warrior spirit is what makes the team so dangerous when their resolve is being tested. It's what helps them stay focused and united when facing setbacks, able to rise above heartbreaks and overcome adversity. And, as the Giants have proven time and again, it's also what turns insurmountable odds into champagne showers and occasions to cheer and be cheered by fans in the streets of San Francisco.

6th Inning

GIANT PERSPECTIVE

Hungry, Grounded, and Focused

20
STAY HUNGRY
Everyone Around You is Constantly Getter Better

Assume just for a moment that you haven't eaten for days and you are ravenous. You are a stark-raving-mad kind of hungry. When you're starving, you are preoccupied, focused, ambitious, and determined. You are flexible and open to trying new things—anything, quite frankly—that will satisfy your hunger, right? You become open-minded enough to entertain cuisine you would never normally try. In the process, you often find new foods you like.

What if you could create a culture that is as hungry for change as that? What if every manager, coach, and player was stark-raving-mad hungry to grow and get better? What if a veteran of 10-plus years was as passionate about improving as when he first came up from the minor leagues?

Athletes who are hungry rarely ever have to be pushed; they are always looking for more. More ways to hone their craft and improve their game. More competitive intel on their opponents. More ways to pump up other players and unify the team. Always thinking about the next step and the next opportunity, they eagerly look for more ways to make the franchise better. This is Madison Bumgarner. This is Buster Posey. And, this is Bruce Bochy. This is the kind of attitude the Giants try to inspire in the clubhouse.

> **Athletes who are hungry rarely ever have to be pushed; they are always looking for more.**

When he came to San Francisco, Boch had had two World Series losses, resulting in two National League Championship rings. He never wore either one of them. Why? Deep down, he watched managers he admires—guys like Tony La Russa, Joe Torre, Terry Francona, and Jim Leyland—win World Championships. They had a sense of career completion Boch was hungry for.

> **Boch:** Had it never happened [winning a World Series] I still would've considered myself fortunate to be in the game, let alone be in it as long as I have. Believe me, I'm thankful and I know how fortunate I am. But honestly, it ate at me. I didn't want to look back and say, "I had so many great memories in this sport, but I never managed a team that won a World Series." It just would've felt incomplete, kind of like not getting to put the exclamation point on a great story.

In an interview with KNBR, the Giants AM flagship station, GM Evans talked about the passion and determination Boch had when he joined the Giants organization. "He came here hungry, he made that clear in his interview. He said he wanted another chance at winning it all, and that was a theme for him: 'I want another chance.' And that hunger still permeates . . . our clubhouse."

Evans got that right. After spending his entire career with expansion teams (Astros, Mets, Padres). Boch could tell there was something different about the Giants. He could feel it when came to AT&T Park. Winning three World Championships hasn't satiated Boch's hunger to get better; it has only intensified it. Especially after a gut-punch loss to the Cubs in the 2016 NLDS.

Boch has a healthy level of ambition. Although it may appear that managing baseball comes naturally for him, Boch is a learner. He's always acquiring new skills to expand his competence. That's the power of being hungry: it prompts you to get better, to do your best work. And if that's how you show up year after year, over the course of 20 years you build a body of work that represents mastery; that makes you one of the best in your field. Boch isn't done looking for the edge or trying to find the advantage. He enjoys the hunt.

> **Boch:** I imagine winning is like any drug. It can be addicting. The more you have it, the more you want it. And for me it's not just winning, it's growing in the game, trying to sharpen your focus and elevate your skills. I still find the process of getting there [trying to win it all] exciting. And even though we've had a lot of continuity among players, there is still so much more I can learn about how Brian and Bobby and our scouting organization bring the right mix of guys into the clubhouse, about what makes each individual tick, and what makes a team gel.
>
> I have a fantastic coaching staff, our training staff is second to none, and our travel secretary is world-class. But I know I can get better at reading these guys, drawing the best out of them, and creating an environment where they can flourish. You are never done.

When you stop bringing something new and fresh and exciting to the game, the game is over. You can't lean on yesterday's headlines. In every field, especially in baseball, you have to create new headlines every year. History is littered with athletes and organizations that set the world on fire and then imploded because they stopped learning. The question, however, is how do you keep from growing stale?

Don't Let Success Become the Enemy

You are never more vulnerable to arrogance, complacency, indifference, and inflexibility than when you are riding the wave of success. Here's why. The more successful you are, the more you have to protect. The more you have to protect, the less you want to change. Change cautions us: "What got you here won't get you there." Change counsels us: "You must leave what's comfortable." That often fosters fear and insecurity. Your brain says, "I like where I am." But, the less you change and grow, the more prone you are to fail.

> **Boch:** The game keeps evolving and we have to change with it. Brian [Sabean] says we have to keep reinventing ourselves, and he's right. Right now there is a more fluid dynamic emerging between the front office and baseball operations. Sabermetrics is changing the game. It requires a different kind of communication.
>
> Technology can give us everything from spin rates and movement on a ball to real-time heart rate, hydration levels, and blood analysis. Training and nutrition regimens are changing. It's likely there will be more expansion teams, and now there are so many more interactive ways for fans to experience the game. All these things just keep getting more sophisticated. So, if you stand still, you're dead.
>
> Good teams change when they have to, when they are losing or not selling out ballparks. Championship teams adjust, adapt, and change strategy constantly to avoid becoming stagnant—even when they are winning.

Given the immense struggles we've had this season [2017] we are taking a hard look in the mirror and asking: "What needs to change? As coaches, what should we be doing differently? What do our players need to be doing differently?" If the answers were evident and easy, we'd be there. Unfortunately, they aren't. But you have to keep asking the questions.

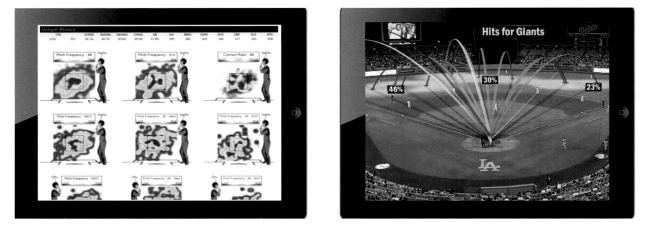

Real-time data and analytics keep getting better, and they are just one of many ways the game keeps evolving.

The question is: Are the changes you evoke opportunity-led or crisis-driven? If they are opportunity-led, then you get to establish the tempo and make your opponents play your kind of game. If the changes are crisis-driven and you are always playing catch up, then you better get comfortable playing by the rhythm and cadence established by your opponents.

Success tempts us to remember selectively. That is, it can lull us into forgetting how hard it is to achieve something great. We can lose the connection between winning and the sense of urgency, sheer resolve, unwavering tenacity, and hard work that got us there in the beginning. Assuming "things will be okay" or "it'll all work out as it did before" stems from overconfidence. Arrogance and complacency can tempt you into believing you have more margin, more room for error, than you actually do. It causes the original passion and work ethic to sag while time runs out.

Success can cause a team to lose focus. It's easy to get caught up in the ongoing hoopla and attention that come with winning. But all of that can become a distraction too. And when it does, a team can fall into the trap of "coasting" into the next season. Maintaining the intensity to repeat, three-peat, and win again at the highest level calls for a play-like-you-have-nothing-to-lose mentality. But playing through October also means you've played so many games that mental fatigue becomes a factor. It becomes more and more difficult to access the psychological resources to win again. The teams that do get there again have extraordinary passion and an invincible level of concentration.

Success can create inertia. If you've been to the top of the mountain enough, you can die of boredom. In baseball it's the idea that we really can't get the adrenaline flowing until the postseason is within sight. Players inaccurately assume that when they need to turn it on they can just flip the switch and get back in the hunt. When they need to rise up, they can and they will. Unfortunately, by the time they realize the error of their ways, it's too late to recover.

Jettison the Incumbent Mentality

An incumbent is the reigning champion, the big dog on the hill that everyone else wants to dethrone. Incumbents are experts—about *the past*. Their knowledge and experience are usually steeped in yesterday's solutions. But as the world of baseball advances, the shelf life of yesterday's solutions keeps getting shorter and shorter. The world takes no pity on the franchise or the person who gets lazy about learning.

Incumbents are susceptible to the often-fatal trap of thinking that the future will be more of the same only a little better, and that what got them to the pinnacle yesterday will get them there again tomorrow. How do you jettison the incumbent mentality? Trade it for the mindset of a challenger or an underdog with an insurgent's mission. Challenge precedent, go to war with the status quo, and put everything you do on probation—constantly. Incumbents that fail to remain scrappy can get blindsided by insurgents who "bring it" because they want it badly.

> **Boch:** I've told our players at the start of spring training: "You should be extremely proud of what you accomplished. You get to wear the horns for a year [as World Champions]. What you did is something you now get to enjoy and savor for a lifetime. But it's a new year, a new season, and a new race. No one is paying us today for what we did yesterday."
>
> I want them to have the confidence that comes with experience, with having won a World Series. But I also want them to *want* it like an underdog, like someone who's never been there before.

Boch is talking about an insurgent's way of thinking. Insurgents are rebels who fight to topple existing regimes. When you are in that frame of mind, you take nothing for granted. Challenging and pursuing are more aggressive than protecting something is. Think of an irrepressible "upstart" in business. The founder's mentality is not that of an incumbent; it is that of an insurgent—a challenger who is deeply connected to a dream and a heroic sense of purpose. The energy and buzz in a start-up are visceral. There is a bias for action. People are hungry. They are restlessly curious, strategically nimble, and eager to do something they've never done before. They are experimenting and learning every day. This is what Boch wants to engender in his players—no matter how many times his team has been to the Fall Classic.

DO SOMETHING NOW

Ask your team: "Are we playing like an incumbent who has been there or an insurgent who wants to dethrone the champion? Do we have the guts to go to war with the status quo; to put everything we do on probation? Or are we trying to protect our success?"

Be Restlessly Curious

Restlessness is both a subtle and sometimes a not-so-subtle agitator. It never lets you get too comfortable with the status quo and it doesn't let you rest on your laurels. Curiosity pushes, prods, and cajoles you to continually ask: What's new? What's fresh? What's next? It's the compulsion to see what's around the corner and over the horizon, and then to go beyond them. If restlessness is the attitude that gets you off your butt, curiosity is what makes discovery happen. Together they push you to explore your own limits and expand the universe of what's possible.

Baseball is a traditional game that has been played the same way almost from the beginning. But that hasn't stopped Boch from regularly visiting the edge. Not only is he open to advice from the outside, he also seeks it. In a game that can be incestuous, he doesn't want to become insular. He reads business books. He is interested in what founder Herb Kelleher has done to create esprit de corps and a culture of unity at Southwest Airlines. Chairman Ratan Tata of India's Tata Group, who has a penchant for thinking big and acting boldly, inspires Boch. He likewise admires Jack Welch's candor and Richard Branson's fearlessness in trying new things. Boch is determined to learn something from everything; he is vigilant about borrowing from outside baseball to reinvent baseball for the franchise.

The more you desire change, the less comfortable you will be with the status quo. If you are comfortable with the status quo, you won't be motivated to change.

Likewise, Boch is a student of coaches in other sports. He learns from what Phil Jackson has done with the Chicago Bulls and the Los Angeles Lakers, how Gregg Popovich leads the San Antonio Spurs, what Bill Belichick does with the New England Patriots, and, most recently, how Steve Kerr has led the Golden State Warriors.

He's even learned from the greats in the entertainment world. The late Waylon Jennings's outlaw spirit challenged Boch to think independently. Bono's passion for creating an experience for the fans and Garth Brooks's ability to connect with them has inspired him to remind his players who they are playing for. No fans, no game.

Many times when a group is kicking around ideas Boch doesn't say much. You wish he would weigh in, and you're left to wonder, "What's going on in his head?" What's going on is that he's practicing curiosity. He listens without judgment. He's not invested in the outcome of what you are talking about in the moment; he's invested in learning. He isn't painting each idea with the brush of his own assumptions and biases; he's trying to be fully present and absorb them. Learning from others is more important to him than pretending to be smart or hearing himself talk.

These sources of knowledge give Boch multiple lenses through which to see and evaluate an issue. More lenses give him a deeper, richer, multidimensional frame in which to think about his club.

Boch involves his players and coaches in his learning process by asking questions and getting their perspectives. "How do you see this problem? What's your take on this issue? What are we missing? Is there another way we should be looking at this?" By asking such questions, he sends a message to the rest of the organization about what *being interested* looks like. Not only does this put his thumb on the pulse of his players and give him new insights; it also lays the foundation for a culture where everybody learns from everybody else.

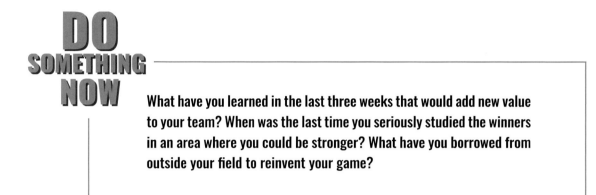

DO SOMETHING NOW

What have you learned in the last three weeks that would add new value to your team? When was the last time you seriously studied the winners in an area where you could be stronger? What have you borrowed from outside your field to reinvent your game?

Be Coachable—Grow

When you are hungry you are willing to be influenced because you know that success is never final. Hopefully, you get better, more experienced, and more confident every year, but you never arrive. Great players don't let false pride and an overly elevated opinion of their skills and contributions close the door to what they can accomplish, where they can take their game, and who they can become. They constantly want to know, "How can I be three times better tomorrow than I was today, and who can help me get there?"

> **Boch:** A player who is reluctant to listen to a hitting coach about a subtle glitch in his swing doesn't really want to change. He'd rather be right than good. Some players want to be right, even when they're not. As a result, the game is difficult for them. That kind of hardheaded attitude conveys arrogance, decelerates learning, and, if it's pervasive enough, damages relationships. Chemistry hinges on building an organization that learns all the time.
>
> You stand a much better chance of building cohesion if the clubhouse is abuzz with players sharing their knowledge with each other, coaches listening to players, players learning from coaches and vice versa. Because it's all about, "How do I make a bigger contribution to the team?" One or two players who don't get this, who are un-coachable, dampen chemistry.

Marquee athletes and world-class business leaders who are coachable share these common characteristics: they are vulnerable, seek advice, demand the truth, unlearn bad habits, and step out in faith. These strengths are also key to people who achieve greatness in many other fields. Try it!

> **Boch:** In 2016, having issues in the bullpen, we got away from clearly defined roles. Were the players happy with this? No. But roles have to be earned. When Rags [pitching coach Dave Righetti] and I sat down with the pen, Javier López asked, "How can we get better?" That's what you want: players who want the truth and who want to get better. When a player can't give himself an honest evaluation, several things happen. First, he's not happy with his role. Second, if he doesn't have an accurate view of his abilities, he doesn't *really* know what needs to improve. Third, it can be detrimental to the club, to what you are trying to accomplish.

If you go for a treadmill test and the doctor inflates the quality of your health, you aren't going to be as concerned about the things you should be doing to improve it. If you die, that doesn't make much sense. I think most people want it real and raw so they can fix what's ailing them and live longer. Players who are coachable are no different.

Players who are coachable are easy to spot. Their hearts are in it. They take charge of success. They have extreme practice habits. They work harder on every aspect of the game by applying what they learn, spending hundreds, maybe even thousands, of hours doing it. Their commitment produces meaningful results.

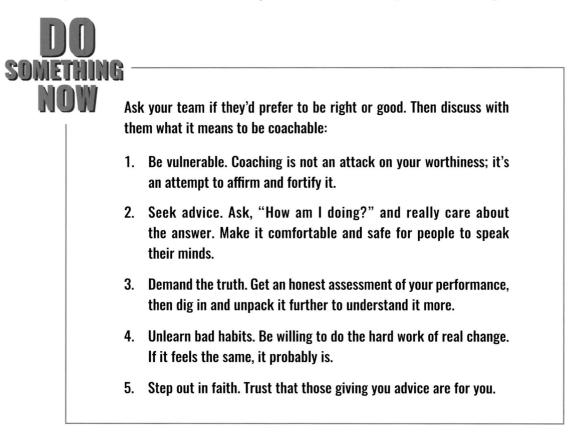

DO SOMETHING NOW

Ask your team if they'd prefer to be right or good. Then discuss with them what it means to be coachable:

1. Be vulnerable. Coaching is not an attack on your worthiness; it's an attempt to affirm and fortify it.

2. Seek advice. Ask, "How am I doing?" and really care about the answer. Make it comfortable and safe for people to speak their minds.

3. Demand the truth. Get an honest assessment of your performance, then dig in and unpack it further to understand it more.

4. Unlearn bad habits. Be willing to do the hard work of real change. If it feels the same, it probably is.

5. Step out in faith. Trust that those giving you advice are for you.

Being coachable is reciprocal. We submit to the influence of those who are for us, who care enough about us to tell the truth and push us beyond where we would be without them. They, in turn, are honored that we have been vulnerable enough to seek their advice and listen. Great coaches and mentors don't abuse our humility, they respect it. They appreciate that we don't take constructive criticism as a personal attack, and they understand the courage it takes to step out of the comfort zone and make seemingly ominous changes. Therefore, feedback is regarded as a powerful multiplier and given with that intent. Feedback is a gift to others that should never be used as a weapon.

What emerges from this dynamic interplay is chemistry: a chemistry that creates an exponential rise in confidence, skill, and performance.

21

STAY HUMBLE
Success Can Make You Vulnerable

Jon Miller, the Giants Hall of Fame broadcaster, frequently does a pregame interview with Bruce Bochy. One day Boch noticed that Miller wasn't wearing his World Series ring and asked, "Where's your ring?"

"Well, it's not like I contributed to winning the Series," answered Miller. "I mean, I wasn't out there on the field."

Boch chided Miller for downplaying his significant role in the larger Giants community. "Well, Jon, I didn't win any of those games either. It's not me who won the World Series; our players got this done."

For Boch, baseball has never been about fame, fortune, or adulation. It's all about making a difference, building upon an already-storied franchise, and, to be sure, winning. Like most professional athletes, Boch is ambitious and driven, but his ambition is directed toward his players and the Giants organization.

"He's not wrapped up in ego," Giants CEO Larry Baer told us. "He's not wrapped up in himself. What he's wrapped up in is putting players in the best place to succeed."

This kind of humility runs throughout the franchise. Brian Sabean defines success collectively, not individually. When it comes to the Giants accomplishments, he is quick to point to his manager and coaches, his scouting organization, his players, and the front office. Considered one of the most knowledgeable guys in the game—a guru really—Sabes doesn't seek attention for himself. As we've said, he prefers to be in the background.

In the beginning of 2014, Baseball Prospectus, the game's analytics think tank, ranked the Giants developmental operation 22nd out of 30, even though homegrown players completely filled the starting infield. That didn't seem to bother Baer. "Whatever acclaim comes will come. And if it doesn't come, it doesn't. We aren't looking for credit."[73]

Giants Hall of Fame broadcaster Jon Miller.

Shortly after Baer made this statement the Giants won their third World Series in five years. Confident humility. It's how the Giants roll. Humility has a profound influence on the culture of a franchise. Plus, it nurtures chemistry. What can we learn from the Giants brand of humility? Here are a few insights.

Play for the Name on the Front of Your Jersey

When you attend one the Giants home games at AT&T Park you will notice something peculiar. There are no last names on the players' jerseys. It is a symbolic gesture that says three things about the character of the organization.

First, symbols have meaning. Washington, D.C., monuments, the Statue of Liberty, and the American flag all say something about our culture. They are part of reinforcing what we value. In the case of the Giants, the jerseys are a simple expression of a franchise that values humility.

Second, the jerseys communicate a kind of level playing field. No prima donnas, no superstars—it's all about the team. Removing names reminds players of the synergy and chemistry that's possible when they play for the name on the front of the jersey rather than for the one that is usually on the back of it. Greatness is defined by ultra-talented players who know how to fit in and play collectively as a team.

No names on the back of the players' uniforms symbolizes all for one and one for all.

Third, zealous Giants fans already know the names of the players. The jerseys create a little bit of family-like exclusivity and promote a special bond with the fans. When the fans of opposing teams visit AT&T Park they are outsiders. They have to work harder to know who's who on the Giants roster. It's a way of the Giants ballplayers saying to their fans: "You know us! You're one of us."

Ignore Your Own Publicity

When you play 162 games in the regular season, there's plenty of room for people to sing your praises *and* cut you down. If your confidence stems from what people say about you, the ride is going to be an emotional roller coaster. For the majority of his 20-year career as a manager, Boch was underestimated and largely unnoticed; until the Giants won their first World Series, that is. It's never bothered him. It doesn't even get on his radar except when the media brings it up. His motivation and drive and confidence in making unconventional decisions come from his love of the game and his passion for drawing the best out of his players.

> **Boch:** As managers, we probably get far more credit and criticism than we deserve. The organization is infinitely bigger than any one person. There are so many moving parts, so many talented individuals who make this franchise work. Sure, as a manager you are in the spotlight and you play an important role, but don't kid yourself; it's one role among many that ultimately get it done.

After the Giants won their third World Series, the press started speculating more seriously about Boch's chances of being inducted into the Hall of Fame. Today, many experts call him a shoo-in for Cooperstown. And, just for the record, this is a conversation he doesn't even want to have.

> **Boch:** I don't ever think about it. It's too humbling to think about. When you think of the Hall of Fame, you think of Willie Mays and great players like that. You don't look at yourself like that.
>
> I feel fortunate that I've been doing what I love for as long as I've been doing it. Of course, moving up to San Francisco and getting the resources from Brian [Sabean] and ownership to help us win three World Championships . . . This game has given me and my family so much. I'm beyond grateful. But the Hall? That is hallowed ground.

Boch is just not a spotlight kind of guy. While he's had multiple opportunities after each World Series win to make appearances on the talk show circuit, he prefers to let his players do so. He exudes confident humility at its best. Boch is not alone here. Ask any of Buster Posey's teammates, for instance, and they will tell you that he is one of the most unassuming people you will ever meet. He has tremendous presence, however. Modest yet confident, Posey is an example of how Giant chemistry works.

> **Boch:** Players see what he has accomplished and then realize he's one of them. He's an MVP who doesn't act like an MVP. It makes him approachable, and that builds chemistry with the rest of the guys. They have so much respect not only for what he's done but also for how he handles it. He doesn't lean on all the accolades; he prepares for every game like he doesn't want to let his teammates down. That rubs off. You get three or four other guys to pick up on that tone and it can unify a clubhouse.

As a favorite to win the 2012 National League MVP award, reporters cornered Posey before it was announced and asked him who deserved the award. Posey was mischievously matter-of-fact in deflecting attention.

"'It's not my choice,' he replied.

'But if you had a vote?'

'I don't have a vote.'

'But if you were a writer?'

Posey smiled. 'I'm not a writer.'"[74]

Confident Humility in Action

Confident humility is fearlessly stepping up to the plate against a marquee pitcher, working the count, patiently waiting for your pitch, and then launching a three-run, walk-off home run to win the game. Humility is *not* ostentatiously standing at home plate admiring your work and then disrespecting the pitcher by flipping your bat. Rather, humility is getting on with it and briskly making your way around the bases.

Confidence *and* humility. Finding the delicate balance between the two is what it means to play the game right and what it means to inspire chemistry on the field. The fusion of these two seemingly paradoxical or contradictory virtues is also what makes the Giants clubhouse both empowering and unique.

Players are attracted to confidence. Not the kind of pop culture bravado that is overly brash and arrogant; that shows up in someone who speaks their mind with little consideration of others and tells a good story, usually about themselves. That kind of show might be intriguing. The stories might be entertaining—for awhile. But eventually they wear thin and people see through the veneer to a poser who is trying to compensate for some insecurity.

Players are drawn to a truly authentic kind of confidence, often demonstrated in a quiet, calm resolve that is understated yet powerfully present and fearless. It is grounded in being overly prepared, extremely competent, and willing to risk big things on behalf of others. It can stand up to a lot of tension and flack; it can also sit back and make room for others to contribute.

Players are also drawn to humility—to leaders who have a realistic awareness of their own limitations, insufficiencies, and need of others. Humility makes them more accepting of themselves and less judgmental of others. In the world of baseball, they are compassionately demanding. That is, they continually raise the bar and ask a lot of their players, but with empathy and a deep-seated appreciation for how hard the game is.

Boch is that kind of person. He's a rock. Players rally around him because they trust his judgment and sense of fairness—even if his decisions don't bend in their favor. He argues with umpires for his guys on the field, stands up for them in the media, and yet, he calls them out in the clubhouse when he thinks they can be more than they have become.

It goes the other way as well. Boch owns it when he makes a mistake. After a recent grueling home game, the conversation with Kevin went like this:

K: How are you doing?

B: Outside of just managing the worst game of my entire career, I'm doin' okay.

K: Really, what went wrong?

B: I went against my gut and left [a pitcher] in too long, he gave up a run, and it cost us the game. I think Kim is standing by the window to make sure I don't jump out.

Kim Bochy is as petite as they come. Stopping Boch from taking that plunge would be like standing a field mouse in front of a Mack truck to block it. But that's classic deadpanning from Boch. He can find humor even in the direst circumstances.

The next day he gathered the players, told them they deserved better, and apologized. "You guys played great. *That game* was on me, fellas." No excuses. No self-justification. Just an unconditional respect for his guys that caused him to

Humility knows the art of the apology.

acknowledge his blind spots and come clean. Part of treating players like people is owning your mistakes and making amends. It sends a powerful signal about unity and how much you care. Humility owns mistakes and practices the art of the apology.

On April 22, 2017, Madison Bumgarner and his wife, Ali, were riding dirt bikes on a day off in Colorado. Bum hit a slippery spot on a trail and crashed. The outcome was significant road rash, bruised ribs, and a partial tear of his left (pitching) shoulder. Adding insult to injury was the speculation all over the media about Bum having potentially violated clauses in his contract and whether he would be fined for the incident.

When GM Evans was asked about it, he said that wasn't even his focus. The club was concerned about Madison's well-being and recovery. Boch said it was a "lesson learned," so now "let's get him healthy." It turns out that the rehab took Bum out until after the All-Star break. Fortunately, he came back in fine form, like his old self.

> **Boch:** When I went to visit him in his hotel room right after the accident, he said, "I'd say I'm sorry, but I don't think I need to because you know I am." It was Bum's way of communicating how bad he felt about the accident and how remorseful he was. He knew he let his teammates and the fans down. Some things just don't need to be said because you are harder on yourself than anyone can be on you. I knew he felt terrible about it. I'm just glad that it wasn't worse. It could've been.

The Giants could've taken a more punitive, legalistic tack. And Bum—who carried the club in the 2014 postseason, and whom most agree is the best deal on the Giants payroll— could have been defensive and essentially said, "After all I've done for this club . . ." But that's not what humility does. Humility doesn't blame; humility takes responsibility, apologizes, and respectfully moves on.

Let the Game Speak for You

In 2010, the race between the Giants and the Padres for the NL West title was heating up. After pitching a 6-3 loss to the Braves in early August, Giants starter Jonathan Sánchez levied some mighty big words that made his teammates and Boch uncomfortable.

Speaking to reporters in front of his locker in the visitors' clubhouse, Sánchez waxed confident about the Giants two-game deficit with the Padres: "We're going to play San Diego now, and we're going to beat them three times. If we get to first place, we're not going to look back."[75]

While inconsistent, Sánchez showed moments of brilliance. In 2009, he was the first pitcher in 35 years to throw a no-hitter for the Giants. But just after yielding four runs in four innings to Atlanta, and with the Giants barely avoiding a four-game sweep by the Braves, his comments seemed uncharacteristically cocky.

Shortly thereafter, Sánchez even predicted that the team was "definitely going to make the playoffs." It wasn't so much that his predictions were not in keeping with the Giants culture; it was his timing and the audience to whom he was speaking. You might think it. You might believe in your heart that it's true. But, you don't make it public prematurely; you let your performance do the talking.

> **Boch:** There is absolutely no upside in making a statement like that. Why provoke the other team? Why fuel a bigger reason for the other team to beat us? It just makes the hill we're climbing that much steeper. This game is hard enough without making yourself a target. These are the kinds of comments that rally their fans and strengthen their resolve, that cause the momentum to shift in their favor.

Sánchez wasn't finished yet. Never mind that up to this point in the season the Giants had dropped seven of eight games to the Padres. Never mind that Sánchez was 0-2 against the Padres in three outings. "That was a long time ago," Sánchez said. "Doesn't matter. We've got a better team now."[76] Sometimes confidence is confused with arrogance and then emasculates humility.

As with politics and most everything else, in the world of baseball context matters. For a Latino player like Sánchez, the remarks were nothing more than demonstrating his love for and loyalty to his team. He told Boch that if he had made these statements to reporters in Puerto Rico, where he is from, they would never have ended up in the paper. Boch reminded Sánchez that he wasn't in Puerto Rico.

While the Padres handled the situation with class, some of Sánchez's teammates were infuriated. Cultural misunderstanding aside, there are some unwritten rules in the clubhouse that must be respected and honored. You don't say things in the press that could be divisive to the team, and you don't unnecessarily agitate your opponent. Sánchez was censured by some of the veterans who basically said, "You don't have the time or tenure on this club to speak for us, so shut it down."

> **Boch:** Some of the guys were pretty put off by it. I think they got on him pretty good. But you know, it's a fine line sometimes. I want our guys to be confident, to believe in what they can do. I've always encouraged them to be themselves. If you manage this way, periodically someone is going to cross the line. So, you don't blow it out of proportion; you correct course and move on. In one sense, I didn't want to break Johnny's competitive spirit. But I did want him to see that some things are better left for the clubhouse and not the media.

This incident had the potential for stirring clubhouse controversy written all over it, but Boch wasn't going to be baited by the media. When asked about it in the dugout the next day, he simply took the high road by essentially telling reporters that it was between them and Sánchez.

* Unwarranted confidence or confidence expressed at the wrong time, in the wrong place, to the wrong audience can cross the line into arrogance. On the other hand, too much humility can border on self-deprecation, on belittling or undervaluing what you or your team is capable of achieving. Self-importance and self-deprecation are simply different sides of the same coin: self-indulgence. And, as we've already pointed out, self-indulgence disrupts team unity.

Tough love is never easy. Perhaps this was a hard lesson for Sánchez. But it was also a good lesson for the Giants because it reinforced the idea that if chemistry is important, confidence and humility must be balanced. There must be a unique blend of both. Here's how Boch explained that balance.

> **Boch:** The kind of players who make our clubhouse special are the ones who carry themselves with class and confident humility. That means you have to:
>
> Be confident enough to have a little swagger. But humble enough to know that you didn't get here by yourself.
>
> Be confident enough to know that you did it and can do it again. But humble enough to never think you've arrived.
>
> Be confident enough to face an opponent from a position of strength. But humble enough to realize that you can never learn enough about him.
>
> Be confident enough to stay focused when it is time to get down to business. But humble enough to take time for the media or be gracious to a kid who wants an autograph.
>
> Be confident enough to call someone out who isn't getting it done. But humble enough to know that you will eventually be on the other side of that conversation someday.
>
> Be confident enough to know that you have earned the right to be here. But humble enough to realize that you have to earn it constantly—each win only buys you an admission ticket to play another day.

Accept Defeat with Dignity and Grace

In 2016, the Giants were, again, the best team in baseball up until the All-Star break. Then, they tanked, losing 27 one-run games and blowing 32 saves. It was one of the worst 66-game stretches in Giants history and one that devoured an 8-game lead over the Dodgers. In the second half of the season, the Giants lost 9 games when leading after eight innings. In 61 games when they were down entering the ninth, they had zero comeback wins. Talk about trying times—this was it.

Then, things began to turn for the better. In the final two series of the season, Boch's boys played brilliant baseball, including a three-game sweep of the Dodgers. Los Angeles still won the NL West, but the Giants were starting to show their Championship Blood, earning a Wild Card spot against the New York Mets.

Madison Bumgarner and Noah Syndergaard, one of the best pitchers in the game, squared off in an epic pitcher's duel. Although Bum outlasted Syndergaard, both were fantastic. With a 0-0 game going into the ninth, Conor Gillaspie, another Giant player without a big contract or mouthwatering pedigree, blasted a three-run homer. The Giants won and advanced to the NLDS to face the Chicago Cubs who had just completed a historic regular season run, winning 103 games.

Conor Gillaspie blasted a three-run homer advancing the Giants to the 2016 NLDS.

After losing the first two games in Chicago, the Giants were in a familiar win-or-go-home scenario. In Game 3, Bum came back and threw what Boch called "one of the gutsiest performances I've ever seen" and "willed his way" through five innings without his best stuff. With the Giants trailing 3-2, one out, and two runners on base, Gillaspie, the hero of the Wild Card Game, smoked a 102-mph fastball off the opponent's flame-throwing closer Aroldis Chapman. Gillaspie's ball dropped into the gap in right-center field, which resulted in two runs. The Giants won and kept their postseason hopes alive.

In Game 4, the Cubs were on their heels all night as Giants starter Matt Moore was dominant. Moore struck out 10 batters and gave up just two hits and two walks. At the end of eight, the Giants had a 5-2 lead. It looked as though they would be taking the series back to Chicago. Then, the wheels came off. With a pitch count at

120, Boch pulled Moore and went to the bullpen. The Cubs rallied for four hits and four runs against five Giants pitchers. Final score: 6-5 Cubs. Players and fans alike were stunned. Instead of forcing a decisive Game 5 at Wrigley Field, the Giants were in unfamiliar postseason territory—they were going home.

The gut-punch ended the Giants heroic streak of winning 11 consecutive postseason series, matched only by the Yankees (1998–2001) for the longest such streak in baseball history. Still reeling from the shock of it all, the organization handled it with class. Here's what Larry Baer said in his letter to the fans: "When the historic streak came to an end this week, we were reminded that Championship Blood is, more than anything, about character. We saw it in the clubhouse after Tuesday's defeat. There was no retreat from addressing the media, no finger-pointing. The players faced their disappointment with grace, reflection, and resolve. They said they would double down on preparation, that they'd never forget how awful this felt. They hugged and consoled and thanked one another. As always, they had each other's backs."

Yes, adversity reveals character, and although they were heartbroken, Boch and his players remained true to who they are—humble, yet hopeful, confident, and resolute. "There's nowhere to point a finger," Gillaspie said. "We win as a team and we lose as a team. What made any of my hits matter is that they allowed us to

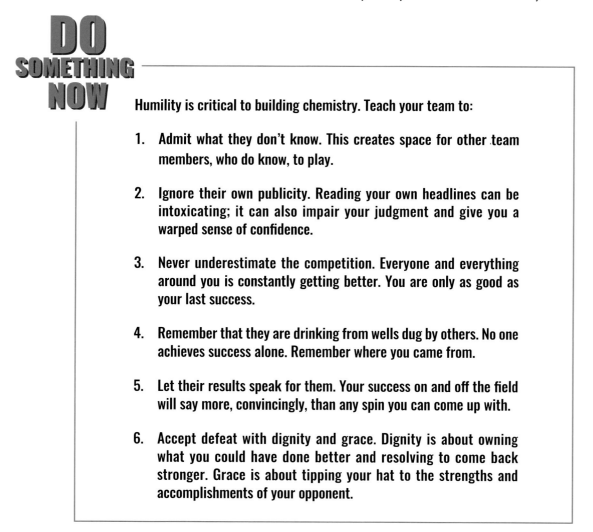

Humility is critical to building chemistry. Teach your team to:

1. **Admit what they don't know.** This creates space for other team members, who do know, to play.

2. **Ignore their own publicity.** Reading your own headlines can be intoxicating; it can also impair your judgment and give you a warped sense of confidence.

3. **Never underestimate the competition.** Everyone and everything around you is constantly getting better. You are only as good as your last success.

4. **Remember that they are drinking from wells dug by others.** No one achieves success alone. Remember where you came from.

5. **Let their results speak for them.** Your success on and off the field will say more, convincingly, than any spin you can come up with.

6. **Accept defeat with dignity and grace.** Dignity is about owning what you could have done better and resolving to come back stronger. Grace is about tipping your hat to the strengths and accomplishments of your opponent.

keep playing, and I'm proud of that. But I'd trade them all to keep playing. That's how important winning is to everybody in this clubhouse."[77]

New to the club, Moore quickly showed what a "fit" he is with the Giants culture. He didn't push to keep himself in the game. And when it was over, Moore stood by Boch's decision to pull him after the eighth inning.

Denard Span, who made several big contributions in the postseason, was asked if having a generally good regular season gave him any solace to cope with the bitter loss. "I'll have this whole off-season to think about this whole season and I'm already hungry to come back and perform and take another crack at it. We'll be back."[78] Acknowledging two uncharacteristic errors he made in the postseason, Brandon Crawford said: "It's kind of a punch to the gut. We just have to come back next year and get better."

> **Boch:** Hunter [Pence] was the first guy to come up to me and say, "Man, this makes me want to come back and win even more now." It's why you play the game. It hurts to not be playing tonight [Game 5]. There's no getting around it. But that's baseball. When you slug through these dark times like we are right now, you take nothing for granted, you get hungrier and you appreciate winning that much more. We'll be back.

These comments are not surprising in the wake of this bitter loss, for this is also how the Giants respond when they are victorious. They celebrate what they've earned but stay humble and always look for a way to recognize the accomplishments of others.

Staci Slaughter, the Giants Executive Vice President, Communications, and Senior Advisor to the CEO, made an interesting observation about the benefits of humility described in this chapter. Remember the Willie Mac Award, which since 1980 has been presented to the most inspirational player on the team? Well, each year the players themselves choose the winner. "The players take this choice very seriously," said Slaughter. "If you look at all the winners throughout the history of this prestigious award, the players have always gotten it right. The winner exemplifies the type of player the team aspires to be."

If you compared all the comments made by all the Giants players during the playoffs and after each of their World Series victories, it's likely you would find a strong sense of self-assurance and a deep appreciation for the *team's* abilities, coupled with a humble view of each player's own importance.

The Giants take C.S. Lewis's famous line to heart: *"Humility is not thinking less of yourself, it's thinking of yourself less."*

22
MAINTAIN PERSPECTIVE
Don't Take Yourself Too Seriously

Socrates is claimed to have said, "What screws us up the most in life is the picture in our head of what it's supposed to be." The antidote? A sense of perspective. It keeps us from making mountains out of molehills and future-tripping over things that may never happen.

Perspective is the ability to focus on what's important in life, to accurately evaluate the weightiness of something in the overall scheme of things. Perspective widens your lens. It helps you see the forest through the trees. Putting life and work in perspective has a way of relieving tension and keeping things light.

Skewed or not, our perspective influences our view of the world—the people in it and our circumstances—which in turn shapes our attitudes and, ultimately, our success and well-being. How do you get a sense of perspective in a game that will eat you alive if you don't? Here are some things we've seen inside the Giants organization.

> **Putting life and work in perspective has a way of relieving tension and keeping things light.**

Your Work Is Not Your Worth

Boch doesn't let the game he treasures define him. His sense of security as a person doesn't lie in his team's performance. Does he care? Does he get emotional behind the scenes? Is he passionate about winning? You bet. Ask his wife, Kim. She'll tell you it can get pretty quiet around their house after a tough loss. Boch is pensive; he's a thinker. But his work is not his worth. His identity is grounded in something bigger.

Boch is quiet about it, but his sense of significance is anchored in his Christian upbringing. He knows *who* and *Whose* he is (someone who has been adopted into the grace and goodness of a loving God). His sister, Terry Bochy, a retired federal customs agent, was the full-time caretaker for their mom, Melrose, who had Alzheimer's for more than a decade. Simply by living her own faith out loud, Terry has had a big influence on Boch's faith. You can see it in the way he speaks about her so reverently. "Believe me," Boch said, "I'm hoping to ride her coattails into heaven." Boch prays. He believes that the game is a gift and that all that is good about his life originates in a God who loves him, likes him, and is *for* him.

Boch is also grounded in family. He has been blessed with an incredible wife who is the anchor of the Bochy household. All of 5 feet 6 inches and maybe 110 pounds soaking wet, Kim is a confident and quiet leader. She will say, "I'm just the wife," but Kim leads their family with dignity, grace, and confidence. Boch affectionately refers to her as "The General." When "just one more" seems like the right thing to do at the end of a late night with our wine tasting–dinner group, Kim is the voice of reason. And we're all grateful for it. She has always had Boch's back. Together, they have two great sons, Greg and Brett, *both* of whom played professional baseball, and now a daughter (in-law).

At a restaurant tucked into the mountainside at Estes Park, Colorado, Boch gave one of the most memorable speeches of his life so far. It was at the rehearsal dinner for son Brett and his fiancée, Kelsey. Boch endeared himself to the entire room when he said to Kelsey's dad, Greg, "She will always be your daughter first, but with your permission we'd like to call her our daughter too; not our daughter-in-law, because she means *that much* to our family."

Financial security also plays a role in Boch's perspective. Bruce and Kim are frugal people. They've always lived modestly. He could have retired comfortably *before* ever coming to the Giants. That financial independence affords one a certain amount of perspective and freedom. And yet, wealth and stuff doesn't define him either.

Kim and Bruce Bochy, enjoying Jordan Winery in Healdsburg, California.

Granted, he manages players who don't have this luxury. They're still trying to establish their place in the game and dealing with whether they'll have a job tomorrow. But Boch was there once too. This has helped him see that there's more to life than baseball. Here's what Kim told us.

You know, I don't know if there was ever a time when Bruce went into spring training knowing for sure that he had made the team. That weighs heavy on you when you're married and have a child. I know that shaped who he is today. You *do* get a sense of perspective when things don't come easy for you. You learn to appreciate those parts of your life that are more stable and consistent. Bruce loves this game, and he certainly wanted another shot at a World Series, but even if he had not been hired by another club after San Diego, he would've been okay.

Sadly, our culture encourages us to buy stuff with money we don't have to impress people we don't know. And unfortunately, things and stuff have become current symbols of success. Bruce and Kim have never gotten sucked into that culture. They appreciate genuine relationships and gravitate to people and places where they can be themselves.

Don't Let Criticism Define You

Bill Bradley, former U.S. senator and two-time member of the World Champion New York Knicks,

Kim and Bruce with daughter (in-law) Kelsey, sons Brett and Greg.

said, "Fame, you learn, is like a rainstorm—it comes on fast and then goes just as quickly, often leaving behind a certain amount of destruction." The more championships you win, the more fame you have. Often, however, this fame comes with a price—the unrealistic expectations imposed by the public that you will do it over and over again. As noted, the Giants won three times in five years—every even year from 2010 to 2014. When they didn't go all the way in 2016, everyone, starting with the players themselves, was brokenhearted. Just when you think it couldn't get worse, in 2017, the Giants turned in the worst year in the history of the franchise.

In baseball, when the fans get their hearts broken they aren't bashful about questioning a manager's decisions and levying their criticism. Talk show pundits, bloggers, and social media groupies are all willing to put you in your place, especially when they don't have to look you in the eye. People on social media can often be visceral, mean, and unfiltered with their comments. They unabashedly make judgments about your intentions. Boch understands this goes with the territory, but he doesn't give it a lot of his attention and he certainly isn't threatened by it.

To be so focused on serving and developing your players—when your primary mission is to put the right player in the right place at the right time, to draw the best out of him, and to do what's best for the team—takes tremendous concentration. You don't have time to read the reviews and feedback on your work. As a manager, even if you *did* have the time, why would you indulge? Still, every manager gets wind of the public's displeasure just by meeting with the press. Boch doesn't let either the praise or the criticism define him.

> **Boch:** Look we're all human. My players are human. I'm human. We're going to make mistakes. It's not like we wake up every so often and say, "How can we lose today?" If you knee-jerk to all the criticism, it'll eat you up inside. That makes for a long season and an even longer career. I tell our players: "If you take it personally, everything you read [in the press], you'll be an emotional pinball. You'll get distracted. You'll play tight. You'll be afraid to take risks. Don't let it define you. If you eliminate it from your diet, you'll have more sanity over the long haul— and you will play better."
>
> Now, that's easier said than done. This year [2017] I've wrestled with not taking it personally— not the public criticism, but my own sense of responsibility to our guys, the front office, and our fans. Three World Series in five years. It's unrealistic to think you can stay on that run forever. But in my wildest dreams I would never have imagined us to be this behind. So, you dig deep to keep it in perspective in the larger scheme of things so you save that mental energy for being creative, for finding a way out of it.
>
> A number of things have happened this year that keeps it in perspective for me. I lost a friend and colleague, Don Baylor [who managed the Rockies and Cubs], to cancer. I have another really close friend, Kevin Towers, who is in the fight for his life against a rare form of cancer. Kevin was my GM in San Diego for 12 years. He is fighting this with so much dignity and optimism. He's a warrior. Just watching him battle makes me think, "Man, if he can do that when the stakes are life and death, I can do it with the kind of season we're having." And then, just recently, Kim and I got news that our oldest son, Greg, and his partner, McKenna, are having a baby. We're thrilled. That has raised my spirit.
>
> So, these major life events keep it real. They put a really rough season in perspective. It doesn't take the sting out of it. It doesn't make it any less painful. But it does give you a reason to be grateful and a reason to keep walking through it.

Don't Take Yourself Too Seriously

A few years back, in January 2014, Boch was honored at the Professional Baseball Scouts Foundation with the Tommy Lasorda Award. The 86-year-old Lasorda has been with the Dodgers as a pitcher, manager, GM, and consultant for better than 65 years and is fond of saying, "If you don't root for the Dodgers, you might not get into heaven."

The night of the awards dinner Lasorda was in rare form. He began by saying how unusual it was for him––"Mr. Dodger"––to be there.

> When I said my prayers last night, first of all I asked God for forgiveness. I said, "Dear Lord, I'm going to have to give a trophy to a Giant." The good Lord said: "Tommy, the guy you're going to honor is great. [An] outstanding manager. A manager that has been so successful, well-liked, [a] nice, easy-going guy. For me to allow him to receive the Tommy Lasorda Award, you know there's something wrong in his dinner tonight." It gives me a great deal of pleasure to introduce the man who has led the Giants to two World Series in the last five years.

Then, as he dramatically pointed to heaven, Lasorda said, "Ladies and gentlemen, my good friend, Mr. Bochy."

Lasorda had sent the packed room into gales of laughter with his introduction, but it was Boch who brought the house down with the last word.

> I'm thrilled to be here with my old friend Tommy Lasorda, who has been so encouraging to me *most* of my career. We used to talk quite a bit; then, when I signed as the manager in San Francisco, he just stopped talking to me. Well, except for one time when he yelled at me, *"I'm done with you!"* in front of everyone in the lobby at our Winter Meetings.

Broadcasters Jon Miller and Dave Flemming dancing Gangnam Style at the Giants 2012 victory celebration.

Seriously though, Tommy, to be here with you is *such* an honor, it really is . . . you were my great, great, great-grandmother's favorite manager.

People rarely succeed in environments or jobs they don't enjoy. In baseball, the job is a no-brainer. Players get paid to play ball, to do what they love. But during the season, they live in the clubhouse as well as on the field. Chemistry requires a healthy rhythm of hard work, fun, and high energy both on and off the field.

When players can joke and laugh with each other—assuming it's not hurtful—it takes the edge off. When you can laugh about things you might not get by with in public, and when that humor offers a sense of relief, the clubhouse becomes an element in growing the team's chemistry. This is why *not* telling players to check their personalities at the door is so important. People tend to more openly express a sense of humor when they can be themselves. Here are some of the benefits.

Humor tames the ego. Not taking yourself too seriously is one of the best ways to keep your ego in check—to give it some perspective. If you can laugh at yourself, it tells people that you have some distance between yourself and the terminal seriousness of your concerns. You become detached from you. Keep in mind that detachment is not the same as denial. Detachment says: "I am fully aware of my situation and willfully choose not to hang on to it too tight. I'm going to look at it from a distance." Denial shows that you are disconnected from reality. For example, a player who is still anxiety-ridden over some constructive feedback he got from a coach several weeks ago, and doesn't think it is affecting his current attitude is too close to it. He's probably in denial.

At 6 feet 4 inches and 245 pounds, Boch is an imposing figure with a powerful presence. He has a deep voice laced with a bit of a Southern whiskey drawl, Popeye forearms, and massive hands that look like bear paws. Stand next to him and he engulfs you. His size intimidates most people.

Boch also has the largest head in baseball—size 8 ⅛. Shortly after he was drafted by Houston in the first round, he took his college batting helmet with him to the club because the Astros couldn't find one his size. The players nicknamed him "Headly" for the size of his melon. Then crisis struck. After one bad at bat, not-yet- "Captain Calm" slammed his helmet onto the dugout floor and cracked it.

Uh-oh.

That sent the club scrambling to find a new helmet. Eventually, they special-ordered one. From that point on, whenever Boch was traded, each new club had to paint his old helmet their team color and then put their own logo on it. The New York Mets mascot, Mr. Met, had an even bigger head. When Boch played for the club, players would tease him saying, "You just need to wear Mr. Met's hat."

That helmet was good for more than just protecting Bruce's head. In perhaps the biggest highlight of his playing career, Boch hit a walk-off home run for the Padres against his former teammate and pitching great, Nolan Ryan.

Boch: We were tied in the bottom of the 10th inning with two outs. I got Nolan when he was tiring a bit, which meant he was probably down to about a 97-mph fastball. After we did the postgame show, I walked into the clubhouse and the guys had laid a red carpet to my locker [and put] a six-pack of beer on ice in my helmet. Terry Kennedy, our starting catcher, said, "There are a lot of helmets that will fit a six-pack of beer, but Bochy's helmet is the only one that will fit a six-pack of beer *with* ice."

At a speech that Boch gave when he managed the Padres, first baseman Wally Joiner started his introduction by making fun of the skipper's head. Joiner told the audience that he remembered playing against Boch and wondering, "Who is this guy with the gigantic melon behind home plate?" Joiner closed by eloquently stating that only after playing *for* Boch did he realize that his head was superseded by the size of his heart.

Where's Boch? Former Padres closer and acclaimed future Hall of Famer Trevor Hoffman told a story about Boch during his playing days as a backup catcher for San Diego. Boch was in the bullpen during a game helping out with some catching duties. The dugout called the pen and said they needed Boch immediately to pinch-hit. "He starts trucking down the back way through the tunnel in Qualcomm and he never shows up," Hoffman recounted. "They're all in the dugout wondering what happened to Bruce. He smoked his head on a beam underneath [the stadium] and knocked himself out. I wasn't there, but just to think about his wrecking-ball head going into one of those beams; we're lucky the stadium didn't come down."[79]

When it comes to the size of his head, Boch gets in on the act. He's not a big joke teller, but he has an extremely quick wit and comes up with some great one-liners. Here are a few he's let loose over the years.

> When asked if the size of his head is where he stores all the genius to manage games, Boch said: "I don't know. There's an awful lot of empty space up there. When I played, if my numbers were better, they'd have accused me of using steroids, as big as my head is."

> When Jake Peavy was being interviewed during the 2014 NLCS, the press asked him how Boch had changed since the two were together in San Diego.

> **Peavy:** "Boch, how have you changed over the years? They're asking me. [To the press] He's gotten older, grayer . . ."

> **Boch interrupting:** "Better lookin!"

> At a Q&A in front of a large audience a fan said some of the Giants games keep him up at night. He asked, "How do you deal with the tough losses?" Boch asked, "When you can't sleep, are you yelling at me or the players?"

> When asked about his favorite last meal, Boch said, "If I was going to the electric chair I probably would order cabbage rolls, a Bochy family favorite. They take a long time to make."

As you can see, Boch is comfortable in his own skin—foibles and all. This opens the door for his players to be themselves as well. There's a certain amount of freedom that comes with being accepted for who you are versus someone you are pretending to be. In Boch's case that freedom translates into a unique clubhouse chemistry as well as players who hold nothing back on the field.

Humor is disarming. Humor levels the playing field and puts people at ease. By not taking himself too seriously, Boch becomes more human, less intimidating, and more approachable. Think about all the things that *don't* get said in a relationship in which someone is prickly. How many small problems get swept under the rug when someone is unapproachable? And when those small problems

> **Think about all the things that don't get said in a relationship in which someone is prickly. Humor makes us more approachable.**

fester into big problems, what is the psycho-emotional cost to the club? How does it hinder performance? Screw up chemistry? Having a manager players and coaches alike can relate to is no small thing.

It makes sense, doesn't it? Authenticity. Self-awareness. Transparency. These are some of the character strengths we look for in every leader. We are much more apt to enthusiastically follow someone who is *real,* someone who has a good grasp on their strengths and weaknesses. Vulnerability helps us identify with these people, and authenticity helps us trust them. Humor helps us disarm ourselves and, in turn, disarm others.

Where's Boch—Again? In 2015, the Giants were playing the Dodgers in Los Angeles. After a Friday night win, the first of the series, the team bus left "enemy territory" without Boch. Brandon Crawford, a UCLA grad who was not staying at the team hotel, offered to give him a ride. Boch didn't want Craw to go out of his way and told him he would take a cab instead. So, there was Boch, standing in a swarm of Dodgers fans while he waited for more than half an hour to flag down a cab. The incident drew some funny responses on Twitter.

"He's lucky to be alive."

"Looks like someone is sitting on the bench."

"Bochy discovers the joys of finding a taxi in L.A."

"This is better than Lane Kiffin [USC's football coach] getting called off of the bus and canned."

"We put a sedated Mattingly on the bus wearing an SF uniform and kidnapped Bochy. No word yet if someone's getting fined for this."

The next day before the game, Fox Sports asked him about it. "The bus left me," he told Fox. "I thought it was like, 'Leave no troops behind.'"

Boch: Standing there outside Dodger Stadium I'm thinking: "I wasn't *that* hard on the players tonight was I? Or, we *are* in hostile territory; could someone have hijacked our bus?" Then it occurred to me, "I might have to fine myself." I'm just glad I had $20 in my pocket for the cab ride. And people think I have a glamorous job.

No one was chastised, no one got fired, and Boch didn't fine himself. In an uptight clubhouse, the ending might have been different. With Boch, this incident sent a different kind of message. It's easier to brush off small inconveniences and bad things that happen with a sense of humor. When your mistakes aren't the end of the world, it's easier to own them.

But when bad things really do happen, this kind of self-detachment also serves to drive home a lesson. No one on a ball club wants to be the guy who loses a game for the team. Players hate that. But when it happens, you can learn from it and either detach from it or dwell on it. Dwelling on it is just another form of self-absorption because it keeps the focus on you and what's gone wrong. Dwelling on it only sets you up for failure the next time. When you laugh at your mistakes, people are

Aubrey Huff shows off his red "Rally Thong" during the Giants 2010 victory parade.

more willing to show compassion and laugh with you. They see that you are not trying to hide behind a facade of perfection.

Humor unites. "There's a little black cloud that hangs over baseball every single day," said Giants broadcaster Mike Krukow. "Nobody talks about it, but they know it's there. Each day you show up could be your last: an injury, lack of ability, the feeling you may never get another hit, throw another strike. The only way to get through that pressure is being able to laugh at it. You look back at every great team and you'll find one or two guys who were the primary comedians, guys who found levity in difficult situations."[80]

On August 30, 2010, the Giants were five games behind the first-place Padres. As they say, "Desperate times call for desperate measures." First baseman Aubrey Huff brought a secret weapon into the Giants clubhouse. A gag gift from his wife, it was a red thong adorned with rhinestones. The Giants needed to win 20 of their last 30 games to make the playoffs and Huff was in a helpful mood.

Donning the red rhinestone thong in the locker room, Huff dubbed it the "Rally Thong," saying, "Boys, this is going to get us 20-10." As the pennant pressure mounted, the Rally Thong took on a life of its own. The media and fans picked up on it. And Isaco, the company that produced Huff's preferred brand of thongs, sent him a box of the products so he could outfit the players and various members of the media.

Going into the final game of the season, the Giants were 19-10. A win on the last day would clinch the division title. Huff doubled in a key run, lifting his team to a playoff berth, and the Giants were 20-10. Was it the red Rally Thong or stellar pitching that brought the Giants through the postseason to a World Series victory in 2010? The smart money is on both.

> **Boch:** He's [Huff] very competitive—took the game very seriously. He just doesn't take himself too seriously. That's so good for our young players, for everyone in fact, because it kept our guys loose. Now the thong, I could do without seeing Aubrey in his thong. It wasn't easy on the eyes. But I will say, it became a symbol of a clubhouse that didn't take itself too seriously either. What can you say? We erased a six-game deficit to win the NL West on the last day. I think there is something to be said for keeping it light.

Huff said he came up into the majors where the veterans were harsh on the rookies. The 33-year-old veteran didn't want to be that way. Instead, he brought a different brand of leadership in the clubhouse. "I don't care if you're a veteran or a younger guy, if you're having fun in the clubhouse and everybody is having a good time and everybody really starts caring for each other, I think that has a lot to do with winning on the field. I don't think you can actually play baseball without a good group of guys that mix well together."[81] We call this chemistry!

On their last road trip of 2015, the Giants lost to the Padres for the second night in a row. This loss was particularly hard to swallow given that it prevented Madison Bumgarner from getting his 19th win and crushed the Giants hopes of catching the Dodgers in the race for the NL West.

Yet, something peculiar was happening as the players boarded the team plane. They were all wearing cream-colored polo shirts and had pulled latex bald caps over their heads. It was a tribute to Tim Hudson's predictable attire. The beloved, bald-headed, 40-year-old right-hander was retiring in a week. Huddy, the major league's active leader with 222 games in the win column, quickly got the message. The joke was on him.

"Looks like this team finally got some style," he said amid smirks and contained laughter.[82] The good-natured Hudson rolled with the prank as he looked around the room and joined his teammates laughing.

Humor is unifying because it builds trust and rapport. In the business of baseball, it reduces the social distance between players and coaches. Humor promotes community and causes people to feel like they belong. We don't horse around and laugh with people we don't like.

Humor is healthy. Here's the thing about people who have a great sense of humor—they're usually stronger physically and emotionally. If they are not in good physical condition, humor will often compensate for that. Humor dissolves stress and rebalances the nervous system. It revitalizes your immune system by releasing endorphins, or feel-good chemicals, into your bloodstream. Humor can help you relax and recharge by helping you let go of resentment, judgment, criticism, and doubt. It's hard to stay angry with someone when you share a laugh.

Well, most of the time.

Boch and Kevin have a friend, Kevin McNamara, whom Boch has affectionately nicknamed "Bad News." The name comes from the early days of their friendship when they lived next door to each other in San Diego. Boch had just come up as the manager of the Padres. Still feeling his way through his first full year as skipper, San Diego went through a tough losing streak. He came home one night to discover that McNamara had pounded a "FOR SALE" sign into the Bochys' front lawn.

Then, there was the time some cattle had broken through a fence and gathered in the street near McNamara's home. "Bad News" herded a couple of cows into the Bochys' backyard. Boch had come home late after a game and went to bed. The next morning, he woke up to a ranch in his backyard.

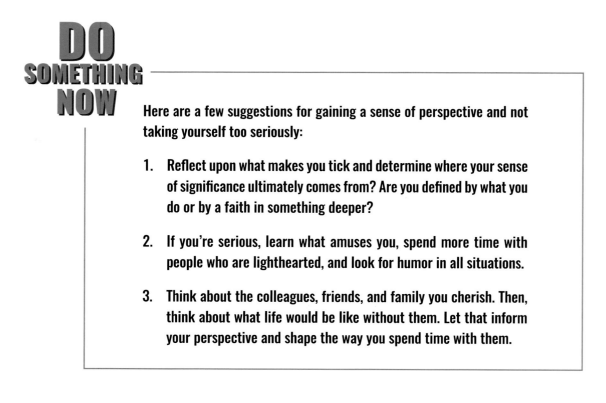

DO SOMETHING NOW

Here are a few suggestions for gaining a sense of perspective and not taking yourself too seriously:

1. Reflect upon what makes you tick and determine where your sense of significance ultimately comes from? Are you defined by what you do or by a faith in something deeper?

2. If you're serious, learn what amuses you, spend more time with people who are lighthearted, and look for humor in all situations.

3. Think about the colleagues, friends, and family you cherish. Then, think about what life would be like without them. Let that inform your perspective and shape the way you spend time with them.

Boch is not beyond pulling his own pranks. He once arranged for room service at a hotel to deliver a $300 order to Flann's door. Of course, it was surprise to his third base coach. Flann responded, "He loves to make the guys laugh at my expense."[83]

Perspective is a choice. Think of the power of what happens when a team of guys shows up saying, essentially, "The world doesn't revolve around me. My work is not my worth. I'm not going to let criticism define me. And, I choose to look for the humor in every situation. I'm not going to take myself too seriously."

In a place like this, players don't escape conflict; they simply deal with it more effectively. They don't avoid hardship, struggles, and pain; they just choose to look at the situation from a different perspective. It's not permanent and pervasive, it's situational and contextual. In a club like the Giants, players hang out longer because they like to be around people who are fun. They get to know each other better and enjoy each other more. They grow closer to their coaches because humor reduces the social distance between traditional levels of hierarchy. In a place like this, there is more acceptance and life. In a place like this, chemistry is abundant.

Conor Gillaspie, Hunter Pence, Hensley Meulens sharing a little chemistry.

23

BE MANIACAL
Stay Focused in the Moment

Think about your favorite brands. Most world-renowned brands do one thing and do it brilliantly. If we said the category is sports cars, you might think Porsche or Ferrari. How about cameras for adventure sports? Your name would be GoPro. Search? Google is a no-brainer. Watches. It's probably Rolex.

What these companies have in common is that they have focused on one thing so single-mindedly they now lead and own the category. They don't get distracted by trying to be all things to all people. They play at full throttle to be the best in class in their space. If you try to build a brand that tries to address everything, you end up with one that stands for nothing. These brands are iconic because they've maintained a laser-like focus. The same maniacal focus that separates these brands from the pack is what separates world-class athletes and championship teams from everyone else.

In a game where there is a significant amount of time between innings and at bats, it's easy to lose your focus, to drift mentally. And when you drift, you lose control, even if only for a moment or two. But a 10th of a second is all it takes to miss a pitch or botch a play.

When the stakes are high, the stage is big and the pressure intense, as it is in the postseason. There's a lot of hoopla and just as many distractions. The media wants more of you: every day the pundits dissect your strengths and weaknesses and analyze

A person who chases two rabbits catches neither.

—Chinese Proverb

your chances of success, and friends you didn't even know you had want to attend games and be part of the excitement. The heightened expectations of fanatical fans intensify all this drama.

And as if that weren't enough, there are internal distractions to contend with. How do you keep your emotions in check when a key player you count on gets injured or another gets suspended? How do you react when, during last night's game, you had to use your bullpen too much and tonight you'll face an umpire who's known for an inconsistent strike zone? Will being in the opponent's house, with its wild and loud fans, get on your last nerve?

All these diversions can cause even the most talented players to crumble under such pressure. Mental toughness—the ability to detach from all the noise and stay confidently and decisively in the moment, regardless of what confronts you—is what it means to have a maniacal focus. It's the power of being present. Some refer to it as being "locked and loaded." Others call it being "in the zone."

You would think that pitching in a one-game, do-or-die Wild Card matchup would be the most stressful scenario you could be in. When asked about it after the Giants defeated the New York Mets in the 2016 Wild

Card Game, however, Madison Bumgarner said: "I try not to look at it that way. I try to leave the pressure out of it, get rid of that and just worry about pitching. That's it." Bum took a nap on the bus on the way into the ballpark before the game. There's a definition of relaxed!

After the same Wild Card Game, Buster Posey was asked about all that he had accomplished in his young career and being in the playoffs four times. Posey brushed it off saying, "I'm just trying to stay in the moment and get ready for the next series."

The Longest Game

In the 2014 NLDS against the Nationals, who had the best record in the National League, Game 2 lasted six hours and 23 minutes across 18 innings! It was the longest postseason game in MLB history.

A workhorse and, perhaps, the unsung hero of the entire 2014 season, reliever Yusmeiro Petit was a warrior. Between July and the end of August, he set an MLB record by retiring 46 consecutive batters, over eight outings. Entering the game in the 12th inning he became just the seventh pitcher in MLB history to throw six or more shutout innings in relief in a playoff game.

"The job Petit did that night, I personally think it was one of the best appearances ever in postseason history," Buster Posey said. "There was a point in that 18-inning game that I think I was borderline delirious."

In the longest game in postseason history (18 innings), Yusmeiro Petit pitched six remarkable scoreless innings.

Approaching midnight, Brandon Belt finally broke the deadlock when he launched a homer into the upper deck in right field in the top of the 18th. Broadcaster Mike Krukow called it "an amazing gut-check victory." Brian Sabean remembered it as a defining moment in the playoffs. Washington literally had 10 "bottom-of-the-ninth" innings in which to beat the Giants and they couldn't do it.

> **Boch:** That game was such a great example of raw determination and grit. Our guys never lost their focus. It just showed the kind of will they have. Petit's resolve was unwavering.
>
> I say "unwavering," but I must admit, I thought he was wavering when I first brought him in. He didn't have his normal great command that we are used to seeing. Given the urgency of the moment, I had Rags get Lincecum going. Well, Petit got out of the inning. I checked on him in the dugout because I didn't know if the moment was getting to him. He said, "I'm fine, it's just that my fingers were so cold when I first came in, I couldn't feel the ball." Then he went back out and gave us one of the gutsiest postseason performances I've ever seen.
>
> I don't know if he ever got the credit he deserved for what he did during the regular season and postseason, but it was truly remarkable.

The Giants sense of resolve and raw determination when someone's foot is on their throats has baffled their opponents and baseball gurus alike. Where does this ability to dig deep come from? What contributes to their presence of mind and their ability to stay cool under pressure? Why do they play some of their best baseball precisely at those moments when adversity teases them with fear, anxiety, impatience, and confusion? What animates their single-mindedness? Here are some of the things that define the maniacal focus they bring to the game.

Be Fully Present—Seize the Moment

Players and coaches who stay in the moment declutter their minds. This means being aware of the emotions that can distract and derail them. For example, fear can cause a pitcher to overestimate the power of a hitter. Instead of attacking, he becomes unnecessarily cautious. Frustration over the umpire's strike zone might drive a hitter to be impatient and overly aggressive. He ends up swinging at junk. Mentally reliving the emotional high of a perfect double play could make an infielder mentally drift just long enough to miss the next gettable line drive.

> **Boch:** When a "catchable" ball is dropped in the outfield, allowing a run to score, the great pitchers maintain their focus because they know that getting irritated is useless. It clutters their mind, clouds their judgment, and frustrates their mechanics just enough to make them vulnerable to a hitter. The emotion seems justified, but in reality, it only gets in the way of what they are trying to accomplish.

Emotions are powerful. Initially, they are stronger than your mind is. Adversity will reveal this. This is why we call it "maniacal" focus. There is a battle within yourself for clarity that demands the utmost intensity and awareness to stay present. How do you do this? It comes through practice and experience. Battle-tested in so many come-from-behind games, the Giants have learned to break the game down into parts, keep it simple, and focus on what needs to be done—right now.

> **Boch:** Maniacal focus is about being present in the moment. You're not thinking about your last at bat or the lousy call the umpire made 30 seconds ago. You're not thinking about who's warming up in the bullpen or the great rally you had going that just ended [because of] a great play from the opposing team or the home run your teammate just stole from the hitter by making an unbelievable leap over the wall. You're not thinking about how stinking hot or cold

it is, how hungry you are, or how the rain that's starting to fall will affect your next at bat. And, you are certainly not spending even a nanosecond on the fight you had last night with your spouse or girlfriend.

Most of our thoughts are about the past or future. But guess what? The past is gone and the future has not yet arrived. A player who becomes so fixated on the mistake he just made or what might happen tomorrow forfeits the clarity of mind to be 100 percent ready to see things for what they are in the moment.

> **Boch:** What happens when an outfielder drops his guard and turns a base hit into a double? What happens when the pitcher forgets to cover first base on a ground ball to the right side? Was the third base coach still ruminating over the last out because he waved a runner home who was tagged out at the plate? These are the things that can take you out of the moment.

Getting in the mindset that this could be your last pitch, your last at bat ever, can bring a sense of clarity and urgency that helps you get locked in, that helps you be in the moment.

> **Boch:** Maniacal focus means you never give away a pitch or an at bat because something went wrong. It's one pitch at a time. If you just made a good or bad pitch, focus on the next one. If you've had three hits, get greedy; get locked in for four. It's about not giving an inch of concentration even though the score is hopelessly unbalanced, you're angry at the umpire, or someone on the other team just looked at you funny. This is why focus is such a game-changer.

Relentless Emphasis on the Fundamentals

Ever since Boch came into the big leagues as a manager he has stressed the importance of the fundamentals—hitting, pitching, base running, run downs, and relays—from spring training through the postseason. Every year when he prepares his spring training talks, he plans to say something to the players about going back to the basics. As an outsider, Kevin didn't feel he had the credibility to question him, but he always thought: "Bruce, these guys are major league players. Don't they have the fundamentals down by now?" Nevertheless, getting better at the fundamentals has been a constant theme in his messages and a long-term, enduring practice on the field.

Clearly, there is wisdom in Boch's approach. Without a solid foundation of fundamentals, you can't get in the frame of mind you need to achieve maniacal focus; it's virtually impossible.

> **Boch:** When you've drilled and drilled and drilled on the basics of the game, the basics become a part of you. They're second nature. You really don't have to think about it. They become unconscious and intuitive, which frees up mental space to be in the moment. Instead of thinking about the three steps to charging a ground ball, you intuitively do it. That gives you the mental capacity to make a split-second decision about what you're going to do with the ball once you get it.
>
> When the fundamentals come automatically, you can improvise. In a lot of cases, plays come up where you must be creative; you must adjust on the fly. Those are the times when being single-minded is more important than ever. Players have to be instinctive and make it up as they go. But that doesn't happen unless the fundamentals are an unconscious reflex reaction.

Relentlessly emphasizing the fundamentals might not be sexy, but it leads to a lot of entertaining baseball. Watch Joaquín Árias take an extremely tough ball hop at third and fire to first to complete Matt Cain's perfect game. Watch second baseman Joe Panik intuitively flip a ball out of his glove to shortstop Brandon Crawford, who turns it into a beautifully executed double play. Watch Gregor Blanco or Hunter Pence make an impossible diving catch in the outfield and you will see that exceptional plays are built on a rock-solid foundation of basic plays, where ordinary becomes extraordinary.

Expecting the Unexpected

To be maniacally focused means your radar is always on and your antenna is up, which gives you a heightened level of awareness, first about yourself and then about your teammates. Think of a service dog that senses the energy of its master, picking up on every movement. The two function as one. This awareness and perceptiveness comes from being in the moment and paying complete attention.

In Game 2 of the 2012 World Series against the Tigers, Marco Scutaro made a spectacular play. Instinct based on having the fundamentals down pat, coupled with being in the moment, gave Scutaro the presence of mind to be in the right place at the right time. In the top of the second inning, with no score and no outs for the Tigers, outfielder Delmon Young shot a double to left field. Gregor Blanco bobbled it long enough for Prince Fielder to attempt to score all the way from first.

It looked like Fielder was going to make it when Blanco's throw badly missed its relay target, shortstop Brandon Crawford. Scutaro anticipated just such a scenario, raced over to back up Crawford, and fielded the ball on the third-base line. Scutaro whirled around, planted, and fired to Buster Posey at the plate. Posey, who had been brutally injured by a crash at home plate the year before, faced Fielder (the largest man in baseball) charging the plate. Scutaro's throw arrived just in time for Posey to slap the tag on Fielder for the out. The game remained scoreless until the seventh inning, when the Giants pulled it out 2-0 on their way to sweeping the Fall Classic.

In Game 2 of the 2012 World Series, Buster Posey tags Prince Fielder for the out. The play was set up by an amazing throw from Marco Scutaro.

You have to ask, "Where does this kind of concentration and composure come from?" It comes from practicing those fundamentals so often that you get it right every time. It comes from not having to think about the fundamentals in the heat of the moment because you are one with them. Execution, in terms of accuracy, speed, and position, is a given.

The Giants mental toughness and ability to focus in the heat of the battle has been honed in repeated gut-wrenching battles. Between the start of 2010 and the completion of the 2014 season, the San Francisco Giants played 47 games where they came from behind in late innings to win.

Staying calm and keeping your wits about you in a high-stakes game doesn't come from some magical formula. Presence of mind isn't relegated to superior intellect, a 007-like bravado, or some focus-enhancing meds. True, unwavering, maniacal focus comes through experience. Maniacal focus under pressure is the result of being tested repeatedly.

> **Boch:** It's uncanny how calm our guys are under pressure. You come to expect it from the veterans, from the guys who've been there [the postseason], but even our rookies have demonstrated a focus that is beyond their years. Posey and Bumgarner in 2010, Panik in 2012, and Duffy in 2015.
>
> I'm not exactly sure how to describe it, but something in the battle-tested veterans rubs off on the younger guys. It's not cocky, it's a calm in the storm and it *is* contagious. And when the young guys make plays and show composure, it lights a fire in the veterans. Pretty soon you have a collective spirit that just won't back down.
>
> I'm sure that the number of close games we played during the regular season prepared our guys for the intensity of the playoffs. And then you think about playing in our park. Our fans are fanatical. They're loud. They're into it every . . . single . . . game, and that makes it feel more like the postseason.

Every time the Giants came back to win an intensely fought battle it made them stronger and better able to stay focused. Each close call equipped them to not panic and to play *their* game. Every time they won like that, it strengthened their faith in the future and increased their confidence in doing it again. Every game reinforced what they know about staying maniacal. A few key lessons: Slow down, never underestimate your competition, and remember that opponents are mortals too.

On paper, the Giants have always faced more talented teams. On paper, the prognosticators have never picked this club to win. In a sense, this has been a gift to the players because it does two things. First, it agitates them. It calls forth a stubborn defiance that says, "We'll prove 'em wrong." Second, instead of assuming their "more talented" opponents *won't* hurt them, they buckle down and do their best to make sure their opponents *can't* hurt them.

> When the young guys make plays and show composure, it lights a fire in the veterans. Pretty soon you have a collective spirit that just won't back down.

> **Boch:** Scouting is the point of reconnaissance in our game. But just because the information is available doesn't mean everyone reads it or looks at the video and absorbs it. *Being there* means that when we are going over scouting reports on another team, the players are 100 percent focused. They're not thinking, "I've heard this stuff before." *Being there* is when a runner gets on base, he's thinking about those reports—what he's learned about the pitcher's delivery or the strength of the catcher's arm—to decide if he can steal a base. He's thinking about every scenario that could unfold in the moment, instead of listening to the first baseman.

The coaches and players who are hungry dig deep to know who they are up against. Going the extra mile is just part of their routine. We assume that opposing teams are capable of more in any given game. We try to expect the unexpected. That means, study it from as many angles as possible so there are no surprises. Every game is different. We want to approach it in a way that doesn't give the other team any unnecessary openings.

Given the number of come-from-behind games the Giants have won, they know that it is possible to be on the other side of that scenario. In the second half of 2016, for example, they lost an extraordinary number (28 blown saves) of one-run games in late innings. The lesson: The game isn't won until the last out is recorded. Even if you are way ahead and the outcome seems like a forgone conclusion, you have to stay hungry. Never underestimate your opponents. Don't kid yourself that they aren't a serious threat. Especially when you're under extreme pressure.

Pat Dobson, Dick Tidrow, Brian Sabean—part of the Giants scouting braintrust.

You hear veterans telling younger players these lessons learned: "Whether the grounder is an obvious out or not, run it out." "On a single don't assume the base runner will stop at second." "On a routine fly ball don't automatically assume the outfielder will catch it." These truisms are code for, "Assume nothing and stay focused; it's not over until it's over."

The Giants reduce the intimidation factor in playing more talented teams by reminding themselves that the players they face are mere mortals who are vulnerable at any given point in time, just like everyone else is. They don't give in to the superstitious notion that some guys are just unbeatable. They believe everyone has chinks in their armor, everyone has insecurities and weaknesses, and everyone can have an "off" day. No one is bulletproof.

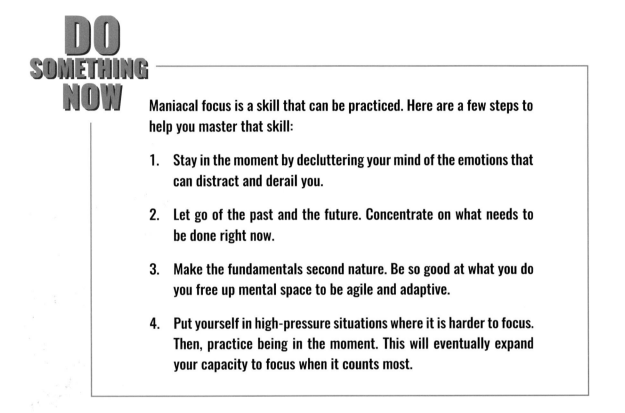

DO SOMETHING NOW

Maniacal focus is a skill that can be practiced. Here are a few steps to help you master that skill:

1. **Stay in the moment by decluttering your mind of the emotions that can distract and derail you.**

2. **Let go of the past and the future. Concentrate on what needs to be done right now.**

3. **Make the fundamentals second nature. Be so good at what you do you free up mental space to be agile and adaptive.**

4. **Put yourself in high-pressure situations where it is harder to focus. Then, practice being in the moment. This will eventually expand your capacity to focus when it counts most.**

It's easy to overestimate your opponent's abilities and underestimate your own. If you can think rationally and not emotionally about this, if you can truly separate the person from the myth, intimidation will yield to concentration and enable you to bear down, with laser-like focus, on the things you can control. You define the game on your terms by executing on the skills that got you there in the first place.

Boch: After three Championships, I've never gotten tired of watching how talented athletes come together and become a band of brothers when they share the same focus and give their hearts, minds, and spirits to something bigger. It's a remarkable thing to experience.

Baseball is a sport that is fast and then slow. It's a game that requires episodic sprints of intense, albeit quiet, concentration for at least nine innings, every day, for seven months. Baseball is about rhythm and balance—you have to be intense yet calm, explosive yet patient, aggressive yet judicious, adaptive yet consistent, and cerebral yet instinctive. None of this can be achieved unless the focus is maniacal and the fundamentals are deeply ingrained.

7th Inning

GIANT SWAGGER

The Guts to be Disciplined, Accountable, and Unpredictable

24
FULL THROTTLE
Play to Win, Not to Not Lose

"Full Throttle." It's the nickname the team gave Hunter Pence because he so personifies what it means to play the game all out, nothing held back. From his trademark high black socks to his unorthodox fielding style and his quirky on-deck practice swings, Pence could easily have fit into Bochy's 2010 band of misfits and castoffs. But everyone, Boch and Sabes at the top of the list, loves the way he plays.

> **Boch:** I can't remember another player who has had the stamina and durability to play every game [383 consecutive regular season games] like he did. He has one speed and that's all out, full throttle, every day. Whether it's the way he plays on the field or the way he encourages other players, his intensity is off the charts. He brings so much energy into the clubhouse. That's why he's so popular. Everything he does, you can just see how much he loves the game. I would pay to watch him play.

Full throttle is about how you approach the game—any game. Whether it's stealing a base, waving the runner on to home plate, or laying down a sacrifice bunt, full throttle is playing to win. It means you take the risk and then commit to making the play with all the passion and intensity you've got. It's striking out because you challenged the pitcher, took a good, hard cut at the ball, and made him throw perfect pitches—*not* because your swing was weak and the pitcher intimidated you.

> **Boch:** It means every at bat, every pitch, every defensive play has got to be delivered with fire in your eyes and the raw determination of a pit bull going on the attack.

Full throttle is about being accountable to yourself and others and realizing that no matter how big you are you are never bigger than the game. So, you work hard. You show up to spring training in shape with focus, purpose, and energy—always looking for ways to make yourself and your team better.

Play Every Game as if It's Your Last

"Literally my goals are to play each game as hard as I can to win," Pence told a Boston sportswriter. "That's what I write down when I'm writing down my goals for the season. I want to give every single game everything I have to win, and the rest, the numbers will take care of themselves."[84] On August 17, 2017, in a game against the Phillies at AT&T Park, Pence showed his all-out, all-the-time approach to the game. Giants left fielder Jarrett Parker smacked a double to center field driving in Denard Span and Pence. Pence ran so hard he came very close to passing Span between third base and home. As it turned out, Pence touched home plate just a step behind Span. "I just knew that he was right on my heels," Span told MLB.com's Jonathan Hawthorne after the game. "That's Hunter being Hunter . . . I didn't hear him. I just felt him. I was just running as fast as I could. In my defense, he had a running start. That was fun. Never had anybody chase me like that before on the bases."[85]

Pence, who had a great read on the ball, said: "He [Span] was coming back, and I was like, 'You gotta go.' Just trying to time it as close as I could behind him to try and score."[86]

Pence goes at it with the kind of consummate devotion that is infectious. He'll do what he needs to do to help the team win even if it means throwing himself at a wall to catch a fly ball, rallying his teammates in the dugout, or walking in bloodied and bruised with no complaint, ready for the next inning. Then, he comes back the next day and does it all over again.

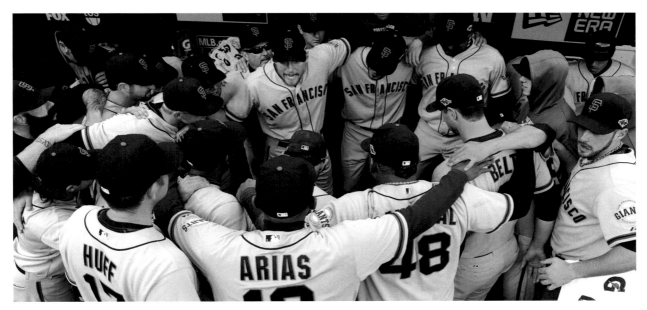

Hunter Pence doing what Hunter does best, spreading his infectious enthusiasm in the dugout.

"Everyone knows about Hunter's speeches in the clubhouse," Brandon Crawford said. "But when he crashed into the bullpen fence face-first to save a run in Arizona, there's nothing that gets your teammates more fired up than that. You see what the guy's willing to do, and everybody's energy is suddenly ramped to the next level."

Every at bat, every ball run down in the outfield, and every time he's on base, you can just see the intensity Boch talked about. It's as if Pence is saying: "This play matters. It calls for everything I've got." Hunter plays every game as though it is his last.

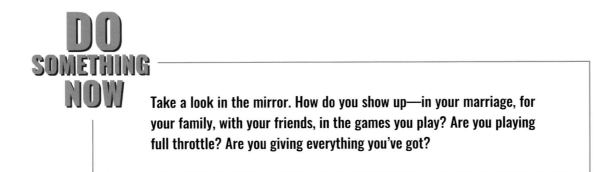

DO SOMETHING NOW

Take a look in the mirror. How do you show up—in your marriage, for your family, with your friends, in the games you play? Are you playing full throttle? Are you giving everything you've got?

Pence is the kind of guy who—through vivid, living, personal example—inspires other guys to look in the mirror and ask: "Am I giving my all? And is my 'all' like his?" This is key, because it's never one guy who wins a game. It's a collective achievement. It's starters and bullpen guys, backup players and everyday marquee guys, and rookies and veterans who show up and give it all every game—guys who love going to battle for each other. They play at their best because they don't want to let their teammates or their fans down.

Say "Yes! Yes! Yes!"

In 2014, rookie Tyler Colvin told Pence that if he hit a home run he, Colvin, would do the special handshake gesture they had worked out, pumping both index fingers in the air while chanting "Yes! Yes! Yes!" Michael Morse got in on the act and then so did the entire team. Anytime someone hit a home run it was "Yes! Yes! Yes!"

Pretty soon, the fans started to catch on and then one afternoon, in front of a packed house at AT&T Park, before the last regular season game of the year, Pence taught the entire crowd the chant. The Giants were leaving to play Pittsburgh in the Wild Card Game. Pence asked the fans if they wanted to see another game at home. Already accustomed to Hunter's brand of enthusiasm, they responded with the euphoric zeal the players have come to know—43,000 Giants fans were on their feet, hands pumping, shouting "Yes! Yes! Yes!" It became the Giants rallying cry for the 2014 postseason and an enduring symbol of what it means to play at full throttle.

Play with Heart and Will

The way Sergio Romo closed out the 2012 World Series against the Detroit Tigers is another example of what it means for the Giants to play at optimal level.

Romo inherited the closer's role late in the season as the Giants made do after their regular closer, Brian Wilson, blew out his elbow and Santiago Casilla struggled with the job. Despite the dire circumstances, most pundits questioned whether Romo had the build or mentality to handle full-time closing responsibilities. Small, at 5 feet 10 inches and 165 pounds, he also took losses hard. The criticism got old. The inferiority complex grew big. The voice of "I am not enough" relentlessly taunted him. But when the Giants needed someone to take hold of the closer's role down the stretch and into the playoffs, Romo said, "Give me the ball."

Before Game 3 of the 2012 World Series, Boch was asked what he had learned about Romo and how he was handling his new role as closer.

> **Boch:** I think, more than anything, what I've learned about Romo is how much he cares about his teammates and that's how he pitches. He wants to win for them and the club. He's a very unselfish player. Even when [Brian] Wilson went down he accepted that role [as closer]. He wants to do whatever he can to help us win. He really cares about the guys around him and he's very appreciative of being out there. There are times when he will come in and thank me for trusting him to help the team win.

Romo had only 14 saves in 2012, and 6 of those were in September. But in the Giants postseason run he saved four games, including Games 2 and 3 of the World Series. Leading three games to none going into Game 4, the Giants had an opportunity to sweep the Tigers. Boch planned to meet with the guys before the game.

> **Boch:** I just wanted to remind them of how far they had come and how good they were. I also wanted them to stay focused and take nothing for granted. We've proven, being on the other side, that a team can be down 3-0 and come back. As it turned out, Pence beat me to it and did a great job of conveying this message in his own way. Ultimately, I was grateful for the momentum we had. I liked the way we were playing. But nothing is guaranteed until that last out is recorded.

After back-and-forth home runs by each team, Game 4 was a seesaw battle, tied 3-3 at the end of nine innings. Even without his best stuff, workhorse starter Matt Cain gave his team seven innings. "That's what the great pitchers do," said Ryan Vogelsong. "They find a way to stay on the field. They win on the days when they don't have their best stuff. Cain's our ace for a reason."

In the bottom of the 10th inning, now leading 4-3, the Giants were just three outs away from another World Series title. Boch gave the ball to Romo, known less for throwing with the typical heat of a closer and more for his wicked Frisbee slider.

After two strikeouts, Romo faced his most dangerous opponent and the best hitter in the world, Miguel Cabrera. In 2012, Cabrera led the American League with a .330 batting average, 44 home runs, and 139 runs batted in. He won the batting Triple Crown epitomizing three separate attributes of a world-class hitter: hitting for average, hitting for power, and producing runs. Cabrera had already hit one home run in this game and everyone knew, with the Giants up by only one run, this guy could hurt you. This was the kind of thriller that induces gray hair.

After throwing Cabrera five nasty sliders, Romo shook off catcher Buster Posey's call for another and threw a fastball as hard as he could right over the middle of the plate into Cabrera's zone. Umpire Brian O'Nora called a third strike on a stunned Cabrera and it was over. The Giants won their second World Series in three years.

Pitcher Sergio Romo celebrates another victory while coming off the mound.

The pitch, which surprised even Boch and Rags Righetti, might have been the "ballsiest" one of the entire Series. While Romo's slider is devastatingly effective, his 88-mph fastball is not. It's certainly not the kind of pitch you would expect when you're facing the most lethal weapon in baseball, in extra innings, in the World Series, with a potential clinching game on the line. But being the perfect pitch for Cabrera to shellac, it might've been the one he was least expecting.

Boch: Sure, we were up by three games, but *we've* proven that you can disrupt that momentum in a heartbeat. You think you're secure and then the momentum shifts. We were down 0-2 to Cincinnati and we came back. We were down 1-3 to St. Louis and came back. We were on the verge of being eliminated six different times, but the momentum shifted and we came back.

We lose that game [Game 4], then we have to face their best pitcher, [Justin] Verlander. Who knows, with the rain and the weather coming in [from Superstorm Sandy], what variables you'll have to deal with. A two-day rain delay can change everything, and we're in *their* house. Better to get it done and get out of there. It's not like we felt we had a lot of cushion.

Shaking his own head in amazement and disbelief, Posey commented: "That guy, he shook to a fastball there. That shows the type of guts he has and faith in what he's got. It's just a great job by him. This is not a knock, but he throws a 88 or 89 [mph fastball], but he's got a plus, plus slider."

Have Faith in Your Team

The source of Romo's faith is his teammates. "And there I was on the mound in Game 4 of the World Series, one pitch away from winning a championship for my teammates, the organization, and the city," Romo said. "At that moment, I was the least nervous I'd been all year. A calm came over me, because I knew my teammates knew how much I cared to get the job done. My teammates looked to me to do it when it mattered, they knew how much I cared to do it for them. I knew I wasn't getting it done alone."[87]

Sergio Romo celebrates in the Giants victory parade with a political fashion statement.

When your teammates have shown confidence in you all year, and when they know you need the faith they have in you, it makes you bigger than you can be on your own. It jacks up the passion and adrenaline you have in the moment and gives you the resolve to play at full throttle.

The baseball gurus say that if you're going to get beat, you ought to get beat on your best pitch. Given the number of sliders Romo throws, why wouldn't Cabrera be expecting another slider? On the other hand, why wouldn't Romo throw another one to Cabrera? Lean on what's reliable, right? It's your signature pitch. With a 2-2 count, he could afford another ball. And, why wouldn't Posey call for another slider? Cabrera had missed the previous five Romo had thrown.

The answer is this: Romo chose to go all in. With so much on the line, going to his most reliable pitch was predictable, except it wasn't. A lot is riding on each pitch when you're going up against the most fearsome hitter in the game: maybe your best pitch isn't your best pitch; maybe it's a different pitch. Perhaps the most unpredictable thing to do is to take a risk and go as hard and as fast as someone can go.

Romo said it was a gut feeling more than anything. Perhaps he saw Cabrera foul off the previous slider with a swing that said, "I'm starting to get your number." When it was over, Posey told Romo he'd thrown "a ballsy" pitch. "I wasn't trying to be ballsy," Romo said. "I was trying to be 'smart.'" Prior to the Fall Classic, in a spirit of respect and friendly competition, Cabrera had teased that he would hit one of Romo's infamous sliders. He later admitted, "From the first pitch to the last pitch, I was looking slider." Romo called it a gut feeling. We'd call it tactical brilliance.

Fellow relief pitcher Javier López paid Romo a great compliment when he said: "He's a little man who pitches like a big man. He's a small dude, but he pitches like he's 6-6, 250 pounds." Even GM Brian Sabean was taken aback. "Santiago Casilla had so many big saves in the first half, and when he faltered, Romo became the guy. I can't say enough about that young man. It is pretty amazing, because he didn't have a track record doing this."

There's another lesson about chemistry to be mined in this risky pitch. Had Romo not had a leader who encourages players to be themselves, had he been part of a fear-based culture that doesn't tolerate going-left-on-red risk taking and mistakes, would he have trusted his gut? If he played in a culture that openly shames players for not making the high-percentage-for-success pitch, in an environment where trust waivers and players blame versus believe in each other—a place where you are constantly looking over your shoulder—would Romo have been comfortable taking the risk?

> **If you want people to play at full throttle, there has to be a culture that says, "It's okay to play on the edge."**

If you want people to play free and loose, if you want them to play all out, there has to be a culture that supports it. There must be a culture that says, "It's okay to play on the edge." As a player, to be "in the zone" you can't be worried about how your manager, GM, or pitching coach is going to respond to what you do. You can't be thinking, "If I blow this, I'm going to have to face some blame and shame." That's punitive, and the prospect of being punished for mistakes causes players to hesitate. It never allows people to bring their best selves to the game.

Instead, you have to believe that regardless of the outcome your team has your back and is all in. If you want people to be creative and innovative, to do something unconventional and unexpected to gain competitive advantage, it must be reinforced and rewarded. Your players have to be thinking: "I'm going to make this pitch *for them*. I'm going to end this game *for us*."

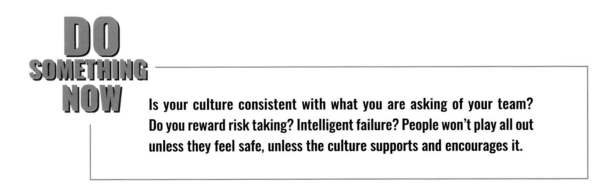

DO SOMETHING NOW

Is your culture consistent with what you are asking of your team? Do you reward risk taking? Intelligent failure? People won't play all out unless they feel safe, unless the culture supports and encourages it.

During the regular season, second baseman Marco Scutaro had counseled Romo about shaking it up after hitters had zoned in on his slider. After watching Romo stubbornly throw too many sliders in a row and then get beaten, Scutaro said, "If you had thrown a fastball to that guy he'd have had no chance."

When Romo shook off Posey, he did it from having learned from history and knowing that he had the support of his team. Boch jokingly said, "If I'd have known he was going to throw it right down the middle, I would've called time out." But Boch liked it. Righetti liked it. Shortstop Brandon Crawford liked it. And, Scutaro empowered it. When you're in a "must get it done" situation, that kind of chemistry is priceless.

"Nobody was expecting a fastball right there," Scutaro said in applauding Romo's decision. And Righetti, one of the preeminent pitching coaches in the game today and has seen so many unbelievable performances, compared Romo to the great relievers. "There's really nobody like him. That was Rod Beck-like. That was Mariano Rivera-like; a guy with total belief in what he is doing out there."

Reflecting on closing the Giants sweep of the Tigers, Romo summed up what the experience meant to him. "I became the player I maybe once thought I never could be, because of them. It was all because of the belief and faith they had in my abilities. Not *my* faith in my abilities . . . *their* faith in my abilities. It sounds clichéd, but now that I think about it, those guys made me become a bigger person, a bigger man."[88]

Under the circumstances, Romo's pitch was epic. A gutsy move to be sure, but that's the heart of a lion and the will of a water buffalo wrapped up in a small package.

It's also what it looks like to exercise maniacal focus, deliver the extraordinary, and play at full throttle.

Go Down Swinging

At the end of the 2014 regular season, the Giants went to Dodger Stadium to play Los Angeles. Three games back and fighting for their lives, the Giants had to win Monday, Tuesday, and Wednesday—in the Dodgers house. To paint an even more dire picture, the Giants had just been swept in San Diego. Still, after a Jake Peavy win in Game 1 and Madison Bumgarner on the mound for Game 2, the Giants held out hope to win the division because nobody wanted to play Pittsburgh in the Wild Card Game.

Bumgarner started out rough. He gave up a home run to Justin Turner and then hit Yasiel Puig in the leg. Puig started toward the mound and emptied both dugouts. The next batter, Matt Kemp, hit a two-run home run to make it 3-0 Dodgers. MadBum was still looking for his first out and Dodger Stadium was going crazy. With Zack Greinke on the mound for the Dodgers, the Giants were in trouble.

Jake Peavy recounted what was going on in the Giants dugout. "Madison Bumgarner did something that showed me what he ultimately would do to single-handedly win the World Series in 2014."

> He doesn't give up a hit for quite a while—retires something like 10 hitters in a row. It's like he said, "No more!" Then, in the third inning he hits a slider off Greinke for a two-run homer. Now we're down by one in a 3-2 ballgame.
>
> Bumgarner finishes the seventh inning with 106 pitches. He's due up to bat second in the top of the eighth inning. Greinke's still pitching. With left-hand pinch hitter Travis Ishikawa on the bench it's pretty clear that Bum is done. Plus, Justin Turner, who's already hit a homer off Bum, is leading off the bottom of the eighth inning. With 106 pitches, you're just not going to send Bum out there to face this right-hand hitter again.
>
> Well, Bum comes into the dugout and I'm sitting right next to Boch and Rags [pitching coach Dave Righetti], who are talking about who's coming in the game to replace Madison. Boch looks at Bum to say, "Nice job" as if, "You're done." But Bum being Bum goes to put his shin guard on, to go hit.

I can see this whole thing unfolding. Boch thinks he's told Madison he's done and Madison ain't even thought about hearing him. Rags and Boch are still talking about [reliever] Hunter Strickland coming into this game. Well, here comes Madison back toward the stairs and Boch turns to say, "Good job" again. Bum looks at Boch and says, "You're not taking me out of this game, are you!"

Boch says, "Look, I've got to put Ishikawa in. We've got to take a chance here." Bum says, "Come on, Boch! I can do it!" Boch says, "I know, I know," trying to put him off so he can get back to talking to Rags because they aren't settled on Strickland yet. Boch turns back toward Rags. Raising his voice, Bum says, "You ain't talking to me like *you know!* I got you the only two runs you've got!"

I said to myself [laughing as he tells us], "Oh shit, he's got a point here." Now, a lot of the team is watching this go down. So Boch looks Bum in the eye and says, "C'mon son, let's go win a game!" Bum ran out to bat like a little kid.

That was a moment in time when Bum became our guy. Our season is on the line. We have to win this game. And, I think Boch made such an emotional call because he knew the other 25 guys wanted to see this happen.

Madison Bumgarner struck out on a 3-2 at bat, Justin Turner hit another home run in the bottom of the eighth inning, and the Giants lost to the Dodgers 4-2. Foolish choice on Bochy's part? Maybe. Did Boch have a great time explaining all of this to the media afterward? No.

The Dodgers stormed the field and celebrated, but many of the players felt something special happened to the Giants in the final innings of that game. Bumgarner demonstrated his heart for the team and his will to win, and he modeled a full-throttle spirit that had a contagious effect on the rest of the club.

A fierce competitor with quiet swagger and imposing stature, MadBum has earned the confidence of his teammates—and Boch.

"We had this collective state of mind that said, 'We went down swinging and we went down with *our* guy!'" Peavy said. "And Boch was right there. He walked through the clubhouse afterward saying: 'Hell of an effort. I'll go down with you boys anytime!' I noticed that something had changed and Huddy [pitcher Tim Hudson] saw it too. We talked about it. It's like Bum became the rallying point and his 'throttle down' mentality elevated every one of us."

Boch went against every rule in the book, but he instinctively endorsed swagger in that moment, a move that propelled Madison Bumgarner and the Giants forward—a swagger the Giants would draw upon in the 2014 World Series. Peavy agreed. "I really believe it set the stage for what Bum did when he made history with Game 7 of the World Series on the line. A lot of people thought Bum would bridge the gap to Romo and Casilla in Game 7, but we all felt that once Bum was in, he wasn't coming out of the game. There was no way that anybody wanted to go down with anyone but Bum out there."

Madison Bumgarner is one of the best October pitchers in the history of the game. In the 2016 Wild Card Game against the New York Mets, he pitched another shutout to advance the Giants to the NLDS. After the game, he defined what it means to play at your best. Speaking with respect for the kind of power the Mets have, knowing they hit a lot of home runs, Bum said: "You can't go out there and pitch scared, like you're afraid to give up that home run. You have to throw every pitch with conviction and believe it's the right one."

No hesitation. All in. Giant swagger. That's full throttle.

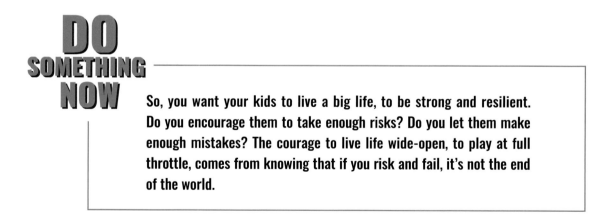

DO SOMETHING NOW

So, you want your kids to live a big life, to be strong and resilient. Do you encourage them to take enough risks? Do you let them make enough mistakes? The courage to live life wide-open, to play at full throttle, comes from knowing that if you risk and fail, it's not the end of the world.

25
HOPE IS NOT A STRATEGY
Relentless Preparation

Hope is the belief that something improbable is possible. How can a team achieve anything difficult and worthwhile without hope? Hope is a critical part of achieving strategy, but in and of itself, hope is not a strategy. Boch puts this in perspective.

> **Boch**: You can hope to acquire the right talent with the right makeup. You can hope you're going to make the right pitch or move a runner over. You can hope to shut down the offense or find a chink in the armor of the defense. You can hope to go deep into the postseason, but hope is not a strategy.

Strategy is about having a goal, a plan to achieve it, the rigor to prepare, the discipline to focus on things you can control, and the courage to execute by making gutsy decisions. In a sense, hope inspires strategy, and it is also animated by it.

Think Like Your Opponent

We've talked about what it means to play at full throttle on the field, but there is another dimension of being all in, and that's what happens before a team ever takes the field. Full throttle is about being so accountable to yourself and your teammates that you hold back nothing when it comes to preparation.

Lioness studies her opponent, a herd of gazelles, Etosha National Park, Namibia.

If you watch lions hunt, there is something extraordinary to be learned from how they prepare for the battle to come. They study—intently. They will follow a herd for days, scanning every movement, picking up patterns, and identifying its weaker members. Rigorous in their observation, they take note of everything and patiently wait for the perfect moment to attack. Their assault is not hasty, nor do they wing it. It is strategic, intentional, well coordinated, and timely.

> **Boch:** One of the biggest upsets in boxing history was when Evander Holyfield pummeled Mike Tyson to win the heavyweight crown. I read where Holyfield, before fighting Tyson, watched every video, of every round, of every fight Mike Tyson ever had. It boils down to work ethic. Holyfield wasn't only in great physical shape, he knew his opponent better than anyone.

Boch devours scouting reports. He watches a lot of video. He quickly grasps sabermetrics. He talks to his coaches and players about other coaches and players. He knows the rule book inside and out. He has a working knowledge of the nuances in each ballpark. And, he studies other managers, trying to understand their patterns and temperaments to think like they do. All this is to say you can be assured that, like a pride of lions stalking their prey, Boch works like crazy pregame to gain a deep working knowledge of every opponent the Giants will face.

In the dugout during a game, this advance preparation enables him to process information quickly and respond to what's happening in real time with speed and agility and the element of surprise. In many cases, it forces his opponents to act before they are ready. Processing the quantitative and objective part of the game in advance also frees him to think intuitively during the game. And it's the balance of these two that makes him so effective.

Boch: In an early matchup between the pitcher and hitter, the pitcher has the upper hand. The hitter doesn't really have a reference point on the pitcher as far as his velocity, his movement, and any patterns he may have. The more a hitter sees a pitcher, the more he learns and the better reference point he develops. Great hitters have an uncanny ability to store that knowledge in their heads.

We all know how Ted Williams [regarded as the greatest hitter who ever lived] turned hitting into a science. He watched a pitcher's every move, identified their pitch sequences and patterns, and picked up on their nuances. He noticed how they would adjust given the count, what they would do different in late innings, and he could see when a hitch in their delivery tarnished their stuff.

Two of the most cerebral hitters I've had are Tony Gwynn and Barry Bonds. Both remind me of Ted Williams. They watched video, studied pitchers, and had a remarkable ability to know what pitch the pitcher was going to throw in any count, in any situation. Both were similar in this regard: instead of being in the batting cage below the stadium before the game, they would be in the dugout watching the opposing pitcher warm up.

Barry Bonds holds all-time home run record (762) in Major League Baseball.

Tony Gwynn was one of the most consistent hitters in baseball (.338).

In a sense, Ted Williams paved the way for players like Gwynn and Bonds, and really, all of today's great hitters. He was like the great generals. They say that Patton read everything he could about his enemies and then used their own strategies and tactics against them. He often knew his enemies as well as they knew themselves.

Boch's thoughts on Ted Williams and General Patton echo what Sun Tzu taught in *The Art of War*. "Know the enemy and know yourself; in a hundred battles you will never be in peril. When you are ignorant of the enemy, but know yourself, your chances of winning or losing are equal. If ignorant both of your enemy and yourself, you are certain in every battle to be in peril."[89]

Demand Timely Intel

You may thoroughly study your opponent, but what you knew about them last year, or yesterday, has most likely changed. Every year the Giants tweak things to try and get better. Every year the questions remain: "How can we be creative? How can we innovate and shake it up to have a better shot at the postseason?" Every off-season the players ask themselves, "What am I going to do different next season to bring my game up?"

If you think you knew your opponent from intelligence gathered last year, think again. They've changed. Just like you. The good ones are studying your patterns. They're trying to figure out how to adjust to changes you are making. They are learning from the tendencies your team is showing—as well as from the things they did right and wrong last season or the season before—and they are adapting. If your reconnaissance is dated, your strategy is weak.

> If you think you knew your opponent from intelligence gathered last year, think again. They've changed. Just like you.

As he approaches spring training each year, Boch just assumes that every other team in the league is smarter and better—that they may not respond to his strategies the same way twice. This means his intel must be deep, broad, and current.

Make Conditioning Your Strategy

Playing at full throttle means you are willing to learn from others outside your space and let their work ethic, intensity, relaxed nature, or whatever it is inspire you. Baseball players who are avid fans of golf, racecar driving, tennis, or basketball have plenty to draw from. Boch has a fear of heights, but he has learned from a high-altitude mountain climber and applied his insights to the Giants.

In 2008, Kevin was asked to give a presentation with a unique twist to the global marketing team at Intel. His hosts asked if he would be willing to present with one of their own, Dave Arnett, one of fewer than 3,000 people who has summited Mt. Everest. Intrigued with the idea of applying the principles from the books he and Jackie had published to Dave's Everest experience, Kevin said, "I'm in."

Little did Kevin know the story went way beyond Everest. Dave had climbed Mt. Baker in Washington State, Denali in Alaska, and Mt. Kilimanjaro in Africa, but he was not an experienced climber in the "Everest" sense. A guide who saw him climb was impressed with his skills and suggested that he could do it.

After a lengthy and heartfelt discussion with his wife, Victoria, and their two daughters, Sarah and Kathryn, Dave made the choice to join an expedition team in 2007. When you make the decision to climb Everest, the experts tell you to get your affairs in order and make sure your will is up to date. It's a nine-week trek of going up and down the mountain to acclimatize, and it's dangerous.

One year before the expedition left for Nepal, Dave began a rigorous training regimen. He got up at 4:00 a.m. to run at altitude, in the snow, in the dark, in subzero weather. He tied aluminum ladders together with climbing rope, spanned them between two platforms 50 feet off the ground, and learned to walk across them wearing crampons (sharp spikes on the bottom of hiking boots made to dig into the ice) and a 60-pound backpack.

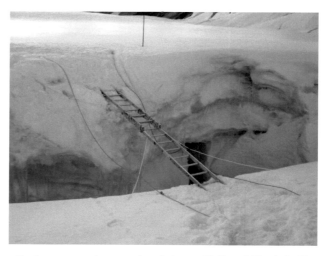

Dave was trying to simulate what it was like to cross Everest's Khumbu Icefall where blocks of ice, ranging from the size of cars to large houses, tumble down the glacier. The icefall is a place where you cross crevasses so deep that, when you look down, you can't see the bottom.

Crossing crevasses so deep you can't see the bottom, Mt. Everest's Khumbu Icefall.

Dave forced himself to climb in the most brutal of conditions. The Lhotse Face is a steep, 40-degree, 3,700-foot-high slope on the way to Everest's Camp III (at 23,625 feet). More climbers lose their lives on this face than on any other part of Everest. Dave practiced self-arresting, which is using an ice pick as a brake when you slip and fall on a face that could kill you.

Why all this conditioning?

Certainly, Dave didn't want to die on Mt. Everest, and being in the best mental and physical shape of his life, along with mastering the necessary technical skills, increased the odds in his favor. But here's what else Dave said about his preparations.

More climbers lose their lives on the Lhotse Face than anywhere on Everest.

"I didn't want to let my team down. I didn't want to be the one the Sherpas tap on the shoulder and say: *You are endangering this expedition. If you continue to climb, someone could get hurt.'* I didn't want to let my wife and daughters down by getting injured on the mountain because I wasn't in 'Everest condition.' I didn't want to prevent a fellow climber from summiting because I was too slow or unskilled."

Dave's story immediately resonated with Boch, who connected it to the preparation, discipline, and accountability necessary to give all your energy and effort and then shared some of Dave's insights with his players.

If you are a climber, you know there are countless life lessons learned from an Everest expedition. Dave Arnett can talk about it for hours, with great humility. And perhaps a comparison to baseball is a stretch. After all, people don't die on a baseball field. But his story impressed the players. The concepts translated to how they take the field, walk into the clubhouse, and engage during spring training. They immediately grasped how Arnett's experience could inform the way they play all season.

Dave Arnett summits Mt. Everest: at 29,029 feet.

Boch: I used Dave's story to talk to our players at spring training about who I wanted to make our climb with. I told them: "I want to climb with someone who has spent most of their life honing their skills for this season—someone who realizes that they are not done improving yet. I want to climb with someone who has the guts to face their fears when adversity strikes, because it will. I want to climb with someone I can trust. Who will be where they are supposed to be at the right time and will do what's best for the team. Who will watch my back and pick me up when I'm down. I want to climb with someone who has the passion to reach the summit—someone who can taste it as bad as I do."

I tried to extend Dave's story a bit more by telling our guys that everyone wants to reach the summit, but no one does it all at once. They break it down to goals that are attainable. They call them base camps. At spring training, the World Series is hard to see, just like the top of Everest, so we try to break it down into manageable goals and take it one series at a time.

Think Future Scenarios

In preparing for a game, Boch gives himself as many options as possible—and tries to offer more alternatives than his opponents do. That's because he's worked through countless scenarios before the game starts. He rejects the kind of rigid, mechanical thinking that assumes there is one right answer. His approach is more fluid. It calls for multiple plans based on multiple scenarios. Giants broadcaster and former big leaguer Duane Kuiper told us: "Boch anticipates as well as anyone. I don't ever remember him not being ready for anything that would happen on the field."

Boch rehearses each game repeatedly in his mind. He's thinking about all the possible matchups for each of those scenarios. While not invincible, he is rarely surprised by what happens during a game. There might be setbacks. A starting pitcher might be done after two innings, but Boch always prepares several contingency plans.

Boch: Usually before a big game, I'll wake up in the middle of the night going over plays with my brain in high gear. It's tough to shut down. When I get to the office I like to have some quiet time just to look at my lineup card and take it inning by inning. If something goes south during a game, who will back up our starter? Who will come off the bench? I think about which pitchers we will need against which hitters, which base runners could give us an advantage in certain situations, and which pitchers we can put a squeeze on. I don't want there to be any surprises on the field.

251

"Boch is as good as anybody in game," Jake Peavy said in a pregame interview during the 2014 NLCS. "No situation is going to arise that we're not ready for. I've already been in Boch's office today watching video of different kinds of defenses and how we're going to handle certain stuff. This man is on top of things. What I love about Boch is we're not going to be caught by surprise."

Reliever Jeremy Affeldt agreed. "I've learned a lot by watching him over the years. I used to think he managed just by gut feel, but now I know it's more than that. He thinks ahead. He plays out these scenarios in his head. He's so well-prepared that he is steps ahead of us and, I think, ahead of most other managers."

Those who manage from the opposing dugout can relate to Affeldt's comments. Former Dodgers manager Don Mattingly has said, "When you go against him, you better be prepared for everything and you are not going to surprise him with anything."[90] Phillies bench coach and former big league manager Larry Bowa concurred that Boch often sees situations before his opponents do. "He is always two steps ahead of everybody. He is an outstanding manager. He knows his personnel and he knows what his guys are capable of doing."[91]

> **When you go against Boch, you better be prepared for everything...you are not going to surprise him with anything.**

Adversity can throw a manager off balance, causing him to be reactive and irrational. When you are caught off-guard and your mind is spinning, it can drown out the voice of intuition. Mastering the details beforehand gives Boch the presence of mind to think clearly. He can be decisive because, in his mind, he's already been there.

Giants broadcaster Mike Krukow says this is especially important during the playoffs. "Once the postseason starts, you have to be proactive. You can't be a hitter late. You cannot be an inning late. You cannot be a pitch late. You just can't have a game get lost and get out of control at any point of the game. So because of that, you watch your great managers . . . they've got plan A, B, C, D and then it just goes on down the line."[92]

One of the guys who have spent more time in a Giants uniform with Boch than just about anyone is Matt Cain. "The biggest thing is, he tries to win every game—and he finds ways to win those games, too," Cain said. "Sometimes he'll do different things in certain situations, and you're wondering why, but he has always got a purpose for everything, and I think that's impressive."[93]

We've talked about how Boch stays calm under pressure and the ripple effect this has on his players. How does he do it? He limits uncertainty. Fear feeds on the unknown. It can cause a manager's imagination to run out of control and flood his mind with angst. But when you've run through so many scenarios in your head with a plan for each, and one of them comes to pass, you are focused on what that scenario calls for, on what you have planned to do. When you are able to stay in the moment, all your brainpower is being utilized; it goes back to the power of maniacal focus. There's no empty space left in your mind for worry or for entertaining an overactive fear-inspired imagination.

Experts have said that Boch takes a lot of risks during a game, but those risks are calculated. Risk taking is always a leap of faith, but in most cases, Boch has already determined there is enough evidence to warrant making the leap.

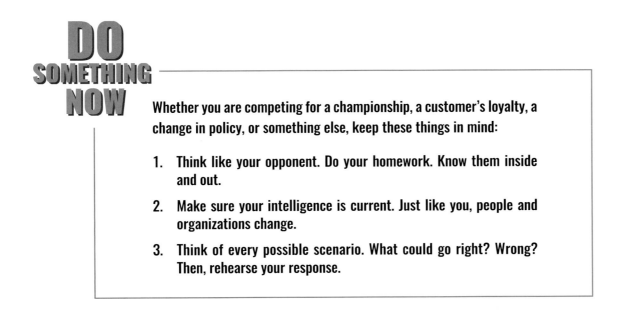

DO SOMETHING NOW

Whether you are competing for a championship, a customer's loyalty, a change in policy, or something else, keep these things in mind:

1. Think like your opponent. Do your homework. Know them inside and out.

2. Make sure your intelligence is current. Just like you, people and organizations change.

3. Think of every possible scenario. What could go right? Wrong? Then, rehearse your response.

Think Chain Reaction

As a manager, not a player, you must be able to see the big picture. That is, you must be totally "in" each game yet thinking beyond it. While Boch has one eye intensely focused on the here and now, he's got another one looking over the horizon, trying to calculate the long-term consequences of what he's doing today. He thinks systemically by asking: "How is the move I'm about to make now going to impact this player, our club, and our ability to win two innings from now, tomorrow, or three weeks from now?" It's having an understanding of the domino effect of each move. It's a balancing act.

> **Boch:** Baseball is a long season. In a sense, you have to break it down and keep it simple. From the players' perspective, we are saying, "Be in the moment, one game at a time." But in management we aren't afforded the same luxury. As a game unfolds, I'm looking ahead one or two at bats, looking at the next several pitches, anticipating the next few hitters, and trying to foresee the next couple of innings. My wheels are always turning, thinking about the next two or three games as we maneuver through an inning.

Tim Hudson has said of Boch, "His ability to think ahead in the game, those moves late in the game, that's what he's really good at."[94] "He's a good manager of the game," Brandon Crawford added. "It seems like he knows what's going to happen a couple innings before they happen. And he'll have something planned already. I don't think I've ever seen a manager as good at seeing something before it happens.[95]

This long-term perspective will influence how Boch sets up his bullpen in a game. Each individual pitcher is a bridge to the next one, and all fit into a larger game plan. Intensely focused on reading a pitcher's body language—each pitch, each inning—to evaluate his stamina and his stuff, Boch is also thinking: "How do we preserve his energy and protect him? What will we need from him a week from now? How important is *that* series going to be?" He thinks in terms of games and series—battles and campaigns.

This is especially true in the postseason. Each game is a battle that is played out in the context of a larger campaign. If the Giants are down three games in a best-of-seven series, the focus is limited to the battle—each win-or-go-home game. If they are up two games in the same type of series, and they have a little margin, Boch is thinking about the campaign—a game or two ahead.

It is rare that something would happen in a game that seduces him into a move he hadn't considered ahead of time—a decision, for example, that might jeopardize the campaign. At the same time, baseball has taught him to expect the unexpected. Future scenario generation and big picture thinking don't always pan out. When something unanticipated happens, Boch has often demonstrated the spontaneity and flexibility to adapt in the moment while keeping the campaign in mind. But sometimes, thinking in scenarios doesn't work.

Earlier we described the Giants heart-wrenching loss to the Cubs in the 2016 NLDS. As one could predict, Boch was criticized for taking starter Matt Moore out of the game at the end of the eighth inning. But here's the thing. Moore is a survivor of Tommy John surgery (elbow ligament reconstruction), and he had thrown 120 pitches. Thinking in future scenarios, Boch knew that although his bullpen was shaky, he would need to protect Moore. He was thinking, "The pen ought to be able to get three outs in the ninth, and if we win Game 5, Moore will be ready to go in the NLCS."

> **Boch:** Yeah, I had a whole season to think about that one. In a do-or-die game, I probably went against my belief: Force a Game 5, then worry about the next series. If you don't win this one [Game 4], there is no NLCS. But we had pushed our starters all season, so pulling Moore seemed like the right thing to do. It *was* a dilemma. Knowing what I know now, I'm not sure I would've done it different. There are just some scenarios you aren't going to account for. I knew our pen was struggling, but I didn't think it would implode that dramatically. Unfortunately, we will live with that one for a long time.

Boch is the first to admit he has made his share of mistakes. Whether or not pulling Moore from Game 4 is one of them will depend on your perspective. But ask the people who've played for Boch and against him and they will tell you that he rarely pulls a pitcher too early or stays with him too long. He knows when a player needs a rest and when to back off so there is still gas in the tank at the end of a long season.

DO SOMETHING NOW

Think strategy and campaign. How are the decisions you are making in this particular scenario going to impact your team, your organization, and your competition today and well into the future? How will your tactics today impact the larger campaign tomorrow or next week?

Never Think You've Arrived

Playing at full throttle is having a stake in the dreams, aspirations, and fortunes of the other 25 guys playing with you. When it comes to preparation that means you never arrive. There is always more to know about your competitors, more to know about your teammates, more skills to hone, and more that can be done to stay in top physical condition. It's a journey, not a destination. Consider the following clichés:

- **You make your own luck.**
- **Fortune favors the prepared mind.**
- **Don't expect success. Prepare for it.**
- **Failing to prepare is preparing to fail.**
- **Luck is where preparation meets opportunity.**
- **It's not the will to win, it's the will to *prepare* to win that matters.**
- **Some people dream of success while others wake up and work hard at it.**

Boch buys into all of them because he believes that freedom and accountability are intertwined. The more accountable you are to your team and the more you respect your opponents, the more diligently you prepare. The harder you work to get inside your opponent's head. The more prepared you are, the more freedom you have to shift and adapt your strategy. If you believe your strategy gives you an element of surprise, a competitive advantage, you execute more confidently, without hesitation. You play your best. Period.

Playing at full throttle is not just about what happens on the field; it's about how you prepare for what happens on the field. Hope is not a solid strategy but it may drive you to an intense level of preparation. Good strategy execution is born out of *doing* the hard work before the game ever starts. It's anticipating various scenarios and the domino effect of each. This kind of due diligence comes from not wanting to be a weak link in the chain for your teammates. When a critical mass of players and coaches adopt this discipline, when players respect the level of prework their teammates bring to the game, chemistry is elevated.

26
BE DECISIVE
Hesitation Kills Opportunity

Whether we're talking about choosing to barehand a ball to throw out a runner or leaving a pitcher in the game whose pitch count is up, decisiveness is a critical part of playing at full throttle. If you hesitate, you lose.

The word "decide" comes from the Latin word meaning "to cut off." It means that you are committing to one direction by choosing to cut off all other options. Wishy-washy comes from wanting to keep as many options open for as long as possible. Often, this stems from the fear of making a mistake or getting it wrong.

The problem with being indecisive is that it creates fatigue and fear. Every time you go back and forth over a choice to be made, it depletes you emotionally and physically. From a leadership perspective, it weakens your credibility. In baseball and in business, the decisive manager has an edge. While an indecisive manager gathers information and analyzes all the options, looking for the perfect choice, the decisive manager decides and moves forward. First movers almost always have a competitive advantage. If it's a bad decision, decisive managers recognize it, learn from it, and let go. Then, they make a new decision and move forward.

Boch's decisiveness comes from everything we've talked about thus far—mapping out scenarios, knowing his players extremely well, and studying opponents. When you are that prepared, you don't hesitate to make bold choices; wishy-washy isn't an option.

Don't Fear Being Wrong

Having the guts to shake it up doesn't come from always being right; it comes from not being afraid to be wrong. No leader can know it all, be it all, or do it all. On the backside of their strategic moves to three World Series titles, Boch and his staff look like geniuses, but on the front side, they had no guarantees that what they were doing was right. If you put yourself out there and do something unconventional, you should expect to be criticized. Boch is a likable guy, but his goal is not to be universally liked and respected; his goal is to make a difference and win games. As for the criticism, he tries to discern the difference between the critics who bring something rare and valuable to the game and those he should ignore.

> **Boch:** If you are trying to win games and do what's right for the organization, there's no humiliation in being wrong. I have my doubts once in a while. And, I make a lot of mistakes. You try not to be predictable so the other club doesn't know what you are doing. Well, guess what? Not every decision is going to be a winner. If you're afraid to be wrong, you'll never step out of the comfort zone. If you are risk-averse, you become more predictable, and that gives your opponent a better chance of disrupting your strategy.

Boch is an other-oriented guy who respects people and cares deeply about the game. But he has learned that in the very public life of baseball you are in a fishbowl where you can't nurse your mistakes and ruminate on scathing comments from the critics. Not if you want to stay sane and survive. Talk show pundits will dissect your every decision—often with the brutality of Attila the Hun. Caustic commentary often makes for better ratings. Still, if you are hypercompetitive, you'll make bold decisions and take calculated risks to win. Worrying about how it will play in the media afterward is a luxury no skilled and winning manager can afford. When it doesn't work out, you own it and move on.

Trust Your Gut

As we have seen and will see some more, Boch has made some unconventional moves over the years. Pitching closer Brian Wilson in the eighth inning or starter Tim Lincecum in relief. Pitching closer Santiago Casilla to preserve a tie game in the ninth or middle reliever Jeremy Affeldt to back up Casilla when the ninth was getting away from him. Giving Travis Ishikawa one more at bat. Leaving Madison Bumgarner in to finish out Game 7 of the 2014 World Series with the tying run on third base. In each of these decisions, Boch poked a finger in the eye of tradition and leaned on gut instinct. And in each case, he earned a win in return.

Close friends, Kevin Towers and Boch worked together for more than 12 years in San Diego.

We've never heard Boch say, "I regret going with my gut." But he *has* said, "I should have . . ." when things didn't go as planned. Describing Boch one of the best in the business, Kevin Towers, former GM of the Padres, said, "He's one of those guys with incredible instincts."

Those instincts come from having multiple kinds of smart. His intelligence and insight have been honed over a thousand players, plus coaches and clubhouse staff, during his career. With 40-plus years in the game, Boch has an ocean full of experiences and lessons to reflect upon.

Think about it: Boch has been managing 162 games a year for more than 20 years. If the average game is three hours long, that's in excess of 9,720 hours. If you add in spring training games, the total is closer to 11,700 hours. But wait, there's more. Boch played as a catcher for 10 years before managing. If you include spring training and regular season games, the total number of hours he has devoted to perfecting his craft is 17,550, a conservative number given that it includes only game time.

That's more than 17,000 hours of hard work building a depth of knowledge, developing analytical skills, reflecting on failures and setbacks, trying to figure out what worked and what didn't, questioning assumptions and practices, connecting dots, and discerning patterns. All with the goal of identifying the deep lessons that would push the edge of the envelope and take his game to the next level.

Boch's "gut" or subconscious has been categorizing and cataloging these experiences for as long as he has been managing. For example, here is a lesson he would put in the bank and draw from many times over.

Knowing when to make a move is part data-driven and part gut instinct. Boch's decisiveness is anchored in both.

Boch: In 2010, we were in Game 3 of the NLDS against Atlanta. We were up 1-0 and our guy, Jonathan Sánchez, had great stuff. He had a two-hit shutout going. Well, we go into the bottom of the eighth with one out and a runner on base. In my infinite wisdom, against my intuition, I pull Sánchez and bring Romo in to face Troy Glaus. Bobby [Atlanta manager Bobby Cox] countered by bringing left-handed batter Eric Hinske to the plate instead.

> With two strikes, Romo hangs a slider and Hinske hits a two-run homer. Now we're down 2-1 and I feel terrible. Sánchez was dealing. And, he had only thrown 105 pitches. We came back to win it, but I learned a hard lesson: You've got to go with your gut. You make certain moves that stick with you. It took me a while to get over that great move.

As is often the case, the greatest lessons we learn are from scenarios that impact us the most. These insights aren't top of mind and immediately available to us all the time. How could we possibly process it all? Rather, everything we have seen and learned and felt is tucked away in our subconscious. But, when faced with a crucial choice in real time, our gut instinct opens the door to flash insights in the moment, usually before our brains even recognize what's going on. In the dugout, Boch can intuit patterns or solutions in an instant as his brain draws from those 17,000-plus hours of information he's internalized.

Most people think of intuition and rationality as mutually exclusive. What if they aren't? What if they are fused and operate seamlessly? For Boch, years and years of analytical thinking and deep reflection about players and games are stored in his memory. When he is consciously thinking about what's going on in a game, his subconscious is free to make sudden connections between the beliefs, experiences, and memories he has collected. These connections help him solve complex problems. This is what it means to "go with your gut."[96]

> **Boch:** We are in a game now where there are so many avenues or channels for people to be critics—and advocates. Being second-guessed has always been part of the game, but now, with social media and real-time everything, it's just more immediate and more pervasive. You can't be swayed by it. At some point, you learn to trust your gut and go with it. Actually, there are a lot of moves that I question myself about that don't get questioned by the media.

"There is something about Bochy's gut and the way he decides things," said John Hickey of the *Mercury News*. "You can't teach it. You can't explain it. It just works. You just want to let him do what he does."[97] Madison Bumgarner described it as an "uncanny ability to make all the right moves."

Boch's decisions do seem to be inspired, and there is genius in his strategy, but it's not because he's a mystic and it's not magic. At some level, we all have gut instincts. Boch just happens to be one of those leaders who take the time to notice, reflect, and pay attention to those instincts. Add in all those hours of doing this and his gut has more to draw from. Like any skill, a good gut instinct doesn't happen overnight. It requires practice and experience. At first, this "intuitive feel" might be so faint that it is hard to identify. But every time we trust it and succeed, our gut instinct grows sharper and stronger. The sharper and more trustworthy it becomes, the more we defer to it.

> **Boch:** So many of our decisions during a game are driven by metrics and logic and experience, but when we're in a dilemma and the decision isn't easy, isn't black and white, I often ask myself how I feel about doing it this way versus that way. I try to ask myself, "How will the player feel about this decision?" Small hunches are worth paying attention to. Those feelings, that sense you get, are legitimate. There is something you know without consciously knowing it.

Combine postseason pedigree with tremendous tactical acumen and you get one of the best managers in the game. Larry Baer said Bochy's "chess-master maneuvering squeezes the very best out of every player on the roster." Veteran and venerated San Francisco Bay Area sportswriter Ray Ratto agrees. "If Bruce Bochy wishes to announce that his [2012] World Series Game 2 starter is [comedian] Louis C.K., you need to be prepared to nod, say, 'Yeah, good call. Well done. Brilliant stroke.' Because while we have always known that Bochy is one of the best pitching manipulators in managing history, it's when his choices hit every note every time, game in and game out, that you see that his true ability is to see things mere mortals do not."[98]

Albert Einstein said: "The intuitive mind is a sacred gift and the rational mind is a faithful servant. We have created a society that honors the servant and has forgotten the gift." Being decisive is about rigorous due diligence and being in the know. It also comes from those quick judgments that flood our consciousness because we've done our homework and accumulated experiences over time. We may not be sure where they come from in the moment or why we feel so strongly about them, but they are compelling enough to make us act.

With sabermetrics so prevalent, perhaps Boch is a dying breed in baseball. Nevertheless, his ability to be decisive results from doing the calculations and trusting his gut; of logically building a case to support his plan and not ignoring a hunch that might disrupt it. This decisiveness is inextricably linked to playing at full throttle and to throwing the gauntlet down in the heat of battle. It is also what garners the respect of his players and gives them a sense of confidence in their skipper.

Avoid hesitation, trust your gut, be decisive—that's a potent combination for potent chemistry.

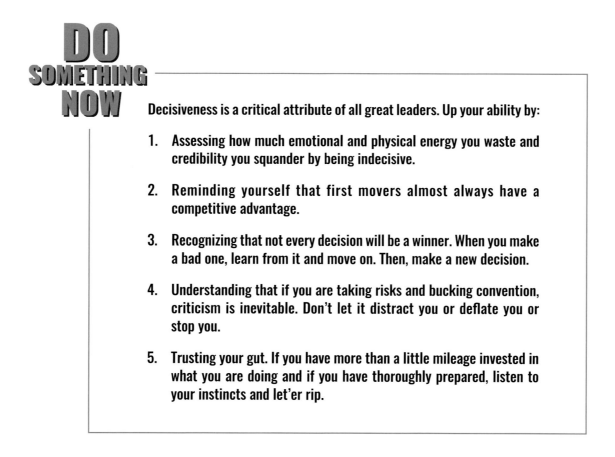

DO SOMETHING NOW

Decisiveness is a critical attribute of all great leaders. Up your ability by:

1. Assessing how much emotional and physical energy you waste and credibility you squander by being indecisive.

2. Reminding yourself that first movers almost always have a competitive advantage.

3. Recognizing that not every decision will be a winner. When you make a bad one, learn from it and move on. Then, make a new decision.

4. Understanding that if you are taking risks and bucking convention, criticism is inevitable. Don't let it distract you or deflate you or stop you.

5. Trusting your gut. If you have more than a little mileage invested in what you are doing and if you have thoroughly prepared, listen to your instincts and let'er rip.

27
KEEP 'EM GUESSING
The Art of Faking Foolish

The Giants are arguably one of the best postseason teams of the modern era. In 2010, they dispatched the Atlanta Braves, the Philadelphia Phillies, and the Texas Rangers. In 2012, they ousted the Cincinnati Reds, the St. Louis Cardinals, and the Detroit Tigers. In 2014, they demolished the Pittsburgh Pirates in the Wild Card Game and then knocked out the Washington Nationals and the Cardinals again, before taking Game 7 and the World Series from the Kansas City Royals. All in all, they toppled 10 consecutive postseason opponents.

The common denominators navigating each of these postseason runs were Sabean and Bochy. Boch is typically the first to admit that he doesn't always get it right. But in the postseason it's hard to identify a move he's made that has gone awry, even though, on the front side of some of his unconventional moves, many "experts" thought he was foolish.

Boch is a nonconformist. His passion for winning is bigger than his fear of shaking it up in high-leverage situations. Boch isn't afraid to "go left on red" and he isn't held hostage by history or the way he's always done it. His unorthodox approach often has pundits scratching their heads and opponents wondering, "What is he thinking?" And then, "What just happened?" Of course, the less they understand, the easier they are to surprise, and surprise puts the competition off balance.

> **Boch's unorthodox approach often has pundits scratching their heads and opponents wondering, "What just happened?"**

Dare to Go Rogue

In 2010, the heart-pounding postseason was in full swing as the Giants battled the Phillies in the back-and-forth NLCS. Managers are notoriously stubborn for refusing to use their closing pitchers in tie games on the road. Their strategy? Save the closer for save situations. In Game 1 of the 2010 NLCS, Boch brought closer Brian Wilson into the *eighth inning* for a four-out save. Then, up 3-2 in the series, the Giants traveled to Citizens Bank Park for the deciding Game 6. Phillies fans came out in full force. Doing their best to get inside the head of Giants starter Jonathan Sánchez, they yelled, "Sannn-chezzz," trying to disrupt the pitcher's concentration.

The Phillies quickly jumped out to a 2-0 lead, but in the top of the third inning, the Giants fought their way into a tie game. After Sánchez hit batter Chase Utley, Boch had seen enough and pulled his pitcher from the game. Jeremy Affeldt came in and held the Phillies scoreless for two critical innings. Then, Boch went rogue again.

In a gutsy move, he gave the ball to Game 4 starter Madison Bumgarner to pitch relief in the fifth and sixth innings. It was an unorthodox approach because, as Boch has pointed out, starters have a different mentality than relievers do. Starters are creatures of habit. They have a definite rhythm and routine to the way they go about their business. Starters know when they are going to pitch and therefore have more control over how they prepare for a game. Unlike relievers, they are not accustomed to not knowing when they will be called upon, and they are not acclimated to getting warm in a matter of minutes. Pitching a starter in relief definitely falls into the realm of unexpected and unpredictable. If you are locked into "the way we've always done it," you miss opportunities to shock your opponent.

Although MadBum put numerous runners on base, he held the Phillies scoreless. Left-hander Javier López dominated the seventh, and Juan Uribe's home run in the top of the eighth gave the Giants a 3-2 lead. Again, Boch showed that he was willing to defy convention by bringing in Tim Lincecum as a reliever in the eighth. Lincecum, the Giants starting pitcher in Games 1 and 5, struck out Jason Werth but gave up back-to-back singles. Boch promptly summoned closer Brian Wilson, again in the *eighth inning*, for a five-out save, and the Giants were on their way to the World Series.

Situations and scenarios, not roles and rules, dictate how Boch maneuvers. The way he manages in the postseason can be radically different from the way he goes about it in the regular season, when you have more time to make up for mistakes. For example, in the postseason his pitchers are on a much shorter leash. If a starter shows early that he's not on his game, Boch will take him off the mound.

Boch is also not going to save a pitcher for a presupposed game that may never get played. If you lose today and fail to advance, it just doesn't make sense. The 2014 NLDS is a case in point. In Game 1, the Giants Jake Peavy faced the Nationals Stephen Strasburg, who was enjoying the best season of his career. Peavy threw 104 pitches. Strasburg tossed 89 in a 3-2 loss to the Giants. Nationals manager Matt Williams indicated that Strasburg would *not* be good to go on three days' rest for Game 4. Boch said he would make Peavy available in relief.

In the postseason, Boch doesn't stick to a batting order just because it's the one he established during the regular season. His focus is maniacal, his preparation is outmatched, and his strategy is full throttle, seize the day, get it done now so you can earn the right to play another day. Giants broadcaster Mike Krukow told us: "We see how he matches up with other managers who have great reputations. He doesn't miss anything and his timing is uncanny. In a short series, his ability to use his team to its maximum strength is such an advantage. When they get into the postseason, everybody in that dugout feels like they have an ace in the hole—and that's Bochy."

Ignore Convention

In Game 5 of the 2014 NLCS, the Giants were up 3-1 in the series against the Cardinals. Boch went to his closer, Santiago Casilla, to preserve a 3-3 tie in the top of the ninth inning. In short order, Casilla loaded the bases, giving up a single and two walks. "The way we've always done it" would dictate leaving your closer in and hoping he will get out of the jam. Instead, Boch replaced Casilla with middle reliever Jeremy Affeldt, who pitched a scoreless inning.

In the bottom of the ninth, Cardinals manager Mike Matheny, one of the best in the game, got handcuffed by baseball orthodoxy. He chose not to use closer Trevor Rosenthal despite the win-or-go-home situation. Instead, he opted for starter Michael Wacha, who had not pitched for 21 days. Trying to shake off the rust, Wacha had no command of his fastball and put two runners on base. Then he gave up a spectacular three-run walk-off home run to Travis Ishikawa that clinched the pennant for the Giants.

Matheny defended his decision to leave his closer in the bullpen saying: "We can't bring him in in a tie-game situation. We're on the road." He was hammered in the media for leaning on an old-school philosophy. In fairness to Matheny, he did what Boch had done—bringing in a starter and someone who hadn't played in days. Had it worked out, he would've been a hero for thinking "outside the box." In every game, you decide whether or not to play the odds. Sometimes it works and sometimes it doesn't. In a 3-1 series there is no tomorrow. If you don't win this game, you go home. Your best bet is to go with the guy who can take you into extra innings and give you another day, another shot at winning. *That*, perhaps, is the ultimate save. Boch can identify with Matheny; he's been there. This is what made pulling Matt Moore in Game 4 of the 2016 NLDS such a dilemma.

Risk More—Gain More

As for Boch, putting Travis Ishikawa in this game was another unusual move. Ishikawa had played only a minor role in the Giants 2010 World Series victory and was then designated for assignment in 2011. In and out of the major leagues with various clubs, but mostly out, Ishikawa found himself back with the Giants in Triple-A in the summer of 2014.

Frustrated, tired, and discouraged, Ishikawa had a now-famous phone call with his wife. The gist of it was about turning 31 and wondering if he should retire and get on with his life. He had had enough. Meanwhile, Boch had been in a strategy meeting where Sabes indicated that Ishikawa, a career first baseman, had played a little bit in left field. Left fielder Michael Morse was out with an injury and the Giants needed someone to fill the gap. Ishikawa was called up in August and given a few starts in left field in late September. Boch liked what he saw.

> **Boch:** When Ishi came up the second time, I could just see that he had matured. I don't know if it was time in the game, the fact that he really had very little to lose, or just age, but he was more relaxed and more willing to step in wherever we needed him. Instead of always pressing, he was enjoying the game more, and I think he played better as a result. Also, I could see that he was getting a good jump on the ball in left field. So, as we went into the postseason, with Morse out, Ishi was our guy in left field. I don't think he had ever started there before September.

That night, in Game 5 of the NLCS, Boch's gut instinct was to give Ishikawa one more at bat before taking him out of the game. That decision will be forever etched in Giants history. Remember Bobby Thomson's "Shot Heard 'Round the World"? Every kid who plays baseball visualizes emulating such a heroic moment and Ishikawa was no exception. On a 2-0 count, Wacha pitched one right into Ishikawa's wheelhouse as he blasted a three-run homer into the history books and became a hero.

Travis Ishikawa blasts a three-run homer in Game 5 of the 2014 NLCS and sends the Giants to the World Series.

The delightful crack of the ball leaving Ishikawa's bat unleashed jubilation, exuberance, and celebration. Frenzied-euphoria reverberated through AT&T Park. The well-traveled journeyman and disenfranchised first baseman, who was placed in left field on an instinct, bought the Giants a ticket to their third World Series. Watching from his box, Sabean, the guy who had re-signed Ishikawa, could only bury his head in his hands and weep.[99] What a punchline to a great story.

> **Boch:** To say that hit was huge is such an understatement. It put us in the World Series. With our guys, you never know who is going to be the next to step in with a big contribution. I don't know how you could write a script any better than that one. For all he'd [Ishikawa] been through, his struggles, his frustration, and now this. It was a storybook moment I'll never forget. I couldn't have been happier for him.

Strategic Madness—Mad(Bum)ness

In 2014, Boch choreographed the rotation so Madison Bumgarner would pitch the Wild Card Game in Pittsburgh against the Pirates. Good move. Supported by a beautiful, crowd-silencing grand slam from shortstop Brandon Crawford, MadBum racked up 10 strikeouts in a shutout (8-0) game that left 40,000 Pirates fans stunned. This is the same Madison Bumgarner who, at 21, tossed eight shutout innings to win Game 4 of the 2010 World Series against the Rangers. And the same Bumgarner who, two years later, pitched seven shutout innings to win Game 2 of the 2012 World Series against the Tigers.

Electric. Vibrant. Down-to-the-wire. Historic. These are the words that characterize the 2014 World Series. With the Royals leading 2-1, the Series moved to AT&T Park in San Francisco. MadBum had thrown seven innings of one-run ball to stymie the Royals formidable offense and give the Giants a 7-1 win in Game 1. Fans prodded and cajoled Boch on social media and the pundits speculated about whether he would pitch Bum on short rest in Game 4 of the Series. He wasn't going to; he played unpredictable.

> **Boch:** Bum was just so "dialed in" that I suspected he would dominate whichever game he pitched. I felt that we needed to win Games 4 and 5 to win the World Series. That meant putting our number five guy against their number five guy. I wanted to go into Kansas City up 3-2 versus down 3-2, which meant we would only need to win one game versus two in their park. It just made sense to give Bum one more day of rest and have him face their ace [James Shields] in Game 5. Even with Bum going in in Game 5, I knew he'd be available for work out of the pen in Game 7.

Another good move. Boch methodically used six pitchers as the Giants won Game 4. Then, Bum threw 117 pitches in a nasty, complete Game 5 shutout against the Royals. Andy McCullough of the Kansas City Star simply stated the brutal facts of reality: "Twice in this series, Kansas City pitted their ace against his San Francisco counterpart. Both nights, Bumgarner reduced the Royals to rubble."[100] Looking for the silver lining in the loss, the Royals speedy center fielder Jarrod Dyson issued some famous last words: "We don't have to face Bumgarner no more."

After a 10-0 routing by the Royals in Game 6, the Giants and Royals were tied three games each. The 2014 World Series would be decided in a drama-filled, winner-takes-all Game 7. There is no bigger stage. You use every weapon you have. This was only the second time in the prior 12 years that the World Series had gone to a Game 7. And in the previous nine times there was a Game 7 in the World Series, guess who won? You got it: the home team. The experts were saying the momentum had swung toward Kansas City. Jeremy Affeldt saw it differently. "Both teams have their backs against the wall."

By the next morning Boch had done what he's learned to do over 20 years of managing; he put Game 6 behind him and focused forward. He had breakfast with his son Brett, a Giants minor league reliever who was part of another epic Giant moment.

Here's a brief aside: When the Giants made a September postseason push, Brett was called up to pitch for his dad. In a game against the archrival Dodgers, Brett's MLB game debut was the first time in history a major league manager handed the ball to his son on the mound. No doubt this will go down as a huge highlight in Boch's career.

Boch: It was a huge emotional moment for me. I didn't get to see a lot of his games growing up. As a manager, I really don't get nervous during games, but as a parent, that one got to me pretty good. And I'm sure for him, when your dad is the manager, there's added pressure to perform as well. It's a little different when your son is a pitcher versus a role player. As a relief pitcher, he's not out there for a long time so you're living on every pitch. I had a lot of confidence in Brett.

Brett Bochy, MLB pitching debut. First time in the history of the game a manager hands the ball to his son on the mound.

He had earned his way. His numbers speak for themselves. Still, I was really nervous for him. The circumstances were less than ideal. I brought him in with two outs and the bases loaded, facing a great hitter. When I got home, Kim [Bochy] barked at me: "You couldn't find a better spot to put him in?" Brett's tough, I knew he could handle it, but when he came in I had to say, "Sorry I put you in this situation in your Major League debut." For me, that moment was as big as it gets. It was like a World Series. I was really proud of him.

Now back to Game 7. Brett said his dad stayed true to form. He kept everything calm. The pundits were already talking about the bullpen and the game hadn't even started. Most everyone suspected they were going to see Bumgarner in Game 7; it was just a question of when. Boch stuck to his game plan.

Boch: I think a lot of people thought we'd bring in Bum behind Huddy [Tim Hudson], hopefully to get us into the seventh or eighth inning, but meeting with Rags [Dave Righetti] and Gardy [bullpen coach Mark Gardner], we decided to use [Jeremy] Affeldt and possibly Timmy [Lincecum] as a bridge to Bum and then Romo or Casilla. The only thing we didn't know was how much gas Bum had in the tank, how long he could go. We were thinking, "If he can give us two or three good innings we'd be fortunate." But it was all new territory.

After pulling Tim Hudson before the end of the second inning, Boch called on the seasoned Affeldt, who did a stellar job over 2 ⅓ innings. Usually a late inning weapon, this was Affeldt's longest relief appearance since 2012, and in Game 7 of the World Series, it was no small feat.

With the Giants clinging to a 3-2 lead in the fifth inning, the visiting bullpen door opened and out stepped the 6-foot 5-inch, 235-pound Madison Bumgarner. Bum made his way to the mound with the confidence of a pitcher who was 4-0 in World Series competition. You could almost sense the oxygen being sucked out of the Royals dugout as Jarrod Dyson's words came back to haunt him.

"When Bum comes in we feel like we're in a really good spot right now," Buster Posey said. "You could almost sense it in the crowd that they're thinking, 'Uh-oh, here comes this guy again.'"

You know what they say, "The best laid plans of mice and men go awry." Boch's plan to use Bum as a bridge to either Romo or Casilla was disrupted by Bumgarner's unbelievable stamina. Except for giving up a single that didn't advance beyond second base

Madbum, Game 7, 2014 World Series

in the fifth, Bum went 1-2-3 in the sixth, seventh, and eighth innings. Posey said he was just as sharp and dominant as he was in Game 5. Always aware of the pitch count but never a servant to it, Boch pays more attention to what he sees physically and how his pitcher is doing mentally and emotionally. Then, he goes with his gut.

Major league pitchers put tremendous pressure on their joints and muscles. That's why you see their shoulders wrapped with huge bags of ice after games. For most, standing on a mound, whipping their arms 100-plus times in a game, requires five days of rest. Perched on the top stair of the dugout, Boch watched Bum intently, looking for signs of fatigue. He didn't see any.

Boch: Bum's usually the one in the dugout pestering me to let him stay in longer, but this time I was just trying to stay clear of him for a different reason. He was showing no signs of wearing down. I didn't want him to say, "I think it's time [to take me out]." That said, I knew we had asked a lot of him physically, so I had Casilla ready to go if he started to fatigue.

Of course, I probably would have had to wrestle him off the mound because that's Bum. I got Casilla up [in the bullpen] because I had to protect him. To think Bum went five innings is unbelievable. He's as strong as a horse. The man just has so much will.

"If Bochy would have told Bum he was done," Affeldt said, "I think he would have had two pitchers out there standing on the mound." Boch's famous quote in the media was: "We just got on this horse and rode it." Before the game, Royals manager Ned Yost said: "Bumgarner's a great starting pitcher. We'll see what kind of reliever he is." Well, here's what they learned. Bum threw 68 pitches for only two hits and five shutout innings on two days' rest. When it was over, the record books would show that Madison Bumgarner:

- threw 52.2 October innings, the most of any pitcher in a single postseason;
- had the lowest ERA of any pitcher in World Series history with at least 25 innings—a mind-blowing, microscopic 0.25;
- became the first pitcher with two wins, a shutout, and a save in World Series history; and
- was named the World Series MVP and *Sports Illustrated*'s Sportsman of the Year, joining the likes of Muhammad Ali, John Wooden, Serena Williams, Michael Jordan, Peyton Manning, and the U.S. Woman's Soccer Team.[101]

Can a starting pitcher really throw five shutout innings on just two days' rest, after throwing 200 regular season and 50 postseason innings, in Game 7 of the World Series? Inconceivable, right? Boch, Righetti, and company had a plan and Bumgarner blew it up. But they were wise and agile enough to adapt, to let baseball—and MadBum—decide "a moment that truly belonged to the game's history."[102]

DO SOMETHING NOW

Where have you been held hostage by "the way we've always done it?" What fears keep you from taking risks? Are these fears real or perceived? Expand your capacity to think big and act bold by asking, "What would I do today if I was going to be really brave?" Then, make a commitment to do one brave thing every day.

Disrupt on Purpose

Boch made a number of moves that kept the Royals off balance, cemented his reputation for being predictably unpredictable, and navigated a path to the Giants third World Championship.

When the final postgame interview of the World Series was over, MadBum, the strapping farm boy from Lenore, North Carolina, got up, turned to Boch, and said in his slow Southern drawl, "I can't lie anymore; I'm a little tired now." The media room erupted in laughter.

MadBum after one of the greatest postseason pitching performances in MLB history.

"You'll never see that again—the way he pitched [his] first two games and then to come back and do what he did," said Jeremy Affeldt, who was also extremely impressive in his own role. "That was epic. To be honest with you, it was the greatest pitching performance that I've ever seen."[103] Every player, announcer, and manager interviewed after the game agreed: "Historic." "Stunning." 'One for the ages." "Never to be seen again." "One of the greatest clutch performances we have ever seen in the World Series."

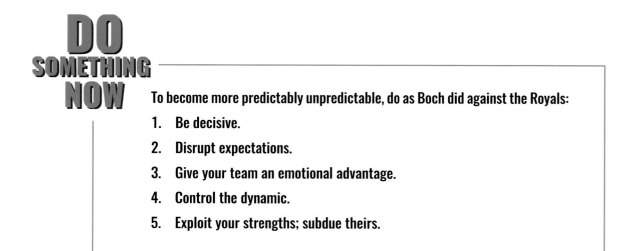

To become more predictably unpredictable, do as Boch did against the Royals:

1. **Be decisive.**

2. **Disrupt expectations.**

3. **Give your team an emotional advantage.**

4. **Control the dynamic.**

5. **Exploit your strengths; subdue theirs.**

Henry Schulman of the *San Francisco Chronicle* asked Buster Posey to comment on pictures of his now-famous "Buster Hugs." In each of the Giants three World Series victories, Buster has charged the mound to hug the pitcher in an emotional release of postseason tension. Looking at the picture of him hugging Madison Bumgarner in the 2014 World Series, Posey reminisced: "The first thing when I see that picture is, I can't believe Bumgarner just did what he did. What stands out to me is the conversation we had after Gordon got on third, and just how calm and confident Bum was. He just said, 'I got this. I'm going to get him out.' There was no other thought in his mind. It definitely made me settle in a lot more once he said that."

Remember the subtitle of this chapter? "The Art of Faking Foolish." Boch in particular has perfected it—to the chagrin of many noteworthy opponents. Take the example immediately above. The Royals may have been thinking of MadBum: "He's on two days' rest, he's pitched five innings, he's thrown 62 pitches, and Salvador Pérez is up. Something's got to give." But they didn't count on the warrior spirit of Madison Bumgarner and the nonconformist way of the San Francisco Giants. This is what Championship Blood does: It challenges the facts, ignores the odds, and says, "I got this."

At 6 feet 5 inches and 235 pounds, MadBum is no easy guy to pick up, but in the adrenaline rush of winning the 2014 World Series, Buster Posey has no problem.

8th Inning
GIANT HEART
Inspiring a Place, an Attitude, and a State of Mind

28
SANCTUARY
Not a House, a Home

Chemistry is not something you can ignite with the flip of a switch. You need an environment that fosters its growth: a place where guys can come together and be themselves; a place where they can know and be known without interference from outside distractions; place where they can be real, where they don't always have to be "on."

If you were to create a place that promotes a sense of belonging, conducive to kinship and a tight-knit band of brothers, where people can let their guard down because they feel emotionally and spiritually safe—a place that encourages people to unleash their gifts and talents and do their most inspired work, a place that makes them feel sacred—what would you call it?

A sanctuary.

The word "sanctuary" has almost become cliché when describing the locker rooms and clubhouses of college and professional athletic teams. But to the Giants it means something more. The word is derived from the Latin *sanctuarium,* or sacred place. The *sanctum sanctorum,* a holy place housing holy people, has been popularized as the inner sanctum, a special place that shields its residents from the outsider and outsiders, from the distractions and toxicity of a crazy, dangerous, and uncivilized world.

Why shouldn't a clubhouse be a compelling safe haven for players? With the demanding schedule of 162 games, half of which are on the road, shouldn't the clubhouse be a place that inspires them and allows them to decompress? Players spend more time in this space than they do on the field and, for some, in their own homes. As a second home, then, the clubhouse gives them a private life within the confines of a public arena.

Make the Place Come Alive

Why shouldn't we create workspaces that speak to the human spirit? Physical space is symbolic. Every home is a statement about the people who live there. Some are inviting and conducive to building great relationships. They beckon you to sit down, relax, and engage in meaningful conversation. Other homes are beautiful and pristine, but they are sterile, uninviting places where you're uncomfortable and afraid to sit on the furniture. In some homes, the decorated walls draw you in and captivate your attention by telling an interesting story. In others, however, the walls are dull, uninspiring, uninteresting, and cold.

Chemistry is affected by all of this. If a house is truly a home, it's because the people who live there are intentional about making it that way. They have a sense about what they want people to think and how they want them to feel when they come into it. They have consciously and intentionally connected the layout, décor, and surroundings to the vision they have for their family and guests.

The Giants newly remodeled clubhouse resembles a comfortable, well-equipped first-class spa and restaurant, except that instead of tranquilizing music you're more likely to hear ZZ Top. With state-of-the-art weight and equipment rooms, big screen TVs, a monitoring station for players' vitals, sleeping rooms, whirlpools, a saltwater float spa, gravity chairs, and leather couches, it's a place you want to be. It's welcoming and inviting. You can watch videos, work out, lounge in your underwear and play cards, and no one will judge. Like AT&T Park itself, it draws you in because it's so full of life. The ambiance inspires players to recharge, refresh, and renew.

The fact is people stay longer in environments where they feel comfortable. The longer players hang around, the more they get to know each other. Most important to Boch, the lockers are configured in a square versus a rectangle.

> **Boch:** When they [front office] asked me about it, I said I'd like to have the players closer together to facilitate more conversation and camaraderie. The clubhouse is now more intimate and much more conducive to meetings. The players' lockers are much nicer and the space we saved bringing players closer gave us more space to expand the team's kitchen and dining area where the players often meet. The training room, the kitchen, the locker room—the whole thing is more player-friendly. The club's investment in remodeling the clubhouse is just another way the front office shows that it understands chemistry and cares about our players.

As up-to-date and comfortable as the Giants clubhouse is, however, the physical environment is only part of what makes their house a home. The rest comes from how family members treat it and use it. When the clubhouse is treated like a sanctuary, players look at it differently and they treat each other differently, which reinforces a sense of community. To adapt a phrase from organization development and community-building author and consultant Peter Block, the architects and designers brought the clubhouse to life, but the players and coaches bring life to the clubhouse.

More Than a Place

We tend to think of a sanctuary as a place, but sanctuary is reflected in the hearts, minds, and relationships of players as well. Players have a choice; they can sow discord or grow deep bonds.

Before a game, the Giants clubhouse, like most, is abuzz with activity. Players are having conversations with other players, moving from the trainer's room to their lockers, giving interviews, and listening to music. Because the clubhouse is the players' inner sanctum, if you have access, you'd better respect it.

When you think about creating a sanctuary, two glaring realities stand out: Meaningful relationships aren't instantaneous, and, they aren't cheap. They require an investment of time, energy, and vulnerability. From everything we've seen, the Giants have worked to create a safe and inviting space and to maintain consistency and continuity on the club's roster. Both are significant reasons the players are such a tight bunch of guys.

The clubhouse doesn't become a sanctuary—and the house isn't a home—until it is animated by love and acceptance, safety and security, and freedom and hospitality. When it is, something powerful begins to happen. Relationships move from shallow and superficial to deep and meaningful. Players who know each other, enjoy each other, and have faith in each other will bear fruit in a special kind of solidarity. Togetherness and unity will be expressed in the Giants undeniable and unencumbered brand of swagger.

Ryan Vogelsong, Tim Lincecum, Barry Zito, Buster Posey, Matt Cain, and Madbum.

Buddies in the clubhouse, warriors on the field.

The Clubhouse Is What You Make It

After winning the World Series in 2010, Boch gave a spring training talk to the players that spoke to issues of togetherness and unity. Essentially, this is what he said.

> **Boch:** Unity is built on the foundation of a healthy clubhouse, and the culture of this clubhouse is your choice. This is the inner sanctum, the safe haven where we gather to get our game face on, console each other when things get tough, and kick each other in the ass when we need it. But make no mistake; we all have to work at this.

Boch wants his guys to see that the culture and the chemistry of the clubhouse and whatever happens on the field are the result of what players and coaches create together. Culture is as much the will of the team as it is the will of the manager. This means players have autonomy in their domain and control the environment they live in.

This act of Boch's is part of a larger picture. If your philosophy is to have players who are accountable to one another on the field and who focus on what they can control, they have to own their choices. If you expect this on the field but shut it down in the clubhouse, you're being inconsistent. If you are asking players to trust themselves and each other but have an authoritarian clubhouse where everyone has to check in with "dad" before acting, you're not empowering them; you're breeding dependency. The price you pay for this type of control is helplessness.[104]

Brian Sabean agrees. "What we've learned here is you try to empower the players. You make it their clubhouse, you make it about them and let them take responsibility for it. You make it where they decide the chemistry and ultimately the season we're going to have. Are we going to help them shape it along the way? Sure. It's a broader collective effort and everyone in the organization has a role. But if you have the right group in the clubhouse and they've got the right focus, they're going make good things happen."[105] Sabean's philosophy applies to his manager and coaches as well. Sabes and Boch talk often and make decisions collaboratively, but you won't find the GM (now Executive VP, Baseball Operations) in Boch's office or lingering around the batting cage before games. "It drives me nuts when you see [GMs] around the back of the batting cage," Sabean said. "That's the office for the manager, the hitting coach and the players. People don't need to hear from me. Our message is best delivered through the people in uniform. The more attention front office people expose themselves to, it's a recipe for disaster."[106]

In leadership lingo, the term "empowerment" is often thrown around loosely, but Boch brings it to life. He gives players the ownership and authority to create a sanctuary, a clubhouse of their own choosing. What could be more empowering than to give players autonomy, connection, and self-expression?

Everyone's a Leader

Giving players ownership of the clubhouse turns them into leaders. It not only gives them the freedom to "self-police" what music is played and when but also paves the way for teachable moments when they can talk to each other about the game and the Giants way of doing things. The words of legendary coach John Wooden ring true here: "Discipline yourself so no one else has to." Boch has earned a great deal of trust and respect among players, but he understands that even his influence has limitations.

> **Boch:** We [manager and coaches] set the tone, no question. We can talk about the importance of choosing service over self-interest, playing with a warrior spirit and the power of love in the clubhouse, but we can't make it happen. Not if we want them to be truly committed. Initiative isn't something that's handed to you; you have to take it. Players learn as much from each other as they do from me, Bobby, Sabes or any of our coaches. They will talk to each other in ways that we can't.

Boch understands that sometimes it's just better to let the players address an issue. Jake Peavy is one of those guys who steps up. Scrappy and passionate, he's a great cheerleader; but, he's also not afraid to call guys out for not giving their all or for being in the clubhouse during a game when they should be in the dugout supporting their teammates.

> **Boch:** Peavy really impacted our clubhouse. His knowledge and experience, the way he went about his business; it just turned up the intensity and focus on our guys. As we've said, when he pitched, he was full bore. He led by example, not only in the way he played but also in the clubhouse. He'd step up and say something if another player's attitude needed to be calibrated. He was a great one-on-one guy in terms of sharing his insights with other players too. And, he was vocal in meetings. He accepted a lot of ownership for the culture of the clubhouse.

The Giants have a culture where leadership is distributed and episodic—it's everyone's job. That is, it shifts easily among players and coaches based on what the team needs at the time. It also means that leaders both shape and are shaped. One moment Boch might be setting the club's direction and taking the lead. The next moment he might be influenced by someone who has his thumb on the pulse of the players, like Pence, Posey, or Bumgarner. With the Giants, leadership is about multiple players and coaches owning the culture of the clubhouse and doing whatever it takes to keep it alive and thriving.

Throw Out the Rule Book

As we've said, Boch is not big on rules. Consequently, the clubhouse doesn't have many. Basically, he's got one rule: Use common sense. Rules are punitive and demeaning. They are designed to control people. More rules mean more things to control and more power to wield. That is oppressive. If you want players to be themselves, if you want a culture that fosters freedom and unity, oppression is not the way to do it.

Two-time World Series Champion Jake Peavy.

Rules focus on "no." Energy, excitement, and enthusiasm are generated from "yes." Rules say, "We don't trust you." Chemistry thrives in an environment of trust where people know they can count on each other. Rules produce a mindless kind of conformity. Chemistry is all about initiative. It's about being the cause of something good, not the effect. Rules are soulless. Chemistry is soul stirring. It's about inspiring people to fully engage—heart, mind, and spirit.

> **Boch:** I watched this coming up as a player. If you hamper players with too many mandatory rules and restrictions, they spend their time testing boundaries or trying to figure out the loopholes. It's wasted energy. If you let them be themselves—within a framework, of course—you've hopefully created a scenario where they are free to access their talents and unleash the best they've got. If they have an opportunity to shape whatever little structure *does* exist, they are more likely to operate within it.

Tim Lincecum had this to say about Bochy's attitude toward the Giants clubhouse. "He gives us the freedom to play. He'll let us police ourselves for the most part."[107] Jake Peavy added, "When you put too many rules out there and suppress guys, you take away their free-spirited athleticism and boyhood that translates to great things on the field."

Instead of rules, Giants players follow an invisible code that has been intentionally communicated over the years through Boch's talks, media interviews, and one on ones with players. It's not written down anywhere, but this code permeates the clubhouse: Choose service over self-interest. Speak the language of respect. Play like a warrior. Have fun. If you've been around for any length of time, you've heard these themes over and over again.

Changing the Rule Makers

In turning the clubhouse over to the players, Boch is not only changing the rules; he's changing who gets to make them. No longer can a player just walk in the clubhouse focused solely on his role and his own functional area. He is now a part of protecting the emotional well-being of the sanctuary. If something goes awry, he has an obligation to speak up and do something about it. If there's someone who should be affirmed and celebrated, he owns a piece of that too.

When the Giants won the 2016 Wild Card Game, it was rookie Conor Gillaspie who came up with a three-run homer in the ninth inning. After the game, a throng of reporters waylaid him, and he was the last player into the clubhouse. Gillaspie was greeted by his goggle-wearing teammates, armed with shaken champagne bottles, shouting, "CONOR! CONOR! CONOR!" *Someone* took charge of organizing that little celebration. *Someone* owned it. And that reinforced the message that the Giants clubhouse is a place where they celebrate the best of everyone and their warrior, full throttle, "leave it all on the field," and have fun spirit.

Certainly, there is a risk to giving players this kind of freedom. The clubhouse could run wild. Less structure might come with less discipline. Without discipline, you can't win games. But here's the thing: When you treat people like adults, they act like adults. And when they don't, you manage the exceptions; or, more precisely, you let the players manage the exceptions. Then, as a manager, you step in when necessary. But you don't change your whole approach by becoming more controlling and dictatorial.

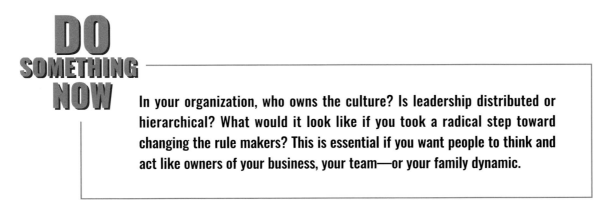

DO SOMETHING NOW

In your organization, who owns the culture? Is leadership distributed or hierarchical? What would it look like if you took a radical step toward changing the rule makers? This is essential if you want people to think and act like owners of your business, your team—or your family dynamic.

Jettison Class Mentality

Boch is serious about leveraging the knowledge and experience of every person in the clubhouse. That's why he doesn't fall into the class mentality that hampers so many organizations. The class mentality essentially says: "Players don't care about culture, they just want to play baseball. The people who clean uniforms don't know anything about running a clubhouse, so what would they have to say about esprit de corps? What could the groundskeepers, chefs, and people who pack equipment possibly know about sanctuary?"

Why are concepts such as autonomy, empowerment, and ownership so overtalked and underpracticed in sports, business, and life? One of the reasons is the class mentality. Boch doesn't stereotype people much. His father was a sergeant major in the U.S. Army so Boch fully understands chain of command. But class divisions are just not a part of how he sees the world.

> **Boch:** If you are playing to win, why wouldn't you tap into every resource you have? More often than not, the players are going to identify an issue in the clubhouse before I do. I want them to play offense in the clubhouse. I don't ever want someone to walk past a problem. I want them to be proactive about protecting the culture and chemistry we have here.

When you pigeonhole people based on your view of their job description, talent, salary, or education, you limit their ability to contribute to reaching your objectives. This view is destructive in three ways. First, it strips the person or the player of dignity and lowers morale. It's another way of ensuring that power resides at the top because only management can know everything. Second, it rips off the franchise by not capitalizing on insight it pays for but never receives. Third, the class mentality crushes people's spirits by stifling their imagination, initiative, sense of responsibility, and—most importantly—their investment in what you are trying to accomplish.

Ownership Breeds Commitment

Command and control breeds compliance to a demand that comes from the outside; a demand that people in authority place on us. Ownership breeds commitment to a demand that comes from within us; a demand that we make of ourselves. It's the difference between "I have to . . ." and "I want to . . ." In a command-and-control clubhouse you run the danger of players trading obedience for passion and true loyalty. When the clubhouse culture is something they help shape, players are invested in it and feel responsible for what it becomes. They are *committed* to promoting and protecting it because they *want* to.

> **Boch:** The kind of guys we want in our clubhouse own it. They aren't afraid to walk in my office and say, "We had an issue and here's how I addressed it." They don't act like victims and they don't make excuses. They care about what this clubhouse becomes. You rarely hear them say, "That's not my place." Or, "I don't have authority." It *is* their place. They *do* have authority. This is their home away from home.
>
> They really do care about each other and love each other, but they're not afraid to get on each other either. If someone needs to be called out in a moment of tough love, it's done *inside* the inner sanctum.

When the clubhouse is a sanctuary it becomes an anchor point, a true shelter, an inner sanctum. But a sanctuary culture can't survive unless it is consciously nurtured. If a rookie comes up from the minor leagues or a veteran player comes from another franchise to the Giants with a prima donna attitude, the culture will call them on it like antibodies reject something foreign in your body. Culture becomes the boss, which makes it easier for someone to say, "That's not the way we do things around here."

At the same time, a sense of sanctuary is not something you can legislate. You can't force players to impose it on other players; it must be something *they* want to create and preserve. You can talk about it and role model it, but if it's to be genuine, the players themselves must own it, promote it, and protect it.

The Giants clubhouse works because the players want to see it as *theirs*—their sanctuary, their quality of life, and their responsibility. People care most when they know someone depends on them. With the Giants, the players know that Boch depends on them to safeguard their unique chemistry by protecting the culture of the inner sanctum. Even more so, they depend on each other to create a place where everyone wants to be and loves to be.

29
FREEDOM
Let the Misfits Be Themselves

Boch first referred to his players affectionately as a band of "misfits, castoffs, and renegades" in 2010. It was a brand that stuck. In the Giants run up to all three World Series, he successfully bridged the gaps between players of different ages, who spoke different languages, had different personalities, and came from different situations.

Take a look at some of the characters Boch has managed in the Giants organization over the years. The ultra-talented but undisciplined Pablo Sandoval, the happy-go-lucky Kung Fu Panda; clean-cut All-American Buster Posey; laid-back Brandon Crawford; the slumbering giraffe, Brandon Belt; and the highly competitive, rodeo-loving rancher from North Carolina, Madison Bumgarner.

 The team was formed of various personalities representing several nationalities and different family backgrounds and cultural upbringings; but they all came together through a love for the game and the talent to play baseball at the highest level.

Misfits.

Add in rodeo clown wannabe Cody Ross (the 2010 NLCS MVP), Mike Fontenot, and Pat Burrell—all of whom were essentially out of jobs before coming to the Giants. You also have Yusmeiro Petit, who cleared waivers twice in 2013; David Huff, who had been designated for assignment three times; and Jean Machi, who a few years prior to the 2014 World Series was pitching in the Mexican League.

Aubrey Huff, Hunter Pence, Tim Lincecum, and Brian Wilson. Each eccentric. But they all found a way to appreciate and leverage their differences.

Castoffs.

And don't forget closer Brian Wilson, with his menacing, jet-black pirate's beard, and Aubrey Huff, with his red rhinestone rally thong. You have the contortionist "freak" in Tim Lincecum, who remembers the words to every song he's ever heard. And rounding out the hodge-podge is the philosopher/preacher Hunter Pence, who joyfully rides his cherished electric scooter to and from AT&T Park and throughout the streets of San Francisco.

Renegades.

Under any other circumstances, these guys might never meet each other much less hang out together. But for more than half the year they live in the same clubhouse and sanctuary, travel together, work side by side, and—most importantly—depend on each other to accomplish their goals and realize a collective *why*.

Let's ask this question one more time: "What would happen if our organizations became as human as the human beings in them?" The truth is, when players are treated like "objectified assets" on a spreadsheet, we place little value on what makes them human. Curiosity, confidence, anxiety, eccentricity, nonconformity, ingenuity, originality, emotions, and passion—just to name a few—are what make us human. All are dimensions of our personalities that are expressed in lots of weird ways, right?

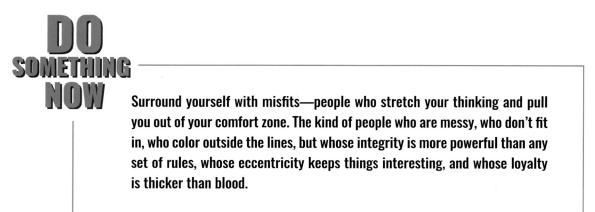

DO SOMETHING NOW

Surround yourself with misfits—people who stretch your thinking and pull you out of your comfort zone. The kind of people who are messy, who don't fit in, who color outside the lines, but whose integrity is more powerful than any set of rules, whose eccentricity keeps things interesting, and whose loyalty is thicker than blood.

Insecure managers don't know how to deal with this. Gutsy leaders, however, understand that blending and balancing diverse personalities under one roof isn't easy, yet it's essential in cultivating chemistry. Difference is unsettling because it challenges us to jettison our dogmas and embrace another person's uniqueness, if only temporarily. We end up with organizations that are only slightly human because we try to manage out and tolerate only a little bit of the "weirdness" that comes with people being themselves.

Express Yourself

Boch isn't interested in forcing his players into some kind of socially prescribed role. He doesn't want them to check their personalities at the door. He wants them to be themselves. Why wouldn't he? When you are together for seven months out of the year, this is crucial. Until 2016, Boch was the only manager Tim Lincecum had played for in his big league career. The two-time Cy Young winner said, "For as long as I've been under him, he's just allowed people to go about themselves and let themselves be free in the clubhouse."[108]

This is what keeps a clubhouse spirited and exciting. When you establish a clubhouse culture that accepts and appreciates players' differences, you have a much more interesting work environment, one that's loaded with mystery and adventure. It's unpredictable yet elevating. As on the field, though, you never know who's going to step up and be "the guy" who infuses the clubhouse with humor or compassion or calls out the warrior spirit. You never know who will be the anchor that keeps the boys grounded in reality or gives them a motivational kick in the ass. When you enter a clubhouse 162 times a year, not to mention spring training and the postseason, wouldn't you rather be in a place that is alive and filled with variety rather than one that says *different day, same routine*?

Appreciating the differences among Boch's misfits, castoffs, and renegades also helps keep the Giants clubhouse healthy. Trying to be someone you're not is stressful. Posing and pretending so you can keep up a façade and "fit in" requires enormous amounts of emotional energy. Asking players to rein in their personalities undermines their dignity, and that diminishes everyone. No one plays well under these conditions.

On the other hand, being yourself is liberating. When players throw away the façade and take off the masks, more often than not their authenticity is endearing. We gravitate to people who are real, don't we? People who are pretentious and deceitful are uncomfortable to be around. We don't know who they are because *they* don't know who they are. And that makes for lousy team chemistry.

Unity Is Not Uniformity

There is a difference between unity and uniformity. Unity is about coming together as one;, uniformity is about control. Our egos are much more comfortable with uniformity. People who look like us, think like us, and talk like us don't pull us out of our comfort zones and disrupt us or confuse us. Yet, being comfortable has a couple of downsides.

First, research clearly shows that when a diverse team is united it will outperform a more uniform "cookie-cutter" team—even if it is more talented.[109]

Second, uniformity hinders a group's capacity to be agile and adapt. When team members run in the same circles, hang with the same people, go to the same meetings, and train under the same regimens, their access to new information, talent, and skills is limited. It's not just diversity, but rather *leveraging the power of diversity*, that has contributed to the Giants success.

> **Boch:** I'm convinced that a key to our success has been the variety of personalities and skills we've had. Diversity creates depth and balance. I know it elevates the spirit of a club. I've seen it too many times. For example, we've got guys like Huddy [Tim Hudson] and Joe Panik or Matt Duffy. These guys are 15 years apart in age. That's a huge gap. But you're blending the experience of a sage in the game with the wide-eyed energy of kids who are hungry and don't know they can't. One instills wisdom; the others keep the clubhouse youthful. That's where the balance comes from.

If a manager says, "We want you to run full throttle with this part of your personality, but we'd prefer you leave this other part at home," that's totally unrealistic. It just doesn't work that way. If a player has to fit into a mold and be like everyone else—that is, he can't think for himself, feel what he feels, and be himself—then you are left with nothing more than a major league robot. How can you play with a sense of security, aggressiveness, and assurance when you are continually trying to figure out which part of you is okay to bring to work?

Boch isn't trying to create robots. By encouraging players to be themselves, he is guarding their distinctness and protecting what brings diversity, creativity, and exponential personality to the clubhouse. You don't get laughter and compassion, abounding life and joy, music and festivity, freedom and passion, intrinsic motivation and discipline when you confuse unity and uniformity. You find it in the mix. The sense of control you think you get from uniformity shuts down a player's natural passion to play the game.

It seems almost paradoxical, but unity is many players with different personalities, quirks, and eccentricities seeing the game from different perspectives yet being one in spirit. They move toward each other, support and fight for each other, and improvise with each other because they appreciate each other. They see the full weight of their differences as an advantage, not a distraction.

The Giants have had class clowns like Aubrey Huff, Pat Burrell, and Ryan Theriot who kept it light by not taking themselves too seriously. Guys like Jeremy Affeldt and Javier López reinforced a bit of "the way we do things around here" to keep pitchers in the bullpen focused. Empathizer Tim Lincecum quietly took younger players under his wing and made them feel like they belong. Andrés Torres, Pablo Sandoval, and Gregor Blanco brought an infectious enthusiasm into the clubhouse every day. They just loved to play ball. Ángel Pagán was a poster child for intensity. And anchors like Buster Posey projected levelheaded confidence and leadership stature beyond their years.

A dozen fiddles in a band might be intriguing, but the music won't be nearly as entertaining as when they are mixed with guitars, drums, a piano, and a banjo. Most everyone in the Giants organization knows that Hunter Pence has been a blessing to the club on and off the field. So has Brandon Crawford. But if you have too many guys with either the fiery personality of Pence or the calm, laid-back demeanor of Crawford in the clubhouse, something is lost. Too much of a good thing isn't good anymore.

Diversity Adds Depth

Unfortunately, we live in a world where many people are obsessed with the differences that divide us. The more we fixate on these differences and amplify them, the more people cease to be people. They become objectified—things we categorize, analyze, and manipulate on spreadsheets. This makes them easier to use. But chemistry doesn't happen when players become assets and variables on a spreadsheet.

Boch has taken a different tack. He wants his players to focus on their mutual goals and aspirations. He wants them not to just tolerate but *proactively explore* how their differences can become a source of strength. He wants them to see that in the clubhouse they have far more in common than not.

> **Boch:** We are different, I'll grant you that. Can you imagine Tim Lincecum and Buster Posey going on a duck hunt together? Can you see Sergio Romo learning to rope steers on Bum's ranch, or Johnny Cueto and Jake Peavy doing a benefit concert together? Can you see Jeremy Affeldt and Ángel Pagán doing a stand-up comedy routine? I'm not seeing it. How about Matt Cain salsa dancing with Pablo Sandoval? We are very different, but we don't let our personality differences drive a wedge between us or limit us. Our diversity is not a source of insecurity; it's a source of strength.

The parade of radically different personalities in the Giants clubhouse could be a headache for some managers, but, as you can see, Boch not only tolerates their eccentricity, he encourages it.

Cultural Kaleidoscopes

In many respects, Boch has created a clubhouse that reflects the city in which the Giants reside. San Francisco is a magnet for eccentricity because the community treats people from all walks of life with respect. San Franciscans are open to new ideas and change, which is why the city has been so influential in shaping our views on culture, religion, politics, and lifestyle.

A fusion of diverse cultures, ethnicities, and personalities, the Giants players are a reflection of the city they play for.

If the Silicon Valley is anything to go by, the Bay Area is gifted with scientists, inventors, entrepreneurs, and artists who are shaping the future of science, medicine, the environment, and the arts. In an article entitled "Diversity Powers Innovation," Scott Page asserts, "On a far larger scale, Silicon Valley's breadth of bright engineers from different academic disciplines and from almost every corner of the globe out-innovates other technology hotspots with equal brainpower but less diversity."[110]

It makes sense, doesn't it? Nonconformists are attracted to San Francisco because it welcomes, even rewards, their weirdness. The Giant misfits fit right in.

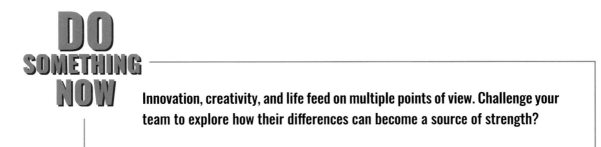

DO SOMETHING NOW

Innovation, creativity, and life feed on multiple points of view. Challenge your team to explore how their differences can become a source of strength?

Manage the Creative Tension

Multiple ingredients make the perfect gumbo[111], and a good gumbo is complicated and messy. Misfits, castoff, renegades—rebels, even—will create confusion and chaos. They tend to question the organization's deeply held, taken-for-granted assumptions. They like to test boundaries. They are not afraid to challenge accepted views and consider contradictory ones. As a result, you have to manage the creative tension that will inevitably arise out of this melting pot of personalities.

Embracing the tension as a positive clubhouse force rather than trying to make it go away starts with getting players to learn from each other without judging. Boch doesn't tiptoe around this issue; he attacks it head-on.

> **Boch:** If you shut down their personalities or their creativity inside the clubhouse, you are sure to shut them down on the field as well. I've always felt that you can play as one; you can reach across cultural boundaries and age differences to collaborate with others without losing your identity.
>
> I've told our players: "Find something you respect and admire in those who are radically different from you. Ask yourself, 'What can I learn from the differences in my teammates? How can I embrace those differences as a source of strength versus a source of insecurity?'"
>
> The more you respect and admire someone, the more you are willing to learn from them and lock arms with them in the trenches. But you won't find it if you don't look for it. Breaking down barriers and embracing the diversity of the clubhouse doesn't mean you have to stop being *you*.

Boch's point is that when you shift from tolerating a teammate's idiosyncrasies and limitations to embracing and leveraging them, you grow stronger. Team members have the potential to grow closer not *in spite of* these personality differences, but rather *because of* them. When you encourage players to be themselves—to bring their unique, sometimes quirky personalities into the clubhouse—you start to see an alchemy in which differences complement, strengthen, and complete rather than compete with one another. The work ethic, attitude, skill, and personality of one player draws something out of another player that makes him reach higher and achieve more.

For example, Aubrey Huff and Pat Burrell brought humor to the clubhouse. Keeping it light is such a critical asset when the intensity of do-or-die games tempts players to take it all too seriously and tighten up.

Pablo Sandoval's love for the game and cheery spirit complement Buster Posey's intensity and all-business-like approach, and Posey's discipline rubs off on Sandoval. Well, maybe! And there's no doubt that Posey's grounded maturity and big picture intelligence beyond his years helped grow the confidence of the entire pitching staff.

Jeremy Affeldt and Javier López are both thinkers who love to learn about leadership. That has an impact on holding a bullpen together and firing on all cylinders. Ángel Pagán's athleticism and intensity will light a fire under some of the more low-key players—particularly after he slam-dunked a Dodger fan who ran out into left field during a home game against their blue rivals.

This fusion of diverse personalities and skills shows up in other ways as well. It's Marco Scutaro coaching Sergio Romo not to throw too many sliders and then absolutely having his back when he throws a fastball to the best hitter in the game—in the biggest game of his life.

It's Hunter Pence, a reader, philosopher, and thinker who gets ribbed for having an awkward throwing motion and the craziest warm-up swing in baseball, who rallied the entire clubhouse to the theme of "I want one more day with you!"

It's Barry Zito "being there" for a struggling Tim Lincecum, and Lincecum being all ears because he saw Zito's class and dignity while struggling through the tough times. It's Gregor Blanco standing on the steps of the dugout supporting the guys on the field even though this could be another day he doesn't play.

It's Brandon Crawford and Joe Panik, two relatively quiet guys with impressive gymnastic abilities, working drill after painstaking drill in spring training to make the double play seamless. And then, logging the miles and building the confidence to intuitively know, in a split second, what the other is thinking when a big play counts in a critical playoff game.

It's Madison Bumgarner, with the weight of the entire team on his broad shoulders, demonstrating what it means to be unflappable and then watching his defense rally behind him. It's Jake Peavy talking to himself on the mound with a fiery intensity that both inspires his teammates and makes them laugh.

And then there are the coaches. Dave Righetti knows the psychology of pitching. No one can get in a pitcher's head, say one or two things on the mound, and get a game back on track better than Rags. A true gift when you consider that he doesn't have five minutes out there to get a pitcher's head right. Tim Flannery's deep knowledge of the game and ability to build intimate relationships with the players was a crucial component of the Giants chemistry. Not to mention that Flann was perhaps the most entertaining third base coach in the game. And, like Boch, Hensley Meulens, the hitting coach who speaks five languages, has a calming effect on the players.

> Ask yourself, "What can I learn from the differences in my teammates? How can I embrace those differences as a source of strength versus a source of insecurity?"

Radically different? Yes. But this cast of characters created a spirited clubhouse where they learned from each other, leaned on their strengths, celebrated their differences, and made history together.

Chemistry, like innovation, feeds on multiple points of view. This makes creative tension inevitable. But tension is where the energy and power of the team resides. If a team is diverse, it's loaded with potential energy—energy that can't be realized without tension. Great leaders see this tension as a positive and lean into it. The more they do, the better they get at making it work.

One Size Fits One

If you are managing multiple personalities, you have to learn to respond to many different signals. One size doesn't fit all; one size fits one. That's not easy. It means you are constantly trying to understand each personality and figure out who needs what. Sabean agrees. "[Bochy] has a knack as to [knowing] who needs a day off, who's a little bit prickly, who needs a little boot in the ass, who needs a pat [on] the back—it's an art form and he's perfected it."[112]

It's also all about who needs love, who needs assurance, who needs a dose of reality who needs data, who needs an intellectual challenge, and who needs something else.

Boch: Every one of our guys has a different way of learning, a different temperament, and a different understanding of the game. They come from different psychological and emotional places. They have different spiritual beliefs and lifestyles. Some are married, many aren't. I've learned that you can't just say something once, in one way, and expect everyone to get it. The lightbulbs go on for different players at different times. So, you have to tailor your message.

One guy is super-concerned about his numbers and job security while another guy just loves to play the game. One is too serious and could stand to loosen up; another is lighthearted and plays the game fluidly. One thinks deeply about things and needs more detail; someone else just needs the Cliff Notes version. When you are trying to bring out the best in these guys, you can't use the same approach.

DO SOMETHING NOW

In no more than five words, create a profile that describes each of the team members closest to you. What are their most significant differences? What battles are they prone to fighting inside themselves? How do these differences dictate what they need from you as a coach or mentor?

One size fits one is an art because everyone has a different tipping point. And the same guys need different things at different times depending on where they are in the season and what's happening in their lives outside the club. You have to be genuinely interested in "reading" them and then adapting to the person, the situation, and the context. It means asking, "How do I insert myself into a conversation so that I'm adding value?" This goes back to finding the story behind the story and then meeting a player where *they* are versus where *you* are.

For Boch, reading his players is both an innate skill and something he continues to work on. "The one thing that I've learned about him in the past couple years is how much he reads, and the knowledge that he gets from books that he reads," Ryan Vogelsong said. "And I think all those books and the knowledge he's taken from other people have helped him learn how to deal with people . . . I've always thought that a good manager is somebody that can manage 25 different personalities, and I think he does it as good as anybody."[113]

Buster Posey agreed. "[Boch's] best quality is how he can take so many different personalities and pull them together and get everybody on the same wavelength."[114]

The Giants major wins have always been the result of a wide array of players stepping up with clutch contributions at different times and in different ways, all arriving at the same place from different directions. These guys are extremely comfortable with each other because they live in a clubhouse where differences are not a threat, but rather a source of strength, energy, and completion. It's a clubhouse that nourishes the human spirit. They are confident about stepping into the breach because they play for a manager who welcomes, celebrates, and draws the best out of his so-called misfits, castoffs, and renegades.

30
TRUST
Chemistry's Bonding Agent

The Giants chemistry rests heavily on the trust that exists between members at all levels of the franchise. Trust is the bonding agent that holds the elements of chemistry together. In fact, it's what makes all the other ingredients in their chemistry work. No trust, no bonds, no chemistry.

The sense of security that comes from counting on others is a great enabler. With it, players find the courage to adapt and change, to be coachable and grow, to be others oriented and self-giving, and to find and spread joy in the journey of being a Giant.

This begs a question every leader must ask: "Am I worthy of the loyalty I desire?" Players don't bust their butts for just anybody. They have to have a compelling reason. If you *didn't* have a title, would anyone follow you? And every player must ask, "Can the guy in front of the locker next to me count on me?" No matter how you unpack the answers, it will inevitably come down to the issue of trust. If you aren't transparent, candid, competent, kind, honest, and *trustworthy*, forget it.

Earn It Again and Again

Boch will joust with the best teasers and pranksters in the business, but he would never knowingly take advantage of someone's vulnerability and embarrass them. He understands that trust, once it has been abused or violated, takes a long time to rebuild. It should never be taken for granted.

> **Boch:** Trust isn't automatically granted to you just because you have the title of manager or coach; it's something you have to earn every time you step into the clubhouse. You're going to make mistakes. The front office is going to make mistakes. But if you do something to violate trust with a player, you have to own it. Be an "adult" about it. Then, immediately start to rebuild it.
>
> Sometimes a GM is working against a trade deadline and things happen very fast. So fast, in fact, that we don't have time to talk about it. I had a situation once where a player came to me feeling insecure about being traded. And I said: "You're not getting traded. Are you kidding? You're going to be here for awhile." And then, unbeknownst to me, we traded him. Man, when that happens you feel terrible. And then, you're in damage control with the other guys. It's made me choose my words more carefully.

What does it look like to build a culture of trust? What elements make up this emotional glue that's so essential to chemistry? And, what is the leader's role in shaping them?

Be Real and Transparent

We live in a world that is increasingly cynical about organizations—about everything, really. We seek leaders who are genuine and transparent. Players trust Boch because he is unvarnished. He knows who he is, faux pas and all, and he owns it. People gravitate toward authenticity—*if* it is skillful, wise, and kind rather than brash and inconsiderate.

Boch may be a lot of things, but he doesn't have a phony bone in his body. He doesn't pretend to be someone he's not. He is not one person in front of the media and another behind closed doors with the players. What you see is what you get. He couldn't make the hard, often unpopular, decisions every baseball manager must make if he weren't comfortable in his own skin.

> **People adapt and change when we give them something worth changing for.**

People easily relate to Boch because he's human; it's what makes him likable and approachable. It's also what gives him presence. Players know he isn't afraid to be bold and decisive. They know he will be straight with them. His inclination to just be who he is sets a tone for the clubhouse too. It gives players the freedom to be themselves as well.

Be Candid

Trust also requires candor, and there's freedom in candor as long as it is kind. When your decisions are framed in words of candor and kindness, people are more willing to adapt and change. This means respecting them enough to define what the organization aspires to become, how it intends to realize those aspirations, and what roles they will play in getting there. It's showing them, as simply and forthright as possible, why you're asking them to take on a difficult challenge. Framing decisions, putting things in context, inspires chemistry and helps make talent dance.

Every time Boch makes a change he sits down with whoever's involved to explain the decision and link it to the broader vision of giving the team the best shot at winning. It's his way of transferring ownership to those who have to implement and execute. Players own it because they want to do what's best for the team and they know their teammates are counting on them. They own it because they trust Boch. They know he wouldn't ask them to do something he didn't think they were capable of doing or something that would jeopardize their careers. They've learned to trust his unconventional decisions because they've seen them work. More than anything, they trust him because he respects and trusts them as well.

Just hours before Game 7 of the 2014 World Series against Kansas City, for instance, Boch had a conversation with reliever Jeremy Affeldt. "He pulled me into the office," Affeldt recalled, "and said, 'I might have to go to you by the second or third inning. If need be, you need to be ready.' And it actually happened."[115] The last time Affeldt came into a game before the fifth inning was in Game 6 of the 2010 NLCS. Boch framed it for Affeldt and put it in context for the reliever. Instead of Affeldt being caught off-guard, he was ready—and pitched formidably.

Javier López, leader for the Giants—on and off the field.

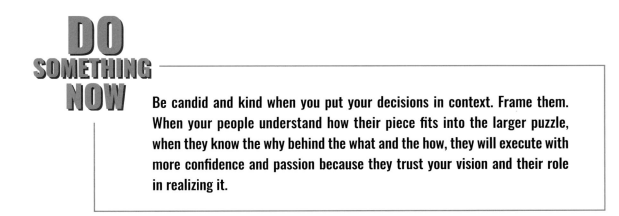

DO SOMETHING NOW

Be candid and kind when you put your decisions in context. Frame them. When your people understand how their piece fits into the larger puzzle, when they know the why behind the what and the how, they will execute with more confidence and passion because they trust your vision and their role in realizing it.

Another of the Giants seasoned relievers, Javier López, said that Boch stands out when it comes to communicating with clarity and candor. He remembered what it was like when he was traded from Pittsburgh to the Giants in 2010. "I'd never met the man and didn't know what we were doing exactly," López said. "The communication started right then and there with, 'Hey, this is why you're coming in, this is what I expect of you.' I think he's got a dry sense of humor; he's witty. But when he's serious, he locks it in. He'll banter with anybody, but when it's time to lock it in, he's the best at it, and that's why we have such good results."[116]

From the board and CEO Larry Baer, to Brian Sabean and Bobby Evans, to his coaches and players, people count on Boch to say what he means and do what he says. Even with his laid-back, other-oriented demeanor, he is anything but tentative—he is decisive. When it comes to making tough decisions about the roster or the lineup, or when talking to players about their performance, he's fearless. He will be painfully, and respectfully, candid with them. Mind you, these guys have lives and families that are affected whenever the organization makes a change. So, these conversations are not easy.

> **Boch:** As a backup [catcher] you see the game differently. You're more sensitive to what these players go through. At the end of spring training, I was one of those players who went to the last cut every year. Talk about stress; there is no pressure worse than that. But it taught me that players want you to shoot straight with them. Be fair, be caring, but they'd rather have you tell it like it is than beat around the bush. I know I appreciated that kind of honesty.

Once, when Boch had a frank discussion with Matt Cain to point out he was not doing enough conditioning, things got worse before they got better.

> **Boch:** Matty didn't speak to me for a week. But then he came back and agreed he needed to work harder. From that day forward he's been unbelievably dedicated. That's what happens with high-character guys. They think about it, take it to heart, and then come around.

When four-time All-Star and two-time Gold Glove awardee Adrian Gonzales was a 23-year-old first baseman with the Padres, he went through a terrible slump in 2006. Boch called Gonzo into the manager's office and didn't pull any punches. "Bruce told me there were other players who were hot at the time and that I wasn't," Gonzales said. "He told me I'd be sitting while I worked on some things . . . but that I wouldn't be pushed to the back of the dugout." Most players would immediately read these comments as code for less playing time. Not Gonzales. "Bochy didn't beat around the bush when I was struggling," the first baseman said. "But he didn't lie to me or anyone. He's honest. He said it was temporary."[117] Gonzales came back and became a four-time MVP for the Padres.

If you are truly going to build a "home" based on trust, candor has to go both ways. Players must have the freedom to confront the brutal facts of reality with their manager. Being calm in the storm is one of Boch's signature strengths, but when he acts out of turn, the players aren't afraid to call him on it.

Once after an emotional outburst, for example, a couple of veteran players pulled Boch aside after the game. "Hey, man, you're throwing the cap and kicking the bucket," they said. "That's not doing anything for us. All that's doing is telling us you're scared. And to be honest, that's not you. And if you're not being *you*, we're not going to be us."

In a situation like this it would be easy to be defensive and to push back, saying something like, "I'm a 20-year manager, who the hell are you to tell me how to manage?" And then kick the players out of your office.

Relief pitcher Jeremy Affeldt told us: "I've actually seen him get these kind of comments, take it in, and then make the adjustments. He's not going to be perfect. I don't know what's going on in his head. I don't know what kind of pressure he's getting from up top, so he might be reacting in the dugout to something else. But if we have the freedom to say, 'You are *reacting*. It's not like you. When you don't react, we play better,' he'll take it the same way he wants us to take it when the roles are reversed."

> **Candor is a two-sided coin. If you are going to build trust, players must have the freedom to confront their manager.**

Boch: I think you have to decide what you're trying to accomplish. If you're trying to win ball games it's not about *you,* it's about figuring out how to draw the best out of your players. And if I'm doing something that gets in the way of *that,* I need to know about it. It's never easy [getting negative feedback], but I appreciated the fact that the guys cared enough to call me out on it.

I'm a competitor. I want to win. But I'm also human. When we make stupid mistakes and things aren't going well, it gets under my skin and I *do* react. But if my reaction is counterproductive, I need to look in the mirror and fix it.

Boch is a good example of what best-selling author Ken Blue says: "Being right is highly overrated." Do you want to stroke your ego, assert your authority, and act like a hypocrite in being right, or do you want to win? Admitting mistakes and acknowledging weaknesses does two things. We show and own our humanness. We also illustrate our concern for the mission and the larger cause over our ego and image. And when we do that, candor becomes contagious.

In a culture where the manager and players are real and are encouraged to be true to themselves, candor says, "I respect you enough to tell you the truth." For players, it works, because in the topsy-turvy world of baseball, they want to know where they stand. Candor means they don't have to guess. For coaches and staff, it works, because when people have the guts to speak up, it gets more people in the conversation, which paves the way for more creativity and better decisions.

Boch has been in baseball long enough to know that you are not in management to win a popularity contest. In a world that brands you a hero in one season and dog meat in the next, popularity can't be your goal. You are there to lead players to a place they couldn't get to without you. That said, however, Boch seems to have mastered the art of making a point without making an enemy.

Candor can be awkward and messy. This is why you don't see much of it in most organizations. If you tell the truth in love, compassion, and kindness, it can be a powerful catalyst to building trust. In other words, if your message is conveyed with a sense of dignity and the right motives—to draw the best out of people, inspire them to unite, and help them win people will start to believe that they can bank on you. No one wants to follow a leader or be on a team with a player who is cowardly, indifferent, or abrasive.

The same is true for dealing with the media. Journalists are not in the business of telling your side of a story. They are going to tell the story as *they* see it. Boch started out being cautious and guarded in front of the media. But he has changed dramatically over his career. Through it all, three principles have dominated his approach to the media: Be accessible. Tell the truth. Take the high road.

This means, in a nutshell, never hide from the media. If the team is in a funk, be visible and say so. No spin, no candy-coating, no scapegoating. It also means that you look for something legitimately positive to talk about. If Boch can truthfully find the silver lining in bad news, that's where he's going to go. Of course, the question is, how do you do this when there really isn't any good news?

For example, how do you find the good after Game 6 of the 2014 World Series when you just got smoked in the opponent's house? The Royals scored seven runs in the second inning on the way to a 10-0 win over the Giants. No road team had won a World Series Game 7 since 1979. So Boch told reporters that the best thing about Game 6 was that the Giants got to "wash it off" and come back for Game 7.

In so many words, he said that this is what the world of baseball longs for: a high-stakes, drama-filled, winner-takes-all Game 7 of the World Series. Something that had only happened once in the past 11 years. *Sports Illustrated's* Tom Verducci echoed the sentiment saying, "It's the best day in sports because it takes the entire season—2,461 games—and distills it to one game."

Be Benevolent

Benevolent leaders look out for others. They choose service over self-interest. When things go wrong, benevolent leaders often assume responsibility and take the hit. We typically equate benevolence with being soft and wimpy—

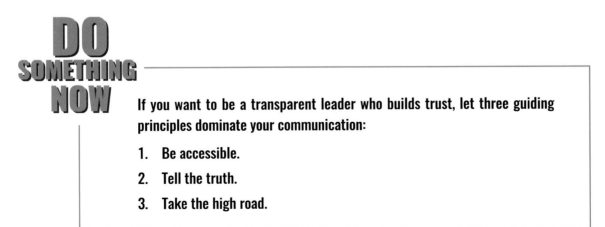

If you want to be a transparent leader who builds trust, let three guiding principles dominate your communication:

1. **Be accessible.**
2. **Tell the truth.**
3. **Take the high road.**

with being a pushover. It's not. Benevolence is gutsy and strong. When a team excels and succeeds, benevolent leaders are generous and altruistic—they give credit to others. You can see why benevolence builds trust.

When the Giants lose, Boch is the first to take responsibility. He doesn't make excuses, bad-mouth, or point the finger; rather, he looks into the eyes of questioning reporters and wears it. You will never see him intentionally throw a player or a colleague under the bus. He'll never use the media to communicate with a player or light a fire under a struggling lineup. It's just not who he is.

Former first baseman and corner outfielder Ryan Klesko played for Boch in San Diego and San Francisco. He had ample opportunities to watch Boch handle the media. "He takes care of his players. He doesn't dog them in the papers. He's been there. He sticks up for his guys."[118]

Behind closed doors Boch might have some very candid conversations with players, but in front of the curtain, it's about absorbing the blows (personally earned or not) and taking pressure off them so they are free to learn, adjust, and move on. Even behind closed doors, if Boch has a problem with a player's effort or attitude, he will never address it in front of other players. He respects the dignity of the player too much, and because he's been there, he knows how it feels to be dressed down in public.

Leaders who are secure with who they are and confident in their own abilities don't have to be the center of attention. When the Giants win and the praises are flowing his way, Boch is a master of deflection. It's all about his players and his coaching staff. If it's not about them, it's about Brian Sabean's genius and Bobby Evans's execution as architects in acquiring the right players; Larry Baer's ability to build a culture and provide the resources for winning; or the hundreds of front office leaders who bring sellout crowds and fanatical fans to the park every game.

> **Leaders who are secure with who they are and confident in their own abilities don't have to be the center of attention.**

And the thing is, it's genuine. He absolutely believes that what the Giants have accomplished—from the front office to the scouting organization, his coaching and training staff, the clubhouse manager, and his players—is a collaborative effort. He appreciates the fact that no one does it alone.

Preaching interconnectedness, the fact that everyone depends on everyone else, rubs off on Boch's players as well. Remember Matt Cain's Game 2 of the 2010 World Series, in which he pitched 7 ⅔ innings to defeat the Texas Rangers? Remember his perfect game in 2012 or when he threw 5 2/3 shutout innings in the series-clinching Game 7 of the 2012 NLCS to beat the St. Louis Cardinals?

In each one of those accomplishments, Cain echoed a familiar theme. He deflected the credit to his defense for making the plays, to his hitters for scoring runs, and to his catcher for calling the games. That's because Matt Cain believes that "we're all in this together" actually means something.

> **Boch:** Over the years I've watched Matty's humility shine through time and time again. In my early days with the Giants, Timmy [Lincecum] became the franchise guy. After the 2012 World Series, Bum [Madison Bumgarner] became an instant rock star. But it never affected Matty in a negative way. It never got in the way of him going about his business. For a guy with his résumé and tenure to carry himself like that, it sets a tone. It's why we have such great chemistry.

Be Firm but Fair

Playing favorites doesn't build chemistry. It destroys it. Boch isn't afraid to give rookies or struggling everyday players more opportunity in high-pressure situations. He'll trust a guy to play a different position when many managers wouldn't even consider it. He has the confidence to look beyond payroll and pedigree with regard to playing the right player in the right position at the right time.

Boch also doesn't let himself get trapped into the kind of rigid thinking that pigeonholes players. He's flexible. Just because a player doesn't perform well today doesn't mean he won't make a huge contribution tomorrow. And lack of experience in one part of the game will not cause him to overlook the potential a player has in another part of the game if that is what the moment calls for.

It's a unique balance. On the one hand, baseball is a meritocracy where performance drives everything. On the other hand, Boch is unwilling to write off a player if he sees an inkling of genius in someone who just needs to spark the pilot light of confidence. If that means giving them a second chance or playing them in a different role, so be it.

As a journeyman player, Boch saw the importance of fairness. He saw the consequences of politics and favoritism—resentment, low morale, selfishness, and players leaving for greener pastures—and he knew how they have the potential to destroy team chemistry.

Ask him to recount the memorable lessons from mentors who shaped his approach to managing and you quickly get the impression that he has learned something from everyone—including how and how *not to* do it. Take, for example, Eddie Stanky, who played in three World Series for the Dodgers, Braves, and Giants, respectively, and went on to manage the Cardinals, White Sox, and later on the University of South Alabama baseball team. Stanky recruited Boch at South Alabama.

> **Boch:** I remember the first time I met Eddie Stanky in his room. He was doing deep knee bends while brushing his teeth. He looked me up and down and said, "Son, it'll take me a while, but I think I can do something with you." It was pretty intimidating for a young kid going into college. Then, I watched one of their drills at South Alabama where Stanky was teaching players how to get hit by a pitch. He had the pitching machine cranked up to around 85–90 mph! That's when I said, "Uh, I think I'm ready to sign with the Astros."

In 1978, Boch signed with the Houston Astros and played for Bill Virdon, who had an illustrious career in MLB as both a player and a coach. Although Boch knows he can learn from anyone, anywhere, anytime, if there is one person who was the single biggest influence on the way he manages today, he would say it was Virdon.

> **Boch:** Bill treated players like he wanted to be treated. He was firm but fair. He demanded that the game be played right, but he never shamed anyone in public. If Bill had a problem with you, he took you into his office, closed the door, and set you straight. No sugarcoating. You knew exactly where you stood. But at the same time, you were never embarrassed. As a player, I appreciated that. I learned a lot from the way he did things.
>
> I've seen the other side of that, too, where a manager yells at players or calls them out in the media. You not only feel bad about making a mistake, now you're embarrassed because you're reading about it in the papers. You feel betrayed. And when you're walking around on eggshells, you don't enjoy the game as much, and I don't think you play your best ball.

Boch also played for Hall of Fame manager Dick Williams with the Padres. Playing for Williams sounded like attending a version of U.S. Marine Corps boot camp. Williams wanted thick-skinned players. Whether it was calling them out in front of other players or talking about them in the press, Williams was demanding and tough. He would do just about anything to "harden" them.

Williams once blamed Boch for failing to execute a rundown between home and third base. Bochy got dressed down in front of the other players. Actually, the third baseman hadn't called for the ball as the rundown called for, but Boch never said anything—even after being sent down to the minor leagues. That's the kind of teachable moment that sticks in your mind, when you say to yourself, "If every mentor is an example to learn from, what are the admired qualities I want to apply in my own managing, and what are the fatal flaws I need to avoid?"

Eddie Stanky, life-size bronze statue at the University of South Alabama.

Fair Isn't Equal

People often confuse fairness with equality, but they are not the same. As our children reached driving age, we made our expectations for buying a car very clear. We agreed to match (up to a certain amount) whatever they saved for a car. We shared our assumption that they would each save different amounts of money and therefore receive different contributions from us. And, when this happened, no one should complain. Now, were we being fair? We think so. Are they being treated equally? No.

Boch is tough. He expects a lot from his coaches and players. He's fair but not always equal. His ability to make tough decisions based on performance has created a meritocracy where players know exactly what to expect and feel that they are treated fairly.

Third baseman Pablo Sandoval had a meteoric rise from the Class A to the majors in just four months. In his first full year with the Giants, Sandoval finished second in the National League with a .330 batting average; third in doubles, with 44; and sixth in slugging percentage (.556) and total bases (318). In 2010, however, an overweight and underperforming Pablo—despite being one of the most likable guys in the clubhouse and beloved by San Francisco fans—barely made it off the bench in the postseason.

> **Boch:** At that time, I just felt that we needed more discipline at the plate and more range at third [base]. We had invested a lot of energy in Pablo in the off-season, in getting him in shape, but he showed up at spring training almost 280 pounds and it showed as the season progressed. Bam-Bam [hitting coach Hensley Meulens] tried to get him to swing at higher-quality pitches. We had him on a strict, low-fat, high-protein diet, but in both cases, not much changed.
>
> Pablo loves the game. He has an infectious clubhouse presence. But his numbers dropped significantly. So, I chose to make a change and play [Mike] Fontenot. I know it was hard on Pablo, and my decision certainly was not popular with some fans. But in the postseason, it's

like you start all over again, except that there is no margin for error. When you lose, you go home—for good. Every game is crucial. Those decisions are tough. But my job is to give our club what I think is the best chance to win.

As we know, Pablo went on to make some heroic contributions in the club's 2012 World Series victory, but in 2010, he was resistant to change and Boch wouldn't have it.

Sandoval's youthful enthusiasm invigorates the Giants clubhouse. He hit an incredible three home runs in Game 1 of the 2012 World Series.

When Boch announced his roster for the 2010 NLDS, excluded from the list was the Giants highest paid player, starting pitcher Barry Zito. It wasn't surprising given Zito's faltering performance in a division-clinching game against San Diego at the tail end of the regular season. Not only that, but in Zito's previous nine starts for the Giants, he went 1-8. No one was more disheartened by Boch's decision than Zito was, and no one took more responsibility. Zito said that he stood behind Boch's decision and that he was disappointed in himself for not making it into the rotation.

> **Boch:** It was another really tough call. You look at what some of these players have done for you in the past and it makes the decision even harder. But no one pays us for what we did yesterday; they pay us for what we can do today and what they think we can do tomorrow. Barry handled it like a true professional. He understood what was best for the team and was willing to subordinate his ego. But that's the kind of player he is—a real class act.

Be Competent

In baseball, dogging it—that is, being halfhearted in your approach to the game—is a good way to lose the respect of your teammates. That's important, because trust is formed through the mutual respect and admiration each team member has for the other players' competencies, which are built from a never-ending effort to get smarter, better, and faster. Buster Posey and Madison Bumgarner are battery mates who have been together a long, long time. They know each other well. They also have a comfort level with each other that rubs off on the rest of the team.

Bum knows how buttoned-up Buster is. Buster has studied. He's read the scouting reports. He's in tune with the umpires' strike zones. He knows how to frame a pitch. He watches the subtle adjustments a hitter makes at the plate to get to a ball. And, he has a game plan. Buster reads his pitchers and tries to call pitches that are within their individual comfort zones, yet aggressive toward the hitter.

Buster knows what Bum can do. Bum is unflappable. He has had the most productive postseason record of any pitcher in the history of the game. If he wants to throw a different pitch than what Buster puts down, it seems like Posey's good with it. Today, they will execute on one well-crafted plan; tomorrow, with a different umpire and a different lineup, it might be a different plan. The point here is that they trust each other's knowledge and skills immensely. When you have chemistry between a catcher and pitcher like that, and it shows up in a rhythm that is so fluid, so in sync, the entire team is galvanized by it.

The trust you see played out on the field echoes throughout the organization. A lot of communication flows back and forth between Boch and the front office. While the relationships are very informal and trustworthy, Boch respects that this level of trust must be re-earned constantly. Sometimes it is earned by taking a stand that's contrary

Posey and Bumgarner, battery mates since (Class A) San Jose Giants days.

to the majority of decision makers. No great enterprise wants a "yes-man" or "yes-woman," and every enlightened leader respects people who have the guts to say, "I think you are wrong."

Other times, trust is earned by creatively leveraging your resources (in Boch's case, ball players) to further the strategic initiatives of the franchise. As with his on-field decisions, he seems to have a good sense of knowing when to stand his ground and when to push back, when to trust his expertise (and gut), and when to back off and fight a different battle another day. Bottom line: If people around you know you are competent to make the data-driven calls, the gut calls, the uncomfortable calls, the left-on-red calls, you earn trust through every single one of those calls.

> **Boch:** When we meet with Larry Baer and the board, even though we have such great camaraderie, I still know it's important to build a business case for what we are trying to do in baseball operations. You can't just go willy-nilly with your emotions in hand and say, "I want to do this or that." You've got to think it through and map it out and then, hopefully, present it clearly and concisely.

It boils down to earned trust. I want all our front office executives and the board to see that while our primary focus is on wining ball games, we are trying to think and act like owners. So, in dealing with Larry or Brian [Sabean], I'm constantly asking myself, "What's best for the franchise as a whole?" In the Giants organization, we don't operate as an island unto ourselves. We operate in the context of something much larger.

Even when Boch was with the Padres, the late Hall of Fame broadcaster Jerry Coleman recognized his managerial acumen. "He's as good as I've ever seen," Coleman said. "Casey Stengel [for whom Coleman played as a New York Yankee] won because he had great teams, but Casey had no personal touch with his players. Bruce is a nice guy, but he also can stand up to people and tell them when they're wrong. And they'll listen—because he treats men like men. Give Bruce players, and he'll win consistently."[119]

Interconnectedness, interdependence, and harmony are what make chemistry possible. But people need a special kind of capital with which to invest—to open up, rely on each other, and lock arms. It is the kind of capital that requires constant attention and scrupulous management because it is so hard to acquire and so easily lost. No meaningful relationship, no comfortable home, and no truly great enterprise was ever built without it, however.

Trust is the social capital of every great team—the bonding agent that chemistry cannot function without.

31
GRATITUDE
The Art of Taking Nothing for Granted

In 2010, down six and a half games in mid-August, the Giants clinched the NL West in the very last game of the regular season. In 2012, it took winning six consecutive elimination games to get to the World Series. In 2014, the Giants squeaked into the playoffs, winning the Wild Card Game against Pittsburgh. Then they took the World Series all the way down to Game 7 before winning on the road.

If there is any beauty in the Giants brand of "torture" baseball, it's that they feel gratitude more *intensely*, more *frequently*, and more *deeply* than do those who have had an easier time getting into and through the playoffs. The pressure to come through in clutch situations has been so intense, so often, that when a teammate does it, the volume on the dial of appreciation is cranked way up. When you are hanging by a thread and someone saves the day to play another day, gratitude intensifies.

> When you are hanging by a thread and someone saves the day to play another day, gratitude intensifies.

Through the five-year run to three World Championships, it seemed as if in every single game a different Giants player made something good happen. For example, in Game 4 of the 2014 World Series, 11 different Giants players got a hit, tying for the most ever for a team in a World Series. To say the least, the opportunities to experience and express gratitude were frequent.

Combine the fact that the Giants have played so many win-or-go-home games, where the threat of going home was immediate, with Brian Sabean's commitment to hire men of character and Bruce Bochy's passion for creating a clubhouse culture where people choose service over self-interest, and it should come as no surprise that the entire Giants organization reeks—of gratitude, that is!

Gratitude Unlocks Chemistry

What do chemistry and gratitude have to do with each other? Well, simply put, gratitude is the emotional response we direct toward others when we benefit from their actions. In baseball, gratitude shows up as a sense of wonder, thankfulness, and appreciation for every aspect of the game: the camaraderie, friendship, lineup, athleticism, culture, loyalty of the fans, and roar of the crowd.

Gratitude is not just superficially saying, "It's a team effort." It's standing in awe of another player's talent and appreciating how that feeds your own goals and the goals of the team. It's getting juiced by having that player on the team.

Put a critical mass of guys together who haven't lost this sense of wonder and you have a team that complains less, trips over petty preoccupations less, and doesn't take one another for granted. You have a team that affirms more, focuses on the larger cause, and seizes every opportunity.

> **Boch:** Our clubhouse is not perfect, not even close, but I think our players know what they have here. I think they know the camaraderie is special and they appreciate it.
>
> We've been through so many heated battles and so much adversity that it's given our guys an appreciation for what they have—what they have in each other, in Larry Baer, Sabes, and the Giants organization, in our trainers, and in our coaching staff. I've been in clubs where people are taken for granted. I don't see that here—not very often.

> In fact, what I *do* see is such a genuine connection among our players that when one of our guys does something special on the field the dugout erupts—they are happy for each other, not just because it advances a runner or scores a run or does something good for the team; they're happy for the guy.

Gratitude transforms your perspective and changes your whole orientation. When you are in awe of what you have, the immediate response is a deep sense of appreciation: "How do I repay my teammates? The club? The fans? What contribution can I make?" These questions leave little room for envy, resentment, entitlement, or an exaggerated sense of self-importance—the toxins that destroy team chemistry.

Gratitude is reciprocal. That is, the more in tune players are with how other players have elevated the entire team, the more they want to do the same in return; and the more frequently and consistently this dynamic occurs, the more accountability, trust, and respect you have in a clubhouse. The ripple effect is more loyalty, a higher level of morale, and better productivity—all of which makes for great bonding among players.

When Friends Move On

In the off-season after the Giants won the World Series in 2014, Boch got a call that he had hoped he would never get. It was from his third base coach and friend of more than 30 years, Tim Flannery. So special is their relationship that MLB Network Presents did a short documentary on Bochy and Flann entitled *The Odd Couple*,[120] and *USA Today* did a lengthy article that picked up on the brotherhood of these two characters.

Flann is a gifted musician whose band has played with the likes of Jackson Browne, Bruce Hornsby, Garth Brooks, and Jimmy Buffet. In fact, during the playoffs in 2012 and 2014, Flann sang the National Anthem with Bob Weir and Phil Lesh of the Grateful Dead. It was time, he told his old friend, to hang up the uniform. He wanted to spend more time with family and pursue his music.

You can tell a lot about a person's impact on a community by the way their colleagues respond to their departure. Will they leave a legacy? Will they be missed? Do they leave a void in the organization? Are people genuinely stunned by the loss? No sooner had Flann made his announcement, social media lit up. Here are just a few of the responses from players.

An emotional Pablo Sandoval says "good-bye" to Tim Flannery.

Twitter
@JeremyAffeldt

first time I've been saddened by a coaches resignation. Tim Flannery u are my friend and enjoyed the ride w you! Love you man @SFGiants

Twitter
@RichAurilia35

@SFGiants Tim Flannery retiring. One of the best coaches I've had. Not only a great teacher, but also a great man. Thanks for the laughs.

Twitter
@bcraw35

This guys is one of the best. We will miss you Flanman. Wish you the best of luck with everything.

Boch reminisced about getting Flann's call.

> **Boch:** Yeah, that was not one of my better days. It was a tough call to take. Flann and I have been down a lot of roads and logged a lot of miles together over 30 years. He brought so much passion and energy to coaching third base. It was entertaining, watching him waving his arms and running down the sideline when he'd send runners. The fans loved it too.
>
> There are so many players out there who will tell you that his knowledge of the game and excitement for it had a big impact on them. We've lost a key member of our coaching staff and a key contributor to what we've accomplished. But more than that, it's the loss of our friendship on the field. We know each other so well he could tell you what my signals would be before I gave them. I lean on our coaches pretty hard, especially Flann, because we had so much trust. But I know this is a good decision for him. He's got such a gift [writing songs and playing music], I'm happy that he's going to pursue it, happy he'll get more time with his family. That said, I miss him terribly.
>
> There's one part of him I won't miss, though. Given the graciousness of so many wine makers who are Giants fans, I've acquired quite a collection of wine in my office. When I went in to do my media interviews after the games, Flann would sneak into my office like a hyena, steal my wine, and take it into the coaches' locker room and share it with all of them. They didn't know what kind of wine to steal so usually ended up with my most expensive bottles. Now, I won't lose so much wine.

A year after the Giants won the 2014 World Series Boch sent a package to the home of each of his coaches just before Christmas. It was a replica of the Tiffany-produced World Series trophy. Flann's retirement was the impetus for the gifts, a tangible way for Boch to say thank you to his coaches and to tell Flann: "Thank you for being by my side for 16 years. You were such a big part of what we accomplished." An emotional guy to begin with, Boch's old friend was moved to tears. When people move on and deep bonds are disrupted, it is because of gratitude—*not loss*—that our emotions arise. We are moved, changed, and enriched by the person's impact on us.

Take Nothing for Granted

No one would ever write "torture" into the script, but adversity is a great teacher because it forces a team to contemplate endings, which in turn makes them more grateful.

In every elimination game there is the possibility of going home that spotlights the significance of the moment. It causes a player to think: "I might not get to play with these guys again—or ever. This could be

Flann and Boch have been together, as players and coaches for three decades.

it." Isn't this what was behind Hunter Pence's now-famous speech to the boys before Game 3 of the 2012 NLDS? It might have been a fiery rant flavored with expletives, but what the players heard was "I appreciate you. I appreciate this game. I appreciate this moment in time that we have together. And, I'm not willing to give it up just yet."

Endings and potential endings wake us up and force us to see the world through a new lens. If we choose to let them, they also can make us stronger, "stronger" meaning more courageous, resilient, and unified.

> **Boch:** With so many injuries and so many lineups over the years, I've learned to take nothing for granted. Even when we lose, if a player is 100 percent healthy, firing on all cylinders, you have to be thankful for that. Because with a season as long as ours, it's not a question of if they will need days off, it's when.
>
> Look at Hunter Pence. [He had] 331 consecutive starts when we went into the postseason in 2014. Then, in 2015, he's hit by a pitch and has a broken arm, and in 2016, he tore a hamstring tendon right off the bone, both of which took him out for big parts of the season. So, you learn—in the blink of an eye, one play—it can all be taken away from you.
>
> I guess you have to look at the silver lining when this happens because you are forced to look at your young players. Believe me, they're grateful for an opportunity to fill the gap. I know they want to do their part to soften the blow of losing one of our starters by playing well. That's what I mean when I say we just have a group of very unselfish guys here.

A Giant Comeback

After a May 2011 collision at home plate with Scott Cousins (described in chapter 18), Buster Posey faced a long road back. Months of rigorous rehab, painful stretching of scar tissue, and mental discipline combined with a lot of patience lay ahead. During the six weeks between two surgeries, one to reconstruct his ankle and one to remove screws, he couldn't bear any weight on the injured leg.

Posey's horrific collision with Marlin's center fielder Scott Cousins at home plate.

The Giants Head Athletic Trainer, Dave "Groesch" Groeschner, shepherded Buster throughout this lengthy, arduous process. It was Groesch who rallied the surgeons and team physicians, asked everyone to put egos aside, and said, "We have to get this right." It was Groesch who formulated the overall rehab plan, feeding it to Buster two weeks at a time. And, it was Groesch who visited Posey in the off-season to make sure the plan was being executed properly.

Part therapist, part trainer, and the executive who would oversee the multidisciplinary community—surgeons, team physicians, nutritionists, and strength and conditioning coaches—charged with putting Buster back together again, Groesch was there every painful step of Buster's way.

"I got to know him pretty well by the end of it. And one of the things I came to realize about Buster is that he's super regimented. He wants to know what to do. 'Here's this week, here's next week.' We're looking down the road, of course, but he wants a plan and he wants to see it. Most of all, the kid busted his ass. That's what amazes me. His motivation to get back is probably the biggest story in all this."[121]

> **Boch:** It was an incredible display of teamwork over a long period. Most of us didn't see the grueling regimen Buster went through, but Groesch was right there from day one, always pushing, encouraging, and mapping out the plan for Buster. And Buster showed true grit and determination to follow the plan. I think Groesch would tell you he exceeded it. Both of them put forth a heroic effort.
>
> When he [Posey] came back to spring training in 2012, I was obviously cautious. He was still feeling some tenderness when running bases so we took it slow. At that point, I'm hoping he'll be good to start maybe 100 games if we give him more time at first base, but he exceeded our expectations. That's just the kind of player he is. It was just an amazing comeback.

Posey started 143 games in 2012, including 111 behind the plate. Who would've guessed? Who would've known, seeing the horrific images of Buster contorted at home plate on May 25, that he would come back in 2012 and be the National League Comeback Player of the Year, the MVP of the National League, the winner of the Hank Aaron Award for being the NL's best hitter, win the Willie Mac Award for being the Giants most inspirational player, and, of course, be the recipient of a second World Series ring?

Talk about gratitude. Everyone in the entire Giants community was thrilled to have Buster back. First baseman Brandon Belt put it this way: "Pretty much everybody in the city loves him. His teammates feel the same way."[122]

Posey was grateful to be back as well. When you've been out for a year you miss the sights and sounds of the clubhouse, you miss the smell of freshly cut grass, you miss the routine of batting practice, and you miss the roar of the crowd and the adrenaline rush of competition. Posey's wife, Kristen, explained it this way: "I think being away hurt him pretty bad. As a player, you're so used to being with those guys, playing every day and feeling that competitive drive."[123]

The benefits of gratitude have been well documented.[124] Grateful people are more alert and enthusiastic, more energetic and attentive, and more determined than are those who take things for granted. Those who replace bitterness and resentment with gratitude report higher levels of fulfillment, vitality, and optimism and lower levels of stress, frustration, and depression. They exercise more regularly, report fewer physical symptoms, and are more likely to live longer than the ungrateful are.[125]

Posey's comeback is just one example of how mutual appreciation and gratitude reverberates through the Giants clubhouse. There are others. The point is, being grateful has a unifying effect that can completely transform the energy and direction of a team.

This unifying effect spills out onto the fans as well. When Posey was down at home plate after the collision, the fans started chanting, "Posey! Posey! Posey!" When he was finally helped to his feet the crowd roared. In the first exhibition game of 2012, a packed house gave him a rousing and prolonged ovation—and he had only gone out to warm up his legs in the outfield.

When you've missed watching a player of his caliber for roughly an entire year, there is a deep sense of appreciation when he returns, particularly when he returns healthy. The fans were with Buster and with the club in this crisis. They hadn't gone through the excruciating pain of rehab, but they were *with him*.

> **Boch:** The response he got from the fans at our first exhibition game was unbelievable. They knew the long road he went down to get back. In a way, even though we weren't sure yet how he'd hold up during the season, it symbolized that his comeback was complete. It was special to watch.

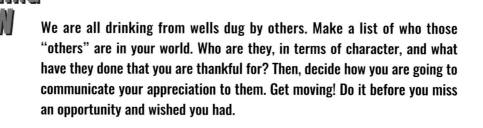

DO SOMETHING NOW

We are all drinking from wells dug by others. Make a list of who those "others" are in your world. Who are they, in terms of character, and what have they done that you are thankful for? Then, decide how you are going to communicate your appreciation to them. Get moving! Do it before you miss an opportunity and wished you had.

Gratitude is a sign of wisdom and maturity, a hallmark of confident humility. Show us a clubhouse, company, or family infused with gratitude and we will show you a group of people who make the most of what they have—people who do more than what is expected of them. And each time they do this, their bond becomes tighter.

This is one more element that makes chemistry possible.

In a different injury, Dave Groeschner escorts Buster Posey from the plate after Posey was hit by a wild pitch.

9th Inning

GIANT REACH

It's Bigger than Baseball, Business, and Money

32
TOGETHER WE'RE GIANT!
Cultivating a Deep Sense of Community

As everyone in San Francisco knows, Hunter Pence rides a now-famous customized motor scooter to every home game. He rides it because he "can't fathom driving" and because he likes to enjoy the views of the city and the bay, connecting with fans on his way to and from AT&T Park. It's such an essential part of his life that the Giants have given away bobbleheads of Pence on it. After signing a $90-million deal with the Giants, the club offered to put him in a town car to get home. Hunter jumped on his scooter instead.

Early in the 2014 season the scooter was stolen outside a restaurant on San Francisco's waterfront after a Sunday game. Pence isn't a materialistic guy, but he was crushed. When he came into the clubhouse the next morning Boch noticed that the guy who is always "up" was uncharacteristically down. "He had a sad face on this morning," Boch said. "I've never seen that from Hunter."

To recover the scooter, Pence appealed to the culprit, essentially saying, "I'll forgive you, no questions asked, if you just bring it back." And then he offered a signed bobblehead to anyone who could help him find it.

The incident blew up on social media and sparked a citywide crusade to retrieve the scooter. People throughout the community were on the lookout for it. Businesses near AT&T Park started promotions as a way of getting the scooter back. Union Square restaurant Lefty O'Douls announced a $200 reward with drink and meal tickets for the scooter's return, and EPIC Roadhouse offered dinner for two. Pence was overwhelmed by the outpouring of support from fans in finding his prized possession. He said they made the gut-shot feel better: "This was like a 'Together We're Giant' kind of story. Everyone had my back."

Imagine being the person who took it. Where would you ride it? Who would you sell it to without the world knowing? And given Pence's immense popularity with now-outraged fans, how would you survive if you were exposed?

The scooter was returned three days later, but the mystery wasn't solved; Pence doesn't know

A happy Hunter Pence is reunited with his beloved scooter.

who took it since he never filed a criminal complaint. Of course, the ordeal gave Hunter's teammates plenty of ammo to tease him with. Sergio Romo wisecracked that the breaking news of the scooter's return was a bigger story than Tim Lincecum throwing a five-inning no hitter. Even Bochy deadpanned a gibe.

> **Boch:** Kim will tell you—I couldn't sleep at night worrying about Hunter's scooter. It might be the most famous scooter in America. Now we can all get some rest. But I will say, the person who took it had to be feeling some real pressure. With people all over the community looking for this thing, he had to feel like a fugitive. When the police brought the scooter into the clubhouse, I know Hunter was relieved. I'm glad the story had a happy ending.

The Reach and the Impact

We've said that chemistry is a product of culture; it's also a product of community. Chemistry is shaped and formed by the individual behaviors of everyone who touches the organization and everyone touched by it. Every day—in the front office, on the air, in the clubhouse, or in the city—people make choices that build chemistry or tear it down.

For example, when people walk out of a meeting with Larry Baer or one of his senior executives, are they left a little better or a little worse? Are players affirmed or deprived, enlarged or diminished by the people they work and play with? Do the coaches and trainers feel humanized or dehumanized by their interactions with Bochy, Sabean, and Evans? Do the conversations throughout the organization draw people closer together or divide them? When a player makes a mistake and blows a game, what's the tone in the clubhouse? Blame or support? Guilt and shame? Or empathy, grace, and a willingness to move on? In other words, what is the reach, what is the impact of the culture? Is it drawing out the best and inspiring competence, confidence, and community, or is it drawing out doubt, fear, and insecurities?

No culture is perfect, and the San Francisco Giants are no exception. Do people blow it in meetings? Sure. Is the organization always as human as the human beings in it? No. Do the flaws of leaders and players periodically spill out when people bump into them? Yes. But what makes the San Francisco Giants special is that the club has cultivated a deep sense of community. The reach is local, national, and virtual. And the impact is about enriching lives by making the business of baseball and everyone connected in this community, as singer/songwriter Jack Johnson puts it, "better together."

> **What makes the San Francisco Giants special is that the club has cultivated a deep sense of community. This community is local, national, and virtual.**

Essentially, there is a network of relationships within the entire Giants organization and between the franchise and the entire Bay Area that is powerfully appealing. There's a connection that goes beyond games, scoreboards, and statistics. It's a relationship in which shared experiences create a shared identity. Fans have endured a "torture" style of baseball, mourned losses, and celebrated victories—together. They don't just identify with the players; they are part of the club. They're not just spectators; they feel responsible for playing their part in creating the chemistry that makes this club unique. Every night the energy of those fans generates another type of electricity that recharges the spirits of the Giants.

In return, the Giants make it a priority to be in tune with the deeply human struggles and needs of people in their community, and then they lean in to lend their support. This is a place where people are visibly jazzed to

Broadcasting duo Mike Krukow and Duane Kuiper are fan favorites and core to the Giants family.

be part of the Giants family and the Giants are ecstatic about being an integral part of the city. The players and fans find their strength in each other.

First and foremost, the Giants are a business. But something is happening here that goes beyond business deals, transactions, and making money. You quickly get the sense that the Giants don't reach into the community just because it is necessary to be a good corporate citizen; they do it because of their love for the city and their compassion for and connection to the people. They have formed a community that has a great vibe and a magnetic pull that makes you think: "In the highs and lows, no one stands alone. I want in. I want to be a part of *that*."

The mutual support and shared identity we are talking about here is multifaceted and multidirectional. It shows up in the relationships between the front office and baseball operations, and among the players, coaches, and training staff. You can see it in the camaraderie among the various broadcasters and in the relationship they have built with the fans. The dynamic duo of Duane Kuiper and Mike Krukow, along with Jon Miller and Dave Flemming, aren't just radio and television personalities; they come into the fans' homes and become their friends And, no matter where you go in the world, when you run into a Giants fan, there is an instant rapport: you're connected and bonded, and you belong to the same community.

Band Together When Crisis Strikes

As of 10 p.m., October 8, 2017 there were 10 wild land fires raging through California's North Bay Area, 11,000 firefighters from all over the world worked tirelessly to contain 250 fires. October 2017 will be remembered as the month thousands would prefer to erase from their memories. But sadly, it will be recorded as one of the most destructive disasters in California history. Wildfires in Northern California scorched more than 220,000 acres—killing dozens and ravaging homes and schools—in Santa Rosa, Sonoma and Napa counties.

Yet, in the darkness there was a glimmer of hope. Tipping Point Emergency Relief Fund founder Daniel Lurie, along with Larry Baer, Salesforce chairman and CEO Marc Benioff, Twitter CFO Ned Segal, Twilio Co-founder and CEO Jeff Lawson, and many other Bay Area leaders joined forces to answer the question, "What can we do?"

This powerful group of Bay Area business and community leaders formed Band Together to support long-term relief, recovery and rebuilding for those hit hardest. A live music event at AT&T Park kicked off the efforts. The best seats were reserved for first responders, volunteers and others impacted by the fires. The event, completely underwritten by sponsors, directed 100 percent of the ticket sales to the Tipping Point Emergency Relief Fund. Metallica, along with G-Eazy, Rancid, Dead & Company, Dave Matthews Band, and Raphael Saadig headlined the concert. As of this publication, the coalition raised over $12 million to support community partners working on the front lines and provide resources to those displaced by the destruction. The coalition effort reinforced the message, "together we are more powerful than any one of us alone."

Here to Enrich

Imagine going to work every day for an organization that you are truly excited about and proud to be a part of. You're excited because you get to make a difference. You're proud because the organization is honorable. It does business in a way that considers the impact of its actions on the social, environmental, and economic well-being of the community. It organizes major relief efforts when tragedy strikes and neighbors are in need.

In the last 20-plus years, the Giants have found new and creative ways to become more deeply entrenched in the community. Each year, the franchise holds more than 375 community outreach programs focusing on everything from youth recreation and fitness to health, violence prevention, education, and literacy. Since its inception in 1991, the Giants Community Fund has donated in excess of $24 million to community efforts. In 2015, more than 45,000 game tickets were donated to 300 community groups, a gift funded by the team's players.

When players come to the Giants, Baer wants to know what they are passionate about in terms of giving back. That's because the Giants organization will partner with players to support their causes. The thinking goes like this: "Why not champion the charities our players choose? They already have ownership in supporting these causes. They're already moved to take action. And, since Together We Are Giant . . . together we can do more."

For example, in the beginning of the 2016 season, Buster Posey made an announcement to the team about a program dedicated to pediatric cancer research and treatment. "Kristen and I have been blessed with two healthy kids and the opportunity to contribute to the community in a meaningful way. We were shocked to learn that only about four percent of cancer funds raised throughout the

Buster and Kristen Posey host fundraiser for pediatric cancer research and treatment.

country are dedicated to pediatric cancer research, and we felt compelled to lend our voices to this important cause. Our hope is that by working with the doctors, patients and their families we can raise significant awareness and funds for pediatric cancer research and treatment."[126]

The Giants support the Poseys' fundraising efforts by selling a special 9FORTY cap, and all proceeds from the sale of the cap go to support pediatric cancer research and treatment. The Poseys—partnering with the Giants—also host an annual fundraiser at AT&T Park to support pediatric cancer research and treatment programs in the Bay Area. And then, once a month, pediatric cancer patients receiving treatment at Bay Area hospitals are invited, along with their families, to attend a Giants game and a pregame field visit to meet Buster and Kristen.

Partnership. The Giants find out what the players are passionate about then help them facilitate that cause. It works because Baer and the front office don't take a one-size-fits-all approach to community involvement. They take advantage of the momentum already created by the players and capitalize on *that*.

> **Boch:** Most clubs and players do a great job of giving back to the community. But I've never been with a club that is as passionate about it or takes it to such an extraordinary level as the Giants. Buster and Kristen are a great example, but there are many others. If a player is committed to doing something in the community here, Larry and the front office are all in; they want to know how to support it.
>
> It just makes you feel proud to be part of an organization that's reaching out in so many ways. And from a coaching standpoint, it gives our players a sense of perspective. We are so fortunate to play this game at this level. And believe me, we are competitive; we want to win. But when you are involved in the lives of people who are disadvantaged or who are going through something very difficult, it puts life in perspective. And, I think all the community things our players do rubs off on them and shapes who they are. I think it contributes to the unselfishness they bring into the clubhouse.

Whether it's Barry Zito's Strikeouts for Troops; Jeremy Affeldt's and Brandon Belt's involvement with Not for Sale, a movement to prevent human trafficking; the Bochys' support of a prenatal program for homeless expectant mothers; Brandon Crawford's sponsorship of Guide Dogs for the Blind; Javier López's Step Up to the Plate Night to raise funds for people living in poverty; or any of the other players' initiatives, getting behind the things your players are passionate about strengthens the bonds between you. Doing it *together* creates chemistry.

In 2016, just weeks after they signed with the Giants, pitchers Johnny Cueto and Jeff Samardzija wasted no time in making community service a priority. Cueto visited kids at the Mission Education Center in San Francisco, a public elementary school serving Latino children who are culturally and academically far below grade level. Samardzija visited the University of California San Francisco Benioff Children's Hospital. Smaradzija, speaking from past experience, said: "Children's Hospital is the epitome of fight and passion. These kids are in there and they are smiling. To give these kids any shred of light is just exciting."

Smardzija asked one young patient who her favorite player is. "Buster Posey," she said. Smardzija responded good-naturedly, "Well, of course it's Buster. I'm gonna get used to that answer." When the child was prompted to say, "Jeff Samardzija," Jeff displayed the kind of humility that characterizes the Giants organization by saying: "No, no. Not yet. Let me do something worthwhile first."

Not Just a Brand—A Sense of Identity

The Giants are first and foremost a baseball franchise, but really, anyone who identifies with the Giants brand does so because they believe in the values driving its championship culture. To say that you are a Giant says something about who you are and what you believe.

No doubt, people are attracted to the brand because of three World Championships—everyone likes to be associated with a winner—but they are also drawn to it because it stands for something bigger than baseball. It's the spirit of enterprise, innovation, and entrepreneurship applied to the well-being of people and planet. If you are not passionate about community, about bringing people together, you won't fit in here. The baseball franchise, Giants Enterprises, the club's Mission Rock real estate development arm, and its philanthropic outreach are all about enriching the human condition.

Everyone is connected—the players, coaches, front office, event organizers, developers, and city officials. Each plays a different role, but everyone shows up dedicated to making the Giant experience and community better.

The Giants Mission Rock project will extend the hub known as AT&T Park into a bayside park, residences, offices, and retail facilities, and a mini-town square where people can hang out. When completed, the project will simply enhance the beauty of an already-spectacular city.

The Giants are a cause-driven enterprise. They are a powerful model that shows how to make a profit while also making a difference. In a world that wants businesses to be a driving force for social, environmental, and economic well-being, people identify with that and, more than ever, are demanding it. Helping players and their families fan out into the Bay Area to support local causes makes the city healthier and more vibrant.

Cause Is a Magnet for Talent

San Francisco's payroll is among the highest in MLB, which shows that the Giants are not afraid to go after great talent. But the franchise hardly relies on payroll alone to make its chemistry click. Being part of a community is a less tangible element, but no less important. Sometimes a player will sign for a little less money or a shorter contract in order to be part of a community that he can stand up for and that stands up for him.

After the 2010 World Series, first baseman Pat Burrell signed with the Giants for $1 million, less than he could've made elsewhere, and relief pitcher Sergio Romo turned down opportunities to be a closer for other interested teams, instead signing a two-year contract with the Giants. Even though Romo is now with the Dodgers, he made it clear that he enjoyed playing for the Giants and loved San Francisco's fanatical fans.

> If you are not passionate about community, about bringing people together, you won't fit in here.

When starting pitcher Jake Peavy re-signed with the Giants in 2014, he pointed out how appreciative he was that the club moved his family across country to San Francisco when he was traded from the Red Sox the year before. In 2015, pitcher Ryan Vogelsong signed a one-year contract for well below what he could've made in any one of four other clubs. His wife, Nicole, was in love with the city of San Francisco.

When Jeff Samardzija was formally introduced by the Giants after signing a five-year contract in 2016, he said, "I can't tell you the excitement I had when they came to me and I was on their radar." Samardzija had done his homework on the Giants. "I talked to some former players I knew, most importantly including Nate Schierholtz, who I played with in Chicago and became a real close friend of mine, and he had nothing but amazing things to say about this organization, almost to a tone of he wishes he were still there. I always picked up on that."[127]

Burrell and Vogelsong could've signed elsewhere for more money, but money wasn't the only factor in their decisions. Romo checked his ego at the door to stay with a club he wanted to be with and play for fans he enjoyed. Peavy did the same. For Samardzija, it was all about the "fit."

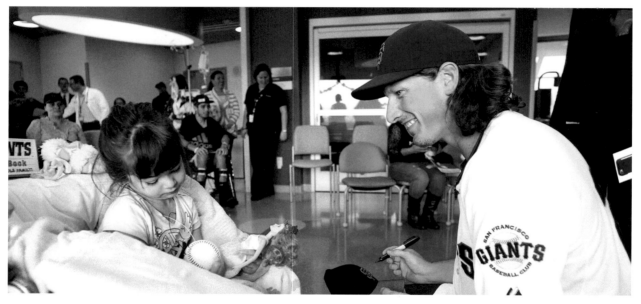

Jeff Samardzija at University of California San Francisco Benioff Children's Hospital.

These individuals each made a choice based on chemistry—a chemistry that springs from a community committed to enriching lives. In a game where players often fall into the trap of measuring their worth by their salary and then simply go to the highest bidder, these guys added another criterion to the mix: community. They were essentially asking: "Is there a community mentality among the players, coaches, and front office executives of this club? Do I want to play in a place that feels like family?"

Community is magnetic because it creates a sense of place, a sense of belonging, and a feeling that you matter to the guys in the clubhouse as well as the coaching staff, the front office, and the fans. Community is about looking out for one another, on and off the field and in the media. Community means that the team is more important than the individual; and every individual, from the executive assistant in the front office to the Cy Young pitcher on the mound, plays a critical role in the team's success.

Community Strengthens Talent

We've always felt that a young married couple surrounded by a strong community has a better shot at success. That is because the community is there to encourage, support, and offer perspective and wise counsel. The couple doesn't feel like they are making their journey through the ups and downs all by themselves. The couple, in turn, feels a sense of commitment and accountability to the community, which often means that when things get difficult, they won't give in or give up as easily. Nosey relatives and helicopter parents aside, there is also a level of comfort and security inside a community because the community has your back. The same can be true in baseball. Here's how Boch described it.

> **Boch:** It's never a perfect world and there are certainly exceptions, but there is a connectedness among our players that resembles family or a band of brothers. We've been counted out so many times. We've been the underdog so often that to come through it and come out on top has made our players stronger. That, combined with the unselfish way they play the game, has made our guys a tight-knit group. It's really kind of a sacred bond between them.

This sense of community sparks strong chemistry. It is part of what makes the Giants so successful as a team. You might well ask, "How does community affect what happens on the field?"

> **Boch:** When our guys know that they are part of a community, where they have each other's backs, it gives them the freedom to play relaxed, to not press so hard. At the plate, it means not feeling the weight of the entire team on your shoulders. A hitter can slow it down, keep it simple, and trust himself. When you feel like you need to carry the day, you'll do too much. And that always takes you out of your normal, good approach.
>
> A pitcher who knows that his tight, crisp defense has his back is more confident and relaxed. That just does so much to his rhythm to keep attacking the strike zone. On a team that has a sense of togetherness, guys are constantly talking to each other. There's better communication. There's less confusion and more collaboration because everyone is on the same page.
>
> I think there's a lot to it [community]. It's pretty evident when it's missing too. In a club where you see dissension, the team just looks out of sync. It isn't as sharp and seems to be missing that togetherness.

Community is a way of thinking. As the Giants have demonstrated, it is galvanized by the kind of interdependence that says, "Every member of our community is a catalytic agent, an instrument of something good, and a beneficiary." That is, the franchise reaches into the community to help it flourish. In turn, the community shows up to the ballpark— loud and rowdy, in sellout numbers—to support the players and help the team rise to the occasion. The uplifting is reciprocal.

This synergy creates a special kind of chemistry that elevates the social, cultural, emotional, spiritual, and financial well-being of every member of the community.

33

MORE THAN A FRANCHISE, IT'S A FAMILY
The Power of the 10th Player

With all its warmth and fan-friendly features, AT&T Park is a hub for the city, the crown jewel of the franchise, and one of the most Instagrammed locations in the world. "We play in the most beautiful ballpark in the country, with the Coke bottle and the old glove, and the sailboats gliding along the bay just outside the outfield walls," Matt Cain said. "We have loud, devoted fans who crank up the energy during every single game."[128]

With an average attendance of 41,500 at each game and a sellout streak that reached 530 games between October 2010 and July 2017, the Giants have the second-longest sellout streak in MLB history (the Boston Red Sox are number one) and the longest sellout streak in the National League. The Giants have consistently been in the top three of all MLB teams in fan engagement. This is based on average home game attendance, social media following, demand, and median ticket price. Almost 60 percent of Bay Area adults identify as Giants fans.

Why?

A house becomes a home when it's inclusive, when it exudes a spirit of welcome and hospitality. For the Giants, there would be no home without the fans. In Larry Baer's 2014 "welcome back" letter to the fans, he showed that "Together We're Giant" is more than a slick tagline; it is quite indicative of how the club feels about its fans. "The connection between this franchise and this community is unlike anything anywhere in professional sports. I can't tell you enough how deeply we appreciate what you give us. You are a key reason players want to sign with the Giants—and stay with the Giants. We begin a new chapter of Giants baseball tonight. Thank you for joining us as stewards of this storied franchise."

Most clubs, especially when the team is winning, will tell you that they have the best fans in the world. But there is something truly remarkable about Giants fans. They show up as consistently and fervently in April and May as they do in September and October. They show up in the rain. They show up when the team is losing and in a funk. They show up in full force on the road. When the Giants play in San Diego, it's not unusual to see as much, if not more, orange and black at Petco Park as there is blue. Fans also show up in a way that gives regular season games the intensity of the postseason—inspired, loud, festive, present, all in. Giants fans are full throttle.

After the 2014 World Series, Boch wrote the foreword to the Giants coffee table book entitled *Champions Together*.[129] In the following excerpt, you quickly get a sense about why the fans are such a critical part of the Giants chemistry.

> **Boch:** It's difficult to put into words the magnitude of your impact. In baseball, the difference between winning and losing can be as narrow as the baseline. A close game can slip away in a moment of fatigue or disappointment. Lucky for us, we have the best fans in baseball—40,000 stomping, cheering, faithful fans at every home game showering us with love and energy. You are like the 10th man on the field. It doesn't matter how far up or down we are in the standings, you fill AT&T Park and you show up on the road in your orange and black . . . your loyalty continues to inspire us.

Empathy Drives Design

AT&T Park was built with energy in mind. That is, a driving question was how do we keep the fans energized? Knowing that the park would serve multiple generations of fans, the designers started with *becoming* the fans. Getting into their heads. Anticipating how they want to experience a game. The Giants put themselves in the shoes of each segment of their fan base and asked, "How do these particular fans want to consume a game?" Then, they built the park accordingly, and now, every year, they change it accordingly. This is what makes AT&T Park one of the most fan-friendly baseball experiences in the nation.

A spacious outfield favors line drive hitters and players who can get a lot of extra base hits. More action, more interest. While the outfield is "roomy," the overall feel of the park is intimate and engaging. Unlike many relatively new ballparks, AT&T is asymmetrical, which means the space is unique and interesting. Think kayaks

Tailgate partying San Francisco style. Kayakers and boaters gather for Game 3 of the 2014 World Series in McCovey Cove hoping to catch a home run ball.

retrieving "Splash Hit" home runs in McCovey Cove. Bullpens are located close to the fans so they can *be there* when a reliever is warming up. The closest front row seats are a mere 42 feet from the batter. And, limited foul territory puts the fans right on top of the action. A lower upper deck outfield results in acoustics that are loud—players can feel the energy of the crowd. Because of this close-to-the-action vibe, there isn't a bad seat in the house.

Understanding that the club is in the entertainment business, CEO Baer is passionate about never letting the fans' experience grow stale. From the Gotham Club and the two restaurants of the Garden (center field) to food trucks in the parking area and a vibrant, jam-packed Giants Dugout stores, the franchise is constantly shaking it up to engage the fans. And Baer is determined, relentless, and creative about giving to fans an opportunity to come together and share their passion for the club.

Giant Fan Fest

Each year, usually in the middle of the off-season, the Giants host a "giant" one-day festival at AT&T Park called FanFest. It's a day when the entire team—including Larry Baer, Brian Sabean, Bobby Evans, Bruce Bochy and his players and coaches, and many of the broadcasters—unite in one big effort to give back to the fans. Each year, more than 40,000 people attend the event.

It's a day when fans have an opportunity to go out onto the field for autographs, photo opportunities, and free giveaways. They can enjoy plenty of ribbing in live interviews and Q&A sessions with the players and coaches, take a photo with the 2010, 2012, and 2014 World Series Trophies, watch a fashion show on top of the Giants dugout, and get the latest gear from the Giants Dugout stores.

Brandon Belt signs baseballs for fans at FanFest.

There's more.

Fans can also visit the Giants Highlight Theater to watch the most exciting moments of past seasons. Then there is the opportunity to visit the team's @Cafe, get a photo taken with one of the players, and then immediately post it to your favorite social network.

FanFest is one more bonding agent in the team's chemistry. It is a major way for the club to reconnect with fans during the lull of the off-season and get people excited about the upcoming season. It allows fans to get to know the person behind the player and allows players to say "thank you" in an up close and personal kind of way.

The Energy of an Electric Crowd

A fan-friendly ballpark. A festival to honor the unwavering enthusiasm of Giants fans. What difference do they make? It's difficult to measure the cause and effect of the fans' influence on the outcome of a game or a season. But the statisticians are getting there. *The Journal of Quantitative Analysis in Sports* suggests that increased attendance at home increases the likelihood of winning.[130] In a sense, though, analysis really doesn't matter. What matters is what the players believe about the role of their fans, and the Giants definitely believe it is huge.

The word "fan" originates from the Latin *fanaticus*, meaning "insanely but divinely inspired, frenzied, furious, enthusiastic, or fanatical." That pretty much describes an authentic, loyal Giants fan.

"I think there's an energy transfer," Baer said. "A lot of times you're coming off of long road trips, Sunday night from an East Coast game, it's hot on the East Coast, you walk in and you may be pretty tired. But the 41,000 screaming and yelling [fans] give you a total boost."[131]

Hunter Pence once described what it's like to be in the opposing dugout. "When I was a visitor, they [fans] would not stop chirping at me the entire game. Now, playing for the Giants, I sometimes forget because they have your back so much here. You want to give 'em everything you've got because you are grateful for how much they believe in you."

When Tim Hudson signed with the Giants in November 2013, he said that one of the things that attracted him to the club was playing in front of a sold-out crowd. "It's a great stadium, it's a great pitchers' park, the fans are awesome—they've had sellouts every game since 2010. Just going in there and playing against the Giants, as an opponent . . . you envy what they have."[132]

Showing his immense appreciation for the fans, Sergio Romo said: "You can't replace what you bring every night to the park. When we Giants talk about how much the fans mean to us, it's real. The fans embrace us. They're what make AT&T Park one of the best places in baseball, maybe in all of sports. It's the real deal. The fans create the energy, the feeling, the passion. Jeez, you guys rock."[133]

How many times have you heard one broadcaster say to another about the Giants, "You can feel the electricity in the air"? They say it because it's palpable; you *can* feel it and the Giants players feed off of it.

> **Boch:** The atmosphere at home is incredible. I stand on that rail, look up, and it's a packed house every day. Our fans are so loud here; it's like Opening Day every day. We really consider ourselves fortunate that we have [enthusiastic fans] what we have here. The support we get from these fans, you take it in and savor it.

Bonded Together

Boch has always had a deep sense of respect for the fans. He knows that the energy they bring to the park comes with a responsibility. He wants his players to keep the power of their loyalty, their bond, in perspective.

> **Boch:** I never want to forget and I don't want our players to forget how important it is to foster a winning relationship between the team and the community. We exist for the fans; the fans don't exist for us. Without our fans there would be no television or talk radio. Without our fans there would be no opportunity for us to compete. We're here to play for *them*—and baseball must never forget that.

Hall of Fame broadcaster Mike Krukow agreed, noting in an interview in 2015 that there is mutual accountability between the players and their fans. "You do not want to disappoint—when you're a Giants player and you walk out onto the field, and there's 41,000 people every night that are supporting you on every pitch. It's a remarkable phenomenon. There is that accountability. When you can stand on the steps of City Hall (during the championship parades) and look into a crowd of over a million and say to yourself that we justified and we validated that support; that's an incredible feeling. And when you don't, it really leaves a void in your accomplishment."[134]

In each of the Giants three victory parades, more than a million fans showed up to celebrate. The view from City Hall looked like this.

In the 2012 NLDS, the Giants lost the first two games at home, then the players showed up for a rather somber travel day to go face Cincinnati in their house. Yes, the pressure was on the Reds to close out the series, but every Giants player knew the odds were stacked against San Francisco. Hunter Pence remembered being in the clubhouse waiting for the bus as Héctor Sánchez was speaking to a lady on the janitorial staff in Spanish.

They were smiling and laughing. Héctor told me, 'She said she loves us, she wished us all the luck in the world and she believed in us.' I don't know, but something changed for me in that moment. I thought, 'Here's someone who believes in us. That is what is so amazing about this place. Tough times and all, the fans are super happy, they wish us luck and they believe.' So, right then and there, I made a decision: That's who we are going to do this for—all the people who believe in us and support us.[135]

That faith and support is what makes the relationship between the club and the fans so special. The Giants organization never has to pump up the fans by reminding them about what's on the line. They don't have to be told, "This is an important series." The fans know. And because they know, they show up ready to be the juggernaut the players need. The players, in turn, take to the field knowing that the people who fill AT&T Park are more than ticket holders—they are family, they are cherished stewards of a storied franchise. And, the worst feeling in the world, as we know, is to let down family members, close friends, the loyal guardians of a legacy.

#RallyZito

In Game 5 of the 2012 NLCS, the Giants were down three games to one against the Cardinals in the Red Birds' house. The Giants were playing their fourth consecutive elimination game and the Cardinals had the momentum. If ever there was a dire situation, this was it.

Madison Bumgarner was due up in the rotation to pitch, but because of a couple of sketchy starts and a mechanical glitch Bum was still trying to work out, Boch decided to hand the ball to a tormented player with a beleaguered past—Barry Zito.

We have already talked about how Zito was left off the roster in 2010 and how he handled it with dignity. For years, Giants fans watched their highest-paid player walk tall, speak humbly, and carry himself with an unwavering level of professionalism while people called for his head. It was a miserable row to hoe. But now, things had changed.

Zito finished the 2012 regular season 15-8, his first winning record as a Giant. And, prior to this do-or-die game against the Cardinals, the Giants won the previous 11 games that Zito started. Boch sensed "Z" had something left in the tank. Apparently, the fans did too.

Giants fans from all over the globe launched one of the most inspirational Twitter hashtag outbursts in history. A hashtag—#RallyZito—had taken over social media, ranking number two in the entire world.

That night Zito pitched 7 ⅔ shutout innings, winning his thirteenth consecutive game and giving the Giants a 4-0 victory over the Cardinals. "He's been through a lot," Boch said. "But this guy, he's some kind of tough. He put on a show." Sabean called Zito one "tough SOB." Zito extended the postseason and gave the Giants a shot at going to the World Series. When Boch went out to get him on the mound, the situation was memorable.

> **Boch:** We all knew what he'd been through. He pitched with so much heart and the same kind of courage that he had demonstrated during all those tough years. Before he left the mound, each one of the guys tapped him and told him how much it meant to them, how much they appreciated him. It was a special moment.

As Zito pitched one scoreless inning after another, tweets flooded the Internet. People everywhere jumped on the #RallyZito bandwagon. Fox Television mentioned it early in the broadcast of Game 5. Even Giants Hall of Famer Orlando Cepeda got in on the fun by tweeting #RallyZito. It galvanized a community. Fans who had never met were united around a clever call to arms that symbolized the team's "Never Say Die" season.

Zito, of course, knew nothing about it. He was focused on the game. So, to say that #RallyZito had something to do with his performance would be a stretch. But it's not too far-fetched to suggest that it made a difference in bringing the momentum, once with Redbird Nation, back to San Francisco. In the next two home games, fans across the country unleashed a tsunami of affection and made their presence known for a team that defiantly refused to lie down. Did the campaign play a role in the Giants taking the NLCS? It's not unreasonable to think so. And, it's not too outrageous to think that #RallyZito had an impact on the pitcher's confidence when he started Game 1 of the World Series against Detroit's ace Justin Verlander—and won.

Barry Zito and wife Amber Seyer at 2012 victory parade.

An Epic Family Reunion

Second only to the sellout crowds at AT&T Park, the uncommon bond between the Giants organization and its fans can be seen in the club's three World Series parades. Baer said they felt "more like joyous family reunions than civic celebrations." From beginning to end along the mile and a half route, the sheer number of people was overwhelming. Exhilarating. Stunning. Surreal. Heartwarming. Elevating. Adrenaline-charged. Jaw-dropping. Mind-blowing. If there was one word to capture all of these, it might come close to describing the experience.

Tens of thousands of orange-and-black-clad fans lined San Francisco's Market Street as confetti rained down. They flooded into the city to be together, to celebrate, to be a part of something big. They perched on light posts and rooftops, filled the windows of high-rises, and unleashed their adoring roars to the beaming faces of their favorite players who were in awe, taking their own pictures and videos. They came to catch a glimpse of history.

Brian and Amanda Sabean were in the staging area of the 2010 parade ready to take their place in a couple of vehicles along with their sons Colin, Sean, Brendan, Darren, and Aidan. Sabes has a tough New England exterior, but people who know him know he is a soft, compassionate guy on the inside. This was the Giants first World Series victory since 1954, and Sabean, like the players, was in awe. "One of our senior officers came over and told us, 'When you turn that corner on Montgomery, you're not going to believe the sea of people.'" "Then it happened, and I got a lump in my throat. I almost lost it, and everybody I talked to was the same way. Just the enthusiasm and the outpouring of emotions . . . we weren't ready for the crowd. City Hall was like something you see at an inauguration, or a visit from the Pope. Everybody was blown away because we really didn't know what to expect. I think all of Northern California was there."[136]

The Giants Hall of Famers, players, and coaches rode in convertibles and motorized cable cars with their families. Students played hooky, businesses closed, music blared, fans cheered and chanted, and players periodically got out and walked the streets to sign autographs. Sixty-five vehicles, 1.5 tons of confetti, helicopters overhead, and 1 million buoyant fans; it was a hell of a party strung out along the mile and a half route. This is the way it went down in 2010, in 2012, and once again in 2014.

Brian, Aidan, and Amanda Sabean. 2012 World Series victory parade.

At the end of the 2010 parade, before all the speeches at the Civic Center celebration, Sabean was once more overwhelmed. "My knees are weak, my heart is racing, and I've [still] got a lump in my throat. We deserved this. San Francisco deserved this. Northern California deserved this. It's the most interesting life experience anyone could ever have. I can only think of one word, and that's closure."[137]

In each run-up to the 2010 World Series, the Giants won on the road. They took the NLDS against the Braves at Turner Field in Atlanta, the NLCS against the Phillies at Citizens Bank Park in Philadelphia, and they won the World Series in Game 5 at the Rangers Globe Life Park in Arlington, Texas. You take a win anywhere, right? But it sucks not to get at least one of these victories in front of the home crowd.

The last time the Giants won a title at home in 2010 was when they clinched the NL West before the playoffs. That afternoon Boch asked the players to take a lap of gratitude around AT&T Park. It would be the last time the Giants would thank their hometown fans in person after a win.

As you now know, Duane Kuiper dubbed the 2010 season "torture." When the much-loved broadcaster took the stage at the Civic Center celebration after the parade, Kuip reminded everyone, "Thanks to these gentlemen here, the torture is over!" Boch picked up on Kuiper's theme and then made sure that the team's expression of gratitude was personal. Looking out at a sea of ecstatic fans in front of City Hall, here's what he said.

> **Boch:** I'd like to apologize to our fans—particularly those of you who acquired a few gray hairs here in the postseason. Believe me, you're not alone. I looked in the mirror this morning and wondered, "What the hell happened?" But if you *did* get a little grayer from those nail-biters, I can bring in my closer [Brian Wilson, who colored his beard]; I think he can help you with that.
>
> Seriously, if you EVER! EVER! EVER! question the role you play in games like these, let me say it very clearly.
>
> We felt your presence against San Diego. We felt your presence in Atlanta. We felt it in Philly. And we certainly felt it in Texas!
>
> YOU showed up in full force and *you* made it an incredible ride. Believe me, this trophy belongs to you, San Francisco, as much as it belongs to any of us.

As you can imagine, Boch, like everyone else, was filled with emotion. It was a cathartic moment. He had come to San Francisco for another shot at winning the big one. He went there to help make a storied franchise "storied" once again. Most gratifying for him was the opportunity to bring a World Series trophy back to the people of San Francisco.

The 2012 parade was no less spectacular and no less emotional. Brandon Crawford, a Bay Area resident and devoted Giants fan since childhood, took it all in with his wife, Jalynne. Even though he had heard about the 2010 celebration from other players, he said there is nothing that prepares you for this kind of outpouring of affection. "I kept expecting the crowds to thin out as the parade progressed, but we'd pass a side street and we'd see people for a half-mile down," Crawford remembered.

> They just wanted to be there, even if they couldn't see us. That's when it began to sink in that we had won and that I was part of it. But how's this for irony? As I was riding in the parade as the World Series shortstop of the team of my childhood dreams, I found myself imagining what it felt like to be one of the fans skipping work or school to join the party! Had my life taken a different turn, I would have been right there on Market Street, maybe perched on a lamppost, thrilled that my team had won it all. [138]

In 2014, parade-goers stood in the rain for hours to celebrate *another* "once-in-a-lifetime" event with the team. Many wondered if the bad weather would keep fans from coming to the parade. Nope, they showed up, full throttle. They turned out in throngs. In fact, city officials estimated the crowds grew successively in each of the three parades.

"I really do believe the big reason we have success in the playoffs is we play in front of a packed house," Buster Posey said. "And they're loud and they're rowdy. So when it comes time in October, we're used to it. We knew a little rain; they weren't gonna let that stop them."[139]

Earlier in the season, Hunter Pence taught a sold-out home crowd the rallying cry "Yes! Yes! Yes!" before the start of a game. In 2014, as he made his way through the parade, he yelled out, "Can we do it again?" Of course, the fans yelled back, "Yes! Yes! Yes!"

One fan, Karen Garcia, put into words what the jubilant die-hards were so obviously feeling: "I am tired, I am wet, I am cold and there's no place that I'd rather be than here."[140] As for the players, Joe Panik captured the moment vividly. "Wow, this is bone-chilling. I had chills the entire time. It was surreal."[141]

When Giants CEO Larry Baer took the podium in front of City Hall after the parade, he talked about unity. "What makes all this work, as corny as it might sound, is a sense of all of us truly being in

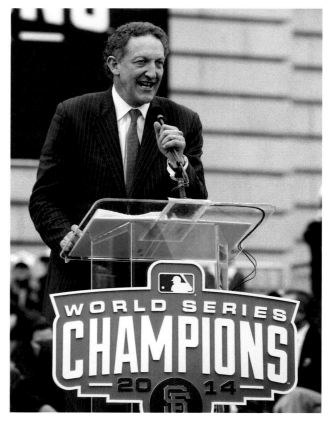

Larry Baer telling fans "they are the difference" at the 2014 victory parade.

this together—the fans, the players, the coaches, the front office, the ownership, and every usher and every vendor in the park. There is a culture with the Giants of genuinely caring for one another and having each other's back. That's the X factor."

Our Magic Is You

Great leaders are gracious; they practice the art of saying "thank you." Each year at the end of the season, Baer writes an open letter to the people of San Francisco. Larry's gratitude epitomizes the special relationship and sense of community the club has with the City of San Francisco and the Bay Area. He speaks as though he is talking to family—because he is. Here are some excerpts from what Larry wrote in 2012, after the Giants won their second World Series.

> As I watched manager Bruce Bochy and his staff spill onto the field, I imagined what was happening in San Francisco. All of us who traveled to Detroit—including every player and coach—knew Coit Tower, the Ferry Building, and City Hall were awash in orange light. We knew that fans had filled every inch of Civic Center Plaza to watch Game 4. We knew that throughout the Bay Area, living rooms and pubs were packed with people wearing Panda and Baby Giraffe hats, fake beards and "Vogelstrong" bracelets.

> We also knew that no matter how talented the players or how ingenious the manager, no team can win a World Series Championship—much less two in three years—without a little magic.

> Our magic is you.

> I wish you could hear how our players talk about you, not just with each other but also with players on other teams. Brandon Belt says base runners on first base tell him they've never heard a park as loud as AT&T. Hunter Pence says that Giants fans are "the ultimate motivator." Matt Cain calls you are their 10th player.

> So believe me when I tell you this: Our players carried all of you with them onto the field at Comerica Park. And they were unbeatable.

> Like 2010, this World Series Championship was truly a shared victory. So, it was humbling during the parade last Wednesday to see fans holding signs saying "Thank You!" The gratitude is ours. We don't win without you. You filled AT&T Park every game. You supported the players and coaches through the highs and lows. You flooded onto Market Street and into Civic Center

Coit Tower in San Francisco. San Francisco's City Hall. Panda-hat-wearin' fan. The Ferry Building in San Francisco.

Plaza in a celebration that felt like the world's biggest family reunion.

On behalf of Brian, Bruce, the players and everyone at the San Francisco Giants, thank you for your tireless support. Thank you for taking us into your lives like family. Thank you for making us better.[142]

The 2015 season ended with the Giants missing the playoffs. Still, the fans poured out in record numbers to say, "We're in this together." Once again, Larry didn't miss an opportunity to express the team's gratitude.

This season revealed the true character of our team. It also showed, once again, the true character of our fan base. No fans are more loyal than ours. You show up no matter what. You sold out AT&T Park every single game this season, a streak of 408 straight dating back to 2010. Our 50 millionth fan walked through the turnstiles. Your energy lifts every player and coach. It's one of the most striking things to our new players—the unusually close relationship between the players and fans. I can tell you that Tim Hudson and Jeremy Affeldt will never forget your outpouring of love and appreciation as they retired from the game.[143]

In his 2016 letter to the fans, after a devastating gut-punch in which the Giants lost the NLDS to the Cubs, Larry told the fans that the players were committed to getting back into the playoffs. Then, he reiterated a common theme that permeates the Giants organization.

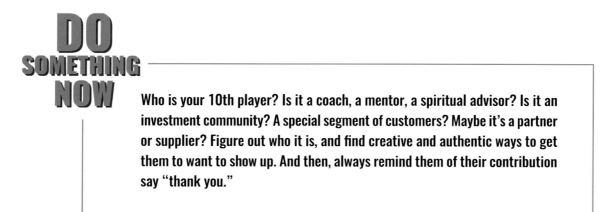

Who is your 10th player? Is it a coach, a mentor, a spiritual advisor? Is it an investment community? A special segment of customers? Maybe it's a partner or supplier? Figure out who it is, and find creative and authentic ways to get them to want to show up. And then, always remind them of their contribution say "thank you."

When the historic streak came to an end this week, we were reminded that Championship Blood is, more than anything, about character. We saw it in the clubhouse after Tuesday's defeat. There was no retreat from addressing the media, no finger-pointing. The players faced their disappointment with grace, reflection and resolve. They said they would double-down on preparation, that they'd never forget how awful this felt. They hugged and consoled and thanked one another. As always, they had each other's backs.

And as always, you had theirs. Despite the ups and downs of the season, they could look up into the stands and see wave upon wave of orange and black. A full house every game. You make it clear: We're all in this together. Every player is so grateful to play in front of the best fans in baseball.[144]

The gut-punch of 2016. A commitment to be in the playoffs again. And then, the worst season in franchise history. What do you say to the fans now? In his 2017 letter, Baer told the fans that they were one of the club's major reasons for being more excited about the future.

> The third reason we're energized is you. We've always seen the team and the fans as a single unit, a family. Families are hit by hard times when frustration mounts and patience wears thin. But they stick together and figure it out. Bruce Bochy spoke for all of us when he was asked recently what he had learned from this season.

> "What I learned, probably as much as any year I've been here, is how great our fans are. They're constantly telling me, 'Hey, we're hanging in there with you.' It's really been amazing, and you're disappointed to not play better ball for them."[145]

Every owner, every GM, every manager, and every player wants to win a World Series in baseball. The question is, "What is the process for getting there and what kind of culture supports that process?" The Giants believe that everything is connected and every connection counts—that includes the passion and energy of the 10th player.

A house becomes a home when the distinction between the club and the fan is blurred. When fans are this deeply bonded, this involved, however, they become not just family but loyal, full throttle, all-in stewards of the storied franchise where legacy and impact grow exponentially. In San Francisco, fans are all of that: they show up, they're all in. And they are because Larry Baer, Brian Sabean, the entire front office, Bobby Evans, Boch, his coaches and players, and all the broadcasters, say and believe . . .

"Together We're Giant!"

34
LEAVING A LEGACY
A Meaningful Way to Win

The reason we study and read about gutsy leaders and great organizations is because they put a face on the principles of success and the practices of lives well lived. Often, they are ordinary people who humanize the extraordinary and make it attainable. And, they take away our excuses. When a band of misfits, castoffs, and renegades—people not all *that* unlike us—rally to achieve what many believe is impossible, and they do it over and over again, their achievements cannot be easily dismissed or marginalized. Instead, their stories act as a wake-up call to those who want examples to learn from and, even more so, to those who say it can't be done. Their lives have the potential to transform our doubt, skepticism, and fears into how-to's, hope, and heroism.

This is why we wrote *Bochy Ball!*

We wanted to take you behind the scenes and give you an inside look at how a World Champion franchise thinks and what it does; how it wins with humility and loses with grace. In doing so, we hope the drama of America's favorite pastime and the leadership insights behind this storied Giants franchise have given you the tools to make your personal and professional journey better.

Larry Baer and the Giants organization have shown us what can happen when you unleash the entrepreneurial spirit that lies dormant in many organizations. You create something that is more than just a business. You create a cause, a movement, a crusade that taps into the creative energy of community—of togetherness. What emerges is a higher degree of collaboration, cooperation, teamwork, and innovation. What emerges is a place where leadership exists at all levels, continuity runs deep, and people enthusiastically assume ownership for playing their role in the crusade. The result is a community that flourishes, a $2-billion enterprise, and a hub of energy, excitement, and connectedness in one of the world's greatest cities.

Who doesn't want more of *that?*

Do the Giants missed years—when they were magnificently horrible—invalidate what we can learn from Boch when his teams were at their historical best? Hardly. Boch's character, leadership capabilities, and strategic moves are consistent with the patterns by which other great leaders in truly phenomenal organizations have achieved success. As in life, so many of the lessons mined in this book come from the Giants failures, defeats, and ability to bounce back from the brink of disaster.

So, we end where we started, *before* he came to San Francisco, when Bruce Bochy ranked with some of the best leaders of our time. Then, together with Larry Baer, Brian Sabean, and the entire Giants organization, they put together an unprecedented five-year run, including three World Championships that compelled the world to tune in and take note. And, as of this publication, it cemented Boch's status as the most successful active manager in the game.

As we have seen, Boch is the first to acknowledge that he didn't do it alone. He did it in a spirit of collaboration with talented colleagues who wanted to win as much as he did. The culture of the franchise and the extended Giants family became the perfect home. It gave him the emotional support and resources he needed to execute Sabean's game plan.

Boch will not only be remembered for winning World Championships, he will be remembered for the way he did it. He has showed us that chemistry is forged in leadership and that leadership is not about you; it's about those you lead. He has shown us the heights to which we can rise when something beyond us—a cause worth fighting for—compels us to keep playing, even through extremely difficult and dark times.

> The Giants organization has shown us that when you create a cause that taps into the creative energy of togetherness, the result is a community that flourishes, a $2-billion enterprise, and a hub of energy, excitement, and connectedness.

Baseball is a roller-coaster ride loaded with unexpected twists and turns, highs and lows. Boch has shown us how to navigate uncertainty with sanity by keeping our perspective and not taking ourselves too seriously. He has demonstrated the payoffs of breaking away from orthodox approaches and encouraged us to be disruptive, to think big, and to act bold. By being himself and letting his players be themselves, he has shown us the power of what can happen when we don't judge others—when we move beyond tolerating differences to appreciating them, learning from them, and leveraging them.

Perhaps one of the greatest insights we can take from Bruce Bochy is that leadership isn't an "either . . . or" practice; it is "both . . . and." Loving people and caring about them deeply don't have to be mutually exclusive with being tough, disciplined, and candid. We can be both at the same time. Many people still believe that leaders who are empathic, loving, and kind cannot be competitive and win. Boch has proved otherwise.

In the end, Boch will certainly be remembered for his myriad achievements, but more importantly, he will be remembered as a leader who loves to see the potential in others blossom; a leader who believes in people and inspires them to believe in themselves. This is why he is a leader people respect and love to follow.

Boch never set out to be all these things. He never intended to be anyone's role model. He just is. That's what endears him to so many. He assumed the mantle of leadership because it came with where he wanted to be in a game he loves. Then, he grew because he worked at it.

When all is said and done, will you be able to look back on your life and like what you see? Will you be pleased with the person you've become? The family you've established? Will you be proud of the battles you fought and the things you stood for? Will you be proud of the impact you've had, the reputation you've built? Were your dreams big enough? Were you courageous, wise, and compassionate when these qualities were needed most? Have you earned the love and respect of those who truly matter . . . and even those who don't?

These are the questions of legacy. They are answered not by a year or two of performances, but rather by a person's entire body of work. Cooperstown or not, in his own quiet, unassuming way, Bruce Bochy has lived a life that matters. And he isn't even finished. There's plenty more he wants to do.

What will your legacy be?

AFTERWORD

I played for some great managers in the Giants organization; both in New York and in San Francisco: Leo Durocher, Bill Rigney, Herman Franks. I think that good players have a head start at becoming good managers, but not every good player can manage. I also think catchers sometimes have the best advantage. Many of them have unofficially managed their teams from behind the plate. They move on up only if they are good thinkers. Just like Bruce Bochy. He is one of the best in the game right now. We are lucky to have him.

Bruce Bochy has won a lot of games. I have been told that there are managers in the Hall of Fame who haven't won as many games as he has won. I think he'll get in one day. He has earned a place there.

You can tell a good manager by how they win or lose. "Bochy"—I call him "Bochy"—puts his players first. He tries to protect them when necessary. When his teams win, he doesn't take credit or stand in the limelight. He stands back and lets his players accept it. When they lose, he doesn't harp on it. He accepts responsibility for the loss and moves on. He respects his players on and off the field.

Bochy has learned that the best way to communicate is to let the guys come to him. They will manage many of their own issues amongst themselves in the clubhouse, if left alone. Bochy's door is always open to his players. He is a good listener, which is the first thing a good communicator does. He is approachable. He is pretty laid-back and levelheaded. He doesn't snap when things go bad. He is calm, open, and smart. He usually knows what's going on before a player does, but he doesn't tip his cards. He knows that you can't jump ahead. You have got to listen first. These guys are professionals. You can't tell them to try harder or that they aren't doing a good job. They are trying hard. Bochy knows to just deal with the problem they bring you. Players respect that.

Bruce Bochy is no pushover. There is never any doubt about who is steering the ship. If he thinks a player is wrong about something, he tells him the truth. But, he isn't one to shout or call attention in public. He always finds a way to take the high road. Managing a ball club is like managing a household. You've got 25 personalities thrown together and, believe me, there are going to be disagreements. And, with injuries and lineups changing, you've got to be able to shuffle the deck without dropping anything. Bruce Bochy is a leader. He expects a lot from his players. That's how he got all of those wins!

> **We have the greatest fans in the greatest city because they are always there. Bochy's guys appreciate this because he has challenged them to play for something bigger than just themselves.**

I mentioned that Bruce Bochy was a catcher and that in my opinion catchers make good managers. They understand how hard this game can be. Think about it; they are in on every play. It's the best spot to learn the whole game from and not just one position. And catchers have the umpire right there watching everything. They learn to stay calm, to listen, and to manage stressful situations. They probably learn the rules better too.

In a game where players can focus on themselves and their individual performances, Bochy challenges his guys to see that they are not just a player on a team, but that they are also part of a larger community. It's about the fans and the City. Three World Series wins in five years. That's amazing! We'd all like to think you can do that every five years. But winning all the time is not realistic. When you play 162 games you are going to have some bad times. I was fortunate. I had more good times than bad times. I bet Bruce Bochy would say the same thing!

This year has been one of those disappointing years, but here's the thing. It's still a game that entertains us. It's still fun to come to the ballpark and cheer on our favorite players. We still look forward to creating good times and great memories at the ballpark.

Can you imagine San Francisco without Giants baseball? Without AT&T Park? I can't. There is a strong bond between the franchise and the fans in San Francisco. We have the greatest fans in the greatest city because they are always there—whether the team is winning or losing. Bochy's guys appreciate this because he has challenged them to play for something bigger than just themselves.

We are a family. The Giants family.

Willie Mays
November 1, 2017

GIANT FANS

JOE MONTANA

TONY BENNETT

HUEY LEWIS

STEVE KERR

E-40, EARL STEVENS

FRANCIS FORD COPPOLA

MARISA MILLER

GOLDEN STATE WARRIORS, FAMILY AND FRIENDS

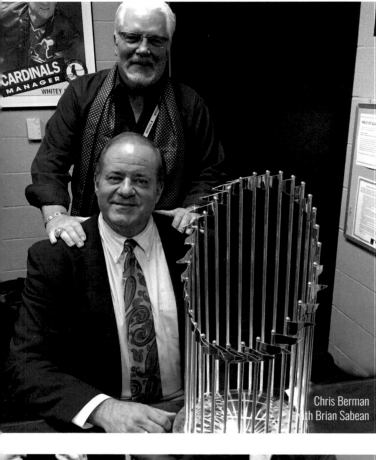

Chris Berman
With Brian Sabean

LIL WAYNE

DANNY GLOVER

ROB SCHNEIDER

MANNY PACQUIAO

METALLICA

STEVE PERRY

BILLY CRYSTAL

OUR ALL-STARS
Acknowledgements

OUR TALENTED TRIBE

This is our eighth book. The process doesn't get any easier. It requires its own brand of focus, grit and determination—and the chemistry of ultra-talented players working together to create something that is bigger and better than any of us could accomplish individually.

Acknowledgements are always riddled with accolades, right? Well, for us, this is really personal so hang on. On this project we had a kick-ass, take-no-prisoners, get'er-done-at-the-highest-level team of All-Stars. We mean, they rocked!

Darcy Lyons. Is our Google docs Maestro. Darcy kept multiple balls in the air, tracked deadlines and became the junction box for managing all the publishing details. All in addition to running our office and serving our clients. All-Star, rock-star, shining star, and friend, Darcy has raised our game in more ways than we can begin to describe. We are certain this book could not have been birthed without her diehard dedication. We can't believe we get to work with you every day. Thank you for being so competent. You are an MVP!

Leslie Stephen. You won't have to talk to very many business authors before the name Leslie Stephen comes up. Successful writers will tell you Leslie is one of the best developmental editors in the business. She has that unique ability to open a manuscript, cut through clutter, move things around, delete redundancies, repurpose content, and make the author(s) sound good. Leslie sees things most people can't. Thank you for saying "yes" to this project and for turning a clunky, cumbersome manuscript into one that makes us look way better than who we are. We loved working with you!

Clint Greenleaf. When our good friend and author, John Blumberg introduced us to Clint Greenleaf, we had no idea Clint would give new meaning to the term, "kindred spirit." Clint is a serial entrepreneur who founded Greenleaf Book Group and grew it into one of Inc.'s fastest-growing companies in America. After selling the company several years ago, we enticed Clint to shake up publishing once again by helping us produce and distribute this book in an unconventional way. Thank you for not only opening your database to everything publishing, but also for being the chief strategist for this project. Your graciousness and can-do spirit is humbling, your transparency and authenticity is priceless.

Linda O'Doughda. Clint introduced us to a woman who might be the most "granular" person we know, which is exactly what you want in a copy editor. If Leslie Stephen was the chief developmental editor, Linda O'Doughda did all the finishing touches. She inspected for accuracy, consistency and everything in between. This manuscript is orders of magnitude more readable and accessible because of Linda's amazing attention to detail. Thank you for being so organized, so focused, so thorough, and so good at what the rest of us can't do. You truly are one of the unsung heroines of this team.

Emma Strong. Design. It's a word we're pretty passionate—maybe even a little persnickety about. If you're visually oriented like us, it means lots of iterations before you come to see something you like. Emma is the person who puts up with our "just-one-more-version" and "can you try it this way" craziness. The very best thing about Emma is she's up for trying anything—design-wise. She has opinions, but her ego is always on a hook outside the door and her go-for-it spirit is invaluable. Thank you for your creative direction, for catching our vision, for carrying such a heavy load without ever complaining, and for being such a team player. You are terrific!

Suzanne von Thaden. Creativity feeds on diversity and it's a good thing it does. Suzanne loves facts and the small precise details that would bury us alive. She went through the final layout of the book with a fine-tooth comb and caught what we couldn't see. If there are any errors, you can reach her at…just kidding. We hope there aren't any, but if there are, we own it. Thank you, Suzanne, for thriving on the intricacies and making this book better in ways *we* never could.

San Francisco Giants Organization. With this project, the San Francisco Giants lived up to everything we've written about them—collaborative, entrepreneurial, enthusiastic, and service-oriented. Staci Slaughter gave us access to everyone and everything we needed, Matt Chisholm can check facts with the speed of the best gun-slingers in the Old West, and Mario Alioto, one of the most creative and innovative people we know, gave us a wealth of ideas. Thank you to Faham Zakariaei and Jason Pearl who helped us secure endorsements. Suzanna Mitchell and Sara Wildman took literally hundreds of requests from us for images, as did Rory Davis. Paul Hodges, Anica Chavez and Katy Batchelder helped us create a book trailer. Finally, Lyz Socha and Karen Sweeney coordinated multiple meetings between the Giants front office and us. They all give real meaning to, "Together we are better."

Interviewees. Giants front office executives, coaches, broadcasters, and players alike, agreed to be interviewed for this project. Their personal experiences, expertise and insights made for a much more interesting read. Thank you to Larry Baer, Alfonso Felder, Staci Slaughter, Mario Alioto, Shana Daum, Russ Stanley, Annmarie Hastings, Brian Sabean, Bobby Evans, Lee Elder, Ron Wotus, Dave Groeschner, Joan Ryan, Javier López, Jeremy Affeldt, Hunter Pence, Ryan Voglesong, Michael Morse, Buster Posey, and Jake Peavy.

Broadcasters and Journalists. A cadre of broadcasters, reporters and photo journalists pretty much live with the team during the season. Thank you to Mike Krukow, Duane Kuiper, Amy Gutierrez, Jon Miller, Dave Flemming, Erwin Higueros, and Tito Fuentes for consistently educating and entertaining us.

As you can see from the endnotes, the work of beat writers and reporters proved to be incredibly valuable to us. Alex Pavlovic, Chris Haft, Eric Alan, Henry Schulman, Brad Mangin, Brian Murphy, Andrew Baggarly, Matt Kawahara, Tim Kawakami, John Hickey, and John Shea, thank you for journalistic excellence.

Chris Berman and Willie Mays. Then, there is the face of ESPN and the man who was so instrumental in growing the network's popularity, Chris "Boomer" Berman. Thank you, not only for writing the foreword, but for being a hell of a nice guy. We look forward to an enduring friendship. What do you say to the greatest all-around baseball player of all time? You say, "Hey Willie, thank you!" Thank you to The Say Hey Kid and Hall of Famer, Willie Mays for sharing your stories, making us laugh and writing the afterword.

Kim Bochy. Kim Bochy gave us her unique insights on Bruce, the team and being a player/coach's wife. The "General" as Bruce affectionately refers to her, read the manuscript, added insights that made it better and dug through personal archives to find photos we didn't have. For 20-plus years we've watched Kim be the bedrock of the Bochy family. She makes it look effortless. Mostly, we cherish your friendship, thank you for leaning in Kimmy.

Bruce Bochy. When you're writing about a friend there is added pressure, to get it right, to not overstep your bounds when mining stories, to not ask too much when there are extreme demands on his schedule. Yet, Bruce never made us feel that way. As he is with everyone, Boch was overly generous with his time, extremely helpful when we needed access to his players and coaches, and always willing to take a call, answer a question or supply a story—even when it was just minutes before taking the field at the start of a game. Thank you for so many great conversations, often over a bourbon, and for the epic speaking, hunting, and wine tasting trips. Mostly, thank you for an incredible friendship. It's been a great ride, loaded with extraordinary memories. Here's to the next great adventure.

Die-hard Friends. All the writers we know share a few things in common: time away from family, lost weekends, sleepless nights, feelings of doubt, and periods of despair. This just seems to be part of the writer's journey. That's when a few special friends show up time and time again with the kind of encouragement that keeps you going. Prakash Idnani, Dan Haggerty, Peter Stark, Steve Williams, and John Blumberg, thank you for jumping in the trench with us. Your repeated challenges to "stay the course" means more than you can ever imagine.

The Greatest Kids in the World. Our most impressive accomplishment in this world and our greatest gift to it are three amazing children. We love them very much, but equally important, we really like 'em. There is no one we'd rather be with than Taylor-Grace, Aubrey and Dylan. As adults, they have become our very best friends. They are our reason for hope and cause for celebration. Thank you for your patience, your belief in us, and for extending so much grace over the years to parents who travel for a living. Now that you are making your own marks in the world, we are thrilled to have a front-row seat! Our lives are rich and full, beyond our wildest dreams, because of you.

ABOUT THE AUTHORS

KEVIN AND JACKIE FREIBERG
International Bestselling Authors and Speakers

Their award-winning books profile gutsy leaders who dare to dream big, fill a room with energy and do things others say can't be done. A blend of rigorous research grounded in real-world strategies and memorable storytelling, their books will stretch your thinking, engage your imagination and challenge you to do something now.

If you're up for a deep dive into how Southwest Airlines became the greatest success story in the history of commercial aviation, the mind-blowing culture of the $3b SAS Institute, what India's Tata Motors did to produce a $2500 car, the CAUSE that catapulted National Life into one of the fastest growing insurance companies in America, or how the San Francisco Giants rose from the brink of disaster to become one of the most successful, enduring sports franchises in the world...

the Freibergs will take you behind the scenes.

If you want to STAND OUT instead of fitting into a sea of sameness, make things happen instead of making excuses and be indispensable instead being someone who won't be missed...their books show you **how.**

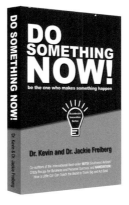

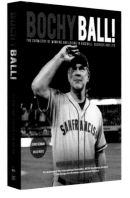

Kevin and Jackie are partners in a firm that equips leaders for a world of change. They have provided keynotes, seminars and retreats to over 2000 companies in 60 industries around the globe.

Their clients don't want to be held hostage by history; they want to understand the threats and opportunities that will shape their future. They are interested in blowing the doors off business-as-usual and finding ways to disrupt themselves before someone else does.

Their clients don't want **dead people working**; they want to create cultures where impassioned people come to work fully awake, fully engaged, firing on all cylinders.

They don't want to be stuck in routine and resignation, they want to think big, act bold, do **epic work** and live **epic lives.**

In a world where everyone and everything around you is constantly getting better, where technology waits for no one and a smarter, more sophisticated customer wants to know what's new, what's next...

you can either **drive** the train departing for the future or **chase it.**

SPEAKING ENGAGEMENTS

AND OTHER RESOURCES

bochyball.com

REFERENCE MATERIALS

PHOTO CREDITS

NOTES

[1] In the world of baseball and sabermetrics, many statistics change on a daily basis. All statistics in Bochy Ball! are as at the time of this publication.

[2] "Matt Cain Throws Perfect Game as Giants Win 10-0," http://www.sfgate.com/giants/article/Matt-Cain-throws-perfect-game-as-Giants-win-10-0-3632764.php.

[3] "A Part of History—Brandon Belt," http://brandon.mlblogs.com/2012/06/14/a-part-of-history-brandon-belt/.

[4] Chris Haft (April 2014), "Bochy quietly building Hall of Fame career as skipper," http://m.giants.mlb.com/news/article/98149330/bruce-bochy-quietly-building-hall-of-fame-career-as-skipper/.

[5] Chris Haft (April 2016), "Bochy: 'I have the best job in baseball,'" http://m.mlb.com/news/article/171727714/manager-bruce-bochy-on-his-time-leading-giants/.

[6] Jerry Crasnick (July 2015), "Who Is Baseball's Best Manager?" http://www.espn.com/mlb/story/_/id/13186480/who-mlb-best-manager-survey-says.

[7] Daniel Brown, The Big 50: San Francisco Giants: The Men and Moments That Made the San Francisco Giants (Chicago: Triumph Books, 2016), 44.

[8] Zach Buchanan (March 2015), "San Francisco Giants May Have Less Talent than 2014, but They Still Have Best Manager," http://www.azcentral.com/story/sports/mlb/2015/03/28/giants-may-less-talent-still-best-manager/70567488/.

[9] Charles Odum (October 2010), "Loss means end of the line for Cox,"https://www.gainesvilletimes.com/sports/atlanta-braves/loss-means-end-of-the-line-for-cox/.

[10] Eno Sarris (August 26, 2015), "What Makes Bruce Bochy and Joe Maddon Great?" http://www.fangraphs.com/blogs/what-makes-bruce-bochy-and-joe-maddon-great/.

[11] Kevin Baxter (August 2014), "No-nonsense approach is a winner for Giants Manager Bruce Bochy," http://www.latimes.com/sports/la-sp-0817-bruce-bochy-giants-20140817-story.html.

[12] Ibid.

[13] Tom Cushman (October 2006), "Playing Bochy Ball," http://www.sandiegomagazine.com/San-Diego-Magazine/July-2006/Playing-Bochy-Ball/.

[14] Baseball players and managers get traded, move around a lot, and retire. We've tried to stay consistent in designating who is an active member of the team and who is not, with the qualifier "former." We apologize to the reader if a player's designation changed during the publication of Bochy Ball!

[15] Jesse Spector (July 2016), "MLB Manager Ranking: Who Tops Sporting News' list?" http://www.sportingnews.com/mlb/list/baseball-manager-rankings-2016-best-worst-bochy-maddon/1bb6iaj2v3zlx1hafy6nniks6h/slide/4.

[16] Yardbarker (March 2017), "Ranking All 30 MLB Managers," http://www.yardbarker.com/mlb/articles/ranking_all_30_mlb_managers/s1__23361706.

[17] Zachary D. Rymer (April 2012), "Analyzing the Importance of Clubhouse Chemistry to Winning MLB World Series," http://bleacherreport.com/articles/1132007-analyzing-the-importance-of-clubhouse-chemistry-to-winning-mlb-world-series.

[18] As quoted in Pat Williams and Peter Kerasotis, Extreme Winning (Deerfield Beach, FL: Health Communications, Inc., 2015), 269

[19] Ibid, 270

[20] Leni Miller (February 2016), "Is San Francisco Giants CEO, Larry Baer, in Right Work?" http://www.huffingtonpost.com/leni-miller/is-san-francisco-giants-c_b_9134746.html.

[21] We have borrowed this phrase from Mehrdad Baghai and James Quigley, authors of As One: Individual Action, Collective Power (London: Penguin Books, 2011), 2

[22] Tom Verducci (November 2014), "Continuity PRINCIPALS," http://www.si.com/vault/2014/11/10/106663750/continuity-principals.

[23] Andrew Baggarly (October 2010), "Giants clinch NL West title," http://www.mercurynews.com/2010/10/03/giants-clinch-nl-west-title/.

[24] Tom Verducci (November 2014), "Continuity PRINCIPALS," http://www.si.com/vault/2014/11/10/106663750/continuity-principals.

[25] Barry Svriuga (October 2014), "On baseball: Maddon's departure and the importance of a manager-GM relationship," https://www.washingtonpost.com/sports/nationals/on-baseball-maddons-departure-and-the-importance-of-a-manager-gm-relationship/2014/10/25/1d7debb0-5beb-11e4-b812-38518ae74c67_story.html?utm_term=.1307dbba1f6f.

[26] Chris Haft (October 2014), "Giants success a testament to Sabean's blueprint," http://m.mlb.com/news/article/99423864/giants-success-a-testament-to-brian-sabeans-blueprint/.

[27] Scott Miller (October 2014), "SF Giants Take Unconventional Path to Cchieving MLB Dynasty Status," http://bleacherreport.com/articles/2249900-sf-giants-take-unconventional-path-to-achieving-mlb-dynasty-status.

[28] David Waldstein (November 2010), "Keeper of the Giants bats and team's history," http://www.nytimes.com/2010/11/04/sports/baseball/04sfgiants.html?mcubz=3.

[29] Mehrdad Baghai and James Quigley, As One: Individual Action, Collective Power (London: Penguin Books, 2011), 2.

[30] Brian Costa (February 22, 2015), "Baseball champions' CEO on creating a culture of success," http://www.wsj.com/articles/baseball-champions-ceo-on-creating-a-culture-of-success-1424664608.

[31] Mark Townsend (April 2015), "Bruce Bochy and Brian Sabean Extensions Reinforce Giants Foundation," http://sports.yahoo.com/blogs/mlb-big-league-stew/bruce-bochy-and-brian-sabean-extensions-strengthen-giants-foundation-232105448.html.

[32] Kevin Lynch (August 2015), "Why the Giants Young Players Succeed," http://blog.sfgate.com/giants/2015/08/11/why-the-giants-young-players-succeed/.

[33] Alex Pavlovic (May 2014), "San Francisco Giants doing wonders with castoffs in the bull pen," http://www.mercurynews.com/2014/05/01/san-francisco-giants-doing-wonders-with-castoffs-in-the-bull-pen/.

[34] ABC News (October 2014), "Kim Hudson talks about Tim Hudson, Madison Bumgarner bromance," http://abc7news.com/sports/kim-hudson-talks-about-hudson-bumgarner-bromance/376127/.

[35] Chris Haft (May 2014), "'Stars are aligned' for grateful Morse with Giants," http://sanfrancisco.giants.mlb.com/news/print.jsp?ymd=20140501&content_id=73959922&vkey=news_sf&c_id=sf.

[36] Matt Duffy (September 2015), "The New Kid," http://www.theplayerstribune.com/matt-duffy-giants-the-new-kid/.

[37] Hayden Higgins (May 15, 2014), "Moneyball 2.0: The New, Team-Oriented Study of Baseball," https://www.theatlantic.com/entertainment/archive/2014/05/moneyball-20-the-new-team-oriented-study-of-baseball/370908/.

[38] Tom Cushman (October 2006), "Playing Bochy Ball," http://www.sandiegomagazine.com/San-Diego-Magazine/July-2006/Playing-Bochy-Ball/.

[39] Demian Bulwa (October 2010), "S.F. Giants Bruce Bochy Has Humble Approach," http://www.sfgate.com/giants/article/S-F-Giants-Bruce-Bochy-has-humble-approach-3170809.php.

[40] Nick Cafardo, "Ex-Red Sox Jake Peavy a different pitcher with Giants," https://www.bostonglobe.com/sports/2014/10/11/red-sox-jake-peavy-different-pitcher-with-giants/XHol947EwZzCMgpTjuOUYN/story.html.

[41] "Oct. 11 Jake Peavy NLCS interview," http://m.giants.mlb.com/news/article/98243394/oct-11-jake-peavy-nlcs-interview.

[42] Brian Murphy and Brad Mangin, Never. Say. Die. The San Francisco Giants—2012 World Series Champions (Petaluma: Camron + Company, 2013), xiii.

[43] Eno Sarris (August 26, 2015), "What Makes Bruce Bochy and Joe Maddon Great?" http://www.fangraphs.com/blogs/what-makes-bruce-bochy-and-joe-maddon-great/.

[44] Kevin Lynch (August 11, 2015), "Why the Giants Young Players Succeed," http://blog.sfgate.com/giants/2015/08/11/why-the-giants-young-players-succeed/.

[45] "Oct. 11 Jake Peavy NLCS interview," http://m.giants.mlb.com/news/article/98243394/oct-11-jake-peavy-nlcs-interview.

[46] Kevin Lynch (August 11, 2015), "Why the Giants Young Players Succeed," http://blog.sfgate.com/giants/2015/08/11/why-the-giants-young-players-succeed/.

[47] "Barry Zito and Tim Lincecum, from riches to scorn to World Series Game 1 triumph . . . together," http://blogs.mercurynews.com/kawakami/2012/10/24/barry-zito-and-tim-lincecum-from-riches-to-scorn-to-world-series-game-1-triumph-together/.

[48] Ibid.

[49] Brian Murphy and Brad Mangin, Never. Say. Die. The San Francisco Giants—2012 World Series Champions (Petaluma: Camron + Company, 2013), xii.

[50] Ibid., 10.

[51] Clair Reclosado-Baclay, "SF Giants' Unity Paves Road to 2nd World Series Title in 3 Years," http://sanfrancisco.cbslocal.com/2012/10/29/sf-giants-unity-paves-road-to-2nd-world-series-title-in-3-years/.

[52] Michael Rosenberg, "Good Chemistry Part of the Science Behind Giants World Series Title," http://www.si.com/more-sports/2012/10/29/san-francisco-giants-chemistry-word-series-title-detroit-tigers.

[53] See these titles by Brian Murphy and Brad Mangin: Championship Blood: The 2014 World Series Champion San Francisco Giants (Petaluma: Camron + Company, 2015); Never. Say. Die. The San Francisco Giants—2012 World Series Champions (Petaluma: Camron + Company, 2013); Worth the Wait (San Diego: Skybox Press, 2011). See also Bay Area News Group's Comeback Kings: The San Francisco Giants' Incredible 2012 Championship Season (Chicago: Triumph Books, 2012); Bruce Bochy and Jeremy Affeldt, Champions Together: The Official Story of the 2014 San Francisco Giants (San Diego: Skybox Press, 2014); and Bruce Bochy et al., One Common Goal: The Official Inside Story of the Incredible World Champion San Francisco Giants (San Diego: Skybox Press, 2013).

[54] Deborah Blagg, "Local Hero," https://www.alumni.hbs.edu/stories/Pages/story-bulletin.aspx?num=1232.

[55] Brian Murphy and Brad Mangin, Never. Say. Die. The San Francisco Giants—2012 World Series Champions (Petaluma: Camron + Company, 2013), 31.

[56] Zach Buchanan (March 2015), "San Francisco Giants May Have Less Talent Than 2014, but They Still Have Best Manager," http://www.azcentral.com/story/sports/mlb/2015/03/28/giants-may-less-talent-still-best-manager/70567488/.

[57] Ibid.

[58] Jorge L. Ortiz (October 20, 2014), "From Wild Cards to World Series, Giants, Royals Endured," http://www.usatoday.com/story/sports/mlb/2014/10/16/royals-giants-mlb-wild-card-teams/17385731/.

[59] Phil Barber (October 9, 2014), "Bruce Bochy is Giants Uncle October," http://www.pressdemocrat.com/sports/2952283-181/uncle-october?artslide=5.

[60] Alex Pavlovic (October 23, 2012), "San Francisco Giants resilience starts with manager Bruce Bochy," http://www.mercurynews.com/ci_21839887/san-francisco-giants-resilience-starts-manager-bruce-bochy.

[61] Eno Sarris (August 26, 2015), "What Makes Bruce Bochy and Joe Maddon Great?" http://www.fangraphs.com/blogs/what-makes-bruce-bochy-and-joe-maddon-great/.

[62] Ibid.

[63] Daniel Brown (October 10, 2014),"Captain Calm: Giant's Bruce Bochy sets even tone," http://www.mercurynews.com/giants/ci_26703070/captain-calm-giants-bruce-bochy-sets-even-tone.

[64] Michael Rosenberg (October 30, 2014), "Scintillating Bumgarner Proves the Ultimate World Series Difference," http://www.si.com/mlb/2014/10/30/world-series-game-7-madison-bumgarner-giants-difference-maker.

[65] Mlblogssfgiants1, "Already Itching to Get Back—Brandon Crawford," http://brandon.mlblogs.com/2015/08/26/already-itching-to-get-back-brandon-crawford/.

[66] Scott Miller (October 2014), "SF Giants Take Unconventional Path to Achieving MLB Dynasty Status," http://bleacherreport.com/articles/2249900-sf-giants-take-unconventional-path-to-achieving-mlb-dynasty-status.

[67] Bruce Bochy et al., One Common Goal: The Official Inside Story of the Incredible 2012 World Champion San Francisco Giants (San Diego: Skybox Press, 2013), 20

[68] Ibid.

[69] Brian Murphy and Brad Mangin, Never. Say. Die. The San Francisco Giants—2012 World Series Champions (Petaluma: Camron + Company, 2013), xiii

[70] Bruce Bochy et al., One Common Goal: The Official Inside Story of the Incredible 2012 World Champion San Francisco Giants (San Diego: Skybox Press, 2013), 53.

[71] Jayson Stark (October 10, 2016), "Why All the Aces Can't Be Bumgarner in October," http://www.espn.com/mlb/story/_/id/17759164/why-all-aces-giants-madison-bumgarner-october.

[72] Andrew Baggarly, A Band of Misfits: Tales of the 2010 San Francisco Giants (Chicago: Prologue Publishing Services, 2011), xvii

[73] Marcos Bretón (October 29, 2014), "Opinion: Giants' success can't be measured by the numbers," http://www.sacbee.com/news/local/news-columns-blogs/marcos-breton/article3191527.html.

[74] John Branch (October 6, 2012), "Posey, the heart of San Francisco, beats quietly," http://www.nytimes.com/2012/10/07/sports/baseball/young-and-talented-buster-posey-is-the-heart-of-the-giants.html.

[75] John Shea (August 9, 2010), "Sanchez's Prediction after Giants' Loss," http://www.sfgate.com/giants/shea/article/Sanchez-s-prediction-after-Giants-loss-3178909.php.

[76] Ibid.

[77] Andrew Baggarly (October 11, 2016), Giants bull pen proves fatal, Cubs mount four-run comeback in ninth to advance," http://www.mercurynews.com/2016/10/11/giants-bull pen-proves-too-fatal-cubs-mount-four-run-comeback-in-ninth-to-advance/.

[78] Jerry McDonald (October 11, 2016), Giants notes: "Panik, Gillaspie fall short of hero status," http://www.mercurynews.com/2016/10/11/giants-notes-panik-gillaspie-fall-short-of-hero-status/.

[79] Henry Schulman (March 2007), "MEET BRUCE BOCHY/NEW HEAD MAN/," http://www.sfgate.com/sports/article/MEET-BRUCE-BOCHY-NEW-HEAD-MAN-San-Francisco-s-2571318.php.

[80] Bruce Jenkins (April 2016), "Baseball humor: The lifeline," http://www.sfchronicle.com/sports/jenkins/article/Baseball-humor-the-lifeline-7222754.php.

[81] John Schlegel (October 2010), "Consistent Huff keeps Giants clubhouse light," http://./news/article/15540412//

[82] Andrew Baggarly (September 2015), "Giants prank Tim Hudson on flight home, etc.," http://blogs.mercurynews.com/giants/2015/09/24/extra-baggs-giants-prank-tim-hudson-on-flight-home-etc/.

[83] Bruce Jenkins (April 2016), "Baseball humor: The lifeline," http://www.sfchronicle.com/sports/jenkins/article/Baseball-humor-the-lifeline-7222754.php.

[84] Peter Abraham (October 2014), "Hunter Pence is high-spirited leader of the Giants," https://www.bostonglobe.com/sports/2014/10/27/hunter-pence-high-spirited-leader-giants/tXLuhxDl88yxLfBQYXc3nI/story.html?comments=all&sort=NEWEST_CREATE_DT.

[85] Adrian Garro (August 2017), "Hunter Pence ran so hard around the bases he nearly eclipsed Denard Span before scoring," http://m.mlb.com/cutfour/2017/08/18/249145414/hunter-pence-nearly-passes-denard-span-on-basepaths.

[86] Ibid.

[87] Brian Murphy and Brad Mangin, Never. Say. Die. The San Francisco Giants—2012 World Series Champions (Petaluma: Camron + Company, 2013), xiii.

[88] Ibid.

[89] Sun-tzu, The Art of War (Oxford: Clarendon Press, 1964; translation by Samuel B. Griffith;), 47

[90] George A. King III (October 2014), "Bochy likely one win away from a ticket to Cooperstown," http://nypost.com/2014/10/27/bochy-likely-one-win-away-from-a-ticket-to-cooperstown/.

[91] Ibid.

[92] Phil Barber (October 9, 2014), "Bruce Bochy is Giants Uncle October," http://www.pressdemocrat.com/sports/2952283-181/uncle-october?artslide=5.

[93] Matt Kawahara (April 2015), "2015 Giants preview: Bruce Bochy deflects attention, but winning doesn't," http://www.sacbee.com/sports/mlb/san-francisco-giants/article17259632.html.

[94] Eno Sarris (August 26, 2015), "What Makes Bruce Bochy and Joe Maddon Great?" http://www.fangraphs.com/blogs/what-makes-bruce-bochy-and-joe-maddon-great/.

[95] Ibid.

[96] Liz Funk (April 7, 2016), "The Hidden Power in Trusting Your Gut Instincts," https://www.fastcompany.com/3058609/your-most-productive-self/the-hidden-power-in-trusting-your-gut-instincts.

[97] John Hickey (October 2014), "Ishikawa makes Bochy's lineup switch pay off for Giants," http://www.mercurynews.com/2014/10/14/ishikawa-makes-bochys-lineup-switch-pay-off-for-giants/.

[98] Ray Ratto (October 25, 2012), "Ultimate redemption for Zito, Lincecum," http://www.csnbayarea.com/giants/ultimate-redemption-zito-lincecum.

[99] Bay Area Sports Guy (October 16, 2014), "Ishikawa's walk-off HR powers Giants back to the World Series," http://www.bayareasportsguy.com/san-francisco-giants-st-louis-cardinals-2014-nlcs-game-5/.

[100] Andy McCullough (October 26, 2014), "Madison Bumgarner stymies Royals again as Giants win 5-0," http://www.kansascity.com/sports/mlb/kansas-city-royals/article3396155.html.

[101] Tom Verducci (December 9, 2014), "2014 Sportsman of the Year: Madison Bumgarner," http://www.si.com/sportsman/2014/12/09/madison-bumgarner-sports-illustrated-sportsman-profile.

[102] Thomas Boswell (October 30, 2014), "Giants' Madison Bumgarner is just scary good as San Francisco wins World Series over Kansas City," https://www.washingtonpost.com/sports/nationals/giants-madison-bumgarner-is-just-scary-good-as-san-francisco-wins-world-series-over-kansas-city/2014/10/30/f1cfe2e8-5faa-11e4-9f3a-7e28799e0549_story.html?tid=a_inl.

[103] Mark Purdy (October 29, 2014), "Giants rode Madison Bumgarner to the finish line," http://www.mercurynews.com/mark-purdy/ci_26827381/purdy-giants-rode-bumgarner-finish-line.

[104] For a broader discussion about freedom and autonomy versus dependency, see Peter Block's wonderful classic, The Empowered Manager: Positive Political Skills at Work (San Francisco: Jossey-Bass, 1987).

[105] Dave Campbell (May 2015), "Clubhouse chemistry in digital age: Winning still cures all," http://www.washingtontimes.com/news/2015/may/5/clubhouse-chemistry-in-digital-age-winning-still-c/.

[106] Jerry Crasnick (November 2010), "Bringing the Giants Forward, from Behind," http://www.espn.com/mlb/hotstove10/columns/story?id=5805953&columnist=crasnick_jerry.

[107] Eno Sarris (August 26, 2015), "What Makes Bruce Bochy and Joe Maddon Great?" http://www.fangraphs.com/blogs/what-makes-bruce-bochy-and-joe-maddon-great/.

[108] Matt Kawahara (April 2015), "2015 Giants preview: Bruce Bochy deflects attention, but winning doesn't," http://www.sacbee.com/sports/mlb/san-francisco-giants/article17259632.html.

[109] Scott Page, The Difference: How the Power of Diversity Creates Better Groups, Firms, Schools, and Societies (Princeton, NJ: Princeton University Press, 2007).

[110] Scott Page (January 2007), "Diversity Powers Innovation," https://www.americanprogress.org/issues/economy/news/2007/01/26/2523/diversity-powers-innovation/.

[111] Thanks to our friend Baxter Kruger, who introduced us to the French term roux as the foundation of gumbo. In Cajun cuisine, a roux is made with various fats or oils combined with flour, to which onion, garlic, celery, and bell pepper are added to create a thick brown sauce, rich in flavor, that permeates the entire dish, whether it's seafood, sausage, chicken, alligator, or what-have-you gumbo.

[112] Brian Murphy (January 2015), "Review: MLB Network presents Bruce Bochy and Tim Flannery as friends who have also worked together for a long time and won world championships," http://www.mccoveychronicles.com/2015/1/19/7546077/mlb-network-bruce-bochy-tim-flannery-bryan-stow-odd-couple-cbs-justified-fx.

[113] Matt Kawahara (April 2015), "2015 Giants preview: Bruce Bochy deflects attention, but winning doesn't," http://www.sacbee.com/sports/mlb/san-francisco-giants/article17259632.html.

[114] Ibid.

[115] Ibid.

[116] Ibid.

[117] Bill Center (October 2006), "Players regret ex-skipper's departure," San Diego Union Tribune. http://legacy.sandiegouniontribune.com/uniontrib/20061028/news_1s28players.html

[118] Tom Krasovic (October 2006), "Loyalty to vets hastened exit," http://legacy.sandiegouniontribune.com/uniontrib/20061028/news_1s28alders1.html.

[119] Tom Cushman (October 2006), "Playing Bochy Ball," http://www.sandiegomagazine.com/San-Diego-Magazine/July-2006/Playing-Bochy-Ball/.

[120] MLB Network Presents (January 2015), "Tim Flannery and Bruce Bochy are The Odd Couple," http://m.mlb.com/video/topic/6479266/v37115087/tim-flannery-and-bruce-bochy-are-the-odd-couple.

[121] Andrew Baggarly (February 2013), "How the Giants put Posey Back together," http://nbcbayarea.csnbayarea.com/blog/andrew-baggarly/how-giants-put-posey-back-together

[122] See Daniel Brown's chapter, "Buster Posey: Giants Missed Their Star Catcher Almost as Much as He Missed the Game," in Bay Area News Group's Comeback Kings: The San Francisco Giants' Incredible 2012 Championship Season (Chicago: Triumph Books, 2012), 39.

[123] Ibid.

[124] Douglas Main (November 2015),"5 SCIENTIFICALLY PROVEN BENEFITS OF GRATITUDE," http://www.newsweek.com/5-scientifically-proven-benefits-gratitude-398582.

[125] Amy Morin (November 2014), "7 Scientifically Proven Benefits of Gratitude That Will Motivate You to Give Thanks Year-Round," https://www.forbes.com/sites/amymorin/2014/11/23/7-scientifically-proven-benefits-of-gratitude-that-will-motivate-you-to-give-thanks-year-round/#43bca209183c.

[126] John Shea (April 2016), "Buster and Kristen Posey Join Fight Against Pediatric Cancer," http://www.sfgate.com/giants/article/Buster-and-Kristen-Posey-joining-fight-against-7258601.php.

[127] Alex Pavlovic (December 1015), "Smardzija's Chemistry with Giants 'Pretty Overwhelming,'" http://www.csnbayarea.com/giants/samardzijas-chemistry-giants-pretty-overwhelming.

[128] Bruce Bochy et al., One Common Goal: The Official Inside Story of the Incredible 2012 World Champion San Francisco Giants (San Diego: Skybox Press, 2013), 157

[129] Bruce Bochy and Jeremy Affeldt, Champions Together: The Official Story of the 2014 San Francisco Giants (San Diego: Skybox Press, 2014), 13.

[130] Erin E. Smith and Jon D. Groetzinger (2010), "Do Fans Matter? The Effect of Attendance on the Outcomes of Major League Baseball Games," Journal of Quantitative Analysis in Sports volume 6, issue 1, article 4.

[131] Matt Kawahara (May 2015), "In 16th season, AT&T still beloved by Giants fans," http://www.sacbee.com/sports/mlb/san-francisco-giants/article21330177.html.

[132] Tom Tolbert and Ray Ratto (November 2013), "KNBR Conversation: Tim Hudson, Giants Acquisition," http://www.sfgate.com/giants/article/KNBR-Conversation-Tim-Hudson-Giants-acquisition-5006654.php.

[133] Brian Murphy and Brad Mangin, Never. Say. Die. The San Francisco Giants—2012 World Series Champions (Petaluma: Camron + Company, 2013), xiii.

[134] Tim Kawakami (April 2015), "San Francisco Giants owe much of their success to AT&T Park," http://www.mercurynews.com/2015/04/12/kawakami-san-francisco-giants-owe-much-of-their-success-to-att-park/.

[135] One Common Goal: The Official Inside Story of the Incredible 2012 World Champion San Francisco Giants (San Diego: Skybox Press, 2013), 95.

[136] Jerry Crasnick (November 2010), "Bringing the Giants forward, from behind," http://www.espn.com/mlb/hotstove10/columns/story?id=5805953&columnist=crasnick_jerry.

[137] Andrew Baggarly (November 2010), "Giants thank their fans on euphoric day in San Francisco," http://www.mercurynews.com/2010/11/03/giants-thank-their-fans-on-euphoric-day-in-san-francisco/.

[138] One Common Goal: The Official Inside Story of the Incredible 2012 World Champion San Francisco Giants (San Diego: Skybox Press, 2013), 145.

[139] ABC News (October 2014), "Buster Posey Credits Giants Fans for Playoff Success," http://abc7news.com/sports/buster-posey-credits-giants-fans-for-playoff-success/375319/.

[140] Laura Anthony (November 2014), "San Francisco Giants Celebrated at Parade, Rally," http://abc7news.com/sports/san-francisco-giants-celebrated-at-parade-rally/374558/.

[141] Mark Emmons, Theresa Harrington, Natalie Neysa Alund, Malaika Fraley, and Thomas Peele (October 2014), "San Francisco Giants parade: Vast throng greets their three-time World Series champions," http://www.mercurynews.com/2014/10/31/san-francisco-giants-parade-vast-throng-greets-their-three-time-world-series-champions/.

[142] Larry Baer (November 2012), "From the Desk of Larry Baer," http://view.ed4.net/v/TSAR2O/NRL1JK/76CPOK/PVFS72/MAILACTION=1&FORMAT=H?partnerId=ed-5517174-55411678.

[143] Larry Baer (October 2015), "From the Desk of Larry Baer," http://sanfrancisco.giants.mlb.com/sf/fan_forum/larry_letter.jsp.

[144] Larry Baer (October 2016), "From the Desk of Larry Baer," http://m.giants.mlb.com/promo/larry-letter.

[145] Larry Baer (October 2017), "From the Desk of Larry Baer," https://sfgiants.mlblogs.com/from-the-desk-of-larry-baer-42df9c23e8fa.

INDEX

team culture and, 80–89
team-first mentality for, 101–102, 142–149
trust in teammates, 150–156
Texas Rangers. *see* World Series (2010)
Theriot, Ryan, 146–147
Thompson, Bobby, 58
Tidrow, Dick, *234*
Tipping Point Emergency Relief Fund, 311
Tobeber,Bob, 76
Torre, Joe, 35, 36, 202
Torres, Andrés, 179
"torture," 170, 194, 323
Totah, Joe, 160
Towers, Kevin, 37–38, 220, 257, *257*
trust, 150–156
Turner, Justin, 244, 245
Tyson, Mike, 247

U

unpredictability, 236–269
decisiveness for, 256–260
"full throttle" playing, 238–246
nonconformity and, 261–269
preparation for, 247–255
Uribe, Juan, 262
U.S. Navy, 52
Utley, Chase, 261

V

Verducci, Tom, 80, 84, 291
Verdugo, Ryan, 183
Verlander, Justin, 18, 145, 321
Virdon, Bill, 293
Vogelsong, Nicole, 313
Vogelsong, Ryan
attitude and, *274,* 286
talent and, 103
team chemistry and, 37
team culture and, 85, 313–314
teamwork and, 151–152
unpredictability and, 241

W

Wacha, Michael, 262, 263
Wallace, William, 161–162
warrior spirit, 193–199
Weiss, George, 85
Werth, Jason, 262
Williams, Dick, 294

Williams, Matt, 262
Williams, Ted, 248–249
Willie Mac Award, 153, 217
Wilson, Brian, 18, 176, 179, *197,* 240, 261, *279,* 280
Wooden, John, 275
World Series (2010)
celebrations, *322–325,* 322–326
"faking foolish" in, 261, 263, 264
pitching and team chemistry in, 170
resilience and, 192
resolve and, 178–179
teamwork in, 161–163
World Series (2012)
celebrations, *111, 322–325,* 322–326
"faking foolish" in postseason games, 261, 264, 266
focus in, 232
teamwork and, 150
World Series (2014)
celebrations, *322–325,* 322–326
composure, resolve, and hope in, 177, 178, 181
"faking foolish" and, 261, 262, *263,* 264–268, *266, 267*
focus during, *229,* 229–230
"full throttle" playing in, *240,* 240–246, *241, 242*
overcoming adversity in, 172–173
players' individual contributions to, 120
team-first mentality and, *148,* 148–149
teamwork and, 155
Wotus, Ron, 34, 87, 172
Wulf, Steve, 133

Y

Yost, Ned, 267
Young, Delmon, 232

Z

Zito, Barry
attitude and, *274,* 285, 295
talent and, 94
team culture and, 312, 320–321, *321*
teamwork and, *144,* 144–146, *145*